Poor Richard's Legacy

POOR RICHARD'S LEGACY

American Business Values from Benjamin Franklin to Michael Milken

Peter Baida

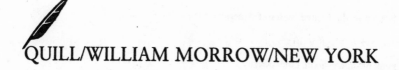

QUILL/WILLIAM MORROW/NEW YORK

Much of Chapter One appeared in somewhat different form in "Flying Kites with Ben Franklin," *Harvard Business Review*, January–February 1986. Copyright © 1985 by the President and Fellows of Harvard College.

Diagrams on page 38 from *The Autobiography of Benjamin Franklin*, edited by Leonard W. Labaree, *et al.* Sponsored by the American Philosophical Society and Yale University. Yale University Press, 1964.

Excerpts from *The Papers of Benjamin Franklin*, edited by Leonard W. Labaree, *et al.* Sponsored by the American Philosophical Society and Yale University. Yale University Press, 1959– .

Quote from *John D. Rockefeller: The Heroic Age of American Enterprise* by Allan Nevins. Copyright © 1940 by Charles Scribner's Sons; renewed 1968 by Allan Nevins. Reprinted with permission of Charles Scribner's Sons, an imprint of Macmillan Publishing Company.

Quote from *The Great Pierpont Morgan* by F. Lewis Allen. Copyright 1945, 1948 by Frederick Lewis Allen. Reprinted by permission of Harper & Row, Publishers, Inc.

Excerpts from *Babbitt* by Sinclair Lewis. Copyright © 1922 by Harcourt Brace Jovanovich, Inc.; renewed 1950 by Sinclair Lewis. Reprinted by permission of the publisher.

It is the policy of William Morrow and Company, Inc., and its imprints and affiliates, recognizing the importance of preserving what has been written, to print the books we publish on acid-free paper, and we exert our best efforts to that end.

Library of Congress Cataloging-in-Publication Data

Baida, Peter.
    Poor Richard's legacy: American business values from Benjamin
Franklin to Michael Milken / Peter Baida.
        p. cm.
    Includes bibliographical references.
    ISBN 0-688-10966-7 (pbk.)
    1. Business ethics—United States—History. 2. Capitalists and
financiers—United States—Biography. 3. Franklin, Benjamin,
1706–1790. 4. Capitalism—United States—History. I. Title.
HF5387.B33   1990
174′.4′0973—dc20
                                                        89-13792
                                                        CIP

Printed in the United States of America

2 3 4 5 6 7 8 9 10

BOOK DESIGN BY PAUL CHEVANNES

For my parents, for Diane, and for Edward
with deepest love and gratitude

Acknowledgments

I would like to thank my agent, Amanda Urban, and my editor, Connie Roosevelt, for their advice, patience, and encouragement.

I also would like to thank Mortimer H. Chute, Jr., vice-president for development at Memorial Sloan-Kettering Cancer Center, whose support has been invaluable.

Most of all, I thank my wife, Diane Cole. Without her this book would not exist. Without her I would not care.

—P.B.

Contents

Introduction

On October 31, 1989, Americans woke to read in their morning newspapers that the Rockefeller Group, the owner of Rockefeller Center, Radio City Music Hall, and other prime real estate in midtown Manhattan had sold controlling interest in the company—51 percent—to the Mitsubishi Estate Company of Tokyo. The Rockefeller Group received $846 million. In return, Mitsubishi acquired a hefty stake in what *The New York Times* described as both "the citadel of one of America's great business dynasties" and "the centerpiece of America's most renowned metropolis."

Politicians worried that the deal might provoke an American backlash against Japan, but in New York City most people in my office merely shrugged. We don't blame Mitsubishi. We don't blame the Japanese for buying CBS Records, Columbia Pictures, Firestone Tire and Rubber, golf courses in Hawaii, real estate in downtown Los Angeles, or anything else that strikes their fancy. They have deep pockets, as people in business say.

Almost everyone believes in capitalism these days, even the leaders of the crumbling Communist bloc. Believing in captialism means believing in the free flow of capital, and let the chips fall where they may. What difference does it make if Michael Jackson and Madonna, through their contracts with CBS Records, work for SONY? What difference does it make if General Electric, NBC, Time Warner, and McGraw-Hill (as tenants of Rockefeller Center) pay rent to Mitsubishi? For decades American companies have owned major assets in foreign countries. We bought what we wanted when we had the cash. We cannot complain if others follow our example.

Still, many Americans feel nervous. And, what may be more remarkable, many Americans do not feel nervous. For a long time I thought I would call this book *While America Slept*. In the 1980s, while America's leaders celebrated the longest peacetime economic expansion in the nation's history, the United States became the world's largest debtor nation. Yet we doze on. What would it take to awaken us? Perhaps if Toyota buys the Statue of Liberty . . . Perhaps if Honda buys Pearl Harbor . . .

Let me repeat: I do not blame foreign competitors. It's not their fault if they outwork, outsave, and outthink us. They have earned their success, as we earned ours in days gone by. What fascinates me is the way that the wheel of fortune, or perhaps I should call it the wheel of history, spins nations in and out of favor. How Spain glittered when the conquests of the conquistadores swelled its coffers! How the Dutch dazzled in the "Golden Age" when they dominated European trade! How the British swaggered in their days of glory!

My title suggests the theme that unifies this book beneath its surface diversity: The wheel of fortune revolves, at least in part, because changing values push it. Values change as conditions change, but not in any simple way. The forces that shape the future act and react, in a process of continuous adjustment. Changing conditions help to bring about changes in values. Changing values help to bring about changes in conditions. Cause and effect blur, yet, inch by inch, whole civilizations are transformed. Anyone who compares Europe today with Europe in the days of Saint Thomas Aquinas will see how momentous a transformation can take place over time.

This book is concerned not only with success and failure in the United States but also with *ideas* about success and failure, with the way those ideas have changed as the nation changed, and with the way success and failure connect with values. Choosing a title was difficult. I considered not only *While America Slept* but also *Tottering Colossus*, *Wealth and Worth*, *Losing Our Way*, *For Richer or Poorer*, and *Fools Make Feast* (from a proverb often quoted by Benjamin Franklin: "Fools make Feasts, and wise Men eat them"). In the end I settled on the title *Poor Richard's Legacy* because, more than any of the others, it not only suggests my theme but also evokes the range of American history and culture that the book explores. In the age of Donald Trump, Benjamin Franklin may not be a name that sells, but my bet is that Franklin's legacy, not Trump's, is the one that will matter in the twenty-first century.

Every book has a story, and I have often wished that writers shared more of the story with their readers than they usually do. Let me say a few words, therefore, about the circumstances that surrounded the birth of this book and about the motives that led me to undertake it.

One day in June 1979, I walked out of a used bookstore in Philadelphia with a nearly new copy of Benjamin Franklin's autobiography and a dusty copy of a book I had never heard of before—Carl Van Doren's big biography of Franklin, published in 1938. I was happy because I had some time available to read for pleasure, something I had not done for nearly two years. I was twenty-nine years old, had just received my M.B.A. from the Wharton School of the University of Pennsylvania, and was scheduled to move to New York City on July 4, to begin work in a management-training program at Memorial Sloan-Kettering Cancer Center.

In the few weeks before July 4, I read both books and wrote the first three or four pages of this book, almost exactly as they appear today. At the time I did not realize that they would be the first pages of a book. Indeed, I did not realize that they would be the first pages of anything. I moved to Manhattan, put my books about Franklin on a shelf, put my three or four pages in a drawer, and started my job.

Four years passed. In the summer of 1983, I took my books off the shelf and my three or four pages out of the drawer. I was thirty-three years old, still worked at Memorial Sloan-Kettering, and was settled in my job and in my personal life. It should have been a comfortable time for me. Instead, it was a restless time. Despite my best efforts, the literary ambitions that I had tried to suppress when I went to Wharton would not lie still. And the ghost of Benjamin Franklin kept talking to me.

By the summer of 1984, I had written not only the forty some pages about Franklin that now begin this book but also a number of short articles, most of which focused on business in some way. One of these articles, "If Willy Loman Read Books, He'd Have Read These," appeared in *The New York Times* on May 13, 1984, and had a most unexpected consequence.

The day after the article appeared, I received a call from an editor of *American Heritage* magazine, asking whether I would like to have lunch. The upshot of the meeting was that from 1985 through 1988 I wrote a column, "The Business of America," for *American Heritage*. I also signed a contract with the book-publishing division at American Heritage based on an early outline of this book. Thus, in the summer of 1984, less than a year after I began to write about business, I found myself with a contract to write a book, a contract to write six articles a year for *American Heritage*, and a full-time job at Memorial Sloan-Kettering. Over the next few years the struggle to balance this triple commitment was a challenge, to put it mildly, but a challenge that invigorated more than it wearied me.

Starting to read any long book is like starting a journey. The reader who is about to accompany me on this journey may be pleased to learn that it will not be as arduous as the one I originally planned. The book I outlined for American Heritage in the summer of 1984 would have been at least eight hundred pages. Early in 1986, however, American Heritage was purchased by Forbes Inc., which promptly closed the book division. The need to find a new publisher gave me a chance to reconsider what I was doing. The result is a leaner book, though not, I hope, a lesser one.

Even in its current form, *Poor Richard's Legacy* stakes a claim to a large chunk of literary, intellectual, and historical territory. My models were Edmund Wilson's monumental study of the literature of the Amercian Civil War, *Patriotic Gore;* Matthew Josephson's group portrait of nineteenth-century American moguls, *The Robber Barons;* and Frederick Lewis Allen's history of the immense business expansion that took place in the United States between the depression of 1893–97 and the Great Depression of the 1930s, *The Lords of Creation.*

Like Wilson, Josephson, and Allen, I felt the urge to work on a large canvas, and I was certain that my subject justified one. Also, the American love of grand enterprises influenced me. "Give me a condor's quill!" Melville exclaims in *Moby Dick.* "Give me Vesuvius' crater for an inkstand! . . . To produce a mighty book, you must choose a mighty theme." However immodest it may sound, I do not hesitate to confess that in this book I wanted to do something that no one had done before, and I wanted to do it so well that no one could easily equal or surpass what I had done.

Poor Richard's Legacy is not a history of American business. It is an exploration of American business, written from a perspective that springs from a schizophrenic education: undergraduate studies in the liberal arts at Harvard, followed eventually by graduate work at Wharton and a decade of managerial experience. From the start I felt that my background put me in a position to write a book of unusual scope. At Wharton I was astonished to meet brilliant people who knew nothing about history or literature and who, even more sadly, did not even know that they knew nothing. Just as astonishing, to judge from my experience at Harvard, is the depth of the ignorance about business that commonly afflicts people who are well versed in the humanities. *Poor Richard's Legacy* attempts to bridge this gap and, at the same time, to fill a void in the realm of American studies. For many years I searched in vain for a book like this one. It did not exist. Now it does.

Poor Richard's Legacy is written for a person I have never met—*you*. In my imagination, you are a man or woman who wants to join me on a stroll through two hundred and fifty years of American history and literature, to share my moments of perplexity and moments of illumination, to examine the lives of some remarkable people, to examine the views of some remarkable people, to take part in a discussion that began long before you were born and will continue long after you are gone.

You might be a young go-getter, a middle-aged manager stuck in a middle-level job, a senior executive, or the chairman of a mighty board. You might be an accountant, a computer programmer, an engineer, a plant manager, a personnel specialist, a venture capitalist, a chief financial officer, a market research analyst, a strategic planner, a consultant, or the owner of a small business. You might be a student of business administration or a student of the liberal arts. You might be a scientist. You might be a writer. You might be a reader in Japan, Korea, West Germany, China, Poland, or Peru. You might be a professor of business history, in search of a book that will instruct, challenge, stimulate, amuse, or provoke your students.

Poor Richard's Legacy is a mixture of biography, social history, cultural history, and business and economic history. Its dominant theme is the persistence, over more than two centuries, of a struggle between opposing views of American enterprise—an affirming tradition that celebrates business values and business success, and a dissenting tradition that questions business values and business success.

To be more precise, the dominant theme is the persistence of these opposing traditions against a background of dramatic change: from the Age of Colonial Enterprise to the Age of the Empire Builders; from the

Age of the Empire Builders to the Age of Organization; from the work
ethic of the eighteenth and nineteenth centuries to the consumption ethic
of the twentieth century; from the affirmation of character in the success
literature of the eighteenth and nineteenth centuries to the revolt against
character in the success literature of the twentieth century; from the affirmation of thrift in the eighteenth and nineteenth centuries to the triumph
of "Buy Now, Pay Later," in the twentieth century; from a time when
Americans worried about affluence and the power of big business to a
time when Americans worry about billion-dollar deficits and the declining competitiveness of big business.

Poor Richard's Legacy is a tapestry in which several major strands are
interwoven. One strand looks at the lives and deeds of representative
figures in the history of American business. A second strand examines
the popular literature, from Benjamin Franklin's day to our own, that
claims to teach Americans how to succeed in business. A third strand
focuses on the work of leading writers who have responded critically or
ambivalently to business. Other threads weave in and out of the tapestry
as the book winds through the centuries.

It is not likely that any reader, even my own mother, will find all
parts of this book equally interesting. Some readers may prefer the biographical chapters to the chapters of intellectual history. Others may
love the chapters of intellectual history, but grow impatient as they read
the biographical chapters. I urge all readers to exercise the privilege of
skipping a few pages if they find themselves getting bogged down. *Poor
Richard's Legacy* has been fun to write, and it ought to be fun to read. I
feel confident not only that the book contains something for everyone
but also that, for most readers, much that it contains will be pure pleasure.

In the biographical chapters, the reader is exposed to one self-made
man with many interests that transcended business (Franklin); one self-
made man with no interests outside business (John Jacob Astor); three
empire builders (Cornelius Vanderbilt, John D. Rockefeller, and Andrew Carnegie); one financier (J. P. Morgan); one inventor-entrepreneur
(Henry Ford); and the prototype of the modern organization man (Alfred
P. Sloan). The advantage of the biographical approach is that it permits
me to write about transformations in American business without losing
touch with the human element and without getting lost among abstrac-
tions. As these lives unfold, the modern world emerges.

Though I do not mind a bit of skimming, I hope that every reader
will read the chapter about Franklin that begins the book. An understanding of Franklin is the foundation of all that follows. You might

think of *Poor Richard's Legacy* as a book that invites you on a journey through the world of American business with Franklin as your guide. As Virgil led Dante on their journey in *The Divine Comedy*, so Franklin has led me on this exploration. I feel confident that most readers will find him, as I have, an agreeable, shrewd, enlightening, and trustworthy companion.

Let me say a word about the prejudices I have brought to this project. I am conservative in my tastes and conservative in temperament, but liberal in my social and political views. I am also liberal in my economic views if you consider a belief in free enterprise to be classically liberal, as I do.

Despite my conservative tastes, few readers will fail to notice that I sympathize with the gadflies and skeptics whose ideas are reviewed in the chapters that examine the dissenting tradition. In truth, I like these "bitter gypsies of dissent," to quote a phrase that the head of General Motors once applied to Ralph Nader, even when I find myself quarreling with them. People who want to comfort the afflicted and afflict the comfortable always win my vote—and my heart—over people who seem content to comfort the comfortable and afflict the afflicted.

Poor Richard's Legacy is not pro-business or anti-business. It does not have an ideological ax to grind. Its aim is to probe a subject, not to score points in a debate. It exposes weaknesses in both the affirming and the dissenting traditions. It marks strengths in both traditions. It explores a persistent tension in American life, but it does not—it cannot—resolve that tension.

Finally, on this matter of liberal and conservative perspectives, I note with pleasure that the judgments offered in the last chapter of this book echo in many ways the judgments offered recently in a much-publicized speech by Richard Darman, the head of the Office of Management and Budget under President Bush. The government's current budget deficit, Mr. Darman charged, is a "Backward Robin Hood" policy, robbing the future to give to the present. The national debt, which has now passed $45,000 for every family of four, is "like a second mortgage—but without the house." In both the public and the private sector, the United States has fallen victim to a severe case of "Now-now-ism," a reluctance to defer gratification for the sake of future gains. "We consume today as if there were no tomorrow. . . . *Like the spoiled '50's child in a recently-revived commercial, we seem on the verge of a collective Now-now scream: 'I want my Maypo: I want it NOWWWWWWW!'* " (Mr. Darman's italics).

Our willingness to run up enormous debts that our children and

grandchildren will pay is not merely reckless, Mr. Darman suggested; it
is an unprecedented "expression of contempt" for the bond that links the
present to the future. As a liberal, I am delighted to concur with this
burst of straight talk from a highly regarded official in a conservative
administration. If liberals and conservatives can agree on this matter, we
might yet give our children a better legacy than we are currently preparing for them.

—Peter Baida
New York City

CHAPTER 1

Benjamin Franklin: "The Way to Wealth"

A Ghost in Spectacles

I entered the M.B.A. program at The Wharton School of the University of Pennsylvania in the fall of 1977, at the age of twenty-seven. Now that I have outlived any urgent need to impress corporate recruiters, I can confess that I disliked business school, and I can confess that what I particularly disliked—what particularly frustrated, irritated, and embarrassed me—was my inability to distinguish myself. I tried my best, but I found much of the work extremely difficult, and some of it I could not even pretend to understand. Not mastery but adequacy became my goal. I worked and worried. I felt stupid.

To make matters worse, I felt out of place. Most of my fellow M.B.A. candidates had spent their undergraduate years sharpening their skills in practical disciplines like accounting. Those who considered themselves impractical had studied economics. I had studied English. Whereas my classmates brought to business school an acquaintance with balance sheets and microeconomic theory, I brought an acquaintance with the poetry of Wordsworth, the prose of Samuel Johnson, and the criticism of I. A. Richards.

When I arrived at Wharton, nine years had passed since I had solved an equation or subjected myself to the perils of examination in a quantitative discipline. Glibness helps greatly in the humanities: Even if you have not read D. H. Lawrence or Jane Austen, you stand a fair chance of bluffing your way through an exam that asks you to compare their views on marriage. Business school makes sterner demands. In a test in accounting, neither native intelligence nor verbal facility will save you if you forget the difference between perpetual and periodic inventory systems.

I survived, but it was not a pleasant time for me. In a dream that woke me more than once, I saw myself shackled by a big black ball and chain to my seat in the school's computer room. The lights overhead threw a glare off the CRT screens. Terminals hummed with digital power, keyboards clicked, and printers clattered. The night sky loomed through a giant window twenty yards behind me. To my right, the clock on the wall was stuck at three. "In the real dark night of the soul," F. Scott Fitzgerald wrote, "it is always three o'clock in the morning."

Despite the hour, the room was full of students who seemed to know what they were doing and seemed not to mind their shackles. I struggled wretchedly to solve a problem I did not understand. Suddenly I felt a tug on my chain. Looking down, I saw my old friend Huckleberry Finn, as scruffy as ever, come to rescue me from business school. Together we would float a raft down the Mississippi, then light out for the territory ahead of the rest.

Carrying my ball and chain, I tiptoed behind Huck down the stairway toward the exit. At the door we were stopped not by the usual guard but by an amiable-looking old gentleman dressed in the plain style of Colonial America, from his old-fashioned coat and loosely knotted neckerchief down to his worsted hose and buckled shoes. It was Benjamin Franklin. Not bothering to take off his spectacles, he spread his arms and moved grimly toward Huck. In the dark they struggled, grunting with the effort. I understood that they were fighting for my soul.

My dream always ended with the famous pair wrestling while I stood helplessly to the side, in the shadows. When I woke, school awaited me. Anyone who has lived in Philadelphia knows that the ghost of its best-known citizen still haunts the city. "University of Pennsylvania—Founded by Benjamin Franklin"—so read the sign that greeted me each morning as I pushed through the doors of Vance Hall, where Huck and Ben struggled in my dream. At dusk each evening I passed beneath the statue of Franklin that gazes toward the library from the walk in front of Col-

lege Hall. My wife worked in the Franklin Building. We drove home via
the Benjamin Franklin Parkway.

All of these signs must mean something, I thought. As a pilgrim trav-
els to the Holy Land in search of his soul's salvation, so I had come to
Wharton in search of the secret of money. Somehow, I thought, Ben
Franklin held the key. But how? I knew about Franklin what every
schoolchild knows: He had served an apprenticeship, flown a kite, signed
a Declaration, and entertained the French. I knew also that it had been
Franklin who popularized the maxims about thrift and pennies and stitches
in time that an earnest teacher had drilled into my head in the third
grade; Franklin who declared, with an economy of language as characteristic as the economy of the sentiment, that "Time is money"; and
Franklin who taught America, in the title of his best-known essay, "The
Way to Wealth." What were my classmates and I doing at Franklin's
university if not struggling to remake ourselves in his image, to lay hands
on his legacy?

If money matters, Franklin matters: So I concluded as I communed
with his statue one crisp evening in that dreary, difficult time at Wharton. But I did not commune for long. There was no time for reverie in
business school, no time for teasing questions, no time for reflection or
speculation. There was not even time to read "The Way to Wealth."
The discovery of ancestors must wait, I told myself, until you have learned
the difference between perpetual and periodic inventory systems. But I
did not doubt that the discovery mattered. My dream needed a new
ending. To earn the blessing of Franklin's ghost, to quiet the spirits that
struggled within me, I would have to step out of the shadows and wrestle the old man myself.

Franklin as Mentor: "Advice to a Young Tradesman" and "The Way to Wealth"

In 1748 Franklin summarized his approach to business in a remarkable
two-page essay titled "Advice to a Young Tradesman." Apart from its
value as an expression of Franklin's views, the essay occupies a position
of unusual interest in the history of ideas. At the start of *The Protestant
Ethic and the Spirit of Capitalism*, German sociologist Max Weber could
find no better way to introduce his subject than to quote "Advice to a
Young Tradesman" virtually in its entirety. Out of the literature of half

a dozen languages, Weber chose these paragraphs to illustrate the spirit
of capitalism:

Remember, that *time* is money. He that can earn ten shillings a day by
his labour, and goes abroad, or sits idle, one half of that day, though he
spends but sixpence during his diversion or idleness, ought not to reckon
that the only expense; he has really spent, or rather thrown away, five
shillings besides.

Remember, that *credit* is money. If a man lets his money lie in my
hands after it is due, he gives me the interest, or so much as I can make
of it during that time. This amounts to a considerable sum where a man
has good and large credit, and makes good use of it.

Remember that money is of a prolific, generating nature. Money can
beget money, and its offspring can beget more, and so on. Five shillings
turned is six, turned again it is seven and threepence, and so on, till it
becomes a hundred pounds. The more there is of it, the more it produces
every turning, so that the profits rise quicker and quicker. He that kills a
breeding-sow, destroys all her offspring to the thousandth generation. He
that murders a crown, destroys all that it might have produced, even scores
of pounds.

Remember this saying, *The good paymaster is lord of another man's purse.*
He that is known to pay punctually and exactly to the time he promises,
may at any time, and on any occasion, raise all the money his friends can
spare. This is sometimes of great use. After industry and frugality, nothing contributes more to the raising of a young man in the world than
punctuality and justice in all his dealings; therefore never keep borrowed
money an hour beyond the time you promised, lest a disappointment shut
up your friend's purse for ever.

The most trifling actions that affect a man's credit are to be regarded.
The sound of your hammer at five in the morning, or eight at night, heard
by a creditor, makes him easy six months longer; but if he sees you at a
billiard-table, or hears your voice at a tavern, when you should be at work,
he sends for his money the next day; demands it, before he can receive it,
in a lump.

It shows, besides, that you are mindful of what you owe; it makes you
appear a careful as well as an honest man, and that still increases your
credit.

Beware of thinking all your own that you possess, and of living accordingly. It is a mistake that many people who have credit fall into. To prevent this, keep an exact account for some time both of your expenses and
of your income. If you take the pains at first to mention particulars, it will
have this good effect: you will discover how wonderfully small, trifling
expenses mount up to large sums, and will discern what might have been,
and may for the future be saved, without occasioning any great inconvenience.

In short, the Way to Wealth, if you desire it, is as plain as the Way to

Market. It depends chiefly on two Words, INDUSTRY and FRUGAL-ITY; i.e. Waste neither Time nor Money, but make the best Use of both. He that gets all he can honestly, and saves all he gets (necessary Expences excepted) will certainly become RICH; If that Being who governs the World, to whom all should look for a Blessing on their honest Endeavours, doth not in his wise Providence otherwise determine.

In Weber's view, these paragraphs express the spirit of capitalism "in almost classical purity." Weber defines capitalism as "the pursuit of profit, and forever *renewed* profit, by means of continuous, rational, capitalist enterprise." The Puritan-capitalist ethic, he writes, takes as its highest goal "the earning of more and more money, combined with the strict avoidance of all spontaneous enjoyment of life." It affirms "the idea of a duty of the individual toward the increase of his capital, which is assumed as an end in itself." Under its influence, "Man is dominated by the making of money, by acquisition as the ultimate purpose of his life."

Franklin's ideas "called forth the applause of a whole people," Weber observes, yet in both ancient times and the Middle Ages, these same ideas would have been condemned "as the lowest sort of avarice and as an attitude entirely lacking in self-respect." It is easy to show that Franklin did not lack self-respect, and it is easy to show that motives other than avarice guided many activities in his life. But to critics who raise these points as "problems," Weber replies testily that "The problem is just the reverse: how could such a philanthropist come to write these particular sentences . . . in the manner of a moralist?" A good question, and Weber's masterpiece may be viewed as an attempt to provide an answer.

"Advice to a Young Tradesman" was neither the first nor the most influential of Franklin's writings on personal economy. Beginning in 1732, Franklin published each year an almanac ostensibly put together by a poor farmer and amateur astrologer named Richard Saunders, better known as Poor Richard. In an effort to make the almanac "both entertaining and useful," Franklin tells us in his autobiography, he "filled all the little spaces that occurred between the remarkable days in the calendar with proverbial sentences, chiefly such as inculcated industry and frugality. . . ." The almanac soon won a large following and "came to be in such demand that I reaped considerable profit from it, vending annually over ten thousand."

In addition to anonymous folk proverbs representing "the Sense of all Ages and Nations," Franklin packed the almanac with maxims that he himself invented and epigrams drawn from writers such as Swift, Bacon, and La Rochefoucauld. He never hesitated to polish popular wisdom. For instance, "Three may keep counsel if two of them are away" was sharpened into "Three may keep a secret if two of them are dead." The Scottish "A gloved cat was never a good hunter" and the English "A muffled cat is no good mouser" became Poor Richard's "The cat in gloves catches no mice."

In 1757 Franklin composed a narrative that brought together in a "connected discourse" approximately one hundred sayings from the almanacs of the previous twenty-five years. The narrative unites the most worldly of Poor Richard's maxims in a speech made by a shrewd old man named Father Abraham to a crowd at a Colonial auction. This piece, Franklin tells us, "being universally approved, was copied in all the Newspapers of the Continent, reprinted in Britain on a Broadside to be stuck up in Houses, two Translations were made of it in French, and great Numbers bought by the Clergy and Gentry to distribute gratis among their poor Parishioners and Tenants." Under the title "The Way to Wealth" or "Father Abraham's Speech," it was reprinted at least 145 times in seven different languages before the end of the eighteenth century, and over the next two hundred years it came to be, with the autobiography, the most widely read of Franklin's writings.

"The Way to Wealth" crams so many proverbs into so few pages that it is difficult to believe that anyone has ever read it without experiencing some discomfort. Most readers probably feel as if they have gobbled too quickly a boxful of very rich chocolates. Franklin is right, however, when he claims that "bringing all these scatter'd counsels thus into a Focus, enabled them to make greater Impression." Here are a few examples of the advice that was calculated, Mark Twain charged, "to inflict suffering upon the rising generation of all subsequent ages."

INDUSTRY

"Dost thou love life, then do not squander Time, for that's the Stuff Life is made of." "He that riseth late, must trot all day." "Since thou art not sure of a Minute, throw not away an Hour." "Lost time is never found again." "The sleeping Fox catches no Poultry." "Little Strokes fell great Oaks." "Plough deep, while Sluggards sleep."

CARE

"If you would have your Business done, go; if not, send." "The Eye of a Master will do more Work than both his Hands." "Not to oversee

Workmen, is to leave them your Purse open." "Want of Care does us more Damage than Want of Knowledge."

FRUGALITY

"If you would be wealthy, think of Saving as well as of Getting." "Beware of little Expences; a small Leak will sink a great Ship." "A fat Kitchen makes a lean Will." "Fools make Feasts, and wise Men eat them." "What maintains one vice, would bring up two Children."

PRUDENCE

"If you would know the Value of Money, go and try to borrow some." "Rather go to Bed supperless than rise in Debt." " 'Tis easier to suppress the first Desire, than to satisfy all that follow it." "Pride that dines on Vanity sups on Contempt." "Pride breakfasted with Plenty, dined with Poverty, and supped with Infamy." " 'Tis hard for an empty Bag to stand upright." "Get what you can, and what you get hold;/'Tis the Stone that will turn all your Lead into Gold."

No work except the autobiography has done more than "The Way to Wealth" to spread Franklin's fame, and no work has done more to expose him to criticism. Melville called Franklin a "maxim-monger"; Keats called him "a philosophical Quaker full of mean and thrifty maxims"; and Twain complained that he worked up his aphorisms "with a great show of originality out of truisms that had become wearisome platitudes as early as the dispersion from Babel." The conventional image of Franklin as a man of narrow practicality might never have won much support had it not been for the success of Franklin's own scheme to mark the twenty-fifth anniversary of the almanac by bringing together the most practical of Poor Richard's precepts in a single narrative.

In his superb biography of Franklin, Carl Van Doren argues that Poor Richard represents only one side of his many-sided creator and that "The Way to Wealth" represents only one side of Poor Richard: "Everyone knows the Poor Richard that has been saved in Father Abraham's speech. Nobody knows Poor Richard as he was in the racy years that made him known to his contemporaries." Van Doren quotes extensively from earlier almanacs to prove that Poor Richard sometimes rejected "the side of calculating prudence"—a point that matters insofar as our aim is to understand Franklin himself, but does not matter insofar as our aim is to understand Franklin's role as an enunciator of business values and a mentor to his countrymen. The image of Franklin that readers have inferred from "The Way to Wealth" may be inaccurate, and the philosophy may be incomplete, but to the extent that readers have accepted them, both the inaccurate image and the incomplete philosophy are facts that have made a difference in American life.

In any case, Franklin's significance rests upon more than the maxims of Poor Richard and the counsel of "Advice to a Young Tradesman." The student of the American business character must examine not only what Franklin said but also the life he lived—a life that he turned, characteristically, into the most celebrated of all American autobiographies. In a remarkable feat of posthumous self-promotion, Franklin did not merely leave us the story of his life; he left us a self-portrait so persuasive it has permanently deprived most of his countrymen of the power to see beyond it.

Franklin as Role Model: Horatio Alger in Colonial America

Among the handful of Americans whose lives occupy a special place in the national consciousness, defining our image of ourselves, shaping our sense of possibility, and providing us with models of aspiration and accomplishment, Franklin presents an especially vivid example of the self-made man: the gifted, persevering individual whose rise from humble beginnings appeals so strongly to the democratic imagination. Only Lincoln, studying incessantly in his dimly lit cabin, offers as striking an image of early struggle in harsh surroundings. In 1862 Horace Greeley expressed a sentiment already common when he observed that "Of the men whom the world currently terms *Self-Made*—that is, who severally fought their life battles without the aid of inherited wealth, or family honors, or educational advantages, perhaps our American FRANKLIN stands highest in the civilized world's regard."

Franklin's story is so familiar that few Americans can recall when they first heard it. We seem to have known it for as long as we have known anything, in the same way that we know the stories of Paul Bunyan or Johnny Appleseed. Hearing the tale again, even in outline, we touch something vital in ourselves. Like the story of Lincoln, Franklin's story revives memories from the depths of childhood, when we began to understand what it means to be American.

Born in 1706, the tenth son and fifteenth child of a Boston soap- and candlemaker, Franklin attended school for two years, after which, at the age of ten, "I was taken home to assist my Father in his Business." His duties included "cutting Wick for the Candles, filling the Dipping Mold, and the Molds for cast Candles, attending the Shop, going of Errands, &c"—responsibilities that seem not to have inspired him, for within two years he found that he had developed "a strong inclination for the Sea." Observing that his son liked to read—"all the little Money that came into my Hands was ever laid out in Books"—Josiah Franklin decided that the boy would make a good printer, and, despite his maritime yearnings, Benjamin signed the papers that made him an indentured apprentice to his brother James "when I was yet but 12 years old."

Although the young man showed "great proficiency in the Business" and developed the skill as a writer that later helped him so much, the brothers did not get along. After five years Franklin broke the contract of apprenticeship, sold some books to raise cash, arranged a secret departure from Boston, and within three days, "found my self in New York 300 Miles from home, a Boy of but 17, without the least Recommendation to or Knowledge of any Person in the Place, and with very little Money in my Pocket."

Finding no work in New York, Franklin resumed the journey that he would describe memorably fifty years later. A stormy passage to Perth Amboy ("30 Hours on the Water without Victuals, or any Drink but a Bottle of filthy Rum"), a three-day walk across New Jersey ("It rain'd very hard all the Day"), and a wretched night lost along the Delaware River ("we made a Fire, the Night being cold . . . and there we remain'd till Daylight") brought him to the city where he would make his fortune.

Franklin's arrival in Philadelphia provides the occasion for one of the most celebrated moments in any American autobiography. Writing in 1771, aware that the youth of future generations might find parts of his life "suitable to their own Situations, and therefore fit to be imitated, " the self-made man permits himself a moment of self-congratulation: "I have been the more particular in this Description of my Journey, and shall be so of my first Entry into that City, that you may in your Mind compare such Unlikely Beginnings with the Figure I have since made there":

> I was in my Working Dress, my best Cloaths being to come round by Sea. I was dirty from my Journey; my Pockets were stuff'd out with Shirts and Stockings; I knew no Soul, nor where to look for Lodging. I was

fatigu'd with Travelling, Rowing and Want of Rest. I was very hungry, and my whole Stock of Cash consisted of a Dutch Dollar and about a Shilling in Copper. . . . Thus I walked up the street, gazing about, till near the Market House I met a Boy with Bread. I had made many a Meal on Bread, and inquiring where he got it, I went immediately to the Baker's he directed me to in second Street; . . . I bad him give me three penny worth of any sort. He gave me accordingly three great puffy Rolls. I was surpriz'd at the Quantity, but took it, and having no room in my Pockets, walk'd off, with a Roll under each Arm, and eating the other. Thus I went up Market Street as far as fourth Street, passing by the Door of Mr. Read, my future Wife's Father, when she standing at the Door saw me, and thought I made as I certainly did a most awkward ridiculous appearance.

One scholar has gone so far as to say that "The boy entering Philadelphia with three loaves under his arm is obviously the prototype of Bunyan's Christian beginning his toilsome ascent to the Heavenly City." Mark Twain took a more skeptical view. Franklin was proud, he wrote, "of telling how he entered Philadelphia for the first time, with nothing in the world but two shillings in his pocket and four rolls of bread under his arm. But really, when you come to examine it critically, it was nothing. Anybody could have done it."

Even after this famous arrival, Franklin did not rise steadily. Indeed, his account of his next five years (in Philadelphia, London, and Philadelphia again) focuses upon what he calls his "Errata"—a printer's term for errors. He misused money entrusted to him, made mistakes with women, and displayed toward his future wife an astonishing thoughtlessness. Yet we see signs of a safe emergence from this "dangerous Time of Youth." At a printing house in London, Franklin's coworkers borrowed money from the teetotaling American when they ran out of credit at the local alehouse: "I watch'd the Pay table on Saturday Night, and collected. . . ." Working next for the Philadelphia merchant Thomas Denham, Franklin "attended the Business diligently, studied Accounts, and grew in a little Time expert at Selling." Denham's death in 1728 pushed the young man, now twenty-two, back into the printing business. He would have preferred a job as a merchant's clerk, but he could not find one.

His mastery of the printer's trade gave Franklin the means to take his first step out of obscurity. But his rise depended upon more than technical skills. He had also acquired qualities of character that enabled him to take full advantage of his trade. One quality that stands out is his craftiness in the art of self-presentation:

I began now gradually to pay off the Debt I was under for the Printing-House. In order to secure my Credit and Character as a Tradesman, I took care not only to be in *Reality* industrious and frugal, but to avoid all *Appearances* of the Contrary. I drest plainly; I was seen at no Places of idle Diversion; I never went out a-fishing or shooting; a Book, indeed, sometimes debauch'd me from my Work; but that was seldom, snug, and gave no Scandal: and to show that I was not above my Business, I sometimes brought home the Paper I purchas'd at the Stores, thro' the Streets on a Wheelbarrow. Thus being esteem'd an industrious thriving young Man, and paying duly for what I bought, the Merchants who imported Stationary solicited my Custom, others propos'd supplying me with Books, and I went on swimmingly.

With the establishment of his own printing business, Franklin began a dazzling entrepreneurial career. An early coup presents a classic example of the self-made man making his own luck. Having noticed "a Cry among the People for more Paper-Money," Franklin wrote and published an anonymous pamphlet titled *A Modest Enquiry into the Nature and Necessity of a Paper Currency*. When the legislature voted to issue an additional forty thousand pounds, the young publisher was hired to print the money—"a very profitable Jobb, and a great Help to me."

Other profitable ventures included the *Pennsylvania Gazette*, which Franklin took over from a bankrupt competitor in 1729 and turned into one of the most vigorous newspapers in the Colonies; and, of course, *Poor Richard's Almanack*. Among printers in Philadelphia, two of Franklin's three main competitors left the business shortly after he entered it, and the third soon settled into semiretirement, so that when the twenty-four-year-old Franklin bought out his partner in 1730, he had the field virtually to himself.

With success in business came, in the words of Carl Van Doren, a "swift accumulation of offices." From 1736 until 1751, when the citizens of Philadelphia elected him their representative, Franklin served as clerk to the Pennsylvania Assembly. Along with a modest title and salary, the position provided an "Opportunity of keeping up an Interest among the Members" and thus "secur'd to me the Business of Printing the Votes, Laws, Paper Money and other occasional Jobbs for the Public, that on the whole were very profitable." In addition, beginning in 1737, Franklin served as postmaster of Philadelphia—another modest position, but it increased the demand for his newspaper, brought him new advertisers, and "came to afford me a very considerable income."

Additional income flowed in from partnerships or working arrangements with printers in the Carolinas, New York, and the British West Indies, as well as from investments in real estate. In 1748, twenty years after the formation of the partnership that launched him, Franklin retired, handing over "all Care of the Printing-Office" to a younger man: "I flatter'd myself that by the sufficient tho' moderate Fortune I had acquir'd, I had secur'd Leisure during the rest of my Life, for Philosophical Studies and Amusements." Thus Franklin took the step that has tripped up any number of nimble businessmen: He stepped aside.

Franklin left business at the age of forty-two, exactly halfway through a remarkably busy life. In Carl Van Doren's 782-page biography, Franklin's retirement occurs on page 123. Ahead lay enough activity to fill the lives of half a dozen men. "Electrician," "Soldier," "Agent," "Speaker," "Agent-General," "Philosopher in England," "Postmaster-General," "Commissioner," "Minister-Plenipotentiary," "Sage in France," "Peacemaker," "President of Pennsylvania"—even a partial list of Van Doren's chapter titles suffices to suggest how little we see of Franklin if we see him only as a businessman.

Yet he began as a businessman, and his success in business paved the way for grander successes. The story of Franklin's rise has entertained and instructed generations of Americans, but its familiarity may lull us into a failure to ask one fundamental question: To what extent did Franklin owe his rise to the virtues he recommended in the writings that made him famous? This question offers our best protection against the charm of Franklin's own voice and the temptation to take a simple view of him.

No one can reasonably deny that industry helped Franklin to gain his fortune and that frugality helped him to keep it. But luck also helped, and natural ability helped even more. Luck led to the apprenticeship as a printer that supplied him with the technical skills on which he based his business success. Natural ability led to mastery whenever he exerted himself. He would not have fared so well if he had been an industrious bumbler or a frugal knucklehead. On the other hand, luck alone would have meant little if he had not worked to master his trade, and natural ability would have meant little if he had not worked to develop his gifts. Franklin was born with a lively intelligence but not with the lively prose style that marked his maturity. He needed luck to succeed, but he needed something more than luck—and something more than industry, frugality, and prudence—to succeed as brilliantly as he did. Imagine Franklin without his eye for entrepreneurial opportunities, or without his humor and his literary skill, and at once it becomes clear that simple economic virtues tell only part of the story. Van Doren's summary puts the issue into perfect perspective:

> In business Franklin was extremely alert to the main chance, adaptable, resolute, crafty though not petty, and ruthless on occasion. . . . Other

men besides Franklin in Philadelphia were as industrious and frugal as he. No other man had a mind so capacious and ingenious and incessant, so able at once to persuade and to charm. It was Franklin's luck that it was easier for him to be outstanding in Philadelphia than it would have been in London. But from the first he was outstanding, and he throve by the exercise of natural gifts of which Poor Richard could not tell the secrets.

Franklin as Team Player: The Junto and Other Groups

In the second half of the twentieth century, successors of Poor Richard have embraced the term "networking" to refer to an activity they see as a key to business success: the cultivation and utilization of professional connections. Here as in so much else, we follow a trail that Franklin blazed. Aspiring youths of any era may usefully study Franklin's accomplishments as a networker.

"Franklin was clubbable," one twentieth-century British admirer has observed, and, indeed, in addition to its lessons of thrift, industry, and prudence, Franklin's autobiography shows how much he loved clubs. In 1727, four years after his arrival in a city where he knew no one, the twenty-one-year-old printer "form'd most of my ingenious Acquaintance into a Club for mutual Improvement, which we call'd the Junto." The members of the Junto were young men not yet respectable or established enough to break into the clubs that served Philadelphia's business elite. Like Franklin, they were tradesmen, sometimes called Leather Aprons, and the Junto was sometimes called the Leather-Apron Club.

Franklin modeled the Junto on the neighborhood benefit societies that Cotton Mather had organized several years earlier in Boston. In his autobiography, Franklin comments upon the influence of his early reading of Mather's *An Essay Upon the Good*, and late in life he wrote to Mather's son that "if I have been, as you seem to think, a useful citizen, the public owes the advantage of it to that book." Franklin may also have been influenced by Mather's *Manuductio Ad Ministerium*, published in 1726. "Form a SODALITY," the eminent Puritan advised. "What I mean is, Prevail with a Fit Number . . . of Sober, Ingenious, and Industrious Young Men, to Associate with you, and meet *One Evening* in a *Week*, for the spending of Two or Three Hours in a *Profitable Conversation*."

Franklin's club exactly followed Mather's recommendation. The Junto was a secret brotherhood that met weekly. Its rules, drafted by Franklin, required new members to "sincerely declare" that they loved mankind in general and truth for truth's sake. Meetings began with twenty-four "standing Queries," also drafted by Franklin, which show that the club did not so much mix business with pleasure as it mixed the business of doing good with the business of getting ahead. A few examples give us the flavor of the enterprise and something of the flavor of Franklin's mind:

> 1. Have you met with any thing in the author you last read, remarkable, or suitable to be communicated to the Junto? . . . 2. What new story have you lately heard agreeable for telling in conversation? 3. Hath any citizen in your knowledge failed in his business lately, and what have you heard of the cause? 4. Have you lately heard of any citizen's thriving well, and by what means? 5. Have you lately heard how any present rich man, here or elsewhere, got his estate? . . . 7. What unhappy effects of intemperance have you lately observed or heard? of imprudence? of passion? or of any other vice or folly? 8. What happy effects of temperance? of prudence? of moderation? or of any other virtue? . . . 11. Do you think of any thing at present, in which the Junto may be serviceable to *mankind*? to their country, to their friends, or to themselves? . . . 13. Do you know of any deserving young beginner lately set up, whom it lies in the power of the Junto any way to encourage? . . . 16. Hath any body attacked your reputation lately? And what can the Junto do towards securing it? 17. Is there any man whose friendship you want, and which the Junto or any of them, can procure for you? 18. Have you lately heard any member's character attacked, and how have you defended it? 19. Hath any man injured you, from whom it is in the power of the Junto to procure redress? 20. In what manner can the Junto, or any of them, assist you in any of your honourable designs? 21. Have you any weighty affairs in hand, in which you think the advice of the Junto may be of service?

In addition to the requirement to love mankind and truth, the rules of the Junto required that "every Member in his Turn should produce one or More Queries on any Point of Morals, Politics or Natural Philosophy, to be discuss'd by the Company, and once in three Months produce and read an Essay of his own Writing on any Subject he pleased." Franklin's own queries show the range of his interests. The man of letters asks, "How shall we judge of the goodness of a writing?" The moral philosopher asks, "Can a man arrive at perfection in this life?" "What is wisdom?" "Wherein consists the happiness of a rational creature?" The ever-curious observer asks, "Whence comes the dew that stands on the outside of a tankard that has cold water in it in the summer time?" The political philosopher asks, "Is it justifiable to put private men to death, for the sake of public safety or tranquillity, who have committed no crime? As, in the case of the plague, to stop infection . . . ?" The future revolutionary asks, "If the sovereign power attempts to deprive a subject of his right . . . is it justifiable in him to resist, if he is able?"

And the man of business who wants also to be a man of virtue asks, "Which is best: to make a friend of a wise and good man that is poor or of a rich man that is neither wise nor good?" "Does it not, in a general way, require great study and intense application for a poor man to become rich and powerful, if he would do it without the forfeiture of honesty?" "Does it not require as much pains, study and application to become truly wise and strictly virtuous as to become rich?"

The Junto survived for more than thirty years and was, Franklin claimed, "the best School of Philosophy, Morals and Politics that then existed in the Province." But it was also, always, an effective source of business assistance for its members, "every one of these exerting themselves in recommending Business to us." In Franklin's mind and in his life, public service and personal welfare went hand in hand. As Carl van Doren remarked, the Junto was Franklin's "benevolent lobby for the benefit of Philadelphia, and now and then for the advantage of Benjamin Franklin."

At the age of twenty-five, with the assistance of the Junto, Franklin embarked on the first in the long line of public projects that amply justified his claim, near the end of his life, that he had "always set a greater value on the character of a *doer of good*, than on any other kind of reputation." The project was the establishment of a public subscription library. Franklin drafted a proposal and, "by the help of my Friends in the Junto, procur'd fifty Subscribers." Fifty years later he could boast that the library had become "the Mother of all the . . . American Subscription Libraries now so numerous."

This was just the start; it is unlikely that any city has ever owed as much to one man as Philadelphia owes to Franklin. After the library (1731), Franklin founded or helped to found Philadelphia's city watch (1735–52), Philadelphia's first fire company (1736), Philadelphia's first college (1749), Philadelphia's first hospital (1751), and Philadelphia's first fire insurance company (1752). He also served as grand master of Pennsylvania's Freemasons (1734), founded the American Philosophical Society (1743), organized Pennsylvania's first militia (1747), and encouraged the paving and lighting of Philadelphia's streets (1751–62).

Each project depended on the assistance of Franklin's network of personal and professional connections, and with each project his network grew, along with his reputation as a doer of good—"a great Promoter of useful Projects." Franklin's skill as a promoter of public improvements fully matched his skill as a promoter of his personal interests. Indeed, we miss the essence of Franklin's success if we try to separate the two.

Throughout his career, the promotion of the public good served Franklin as the most effective possible self-promotion.

In his autobiography, Franklin reveals with characteristic candor—or at least with a characteristic *appearance* of candor—some of the tricks that made him so effective in his public ventures. The key lesson was one that he learned in his very first campaign, the effort to establish the subscription library. The resistance that he encountered, he tells us, "made me soon feel the Impropriety of presenting one's self as the Proposer of any useful Project that might be suppos'd to raise one's Reputation in the smallest degree above that of one's Neighbors, when one has need of their Assistance to accomplish that Project. I therefore put my self as much as I could out of sight, and stated it as a Scheme of a *Number of Friends*, who had requested me to go about and propose it to such as they thought Lovers of Reading. In this way my Affair went on more smoothly, and I ever after practis'd it on such Occasions."

This apparent self-effacement on the part of a brilliant self-promoter may strike us initially as a baffling contradiction, sufficient to compel a reconsideration of Franklin's character. But the contradiction disappears when Franklin explains his strategy. "The present little Sacrifice of your Vanity," he writes, "will afterwards be amply repaid. If it remains a while uncertain to whom the Merit belongs, some one more vain than yourself will be encourag'd to claim it, and then even Envy will be dispos'd to do you Justice, by plucking those assum'd Feathers, and restoring them to their right Owner."

This kind of wily insight animates many passages in the autobiography, giving the book much of its charm. From Franklin we learn, for instance, that "a perfect Character might be attended with the Inconvenience of being envied and hated," so "a benevolent Man should allow a few Faults in himself, to keep his Friends in Countenance." From Franklin, too, we learn how to turn an enemy into a friend. Request that the enemy do you some favor, and once the favor has been done, express your gratitude in the strongest terms. It is an old maxim, Franklin explains, that *"He that has once done you a Kindness will be more ready to do you another, than he whom you yourself have obliged."*

As Franklin recommends self-effacement to the promoter of any project, so he recommends self-effacement in conversation. His rules for the Junto included a stipulation that the weekly discussions were to be conducted in "the sincere Spirit of Enquiry after Truth, without Fondness for Dispute, or Desire of Victory"—a stipulation that the members took so seriously that eventually "all Expressions of Positiveness in Opinion, or of direct Contradiction, were . . . made contraband and prohibited under small pecuniary Penalties." Outside the Junto, Franklin "made it a Rule to forbear all direct Contradiction to the Sentiments of others, and all positive Assertion of my own. I even forbid myself . . . the Use of every Word or Expression in the Language that imported a fix'd Opinion; such as *certainly, undoubtedly,* &c. and I adopted instead of them, *I conceive, I apprehend,* or *I imagine* a thing to be so or so, or it so appears to me at present. When another asserted something, that I thought an error, I deny'd my self the Pleasure of contradicting him abruptly, and of showing immediately some Absurdity in his Proposition; and in answering I began by observing that in Certain Cases or Circumstances his Opinion would be right, but that in the present case there *appear'd* or *seem'd* to me some Difference."

On humility in general, Franklin admits that "I cannot boast of much Success in acquiring the *Reality* of this Virtue; but I had a good deal with regard to the *Appearance.*" The appearance sufficed to produce definite benefits: "The Conversations I engag'd in went on more pleasantly. The modest way in which I propos'd my Opinions procur'd them a readier Reception and less Contradiction; I had less Mortification when I was found to be in the wrong, and I more easily prevail'd with others to give up their Mistakes and join with me when I happen'd to be in the right." Indeed, Franklin claims to have succeeded so well in overcoming his youthful habit of "abrupt Contradiction" that "perhaps for these Fifty Years past no one has ever heard a dogmatical Expression escape me," and he credits his modesty of speech, after only his "Character of Integrity," for the fact that he acquired early in life "so much Weight with my Fellow Citizens, when I proposed new Institutions, or Alterations in the old. . . ." In summary, he tells us, with the conviction of sixty years of worldly experience, "these disputing, contradicting, and confuting People are generally unfortunate in their Affairs. They get Victory sometimes, but they never get Good Will, which would be of more use to them."

Self-effacement not in the expression of his views but in the manner of the expression, self-effacement not in the promotion of public works but in the pursuit of credit—or at least the *appearance* of pursuit—those are the lessons that Franklin teaches. He would not have found anything new in Dale Carnegie's *How to Win Friends and Influence People* or in the self-help books of Carnegie's successors in our own generation. He would not have found anything new in the ten generations of self-help writers who have followed his own Poor Richard. He was an accomplished "net-

worker" and an invaluable team player—a master of what social psy-
chologists of the twentieth century call "group dynamics." To an
unsympathetic commentator, he was "the father of all the Kiwanians";
to a sympathetic one, "the first of the joiners and boosters and glad-
handers." His career as a team player began with the group of young
tradesmen he brought together in his Junto and ended with the teams
that hammered out the Declaration of Independence and the Constitution of the United States. His last public speech, made at the age of
eighty-one to close the Constitutional Convention, gives us a chance to
overhear the consummate team player as he makes perhaps the finest
locker-room talk in history:

"I confess," the sick old man wrote in the speech that James Wilson
of Pennsylvania delivered on his behalf on September 17, 1787, "that
there are several parts of this Constitution which I do not at present
approve, but I am not sure I shall never approve them; for, having lived
long, I have experienced many instances of being obliged by better information or fuller consideration to change opinions, even on important
subjects, which I once thought right but found to be otherwise. It is
therefore that the older I grow the more apt I am to doubt my own
judgment and to pay attention to the judgment of others. . . . Thus I
consent, Sir, to this Constitution because I expect no better, and because
I am not sure that it is not the best. The opinions I have had of its errors
I sacrifice to the public good. I have never whispered a syllable of them
abroad. Within these walls they were born, and here they shall die. . . .
On the whole, Sir, I cannot help expressing a wish that every member
of the Convention who may still have objections to it would, with me,
on this occasion doubt a little of his infallibility, and, to make manifest
our unanimity, put his name to this instrument."

Here is a speaker who knows that honey catches flies. In France during the Revolutionary War, Franklin had won a formidable reputation as
a ladies' man, but it seems unlikely that he wooed the women of French
society any more sweetly than he wooed his recalcitrant colleagues at the
Constitutional Convention. Other men may have been more modest, but
no one has ever sounded more modest.

Franklin as Moral Bookkeeper: The Art of Virtue

The humility to "doubt a little of his infallibility" did not come easily to
Franklin. Though he tried to subdue his pride, he recognized that "Dis-
guise it, struggle with it, beat it down, stifle it, mortify it as much as

one pleases, it is still alive, and will every now and then peep out and show itself." He concedes that the reader will "see it perhaps often" in his autobiography, and he adds characteristically that "even if I could conceive that I had compleatly overcome it, I should probably be proud of my Humility."

Only a proud young man could have undertaken the project that provides the subject for one of the most revealing sections of the autobiography—"the bold and arduous project," as Franklin says with some understatement, "of arriving at moral perfection." It is the kind of project that only youth could embrace, and Franklin conceived it at about the age of twenty-five, in the same period when he founded the library and prepared the first edition of *Poor Richard's Almanack*. What makes the episode revealing is not the idea itself but the extraordinary plan that Franklin developed to put the idea into effect. Franklin began with a list of thirteen virtues, "all that at that time occurred to me as necessary or desirable." The virtues were temperance, silence, order, resolution, frugality, industry, sincerity, justice, moderation, cleanliness, tranquility, chastity, and humility. Recognizing that moral perfection might be a tall order, Franklin "judg'd it would be well not to distract my Attention by attempting the whole at once, but to fix it on one of them at a time, and when I should be Master of that, then to proceed to another, and so on till I should have gone thro' the thirteen." In keeping with this approach, he arranged the virtues in order of priority, with the intention that the acquisition of the first should facilitate the acquisition of the second, the acquisition of the first and second should facilitate the acquisition of the third, and so on through the thirteenth. What is striking is that Franklin approaches the task of achieving moral perfection in exactly the way that he would approach any large task in business. In other words, he brings to moral and spiritual affairs exactly the spirit that he brings to worldly affairs—a spirit of discipline, order, and precise calculation.

"I made a little Book," he tells us, "in which I allotted a Page for each of the Virtues. I rul'd each Page with red Ink, so as to have seven Columns, one for each Day of the Week, marking each Column with a Letter for the Day. I cross'd these Columns with thirteen red Lines, marking the Beginning of each Line with the first Letter of one of the Virtues, on which Line and in its proper Column I might mark by a little black Spot every Fault I found upon Examination to have been committed respecting that Virtue upon that Day."

This moral ledger was only one part of the plan. Since the virtue of order required that "*every Part of my Business should have its allotted Time,*"

Form of the Pages

TEMPERANCE.						
Eat not to Dulness. *Drink not to Elevation.*						
S	M	T	W	T	F	S
T						
S	••	•		•		•	
O	•	•	•		•	•	•
R			•		•		
F		•			•		
I			•				
S							
J							
M							
Cl.							
T							
Ch.							
H							

and since the virtue of industry required that he "Lose no Time. Be always employ'd in something useful. Cut off all unnecessary actions," Franklin devoted one page of his book to a "Scheme of Employment for the Twenty-Four Hours of a Natural Day":

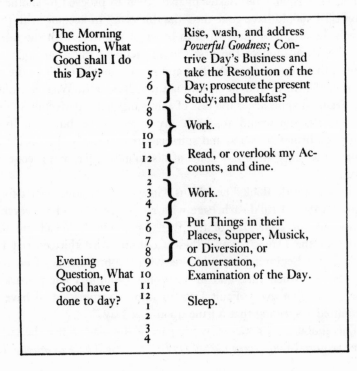

The Morning Question, What Good shall I do this Day?

5	Rise, wash, and address *Powerful Goodness;* Contrive Day's Business and take the Resolution of the Day; prosecute the present Study; and breakfast?
6	
7	
8	Work.
9	
10	
11	
12	Read, or overlook my Accounts, and dine.
1	
2	Work.
3	
4	
5	Put Things in their Places, Supper, Musick, or Diversion, or Conversation, Examination of the Day.
6	
7	
8	
9	
10	
11	
12	Sleep.
1	
2	
3	
4	

Evening Question, What Good have I done to day?

Here the spirit of capitalism—in Weber's definition, "that attitude which seeks profit rationally and systematically"—is applied to the pursuit not of material but of moral well-being. It makes no difference whether Franklin seeks wealth or moral perfection. His method will be the same— a systematic approach, with precisely defined objectives and a timetable.

We will never know how many of Franklin's readers followed his example, but we do know of one prominent follower in fiction. In F. Scott Fitzgerald's novel *The Great Gatsby*, a poignant scene occurs when Gatsby's father comes East after the death of his son. He brings with him a ragged old copy of a *Hopalong Cassidy* book, which he has saved because of a "SCHEDULE" that his son wrote on the flyleaf:

Rise from bed .... 6:00 A.M.
Dumbbell exercise and wall-scaling 6:15–6:30
Study electricity, etc. 7:15–8:15
Work 8:30–4:30
Baseball and sports 4:30–5:00
Practice elocution, poise and how to attain it 5:00–6:00
Study needed inventions 7:00–9:00

GENERAL RESOLVES

No wasting time . . .
No more smoking or chewing
Bathing every other day
Read one improving book or magazine per week
Save $5.00 [crossed out] $3.00 per week
Be better to parents

Like Franklin, Jay Gatsby runs away from home to make his fortune, but unlike Franklin's, his story ends in loss and corruption. He never seems more American than in his father's remembrance: "Jimmy was bound to get ahead. He always had some resolves like this or something. Do you notice what he's got about improving his mind. He was always great for that." It is Gatsby's epitaph, but it could be Franklin's, spoken by the father he left behind in Boston.

Franklin as Symbol: Posterity Talks Back

Almost since the day he died, America has been talking back to Benjamin Franklin. Some of us love him, others loathe him, but few are neutral. He is not like anyone else, yet somehow he is representative—a figure we must understand if we want to understand the American character. All of us see ourselves in him, or see an antiself.

His contemporary John Adams saw, perhaps jealously, a man whom posterity would overrate. To a correspondent he complained that "The history of our Revolution will be one continued lie from one end to the other. The essence of the whole will be that Dr. Franklin's electrical rod smote the earth and out sprang General Washington. That Franklin electrified him with his rod, and thenceforward these two conducted all the policy negotiations, legislatures, and war."

Adams seems reverent compared with William Cobbett, a Federalist pamphleteer who saw Franklin as "a crafty and lecherous old hypocrite . . . whose very statue seems to gloat on the wenches as they walk the State House yard." Another Federalist, Joseph Dennie, sneered that "The fact is, that 'our Benjamin' was no more distinguished for the originality of his conceptions, than for the purity of his life, or the soundness of his religious doctrine. . . . Above all he was the author of that pitiful system of Economies, the adoption of which has degraded our national character."

Adams speaks only for himself, and Cobbett and Dennie speak for a minority. The majority made Franklin's autobiography the most famous of any ever written by an American and made Franklin himself one of the two or three most popular subjects of American biography. Franklin's name has become a public possession. In 1831, when a group of Bostonians decided to sponsor lectures to encourage young men to lead sober and industrious lives, they found it natural to call them Franklin lectures. Even today, nearly two centuries after his death, hundreds of savings institutions call themselves Franklin banks.

Testimonials to Franklin's influence could fill a book. Thomas Mellon, the founder of one of America's greatest fortunes, provided one of the best. Mellon was a fourteen-year-old living on a farm outside Pittsburgh when he stumbled upon a copy of the autobiography. "I had not before imagined any other course of life superior to farming," he said later, "but the reading of Franklin's life led me to question this view. For so poor and friendless a boy to be able to become a merchant or a professional man had before seemed an impossibility; but here was Franklin, poorer than myself, who by industry, thrift and frugality had become learned and wise, and elevated to wealth and fame. The maxims of 'Poor Richard' exactly suited my sentiments. . . . I regard the reading of Franklin's *Autobiography* as the turning point of my life." Not long after he discovered Franklin, Mellon set out from his home in Poverty Point, Pennsylvania, for Pittsburgh, twenty-one miles away, with ninety-nine cents in his pocket. Years later, the financier put a statue of Franklin in his bank, and late in life he printed one thousand copies of the autobiography to give to the young people who flocked to him for assistance or advice.

The most incisive portrait of Franklin to appear in the nineteenth century is tucked into the middle of Herman Melville's novel *Israel Potter*. Melville describes the venerable Franklin as a "serene, cool and ripe old philosopher . . . the grave man of utility . . . the homely sage, and household Plato . . . the lean and slippered metaphysician." In his invented encounters with Melville's innocent hero, Franklin plays so cunning a series of tricks that at last the forlorn youth reflects, "Every time he comes in he robs me, with an air all the time, too, as if he were making me presents." Amid the horseplay, something extraordinary happens. Melville gets interested in Franklin, forgets that his novel only needs a comic stereotype, forgets that he is only writing a potboiler, and dashes off the most brilliant portrait of Franklin that anyone has ever written. In these paragraphs, just for a moment, Melville drops his satirist's mask and looks Franklin straight in the eye, genius to genius:

> Franklin all over is of a piece. He dressed his person as his periods; neat, trim, nothing superfluous, nothing deficient. . . . labyrinth-minded . . . plain-spoken . . . thrifty, domestic, dietarian . . . didactically waggish. . . . Having carefully weighed the world, Franklin could act any part in it. By nature turned to knowledge, his mind was often grave, but never serious. . . . Printer, postmaster, almanac maker, essayist, chemist, orator, tinker, statesman, humorist, philosopher, parlor man, political economist, professor of housewifery, ambassador, projector, maxim-monger, herb-doctor, wit:—Jack of all trades, master of each and mastered by none—the type and genius of his land. Franklin was everything but a poet. . . . There was much benevolent irony, innocent mischievousness, in the wise man. Seeking here to depict him in his less exalted habitudes, the narrator feels more as if he were playing with one of the sage's worsted hose, than reverentially handling the honored hat which once oracularly sat upon his brow.

Whereas Melville struggles to take Franklin's measure, Mark Twain contents himself with a tweak of the great man's nose. Franklin, he declares, was "of a vicious disposition" and "full of animosity towards boys." He "early prostituted his talents to the invention of maxims and aphorisms calculated to inflict suffering upon the rising generation of all subsequent ages. . . . It was in this spirit that he became the son of a soapboiler, and probably for no other reason than that the efforts of all future boys . . . might be looked upon with suspicion unless they were the sons of soap-boilers."

The general acceptance of Franklin as a model for the young offered Twain a target he could not resist. He complains that "with a malevolence which is without parallel in history," Franklin would "work all day, and then sit up at nights, and let on to be studying algebra by the light of a smouldering fire, so that all other boys might have to do that also, or else have Benjamin thrown up to them. Not satisfied with these proceedings, he had a fashion of living wholly on bread and water, and studying astronomy at meal time—a thing which has brought affliction to millions of boys since, whose fathers had read Franklin's pernicious biography."

In the twentieth century, critics of Franklin have hit harder. The literary critic Charles Angoff charges that

> Franklin represented the least praiseworthy qualities of the inhabitants of the New World: miserliness, fanatical practicality, and lack of interest in what are usually known as spiritual things. Babbittry was not a new thing in America, but he made a religion of it, and by his tremendous success with it he grafted it upon the American people so securely that the national genius is still suffering from it. . . . Not a word about nobility, not a word about honor, not a word about grandeur of soul, not a word about charity of mind!

Franklin was, Angoff concludes, "a cheap and shabby soul."

The bitterest denunciations of Franklin, as well as the most sweeping and the least conventional, have come from the American poet William Carlos Williams and the stormy Englishman D. H. Lawrence. Both of them associate Franklin with values they detest, and both of them launch long, complex, vigorous attacks. Williams complains that in his experiments with lightning, Franklin "didn't dare let it go in at the top of his head and out at his toes. . . . He sensed the power and knew only enough to want to run an engine with it. His fingers itched to be meddling, to do the little concrete things. . . . He was the dike keeper, keeping out the wilderness with his wits. . . . His mighty answer to the New World's offer of a great embrace was THRIFT. Work night and day, build up, penny by penny, a wall against that which is threatening, the terror of life, poverty. Make a fort to be secure in." Franklin, Williams concludes with a sigh, is "our wise prophet of chicanery, the great buffoon, the face on the penny stamp."

Like Williams, D. H. Lawrence sees Franklin as a spiritual enemy—

an enemy of life itself. When Franklin says that God "governs the world by his Providence," Lawrence protests that Franklin's God is "the supreme servant of men who want to get on. . . . The provider. The heavenly storekeeper. The everlasting Wanamaker." When Franklin says that "the soul of man is immortal," Lawrence exclaims, "Why, the soul of man is a vast forest, and all Benjamin intended was a neat back garden. . . . Benjamin fenced a little tract that he called the soul of man, and proceeded to get it into cultivation. . . . This is Benjamin's barbed wire fence. He made himself a list of virtues, which he trotted inside like a grey nag in a paddock."

Of all Franklin's offenses, his scheme of moral perfection strikes Lawrence as the most obnoxious. "I am a moral animal," he counters. "But I am not a moral machine. I don't work with a little set of handles or levers. The Temperance-silence-order-resolution-frugality-industry-sincerity-justice-moderation-cleanliness-tranquillity-chastity-humility keyboard is not going to get me going. I'm really not just an automatic piano with a moral Benjamin getting tunes out of me."

Franklin had all the qualities of a great man, Lawrence says, but he never became more than a great citizen. He was "the first downright American . . . the pattern American." Mark Twain's account of Franklin's "pernicious" influence is revealed for what it is—a good-natured and perhaps even affectionate joke—when we compare it with Lawrence's protest:

> I can remember, when I was a little boy, my father used to buy a scrubby yearly almanac with the sun and moon and stars on the cover. And it used to prophesy bloodshed and famine. But also crammed in corners it had little anecdotes and humorisms, with a moral tag. And I used to have my little priggish laugh at the woman who counted her chickens before they were hatched and so forth, and I was convinced that honesty was the best policy, also a little priggishly. . . .
>
> And probably I haven't got over those Poor Richard tags yet. I rankle still with them. They are thorns in young flesh.
>
> Because, although I still believe that honesty is the best policy, I dislike policy altogether; . . . It has taken me many years and countless smarts to get out of that barbed wire moral enclosure that Poor Richard rigged up. Here am I now in tatters and scratched to ribbons, sitting in the middle of Benjamin's America looking at the barbed wire. . . . And I just utter a long loud curse against Benjamin and the American corral.

The extreme responses to Franklin, whether pro or con, are more vivid and entertaining than balanced appraisals, which have nothing to recommend them except the wish to be fair. A balanced appraisal must concur with Carl Van Doren's statement that Franklin "seems to have been more than any single man," as well as his assertion that nothing seems to have been omitted from Franklin's character "except a passionate desire, as in most men of genius, to be all ruler, all soldier, all saint, all poet, all scholar, all some one gift or merit or success." Franklin was indeed, as Van Doren says, "a harmonious human multitude." He might have taken as his epitaph Turgot's famous epigram "He snatched the lightning from the sky and the sceptre from tyrants." But the grand style did not suit him, and, though he stood before kings, he never forgot his roots. His will begins, "I, Benjamin Franklin, Printer . . ."

Benjamin Franklin and Huckleberry Finn, the ghost in spectacles and the boy in rags, always will wrestle for the soul of America. It is not as bitter a struggle as it might seem at first, nor is Franklin an unfriendly spirit. Having listened to the best and the worst that posterity has said of him, we might end by listening to the ghost himself. He has saved one last story, and he will not let us go until he tells it. The year is 1755, and Franklin has gone on an excursion with friends. But let him speak for himself:

> Being in Maryland, riding with Colonel Tasker and some other gentlemen to his country seat . . . we saw, in the vale below us, a small whirlwind beginning in the road and showing itself by the dust it raised and contained. It appeared in the form of a sugar loaf, spinning on its point, moving up the hill towards us, and enlarging as it came forward. When it passed by us, its smaller part near the ground appeared no bigger than a common barrel, but, widening upwards, it seemed at forty or fifty feet high to be twenty or thirty feet in diameter.
>
> The rest of the company stood looking after it, but, my curiosity being stronger, I followed it, riding close by its side, and observed its licking up in its progress all the dust that was under its smaller part.
>
> As it is a common opinion that a shot fired through a water-spout will break it, I tried to break this little whirlwind by striking my whip frequently through it, but without any effect. Soon after, it quitted the road and took into the woods, growing every moment larger and stronger, raising instead of dust the old dry leaves with which the ground was thick covered, and making a great noise with them and the branches of the trees.
> . . . By the leaves it was now filled with I could plainly perceive that the current of air they were driven by moved upwards in a spiral line; and when I saw the trunks and bodies of large trees enveloped in the passing whirl, which continued entire after it had left them, I no longer wondered that my whip had no effect on it in its smaller state.

I accompanied it about three-quarters of a mile, till some limbs of dead trees, broken off by the whirl, flying about and falling near me, made me more apprehensive of danger; and then I stopped, looking at the top of it as it went on, which was visible by means of the leaves contained in it for a very great height above the trees.

This is not the voice of Franklin the prudent aphorist or Franklin the philosopher of common sense or Franklin the self-made self-promoter. It is not even the voice of Franklin the scientist. It is the voice of Franklin the man—the most inquisitive American of his time, as well as the most versatile and the most observant.

Franklin is ours forever—"the type and genius of his land." We may love him or hate him, but we cannot escape him: His ghost will not let us go. When we recall the familiar stories that deceive us into thinking that we know everything about him, when we recall the writings that led Weber to choose him as the embodiment of the spirit of capitalism and led others to dismiss him as "mean and thrifty" or "cheap and shabby," and when we recall the characteristics that led Lawrence to renounce him as "the sharp little man . . . Middle-sized, sturdy, snuff-coloured Doctor Franklin," we should also take a moment to remember Benjamin Franklin and the whirlwind: "The rest of the company stood looking after it, but, my curiosity being stronger, I followed it, riding close by its side. . . ." We shall meet many remarkable men and women in our examination of business in America, but we shall not meet a match for Benjamin Franklin.

CHAPTER 2

John Jacob Astor: "A Self-Invented Money-Making Machine"

The Fascination of Wealth

How are we to justify our interest in the rich? We cannot say of John Jacob Astor, Cornelius Vanderbilt, or John D. Rockefeller what we must say of Benjamin Franklin—that they helped to define the national character and to shape the way that generations of Americans thought and lived. Nor can we say with absolute assurance that they exercised decisive influence as shapers of the nation's economic destiny. The fur trade would have developed without Astor; shipping lines would have been opened and railroads built without Vanderbilt; oil would have found its way to market without Rockefeller. However powerful they may have appeared to their contemporaries, to the historian these potentates may seem no more significant than pebbles hurled into the sky when a volcano blows its top. What matter are the forces that triggered the explosion, not the sparks that happened to soar in the aftermath.

It might be argued that the prodigiously wealthy deserve attention on the ground that they possess a prodigious gift for making money, as Mozart possessed a prodigious gift for making music. This view has merit,

46

but less than meets the eye. Unless he is exceptionally stupid, a man worth $50 million today can scarcely help being worth $100 million in seven years and $200 million in another seven. By the exercise of an equal gift, a man worth $50 today can scarcely help being worth $100 in seven years and $200 in a mere fourteen. The same return on investment produces the appearance of remarkable financial acumen in one case and the appearance of financial incompetence in the other.

What matters, then, is the making of the first $50 million. How exactly was it done, and by what kind of man or woman? What role did luck play? What role thrift, prudence, and industry? What role discipline and intelligence? What role general ability? What role courage, cunning, greed, ferocity, duplicity, or calculation?

Aside from the size of their fortunes, does anything unite the prodigiously wealthy of different eras or nations? Will an examination of their lives teach us any lessons we can put to use in our own lives? Will it teach us anything about the world and the qualities the world rewards? Are the rich admirable, and if so, do we find ourselves admiring their virtues or their vices? What does our fascination tell us about ourselves? An interest in any of these questions may justify an interest in the rich. But what justifies it most of all is simple curiosity. The sparks that light the sky when a volcano erupts may not matter, but that is no reason to disdain the spectacle. The rich are a blazing part of the human spectacle, and they hold our attention for that reason even if for no other. In the cases examined here, moreover, the sparks do more than light the sky. The lives of prominent figures illuminate the development of American business more vividly than it could possibly be illuminated if biography were neglected.

Seven Flutes

On May 22, 1786, four years before the death of Benjamin Franklin and eight years before the birth of Cornelius Vanderbilt, an advertisement appeared in the *New York Packet:* "Jacob Astor . . . has just imported from London an elegant assortment of musical instruments, such as Piano Fortes, spinnets, guitars . . . and all other kinds of strings; music boxes and paper, and every other article in the musical line, which he will dispose of for very low terms for cash."

The man who placed this advertisement was a twenty-three-year-old immigrant who had left his native Waldorf, in Germany, six years earlier with little more in the way of worldly possessions than the clothes on his back. He had left behind a stepmother whom he did not like and a father whom an early biographer describes as "a jovial, good-for-nothing butcher," and he had made his way to London, where he had taken a job working for his uncle in a firm of musical instrument-makers. After four years in London he had accumulated a capital of $75, of which $25 remained after he purchased seven good flutes and a berth in steerage on a ship bound for the United States. The seven flutes may be regarded as the foundation of the fortune of $20 million to $30 million that made the butcher's son, at his death in 1848, the richest man in America.

Astor is as emblematic a figure as Benjamin Franklin. Franklin shows us the self-made man at his best, with interests that transcended business and talents that transcended money-making. Astor shows us the self-made man at his narrow worst—an icy figure with one interest and one talent.

The voyage to America brought young Astor into contact with a German passenger who, on a previous visit, had made a handsome profit trading for furs with Indians. By the end of the voyage, legend has it, Astor's interest in flutes had begun to wane. On his arrival in New York, after several weeks peddling pastries up and down Broadway, he took a clerkship with a fur merchant at a salary of $2 a week, plus room and board. He proved sufficiently reliable that in the spring of 1785 his employer sent him up the Hudson into the Iroquois country, to trade with the Indians of the once-mighty Six Nations.

By 1786 Astor had married and, with the assistance of his wife's dowry, had set up the small shop where he offered the public musical instruments "for very low terms for cash." Furs were not advertised, but on the day that the notice appeared, Arthur D. Howden Smith tells us in his vivid though not entirely reliable biography, Astor was "plunging through the forests on the Niagara frontier, back bent beneath the weight of his pack, rifle in hand, bullet-pouch, powder-horn, hunting-knife and haversack slapping his thighs." In a life distinguished by an unusually intense acquisitiveness, this is perhaps the only moment when John Jacob Astor presents an attractive image—indeed, a romantic one. Later he sat in his office raking in profits while his agents radiated to every corner of the American wilderness, but in this period Astor himself made the journeys: "He knew the tricks of the frontier," Smith writes, "how to find his way by the stars and the sun, how to tell which was north by the moss on tree-trunks, how to throw up a lean-to and build a fire in the rain. . . . He was tireless on the trail, plodding, plodding, plodding, never less than sixty pounds weighing down his broad shoulders—and never content unless his load grew heavier with the substitution of stiff pelts for the lighter bulk of the knickknacks that paid for them. Thousands of miles he walked every year, and always burdened."

In January 1789, a new advertisement appeared in the *New York Packet*. John Jacob Astor, it informed the public, "has for sale an assortment of Piano Fortes of the Newest Construction, made by the best makers in London. . . . He gives cash for all kinds of Furs and has for sale a quantity of Canada Beavers and Beavering Coating, Raccoon Skins, and Raccoon Blankets, Muskrat Skins, etc., etc." In the same year, Astor made the first of his many investments in the real estate of his adopted city: two lots on the Bowery Lane in Manhattan, purchased for $625 in cash.

The 1790s brought new opportunities for Astor. The Jay Treaty of 1794 led to the modification of trade restrictions between the United States and Canada and to the evacuation of the frontier military posts by which the British had kept Americans from occupying the territory immediately south of the Great Lakes. Astor's agents spread through the land as soon as it opened to them. Furs poured in at an astonishing rate, but demand was high: It was an age when every gentleman in Europe and America required a beaver hat. By 1800 Astor was America's leading fur merchant, worth $250,000.

Furs and Tea

Unlike Benjamin Franklin but like many other self-made men, Astor never distinguished himself as a prose stylist. He "wrote a wretched scrawl," one historian reports, "setting spelling and grammar equally in defiance." His voice comes through clearly in a letter that he sent to a business associate in 1798, in the middle of vexing legislation: ". . . it is evident that Mr. B. Levingston has not paid that attention to the Busniss which it Requird and has Sufferd those fellawes who are employd against us to get every advantage thy wishd—I am very Sick of the Busniess all the mony I Can muster goes for this Damd businiss it is too much for me to Lay aut of and I Do Sincerley wish you would Sent me Som Cash Soon . . . if we have no prospect of Success Lets be Done with it at ances and thraugh no more mony away for if no Stop is put to it I shall yet be ruind by it."

In view of his success, it is disconcerting to find that, on a trip to

London in 1799, Astor took a berth in the steerage, exactly as he had fifteen years earlier, when he owned nothing but the clothes on his back and seven flutes. "Poor Jacob!" even his sympathetic biographer Smith exclaims. "Parsimoniousness turned into acquisitiveness and acquisitiveness developed a passion for hoarding, and hoarding, once it was a confirmed habit, created the churlish penuriousness of the miser. Money! Everything was money."

A chance meeting on this trip to London launched Astor on the next stage of his career. The meeting was with a governor of the British East India Company who had been born in Germany and who presented his fellow emigrant with a permit authorizing any ship that carried it to trade at ports that the company controlled. An examination of the price list disclosed that furs were traded at the seaport of Canton in China.

Astor persuaded a merchant friend to outfit a voyage to Canton—a voyage that netted Astor a profit of $55,000, a remarkable sum for a single venture in 1800. More important, the episode convinced Astor to commit his resources to the China trade. Never a man to share profits, by 1803 he was building his own ships, and before long he had, as he liked to say, "a million dollars afloat." Now his empire had a foot in each of three great cities: New York, London, and Canton. Though it spanned continents, his business had an underlying simplicity. The basic principle was to keep furs moving out of the United States and tea moving in.

This period provides an amusing example of Astor's attitude toward the laws of his adopted land. The embargo of 1807 forbade American ships to embark for foreign ports; yet in 1808 Astor's ship *Beaver* sailed for China—the beneficiary not of favoritism, American officials explained, but of a waiver that the government had granted so that a distinguished mandarin could return home to Canton. Upon investigation, the visitor was revealed to be "no mandarin, not even a Hong Kong merchant, but a common Chinese dock loafer," whom Astor had dressed in a fancy robe to fool the authorities.

At about this same time, Astor was making plans for what turned out to be the grandest failure of his career. Jefferson's purchase of the Louisiana Territory from France in 1803 had opened almost unlimited possibilities for the expansion of the fur trade. To exploit those possibilities, Astor conceived a colossal scheme that involved the establishment of a chain of trading posts along the Great Lakes and down the Mississippi to St. Louis, a second chain from St. Louis along the Missouri to the Rockies, and a third chain from the Rockies down to the Pacific, where he would establish a great fort and trading post at the mouth of the

Columbia River. St. Louis would serve as the focal point for the east-
bound trade, while the post at the mouth of the Columbia, close to the
rich northwestern trapping grounds, would serve as the focal point for
the trade with China. Astor planned to call this post Astoria.

A curious blindness on Astor's part doomed this scheme almost from
its inception. When he organized the Pacific Fur Company in 1810, Astor took as partners four Scotsmen whom he lured from his great Canadian rival, the Northwest Company. At a time when almost everyone
foresaw war between the United States and Britain, it seems never to
have occurred to Astor that it might be unwise to entrust the establishment of an American post to an expedition led by British subjects. In
October 1813 Duncan McDougal, the partner temporarily in charge at
Astoria, sold the post and its property to the Northwest Company at an
absurdly low price—a service that his former employers rewarded by
offering him a new and more lucrative partnership. By the end of 1813
Astoria had been renamed Fort George, and the British flag flew over it.

Though it cost him Astoria, the war was not a complete loss to Astor.
To pay for the war, the government needed money. In 1813, with businessmen David Parish and Stephen Girard of Philadelphia, Astor formed
a bond syndicate to purchase bonds from the struggling government. It
was not a deal that enhanced his reputation as a patriot. Astor, Horace
Greeley complained later, "must have cleared more than a million of
dollars in hard money on every two millions of paper thus lent."

Monopoly

The loss of Astoria did not diminish Astor's determination to dominate
the trans-Mississippi fur trade; if anything, the defeat intensified his drive.
On April 29, 1816, partly in response to Astor's lobbying, Congress
passed an act that forbade noncitizens from participating in the fur trade
as proprietors. This act left Astor's old nemesis, the Northwest Company, with little choice but to sell to Astor all of its posts below the
Great Lakes, so that the entire fur trade east of the Mississippi came
under Astor's control. Not satisfied, Astor lobbied Congress to abolish
the trading posts that the government had operated since 1796. When
Congress complied in the winter of 1821–22, the stage was set for one
of the classic battles in the history of the American frontier, as well as
one of the most uneven battles in the history of American business: the

battle between Astor's giant American Fur Company and scores of independent small trading firms and individual trappers.

One by one over the next decade, Astor's competitors were driven out of business or absorbed at terms that Astor dictated. The Missouri Fur Company; Bernard Pratte & Company; Stone, Bostwick & Company; the Columbia Fur Company—all folded or were absorbed. "Never," Astor's friendly biographer Arthur Smith concedes, "in the economic history of this country, has a corporation marched more ruthlessly across the prostrate corpses of opponents to attainment of monopoly."

Astor's own employees did not necessarily fare better than his competitors. The company furnished its agents with trade goods at rates that assured Astor's profit but that offered no such assurance to anyone else in the organization. The entire operation was designed to maximize the return to Astor while letting any risks fall on other shoulders. Fortunately for the traders, they could exploit the Indians even more effectively than they themselves were exploited. Despite laws intended to prevent such abuses, diluted alcohol was traded to Indians for pelts a dozen times more valuable or sold at rates of $25 to $50 per gallon. In 1831, the attitude of Astor's agents was summarized in a letter written to the secretary of war by an official on the scene: "They entertain, as I know to be a fact, no sort of respect for our citizens, agents, officers or the Government, or its laws or general policy."

The American Fur Company was a huge enterprise, but Astor did not need a huge staff of salaried executives to manage it. Astor's life as a businessman resembled the life of a merchant banker of the Renaissance much more than it resembled the life of a modern corporate executive. Here is a description of a particularly busy day written by a merchant of the period:

> To rise early in the morning, to get breakfast, to go down town to the counting house of the firm, to open and read letters—to go out and do some business, either at the Custom house, bank or elsewhere, until twelve, then to take a lunch and a glass of wine at Delmonico's; or a few raw oysters at Downing's; to sign checks and attend to the finances until half past one; to go on change; to return to the counting house, and remain until time to go to dinner, and in the old time, when such things as "packet nights" existed, to stay down town until ten or eleven at night, and then go home and go to bed.

Thus passed the days of a man like John Jacob Astor in the early years of the nineteenth century, before the Industrial Revolution changed the pace of life forever.

The Landlord of New York

In 1834, exactly fifty years had passed since Astor began in the fur business. From London the previous year he had written, "I much fear beaver will not sell well very soon unless it is very fine. It appears that they
make hats of silk instead of beaver." On June 1, 1834, partly out of
weariness, partly out of an intuition that the glory days had passed, and
partly out of grief at the death of his wife, Astor sold his interest in the
American Fur Company and retired from active business.

By this time he had become not only the wealthiest man in America
but also "the landlord of New York." Throughout this period, if furs
were Astor's business, real estate was his pleasure. In late afternoon or
early evening, after the day's work was done, he would ride his horse
through undeveloped parts of his adopted city—"ride out the Bowery,
lined by rows of quaint, low-roofed, old Dutch houses," or ride along
the lane later to be called Bleecker Street, "where wild roses and black-
berries stirred in the soft wind," or ride "across the Stuyvesant meadows
and the thickets, swamps and farms stretching northwards beyond
Greenwich Village to the Harlem Hills." New York had grown from a
city of twenty-five thousand when he arrived in 1784 to sixty thousand
in 1800, and Astor had faith that its growth would continue far into the
future. Year after year he kept buying farmland and pastureland, rocky
fields, swamps, wasteland—anything at all, it seems, as long as the land
lay on the isle of Manhattan. For $25,000 he acquired the farm of Medeef
Eden, which extended from what is now Forty-second Street to Forty-
eighth Street in New York City, and from Broadway west to the Hudson River—an area whose value was estimated at $50 million in 1930.
For about the same amount he acquired the farm of John Cosine, which
reached from Fifty-third Street to Fifty-seventh Street and, again, from
Broadway to the Hudson—an area valued at nearly $20 million in 1930.
There was also the farm of John Semlar, on the East Side of the island,
purchased for $20,000 and valued at $16 million to $20 million in 1930;
and a block in Harlem, purchased for $2,000 and valued at $2 million in
1930; and a large portion of Governor Clinton's country estate in the
area now called Greenwich Village; and so on. Legend has it that Astor
never sold a piece of property, and though the legend is false, it does not
err by much. In all, Astor invested approximately $2 million in New

York real estate—an investment that formed the basis of a family fortune estimated at nearly $500 million in 1930.

The best known of Astor's real-estate transactions throws a vivid light on his character as a businessman. During the Revolutionary War, New York State confiscated an immense tract of land in Putnam County— 51,012 acres—owned by a Tory major, Roger Morris, and his wife, Mary. Afterward the state sold the land in pieces to various farmers. By 1809, seven hundred families were settled on what had been the Morris estate.

In that year a lawyer (possibly Aaron Burr) informed Astor that the seven hundred families had no legal title to the land, for the Morrises had held only a life lease, and by law the state did not have the authority to confiscate a life lease. Thus the property was still owned by Mrs. Morris and would become the possession of her three children when she died.

Astor located the heirs and purchased their claim for $100,000. Then he notified the farmers that when Mrs. Morris died, he would own not only the land but also everything that they had built upon it in the decades since they took possession. His intention, it seems, was not to evict the farmers but to pressure the state into purchasing his claims, since if it failed to do so, the state opened itself to the charge that it had violated the trust of the farmers by selling them land it did not own.

Astor waited—waited until 1825, when Mrs. Morris died at the age of ninety-six. At that point Astor sent eviction notices to the seven hundred farmers. They appealed to the legislature, which at first refused to recognize Astor's title. Despite the efforts of Daniel Webster and Martin Van Buren representing New York State, the courts upheld Astor's claim. Astor repeated an earlier offer to sell the land to the state, but his offer was rejected. The public failed to see why a man already rich should grow richer because he had purchased an ancient claim from the descendants of people generally regarded as traitors; nor could the public see why several hundred families should lose their life's work on account of a technicality that no one understood except a few lawyers. Astor stood firm, and in the end, rather than allow the families to be evicted, the state purchased the land through a special issue of stock.

Few episodes in Astor's career have excited more bitter condemnation than his behavior in the Morris affair. To many people it seemed an example of extortion rather than honest enterprise. The muckraking historian Gustavus Myers cited the case as an example of Astor "the insidious and devious schemer, acting through sharp lawyers instead of by armed force." Arthur Smith called it "the most ruthless coup of Astor's career—a coup . . . perhaps more cold-bloodedly selfish, more directly antisocial, than any undertaken by any American, of Astor's time or since."

Astor seems not to have cared much what his contemporaries thought of him, but in retirement he began to worry about the judgment of posterity. He hired Washington Irving to write a history that would set in proper perspective the most conspicuous failure in his career—the effort to establish Astoria. Irving was given a suite of rooms in Astor's country house, and in due course a satisfactory history appeared. "The remarkable form of John Jacob Astor stands out like a statue of granite," Henry Wadsworth Longfellow commented: "a sublime enterprise."

Wealth enabled Astor to purchase what he enjoyed, and he enjoyed the company of literary men. Aside from his son William, the main companions of Astor's retirement were a poet, Fitz-Greene Halleck, and a man of letters, Joseph Cogswell. Cogswell often accompanied the old man on excursions by carriage or boat. On one such outing, legend has it, the pair stopped at a hotel on the Hudson for tea. Pointing to the proprietor, Astor said, "That man will never succeed."

"Why not?" Cogswell asked.

"Don't you see," Astor replied, "what large lumps of sugar he puts in the sugar bowl?"

Another time, as they walked toward a boat that Astor had chartered for a sail, Cogswell remarked that every minute he kept the boat waiting cost Astor twenty-five cents. At this, it is said, the richest man in America "broke into a worried trot."

The poet Walt Whitman, then a child, saw Astor in this period and later preserved the image: ". . . a bent feeble but stoutly built old man, bearded, swathed in rich furs, with a great ermine cap on his head, led and assisted, almost carried down the steps of the high front stoop . . . and then lifted and tucked in a gorgeous sleigh, envelop'd in other furs, for a ride. The sleigh was drawn by as fine a team of horses as I ever saw. . . . I remember the spirited champing horses, the driver with his whip, and a fellow driver by his side, for extra prudence."

Astor's feebleness in old age shocked many visitors. At dinner, noted former New York City mayor Philip Hone, a servant stood behind the host "to guide the victuals which he was eating, and to watch him as an infant is watched." "I am broken up," Astor said to a friend. "It is time for me to be out of the way." In his last months, according to contemporary accounts, the man who owned much of New York lived on the milk of a wet nurse, was "daily tossed in a blanket for exercise," and

could not "*converse* . . . neither listen nor reply." Yet, it is said, Astor
retained a strong interest in the management of his property.

The Will That Enraged a City

In his diary on March 29, 1848, Hone wrote: "John Jacob Astor died
this morning at eight o'clock, in the eighty-fifth year of his age; sensible
to the last, but the material of life exhausted, the machinery worn out,
the lamp extinguished for want of oil. Bowed down with bodily infirmity for a long time, he has gone at last, and left reluctantly his un-
bounded wealth."

Hone did not doubt that Astor's life had been a success, nor did he
doubt that the source of the success had been the strength of Astor's
character. "He was the richest man in the United States in productive
and available property, and this immense, gigantic fortune was the fruit
of his own labor, unerring sagacity, and far-seeing penetration. He came
to this country at twenty years of age; penniless, friendless, without inheritance, without education, and having no example before him of the
art of money-making, but with a determination to be rich, and ability to
carry it into effect. . . . All he touched turned to gold, and it seemed as
if fortune delighted in erecting him a monument of her unerring
potency."

Many public commentators agreed. William Cullen Bryant's *New York
Evening Post* attributed Astor's success to "the steady application of more
than common powers of intellect." The *New York True Sun* paid tribute
to Astor's "iron memory," to his "lucidity of combination which nothing
could confuse," and to his "instinctive knowledge of every detail that
occurred in his vast transactions." "There are few men whose biography
would prove more instructive or acceptable to the present age," the *True
Sun* declared, "than the life of John Jacob Astor."

The chorus of praise was not unanimous, however. Horace Greeley's
New York Tribune commended Astor for his "farseeing sagacity," his "vigorous intellect," and his "promptness and regularity" in business affairs,
but it added that "It is a melancholy, insane perversion of human life to
make it mainly subservient to the acquirement of such a fortune." James
Gordon Bennett's *New York Herald* went so far as to suggest that Astor's
success in business might have owed something to qualities of character
that were neither praiseworthy nor honorable: "If Mr. Astor was industrious in the accumulation of riches, he was likewise very penurious and

niggardly in money matters. What he saved he kept and locked up to the day of his death. . . ."

Other newspapers measured Astor against traditional moral and religious standards and found him deficient. The *Concord Congressional Journal* declared: "His pleasure was in the acquisition, not the use of money—the most sordid and unworthy passion of which the heart is capable." "For more than three score years and ten," the *Boston Traveller* said, Astor had toiled to heap up a "vast pile of wealth—not a farthing of which he can take with him whither he has been called from his sordid labor." The *New-York Organ and Temperance Safeguard* treated its readers to a detailed description of Astor's coffin, after which it commented: "So a rich man has the advantage of rotting in *velvet, gold,* and *silver* trappings . . . while the dust of a poor man must decompose in plain wood! What a compliment to the *immortal spirit* of the departed."

The publication of Astor's will a week after his death fueled the controversy. Yielding to the entreaties of Joseph Cogswell, Astor left $400,000 to establish a public library in New York City, thus planting the seed of one of the world's great libraries. Beyond this one bequest, however, Astor showed virtually no interest in charity. The bulk of his fortune was left to his eldest mentally competent son, William Backhouse Astor, with smaller legacies provided for his mentally ill eldest son, John Jacob, Jr.; his daughter Dorothea; his grandchildren; his nieces; and his nephews. The only legacy to a person outside of Astor's family was an annuity of $200 to his employee of sixteen years, Fitz-Greene Halleck.

Astor's will contrasted sharply with the will of his predecessor as the richest man in America, Philadelphia banker and merchant Stephen Girard. When he died in 1831, Girard left only about $200,000 to relatives, friends, and retainers out of an estate of $7.5 million. The rest went for various public purposes. Astor's relative indifference to these purposes did not go unnoticed: "During the greater portion of the last years of his life," Bennett's *New York Herald* observed, "[Astor] was the associate and Maecenas of Washington Irving, Mr. Cogswell, Mr. Halleck, and several other literary, philosophical and poetical gentlemen. . . . The results of their doctrines . . . appear in the will; and judging from that document, we must say that we don't think too much of their teachings. If we had been an associate of John Jacob Astor . . . the first idea we should have put into his head, would have been that *one-half of his immense property—ten millions, at least—belonged to the people of New York.*"

Half of the property belonged to the people of New York, the *Herald* argued, anticipating an argument that Henry George would later make famous, because the property had been "augmented and increased in value by the aggregate intelligence, industry, enterprise and commerce of New York, fully to the amount of one-half of its value." Thus, in the unlikely event that Astor had sought the assistance of the editors of the *Herald* in drawing up his will, "we would have counselled [him] to leave at least the half of his property for the benefits of the city of New York. . . . But instead of this, he has only left less than one-half a million for a public library. What a poor, mean and beggarly result!"

Even Astor's legacies within his family seemed sinister to the *Herald*. In leaving the bulk of his fortune to one son, Astor had sought "to get round and evade . . . the American law which prohibits primogeniture, or the concentration of the whole of a man's property upon one heir, to the exclusion of the others. . . . The great object of the will, is to create an Astor dynasty."

In view of the evidence provided by the will, the editors of the influential *Herald* declared, they could not "pronounce the highest species of eulogy upon the character of the late John Jacob Astor." He had "exhibited, at best, but the ingenious powers of a self-invented money-making machine," and his associates, "seem to have looked no further than to the different pins, cranks and buttons of this machine, without turning it to any permanent benefit to the community from whose industry he obtained one-half the amount of his fortune, in the indirect values added to his estates in the course of years."

Astor himself, one imagines, would have shrugged off the assaults of America's moralists with a smile of wry contempt. When he remembered his first weeks in New York, hawking pastries on streets he would later own, he must have felt a satisfaction that bordered on ecstasy. Furs and tea, tea and furs, and land—always more land. Let the moralists sneer. To end as a symbol of unredeemed wealth might not have distressed the butcher's son who had begun his life in America with seven flutes and $25 in cash.

CHAPTER 3

Cornelius Vanderbilt: "I Never Cared for Money"

Young Vanderbilt

On May 27, 1794, five years after John Jacob Astor made his first small purchase of real estate in Manhattan, a child was born in a tiny farmhouse on Staten Island to Phebe Hand Vanderbilt and her husband Cornelius—a hardworking farmer and boatman described by one of his son's biographers as "an industrious plodder" who "seemed destined to eke out no more than a precarious living on the island." The infant, Phebe's fourth child and second son, must have been healthy, for it grew into a "big-bodied, husky, black-eyed lad" who could outwork any other youth on the waterfront, and then into a man who outworked, outfought, and outthought his rivals for sixty years, never backing from a fight, and never fighting with anything less than ferocious energy and determination. In the end the son of the plain Dutch couple built a fortune that lifted the name Vanderbilt to a special place in the national consciousness, like the names Astor before it and Rockefeller afterward—a place we set aside in imagination for the unimaginably rich, the favored few who pile up fortunes beyond our capacity to count or comprehend.

Until Cornelius, says Wheaton Lane in his fine biography, the Van Der Bilts of Staaten Eylandt, as the original Dutch settlers called it, had been "plodding, unimaginative tillers of the soil, with here and there a petty tradesman, fisherman, or tavern keeper breaking away from the wearying routine of farm labor." Their outstanding characteristic seems to have been "a steadfastness of purpose which drove them to make their living in relatively unfavorable surroundings, and rear large broods of children successfully." Cornelius himself was the fourth of nine children and would be the father of twelve.

Young Vanderbilt disliked books and school, and, indeed, it seems possible that he read only one book, *The Pilgrim's Progress*, after he left school at the age of twelve. Already at that age he could manage the sailboat his family used to carry produce from their farm on Staten Island across the bay to the markets on the tip of Manhattan. At sixteen, with $100 advanced as a loan by his parents, he bought his own boat, a small two-masted sailing vessel called a periauger, and immediately went into business carrying freight and passengers between the island and the city.

At a time when ferrymen charged eighteen cents for the seven-mile trip, with a round trip going for a quarter, Cornelius earned more than $1,000 in his first year of work. Ferrying and freighting by day, taking parties of young people on pleasure trips when weather permitted in the evening, he seems never to have tired, never to have rested, and never to have turned down a job. The men who had the bad judgment or bad luck to oppose him later in his business career would have recognized him at sixteen: "In a competitive business, his prices were low and nobody underbid him. He was perfectly willing to undertake any job, however dangerous, and when, in stormy weather, the other boatmen were reluctant to venture upon the day, Cornele was always ready for any emergency."

In 1814, Vanderbilt entrusted his ferry business to a subordinate and turned his attention to more ambitious ventures. He built a schooner to make the long run to Long Island Sound and, the next year, two larger schooners for trips along the Atlantic coast from Boston down to Charleston. Business boomed, and at the end of the year 1817, seven years after he had borrowed $100 to buy his first vessel, Vanderbilt found himself worth $15,000. At this point he astonished his family and friends by announcing that he intended to sell all of his sailing ships and take a job as a salaried employee.

Vanderbilt had come to the conclusion that the future of navigation lay with steamships rather than with sailing ships, and Thomas Gibbons of Elizabeth-Town, New Jersey, owned a steamship. Unfortunately for Gibbons and other potential entrepreneurs, the New York State legislature had granted to Robert Fulton and his partner Robert Livingston a monopoly on steam navigation in New York waters, and this monopoly had given a sole license on the run from New Jersey to New York to a former partner of Gibbons, now his bitter enemy, Colonel Aaron Ogden of Elizabeth-Town.

Gibbons offered Vanderbilt command of his steamship plus $60 a month to make the run from New Brunswick to New York in defiance of Ogden's exclusive license. He had picked the right man. Vanderbilt loved a fight, cared little about the law even when it happened to favor him, and cared even less when it did not. For six years, learning his trade, he ran Gibbons's steamship *Bellona* between New Jersey and New York, while his wife Sophia added to the family's income by transforming a run-down, riverside tavern in New Brunswick into a successful hotel. A dispute involving this hotel provided the occasion for a characteristic letter from Vanderbilt to his employer:

> Last evening New Brunswick wais in an uproar. Letson toald the passengers that retaining them their was all my falt that all I did it for was to get their supper and lodging from them he offered to take 7 of them for 3 dollars each in one of the Line Stages the bargain wais maid and upon reflection Letson flew. Cannot you stop Letsons mouth?

Gibbons was less concerned with Letson's mouth than he was with the license the Fulton/Livingston monopoly had granted to his enemy Ogden—a license that put Vanderbilt at continuous risk of arrest. This risk seems to have cheered the young captain more than it worried him; his letters ring with energy and enthusiasm. Meanwhile, Gibbons had taken his case to court with Daniel Webster as his counsel, arguing that the action of the New York State legislature violated the clause of the Constitution that gives control of interstate commerce to the federal government. In 1824, in an opinion written by Chief Justice John Marshall, the U.S. Supreme Court ruled in favor of Gibbons, and the stranglehold of the Fulton/Livingston monopoly was broken.

Biding his time and slowly building his capital, Vanderbilt continued to work for Gibbons until his death in 1826 and then for the Gibbons family until 1829—a total of eleven years. His salary was raised to $2,000 a season, but legend has it that he refused an increase to $5,000. "I did it on principle," his early biographer James Parton quotes him as saying. "The other captains had but $1,000 and they were already jealous enough of me. Besides, I never cared for money. All I ever cared for was to carry my point."

On His Own

Vanderbilt was thirty-five years old when, in 1829, he resigned his salaried position and went into business for himself. In a decade he had won a reputation as a master of steamships that matched the reputation he had won earlier as a master of sailing ships. Now, with characteristic verve, he launched a fierce rate-slashing war against a solidly entrenched competitor in the run from New York to Philadelphia. Though not decisive, the evidence suggests that Vanderbilt made such a dent in the profits of his rival that, within a year, it became the first in a long line of foes that paid the stubborn Dutchman to withdraw from competition.

Vanderbilt turned his attention to the rich traffic of the Hudson River— a traffic that had boomed dramatically after 1825, when the completion of the Erie Canal opened the markets of the Eastern Seaboard to the farm products of the Great Lakes region. Again Vanderbilt threw his line into a rate-cutting war against an entrenched rival; again he brought down his rival's profits; again his rival came to the conclusion that it would be easier to pay off the upstart than to compete against him. This time, in exchange for his agreement to withdraw from the Hudson, Vanderbilt received a $100,000 "bonus" plus $5,000 a year for ten years.

With the Hudson off limits, Vanderbilt established routes on Long Island Sound and then, beyond the sound, up the coast as far north as Boston. At about the same time, returning to familiar waters, he purchased a half interest in the Staten Island ferry. Meanwhile, he kept buying and building steamboats—always bigger, always faster, always more luxurious—until there came a point, sometime in the 1840s, when he owned and operated more steamboats than any man in the country. By this time his contemporaries had began to call him "Commodore." In 1845 his fortune was estimated at $1.2 million. Three years later, after the death of John Jacob Astor, he expressed great interest in the size of the estate, as if it were a target.

Vanderbilt's Revenge

In 1849, the discovery of gold in California sent thousands of fortune-hunters hurrying West. While the minds of his contemporaries turned to gold, the mind of Cornelius Vanderbilt turned to transportation routes. A scheme to dig a canal across Nicaragua collapsed, but by 1851, the Accessory Transit Company, with Vanderbilt as president, could offer the traveler a route of 4,531 miles from New York to San Francisco via Nicaragua, as compared to its competitor's route of 4,992 miles via Panama. Known for their speed and low fares, Vanderbilt's steamships usually carried five hundred or six hundred passengers on the journey West and made enormous profits.

In 1853 Vanderbilt confided to a friend that his fortune had reached $11 million, invested so as to yield 25 percent annually. In the same year, the fifty-nine-year-old titan took the first vacation of his life: a grand tour of Europe in a steamship built especially for the voyage and "fitted up," a contemporary newspaper reported, "with all that can tend to gratify the eye and minister to luxurious ease." Before leaving, Vanderbilt resigned the presidency of the Accessory Transit Company and turned over its management to a pair of aggressive but overly grasping associates, Charles Morgan and Cornelius M. Garrison. In the commodore's absence, these gentlemen took steps that challenged his interests, thus provoking what is probably the most pointed letter in the history of American business:

Gentlemen:

You have undertaken to cheat me. I won't sue you, for the law is slow. I'll ruin you.

Yours truly,
Cornelius Vanderbilt

It would be interesting to know what thoughts went through the minds of Morgan and Garrison when they realized that the lion intended to reclaim his lair. If they supposed that age had weakened or success softened the commodore, they soon learned how badly they had miscalculated.

By February 1856, Vanderbilt had regained the presidency of the Accessory Transit Company. Morgan and Garrison were not yet ruined, however. In 1855 the government of Nicaragua had been overthrown by a band of fifty-eight adventurers led by American filibuster William Walker, a soldier of fortune who liked to call himself the "grey-eyed man of destiny." Morgan and Garrison had helped Walker, and now they proposed that he might help them in return. Accordingly, less than two weeks after Vanderbilt resumed the presidency of the Accessory Transit Company, Walker rescinded its charter, seized its property, and granted a new charter (along with control of the confiscated property) to his friends Morgan and Garrison.

The man of destiny had gone too far. Having failed in an effort to persuade the U.S. government to intervene against Walker, Vanderbilt decided to organize his own army. Late in 1856 two of his agents, William R. C. Webster and Sylvanus H. Spencer, invaded Nicaragua from Costa Rica with a force of 120 men. The men were armed with Minié rifles and ammunition supplied by Vanderbilt. They hacked their way through miles of jungle, took rafts and canoes down the San Carlos and San Juan rivers, and won a series of victories that put Walker in a hopeless position. On May 1, 1857, he surrendered. Destiny, in the person of a sixty-two-year-old American businessman, had caught up with him.

With the fall of Walker, Vanderbilt regained control of the Nicaraguan transit route and thus completed his revenge against Morgan and Garrison. Vanderbilt did not reopen the route, so the Panama lines continued to operate without competition—a courtesy for which Vanderbilt charged $56,000 a month. Eventually the details of this arrangement were made public, and on February 9, 1859, *The New York Times* paid a reluctant tribute to the commodore: "If ever there was a man who has made his own way in the world, it is Mr. Cornelius Vanderbilt. . . . Like those old German barons who, from their eyries along the Rhine, swooped down upon the commerce of the noble river, and wrung tribute from every passenger that floated by, Mr. Cornelius Vanderbilt, with all the steamers of the Accessory Transit Company held in his leash, has insisted that the Pacific Company should pay him toll. . . . There are honorable and high-minded merchants, American gentlemen of the best stamp, among the directors who have thus bowed the knee to this man's dictation. . . . They must doubtless have writhed under the consciousness of the true part that they were playing."

Across the Atlantic

While he fought a private war in Nicaragua, Vanderbilt found time to get involved in a new business: transatlantic steam transportation. In its early years, ocean steam navigation was dominated by Britain's famous Cunard Line, founded by Samuel Cunard of Halifax in 1839. The chief American competitor was Edward M. Collins, whose U.S. Mail Steamship Company began regular operations between the United States and Liverpool in 1850.

Collins was assisted by an annual mail subsidy of $858,000 ($33,000 per round-trip voyage) provided by the U.S. government. Though the speed of Collins's vessels dazzled the public, the line needed the subsidies to operate, and it never paid a cent in dividends to its stockholders. Vanderbilt viewed it with contempt.

In 1854 Vanderbilt offered to start a biweekly service, alternating with Collins, for a subsidy of only $15,000 a trip—$1,000 less than the subsidy the British government paid the Cunard Line. For reasons that had much to do with politics and nothing to do with economics, Congress turned down Vanderbilt's offer and continued the subsidy to Collins. Unsubsidized, Vanderbilt began a transatlantic line with a terminus in Havre. In 1856 Congress reduced the subsidy to Collins, and before long his ships were being sold to meet the claims of creditors. The Vanderbilt line, on the other hand, operated at a profit from 1858 until the outbreak of the Civil War—a period in which Vanderbilt was, in the words of one biographer, "the principal figure in upholding the prestige of the American ocean steam marine."

Vanderbilt Versus the Merrimac

On March 15, 1862, the commodore received an urgent telegram from an official of the U.S. War Department: "The Secretary of War directs me to ask you for what sum you will contract to destroy the *Merrimac* or prevent her from coming out from Norfolk—you to sink or destroy her if she gets out." At a meeting with President Lincoln and Secretary of War Edwin M. Stanton, Vanderbilt suggested that he could stop the Confederate ironclad by ramming her with his steamship *Vanderbilt*. Asked how much money he would require for this service, the commodore replied that he would give his steamship—and his own services as commander—free to the government.

On March 23 the *Vanderbilt* arrived at Fortress Monroe, outside Norfolk. "How can we help you?" an officer asked Vanderbilt. "Only by keeping severely out of the way when I am hunting the critter," he replied. As it turned out, there wasn't much of a hunt. The *Merrimac* probably was not worried about the *Vanderbilt*, whose paddle wheels made it vulnerable to gunfire. But it was worried about the *Monitor*, which also stood on guard, and it never ventured out of Norfolk for a second engagement with the Federal ironclad. Later, the Confederates themselves blew up their ship before abandoning the city.

The Navy Department used the *Vanderbilt* in various other ventures, and Congress eventually passed a resolution thanking the commodore for his "magnificent gift." Informed of the resolution, Vanderbilt exclaimed, "Congress be *damned*! I never gave that ship to Congress. When the Government was in great straits for a suitable vessel of war, I offered to give the ship if they did not care to buy it; however, Mr. Lincoln and Mr. Welles [Secretary of the Navy Gideon Welles] think it was a gift, and I suppose I shall have to let her go."

On receiving a large gold medal that Congress had ordered to be struck as a token of the nation's gratitude, Vanderbilt expressed the hope that "those who come after me as they read the inscriptions of the medal . . . will inflexibly resolve that, should our government be again imperilled, no pecuniary sacrifice is too large to make in its behalf." In 1870, however, an interviewer from *The New York Times* found him in a less patriotic mood. "I was served meanly on that," the commodore complained, "meaner than ever any government served a man before or since. Why, they never gave me my vessel back."

"Hain't I Got the Power?"

In 1864 Vanderbilt sold the Panama line, his last major shipping property, for $3 million. At the age of seventy, after more than half a century of hard work, he might have retired to enjoy his wealth. But he was not retiring. He was thinking about new work, new battles—a new business. He was thinking about railroads.

At seventy, Vanderbilt was not tired. He owned a pair of fast trotting horses, and late in the afternoon, on Bloomingdale Road (now upper Broadway), he liked to race his team against the teams of other sportsmen. A reporter for the *New York Herald* gives us a glimpse of him in his sixties: "What fine looking man is that with a segar in his mouth, who is passing all those roadsters on the right? He dashes past everybody but Bonner. His bays must be well trained; he handles the ribbons as though he was used to it. . . . Yes, sir. That is Commodore Vanderbilt, who has four of the best horses that appear on the road, every one of them exceedingly fast."

Vanderbilt had begun to buy stock in the New York and Harlem Railroad in the 1850s and had become a director in 1857. The railroad was not highly regarded as an investment, but Vanderbilt knew that its charter gave it the right to lay tracks in New York City north of Forty-second Street, and he knew that if it could obtain the right to lay tracks south to the Battery, the Harlem would have a line that ran the length of Manhattan Island—a line of immense potential value.

The right to lay tracks to the south required the approval of the Board of Aldermen and the Common Council of New York City—an approval that was secured in 1863, in accordance with the standard political morality of the times, through the payment of bribes. With the announcement that the city had granted the franchise and the subsequent announcement that the board had elected Vanderbilt to the office of president, the stock of the Harlem soared.

The rise in the price of the Harlem's stock set the stage for a contest between Vanderbilt and one of the line's other directors, Daniel Drew. Born in 1797, Drew had begun his career as a cattle trader, had competed against Vanderbilt in the steamboat business in the 1830s, and in 1844 had opened the Wall Street brokerage firm of Drew, Robinson, and Company, where he had gained a reputation as one of the shrewdest stock market operators of his time.

Now Drew schemed to sell the Harlem short—that is, to sell shares he did not own, but would have to purchase later to cover his sales. The scheme would make money for Drew if the current price—the price he received—exceeded the price of the purchases he made later. But why should the price of the Harlem go down? It would go down, Drew figured, because he would secretly invite members of the city's Board of Aldermen to take part in his scheme. On June 25, 1863, the board rescinded the franchise for the Harlem to lay tracks south of Forty-second Street.

On the day the franchise was repealed, the price of the Harlem dropped to a low of 73. Then it steadied, and then it began to rise. Vanderbilt and his associates were buying—buying every share that was sold short, and buying every other share they could get their hands on. The short-sellers had made a gigantic blunder. They had sold more shares than existed. It may have been at about this time that Drew composed a jingle that is still remembered:

> He that sells what isn't his'n,
> Must buy it back, or go to prison.

The short-sellers had to cover their sales, but Vanderbilt and his associates owned all the stock of the Harlem, and they were not eager to sell, not even after the aldermen, desperate to stop their losses, annulled the repeal of the franchise. When the last of the short-sellers covered their sales, it was at a price of 179, up from 73.

Drew had not learned his lesson. In 1864 he made a second attempt at a bear raid on the Harlem, this time with the help of members of the state legislature. Again Vanderbilt outmaneuvered the short-sellers, cornering the market and forcing them to pay $285 for shares once available for $100. "We busted the whole legislature," Vanderbilt boasted. Drew's loss was estimated at between $500,000 and $1 million, while the commodore made $2 million.

Now Vanderbilt turned his attention to the New York Central, a highly profitable line that had been formed in 1853 by the consolidation of nine little railroads linking Albany and Buffalo. The Central enjoyed an important strategic advantage in its relations with both the Harlem and the Hudson River railroads. Those lines had to transfer westbound freight to the Central, but for nine months of the year the Central could ignore the railroads and send freight from Albany to New York City via the Hudson River. Only in winter, when ice choked the river, did the Central rely on rail lines to Manhattan.

Vanderbilt began buying stock in the Central, and by 1864 he had acquired enough clout to protect his interests. At that point, the Central agreed to pay Vanderbilt's Hudson an annual "bonus" of $100,000.

This arrangement collapsed when a new group gained control of the Central after the sudden death of its president in 1866. Power seems to have had an unhappy effect on the judgment of the new management: Vanderbilt's representatives were thrown off the board, and the annual payment to the Hudson River line was revoked.

Vanderbilt did not take long to strike back. On January 14, 1867, he announced that he would halt his trains on the eastern side of the river, a mile from Albany. Passengers bound for New York now had to walk across the ice; freight bound for New York piled up in the Central's terminal. The directors of the Central held out for forty-eight hours, then capitulated.

In hearings later conducted by the Railroad Committee of the state legislature, Vanderbilt had an interesting exchange with a legislator who thought he should have sued the Central when it canceled the bonus.

"Did you not know," the legislator asked, "that the law provides a remedy for all wrongs, and that railroad corporations have no right to take the redress of their own wrongs into their own hands to the detriment of the public?"

"The law, as I view it, goes too slow for me when I have the remedy in my own hands," Vanderbilt replied. ". . . I for one will never go to a court of law when I have got the power in my own hands to see myself right. Let the other parties go to law if they want, but . . . I know what the law is. I have had enough of it."

This exchange appears to be the source of a statement often attributed to Vanderbilt: "Law! What do I care about law? Hain't I got the power?"

By the end of 1867, with the support of disgruntled shareholders representing $13 million worth of stock, Vanderbilt had gained control of the New York Central. In 1869, by act of the state legislature, the Central and the Hudson were united as the New York Central & Hudson River Railroad, and in 1872 the Harlem River Railroad joined the other two. The consolidation of the three lines was a triumph for the commodore. The steamship king had become a railroad king.

The Battle of Erie

His stake in the Central gave Vanderbilt control of a railroad that connected New York with the Midwest. But that was not enough for him. There was a rival line, the Erie, and the commodore wanted to control it, too. His effort sparked one of the most famous contests in the history of American business. Sometimes known as the "Battle of Erie," sometimes known as the "Erie War," that contest brought Vanderbilt into furious conflict with a group of adversaries who matched his energy, his cunning, and his contempt for law.

The story of the Erie War has been told many times, most notably in two masterful articles published by Charles Francis Adams, Jr., in the *North American Review* in 1869 and 1871. Of the contest that flared up in 1868, Adams wrote: "It was something new to see a knot of adventurers, men of broken fortune, without character and without credit, possess themselves of an artery of commerce more important than was ever the Appian Way, and make levies, not only upon it . . . but, through it, upon the whole business of a nation."

The "men of broken fortune" were Vanderbilt's crafty opponents— old Daniel Drew, president of the Erie, and his two younger allies, James Fisk, Jr., and Jay Gould.

Fisk was a flamboyant character who won a variety of nicknames in his short career, including Jubilee Jim, the Prince of Erie, and the Barnum of Wall Street. A roly-poly fellow with blond hair and a moustache that made him look like a walrus, he had a taste for flashy clothes and willing women. During the Civil War, as a salesman for Jordan, Marsh & Company of Boston, he made big money selling dry goods to the government. The money was lost in stock-market speculations, but Fisk emerged as an independent broker in the firm of Fisk, Belden & Company. His alliance with Daniel Drew—an alliance that set the stage for Fisk's participation in the Battle of Erie—began when he came up with a scheme that led to the profitable disposition of some worthless securities that Drew had acquired. Later Fisk worked with Jay Gould in an attempt to corner the gold market, an effort that led to the panic that rocked Wall Street on "Black Friday," September 24, 1869. In the end, his love of the good life undid him: He was shot to death in 1872, at the age of thirty-eight, by a rival for the affections of his showgirl mistress, Josie Mansfield.

Jay Gould was a quiet man with a big beard, dark eyes, and a manner so secretive that the word "enigmatic" crops up in virtually every description of him. Born in Roxbury, New York, in 1836, he worked as a surveyor in his teens; then was involved in suspicious dealings as the manager of a tannery; then, with the assistance of his well-to-do father-in-law, began to invest in railroad securities. By the age of twenty-five he was a partner in a brokerage firm that specialized in trading the stock of the Erie—a position that led to an invitation to join the board of the railroad in 1867.

Gould's business activities did not win him an enviable reputation. Joseph Pulitzer called him "one of the most sinister figures that have ever flitted bat-like across the vision of the American people," while the *New York Herald* suggested that "he should be called the Skunk of Wall Street, not one of its ubiquitous Wolves and Wizards." In his *History of the Great American Fortunes* (1909), the muckraker Gustavus Myers took a deep breath and described Gould as "one of the most audacious and successful

buccaneers of modern times . . . a freebooter who, if he could not appropriate millions, would filch thousands; a pitiless human carnivore,
glutting on the blood of his numberless victims." Gould himself conceded—or perhaps boasted—that he was "the most hated man in America." Yet some mystery remains. A recent biographer has challenged the
conventional image at almost every point, and offered in its place the
poetic, though not entirely persuasive, image of "a shy, furtive creature
feeding at twilight at the forest's edge."

Thanks to the activities of Daniel Drew, the Erie had come to be
known as the "scarlet woman of Wall Street." The battle of 1868 began
quietly, with the purchase of the judiciary. Judge George G. Barnard,
the agent of the Vanderbilt group, granted an order that forbade the Erie
board from issuing any new capital stock, temporarily suspended Drew
from his position as treasurer, and forbade Drew from trading Erie stock
until he returned the securities he had received as collateral for a loan
two years before. Not to be outdone, the Erie group produced its own
judge, who canceled Barnard's injunctions as quickly as he could
issue them.

Now, with misplaced confidence in the force of Judge Barnard's orders, Vanderbilt began to buy Erie stock. Drew and his associates sold.
Indeed, they sold shares as fast as they could print them, for Fisk and
Gould had got hold of a printing press. "If this printing press don't break
down," Fisk said, "I'll be damned if I don't give the old hog all he wants
of Erie."

Judge Barnard ordered the arrest of the Erie trio. They promptly
packed up $6 million in cash, along with the records of the company,
and (in the words of Charles Francis Adams, Jr.) "looking more like a
frightened gang of thieves, disturbed in the division of their plunder,
than like the wealthy representatives of a great corporation"—made a
dash for the ferry. Arriving in New Jersey, they took up residence at
Taylor's Hotel in Jersey City. To discourage any thoughts of violence
that the commodore might have entertained, a small army of Jersey City
policemen and hired thugs was placed on permanent guard. Three twelve-
pound artillery pieces offered additional discouragement.

Judicial action having produced a stalemate, the battle moved to the
New York State legislature in Albany. There, as in the courts, cash was
the weapon that carried real weight. In the view of one newspaper, the
legislature of 1868 was the "worst assemblage of official thieves that ever
disgraced the Capitol of the Empire State"—no small distinction, considering the competition.

With a valise containing $500,000 in cash, Gould himself traveled to Albany, where, Adams tells us, he "assiduously cultivated a thorough understanding between himself and the legislature." In 1868, a later investigation showed, the Erie group spent more than $1 million for "extra and legal services." Perhaps because he had entered secret discussions with Drew at about the same time, Vanderbilt allowed his opponents to outbid him.

The negotiations that brought the Battle of Erie to a close began with a simple note: "Drew: I'm sick of the whole damned business. Come and see me. Van Derbilt." Despite his defeat in Albany, Vanderbilt might have filed suits and injunctions that would have kept his opponents in Jersey City for a long while—a fate none of them relished. A complicated settlement was reached, with Vanderbilt selling fifty thousand shares of stock for $2.5 million in cash and $1.25 million in guaranteed bonds. He also received a cash bonus of $1 million, ostensibly in return for an option to buy another fifty thousand shares of his stock. Even with this bonus, it has been estimated that the Erie War cost the commodore between $1 million and $2 million. "From now on," he declared, speaking of Fisk and Gould, "I'll never have anything more to do with them blowers." To Drew he confided, "This Erie War has taught me that it never pays to kick a skunk."

Watered Stock and a Grand Depot

An early biographer offered an amusing and generally accurate summary of Vanderbilt's approach to the railroad business: "1, buy your railroad; 2, stop the stealing that went on under the other man; 3, improve it in every practicable way within a reasonable expenditure; 4, consolidate it with any other road that can be run with it economically; 5, water its stock; 6, make it pay a large dividend."

Stock-watering deserves particular attention, since it is one of the charges against Vanderbilt that his critics have emphasized. The phrase itself appears to have originated in the 1820s, when young Daniel Drew worked as a cattle drover. Drew, legend has it, would feed his cattle salt as they approached the marketplace, then let them drink their fill just before they were weighed. The purchaser of "watered stock" might think he was paying for beef, but to the extent that Drew's trick worked, he was paying for water.

A similar technique soon flourished on Wall Street. Adams devotes a chapter to the subject in *Chapters of Erie*. He defines stock-watering as "the reappraisal by its owners of a corporate property which has, or is alleged to have, increased in value on their hands, without any new outlay upon their part, and the issue to themselves of new evidences of value equal to such supposed increase." Stock-watering must be distinguished, he says, from "fraudulent and secret issues of stock by corrupt managements," which are "mere fraud."

Though he distinguishes it from fraud, Adams contends that stock-watering "has been very grossly abused," and he declares that these abuses "now impose a very heavy additional burden upon the cost of transportation" in the United States. Examining the books of the New York Central, he finds that the cost of the road is listed at $60 million, or about $70,000 per mile, while the capital stock of the company is listed at $103 million, or about $122,000 per mile. Thus, "According to the books of the company over $50,000 of absolute water has been poured out for each mile of road between New York and Buffalo."

In answer to such criticism, Vanderbilt argued that it was earnings, not initial capitalization, that determined the value of any business. If a company doubled its stock while earnings remained constant, then dividends would be cut in half, and each shareholder would receive exactly what he had received before—half the dividend on twice the number of shares.

On this point, most financial analysts now agree, Vanderbilt had a better case than his critics. The dilution of earnings balances any watering of the stock. Daniel Drew's trick works if the water is poured into a cow, but not if it is poured into a company.

Having failed in his effort to gain control of the Erie, Vanderbilt sought an alternative route to the Midwest. To the New York Central, the Harlem, and the Hudson he added, in the last years of his life, the Lake Shore, the Michigan Southern, the Canada Southern, and the Michigan Central railroads. These acquisitions made him the master of one of the great systems of American transportation—a continuous line of 978 miles that linked New York to Chicago.

In 1871, even before making the purchases that completed the system, Vanderbilt opened a great new terminal, the largest in the world, in the heart of New York City. The Grand Central Depot, at Forty-second Street and Fourth (now Park) Avenue, cost $3 million and stood upon five acres of the most expensive real estate on earth. From the front of the even grander terminal that occupies the same location today, facing the automobile ramp that rises from lower Park Avenue, an undistinguished statue of the commodore has gazed south since 1929. Behind the statue, pushing deep into the heartland, stretches the railroad empire that the steamship king built in his fierce old age.

The Lion in Winter

On August 21, 1869, almost a year to the day after the death of his wife, Sophia, Vanderbilt married a distant cousin, Miss Frank Crawford of Mobile, Alabama. The groom was seventy-five; the bride, a handsome woman of about thirty. The marriage appears to have been happy. A prenuptial agreement limited any claim that the new Mrs. Vanderbilt might make upon her husband's estate.

The aging commodore loved to vacation in Saratoga, where he would go to the races, drive his trotters, and play whist with old friends. He developed an interest in spiritualism and attended séances conducted by a seer on Staten Island.

For the first time in his life (not counting the "gift" of the steamship *Vanderbilt* to the government during the Civil War), the commodore began to take an interest in philanthropy. He gave $50,000 to a church whose pastor was a friend, and he gave $1 million to the Central University of the Methodist Episcopal Church of the South at Nashville, Tennessee, which promptly showed its gratitude by renaming itself Vanderbilt University. But he was not a soft touch. He might say that "A million or two is as much as anyone ought to have," but if anyone suggested that it ought to be easy to get rid of his extra millions, he would shake his head wearily: "What you have got isn't worth anything unless you have got the power, and if you give away the surplus, you give away control."

His body began to fail—doctors later reported that ulceration had left him with "scarce a sound organ in his body"—but the will that had sustained him through so many battles did not falter. Once a reporter came to his home to ask about rumors that his health was failing—rumors that had led to heavy sales in the stock of the Lake Shore. Dragging himself out of bed, the commodore shouted down the stairs that he was still strong enough to "knock all the lies out of the wretches" who were spreading the rumor.

In the last months of his life, in 1876, he fought his last business battle—a rate war that pitted Vanderbilt's New York Central and Hudson River lines against the Grand Trunk of Canada, the Pennsylvania

Railroad, and the Baltimore and Ohio. The leaders of the rival roads may have supposed that their eighty-two-year-old adversary, however formidable he had been in his prime, would have no stomach for the fight. They soon learned how wrong they were. Rates were slashed and slashed again. Goods were being hauled so cheaply, one rival official complained, that the company could barely pay for the axle grease. In December 1876 Vanderbilt's antagonists trooped to New York and signed an agreement that gave him the concessions he wanted.

Less than three weeks later, his heart gave out at last. Between 1875 and 1877, the three richest men in America had died. Alexander T. Stewart, the department-store magnate, left an estate of about $40 million. William Backhouse Astor, the dull son of John Jacob, also left about $40 million—double the amount he had inherited. Cornelius Vanderbilt, who in 1848 had expressed such interest in the size of Astor's estate, left $104 million. Ninety percent of Vanderbilt's fortune had been amassed in the last dozen years of his life, when he turned his attention to railroads.

As always, the public was eager to know how the modern Midas had disposed of his estate.

To his wife, in accordance with their prenuptial agreement, the commodore left $500,000 in cash, the modest home they had shared at 10 Washington Place in lower Manhattan, and two thousand shares of New York Central stock. To his eight daughters he left bequests ranging from $250,000 to $500,000—a total of $2,450,000. And to his younger son, Cornelius Jeremiah, a ne'er-do-well whom the commodore neither liked nor trusted, he left $200,000.

The will contained no new bequests, though it has been said that Vanderbilt asked his son William to take care of his charitable interests. William could afford it. As John Jacob Astor had sought to keep his fortune intact by leaving virtually all of it to one son, so Vanderbilt left nearly all of his estate—more than $90 million—to William.

A tremendous legal battle followed. The will was challenged by Cornelius Jeremiah and two of his sisters. A contest that Dickens might have invented dragged on in the courts for nearly a year. At last William offered a compromise. The exact figures are not known, but it seems that each of the disgruntled siblings received about $500,000 more than the commodore had thought necessary.

In 1882, after a night at a gambling house, Cornelius Jeremiah shot himself to death in his rooms at the Glenham Hotel in Manhattan. Nothing in his life suggests that his father had judged him unfairly. His respectable older brother William died of natural causes in 1885, at the age of sixty-four, leaving an estate worth nearly $200 million, to be divided among the many heirs who would carry the Vanderbilt dynasty into the twentieth century.

"One Honest, Sturdy, Fearless Man"

Even before his death, the contemporaries of the commodore debated the meaning of his career. In an open letter published in 1869, Mark Twain wrote:

> How my heart goes out in sympathy to you! how I do pity you, Commodore Vanderbilt! Most men have at least a few friends . . . but you seem to be the idol of only a crawling swarm of small souls, who love to glorify your most flagrant unworthiness in print; . . . All I wish to urge you now, is that you crush out your native instincts and go and do something *worthy* of praise. . . . Go, now, please go, and do one worthy act. Go, boldly, proudly, and nobly, and give four dollars to some great public charity."

Twain was an ambitious smart aleck, not to be taken seriously. To men of mature judgment, there could be no doubt that Vanderbilt's career had been a success and no doubt that that success had sprung from the strength of his character. The obituary in James Gordon Bennett's *New York Herald* epitomized this view: "Energy, application, painstaking patience and persistence, made the dead Commodore what he was, and they constitute a set of virtues of which the best man alive might be proud. . . . The lesson to be learned from the life of Vanderbilt is simple and impressive. . . . It was one honest, sturdy, fearless man against the world, and in the end the man won."

A few commentators dissented. The editor of *The Nation*, E. L. Godkin, agreed that Vanderbilt's success had been rooted in his character, but he did not find that character wholly admirable. Moreover, he disliked the crudeness of the self-made man: Vanderbilt's "early education was scanty," Godkin wrote, "and he had few of the requirements of culture; his language was always illiterate and often profane. In his business transactions he was overreaching and exacting, often availing himself of questionable practices. . . . He was a kind of man whose like we should be sorry to see many of—the typical result of strong character developed by energy and perseverance to the highest point of business success."

Henry Ward Beecher, one of the nation's best-known clergymen, also expressed doubts. "Looking at his commercial life," Beecher told his congregation, "few have equalled, none have surpassed him, but there it stops." Vanderbilt's pastor, the Reverend Charles F. Deems, had noted approvingly that the old man liked to sing certain hymns. "Yes," Beecher said, "I am glad he liked the hymns, but if he had sung them thirty years ago it would have made a great difference. He did not sing hymns as long as he could get about. We don't want to give God the fag end of our lives."

Others criticized the commodore for giving too little to charity. But his defenders had an answer: "By some the usual lamentations are uttered because no large bequests were made to benevolent objects. Whatever Cornelius Vanderbilt acquired he did not owe to public favor, and he had a very clear right to use it as he deemed best. If he believed that $60 million would be better employed in building up, maintaining, and defending against all competition, the great railway which now forms the main artery of the commerce of this city, it is at least possible that he thereby established a more useful benevolent institution than any other which his money could have founded. It is better to permanently promote the industry, commerce and prosperity of a great state and city, thereby giving millions of workers a better chance to earn a living, than to found any number of hospitals."

This argument was made again and again in editorials all over the country. It was a useful argument, which allowed editors to affirm the value of business activity while relieving them of any need to make absurd claims about the character of the titans who were beginning to dominate the commercial life of the nation. It was not necessary to say that the commodore had been a saint. Men like Vanderbilt work for the public good, this line of thought suggested, "whether they want to do it or not."

It was a new argument—an argument that did not apply to John Jacob Astor, collector of rents, but did apply to Cornelius Vanderbilt, builder of railroads. It was an argument that suited the nation that was emerging in the 1870s—a nation that soon would see larger fortunes than Vanderbilt had made and larger enterprises than he had built, though it might never see a more eager appetite for business combat. The son of Staten Island farm folk had built a fortune that made his name seem to glitter and dazzled even the moralists who disliked his motives and condemned his methods.

CHAPTER 4

The Literature of Success in the Nineteenth Century

"Ours Is a Country . . ."

Success has always fascinated Americans, and, for most Americans, success has meant money. This equation goes far back in our history. "The only principle of life propagated among the young people is to get money," one New Yorker complained in 1748. William Ellery Channing, the pastor of the Federal Street Church in Boston, made a similar observation shortly before his death in 1842: "How widely spread is the passion for acquisition, not for simple means of subsistence, but for wealth! What vast enterprises agitate the community! What a rush into all the departments of trade!"

The commercial exuberance of Americans in those early years was related to the break from Europe, which meant a break from rigid class structures. The idea that all men were created equal, and that all ought to be free to rise as high as their own efforts could lift them, stirred everyone it touched in the young nation. For white males, at least, no country in the world raised fewer barriers to success, and none came closer to realizing the idea of equal opportunity.

America was open, self-created, invigorating. America was different—different from anyplace else in the world. A thousand passages like this one, from a volume published in 1844, might be quoted: "Ours is a country, where men start from an humble origin . . . and where they can attain to the most elevated positions, or acquire a large amount of wealth. according to the pursuits they elect for themselves. No exclusive privileges of birth, no entailment of estates, no civil or political disqualifications, stand in their path; but one has as good a chance as another, according to his talents, prudence, and personal exertions. This is a country of self-made men, than which nothing better could be said of any state of society."

The eagerness to make a fortune was accompanied by an eagerness to read about the fortunes others had made. In 1842, the editor of the *New York Sun*, Moses Yale Beach, published the first directory of wealthy Americans. Beach's *Wealth and Pedigree of the Wealthy Citizens of New York City* provided brief biographies of all residents of New York with an estimated worth of $100,000 or more—no small amount at a time when room and board at the luxurious Astor House Hotel, including four meals with "all the delicacies of the season," cost $1.50 a day.

The first list included fourteen millionaires, headed by John Jacob Astor. Beach called special attention to those who "by honest and laborious industry have raised themselves from the obscure walks of life, to great wealth and consideration." He himself had been born poor in Connecticut and apprenticed to a cabinetmaker at fourteen. "By overwork and working nights," according to the entry on his own life in the list published in 1845, he "managed to save, by . . . his 18th year, $400," and by 1845 he was worth $250,000. He published twelve editions of his list and made enough money, from that source and others, to retire at forty-eight in 1848. When *Forbes* magazine began to publish its own "rich list" in the 1980s, it acknowledged Beach as a forerunner.

Beach was not the only person who catered to the pre-Civil War interest in America's money-makers. A member of the Philadelphia bar published *Wealth and Biography of the Wealthy Citizens of Philadelphia* in 1845. Freeman Hunt founded *Hunt's Merchants' Magazine* in 1839, published hundreds of business anecdotes and maxims in *Worth and Wealth* (1856), and offered two volumes of business biography in his *Lives of American Merchants* (1858). Edwin T. Freedley of Philadelphia emphasized manufacturers rather than merchants in his *Practical Treatise on Business* (1852) and in *Leading Pursuits and Leading Men* (1856).

Timothy Shay Arthur of Philadelphia argued that biographies of self-made businessmen served the public good: "Hitherto, American biography has confined itself too closely to men who have won political or literary distinction. . . . Limited to the perusal of such biographies, our youth must, of necessity, receive erroneous impressions of the true construction of our society, and fail to perceive wherein the progressive vigor of the nation lies. . . . We want the histories of our self-made men spread out before us, that we may know the ways by which they came up from the ranks of the people." The inspiring stories in Charles C. B. Seymour's *Self-Made Men* (1858) almost seemed to answer Arthur's plea.

Benjamin Franklin remained a central figure in the American consciousness—the prototype of the self-made man. The rhetorical excess he inspired gives us one measure of his significance. Here is a passage from a speech made at the unveiling of a statue of Franklin in front of Boston City Hall in 1856:

> Behold him, Mechanics and Mechanics' Apprentices, holding out to you an example of diligence, economy and virtue, and personifying the triumphant success which may await those who follow it! Behold him, ye that are humblest and poorest in present condition or in future prospect,—lift up your heads and look at the image of a man who rose from nothing, who owed nothing to parentage or patronage, who enjoyed no advantages of early education which are not open,—a hundred fold open,—to yourselves, who performed the most menial services in the business in which his early life was employed, but who lived to stand before Kings, and died to leave a name which the world will never forget.

Franklin did not merely help create the cult of the self-made man in America. He became, in the words of historian Irvin G. Wyllie, "the first object of adoration in this cult." Through Franklin, the success traditions of the eighteenth and nineteenth centuries were united.

Wealth Through Virtue

A staggering amount of advice was available to nineteenth-century youths who yearned to succeed—not only biographies and autobiographies of business leaders but also didactic novels, self-help manuals, essays, lectures, sermons, and orations. This vast literature taught a single lesson: Success was a function of character.

Character mattered because it was developed through personal effort. To the extent that they were a gift of birth, intelligence and physical strength did not matter. As Theodore Roosevelt wrote in 1900, "No brilliancy of intellect, no perfection of bodily development, will count when weighed in the balance against that assemblage of virtues . . . which we group together under the name of character."

Adversity was good because it strengthened character. Henry Ward Beecher, pastor of Plymouth Congregational Church in Brooklyn from 1847 to 1887, advised his wealthy congregation not to fear misfortune: "How blessed, then, is the stroke of disaster which sets the children free, and gives them over to the hard but kind bosom of Poverty, who says to them, 'Work!' and working, makes them men."

Andrew Carnegie agreed. Poor boys "appear upon the stage," he wrote, "athletes trained for the contest, with sinews braced, indomitable wills, resolved to do or die. Such boys always have marched, and always will march, straight to the front. . . . They are the epoch-makers." No school taught more than the school of poverty: "Abolish luxury, if you please," Carnegie wrote, "but leave us the soil, upon which alone the virtues and all that is precious in human character grow; poverty—honest poverty."

The qualities of character that led to success, in the view of the self-help advisers of the nineteenth century, were the same qualities that Benjamin Franklin had recommended: industry, frugality, sobriety, honesty, perseverance, and so on. Also vital were the characteristics that employers looked for: punctuality, reliability, loyalty, and obedience. If adversity failed to develop these qualities, America's youths could learn their importance from the famous McGuffey readers:

> Work, work, my boy, be not afraid;
>   Look labor boldly in the face;
> Take up the hammer or the spade,
>   And blush not for your humble place.

America's clergy preached this lesson with tremendous enthusiasm. We may never know which came first, the Protestant ethic or the spirit of capitalism, but it is clear that Protestantism not only sanctioned accumulation but also sanctioned the economic virtues—industry, frugality, etc.—that were presumed to lead to accumulation. A book published by the Reverend Thomas P. Hunt in 1836—*The Book of Wealth; in Which It Is Proved from the Bible that It Is the Duty of Every Man to Become Rich*—tells the whole story in its title.

"Religion," wrote Daniel Wise, a Methodist minister, "will teach you that industry is a SOLEMN DUTY you owe to God, whose command is 'BE DILIGENT IN BUSINESS!' " Writing in an article titled "The Elements of Business Success" in *Hunt's Merchants' Magazine* in 1854, Matthew H. Smith argued that Adam's sin was a failure to attend to business: "The race was made for employment. Adam was created and placed in the Garden of Eden for business purposes; it would have been better for the race if he had attended closely to the occupation for which he was made."

Theodore Parker of Boston, a Unitarian clergyman best known for his role in the antislavery movement, suggested that a new kind of saint had emerged in the nineteenth century. The merchant who thrived through honest industry was "a moral educator, a church of Christ gone into business—a saint in trade. . . . The Saint of the nineteenth century is the Good Merchant. . . . Build him a shrine in Bank and Church, in the Market and the Exchange. . . . No Saint stands higher than this Saint of Trade."

As the way to wealth was the path of righteousness, so the possession of wealth was proof of virtue. "Godliness is in league with riches," said William Lawrence, the Episcopal bishop of Massachusetts and son of industrialist Amos Lawrence. Money, a Unitarian minister told his congregation, "is a *blessing from the Lord*. It is a sign of the divine approval." John D. Rockefeller, a Baptist who taught Sunday school classes, stood squarely in the mainstream of nineteenth-century thought when he said, in reply to his critics, "God gave me my money."

Neither clergymen nor nonclerical preachers of the get-ahead gospel glorified men who cheated or bullied their way to success. "Riches got by fraud," Henry Ward Beecher wrote in his *Seven Lectures to Young Men* (1844), "are dug out of one's own heart and destroy the mine. Unjust riches curse the owner in getting, in keeping, in transmitting." "It is folly supreme, nay madness," the author of *Mercantile Morals* warned, "to make the acquiring riches, and enjoying them, the chief end of life." The author of *Money for the Millions* agreed: "A *little*, justly gained, is better than *thousands* secured by stealth, or at the expense of another's rights and interests." Whatever else he might sell, the man of business was not supposed to sell his soul.

Honest industry in the accumulation of a fortune was not the only mark of good character. The businessman who wanted to earn public approval was required to be charitable. As Irvin Wyllie observes, "If critics charge Jay Gould, Jim Fisk, and Daniel Drew against the gospel of self-help, they must also add to its credit more respectable operators such as George Peabody, Peter Cooper, Ezra Cornell, and Andrew Carnegie, for it was the latter, not the former, who were acknowledged as the heroes of the cult."

The doctrine of the stewardship of wealth—the idea that the rich man held his money in trust, to be used in doing God's work on earth—sealed the partnership of God and Mammon. "I do not recognize myself as the owner . . . of one dollar of the wealth which has come into my hands," said New York industrialist and philanthropist Peter Cooper. "I am simply responsible for the management of an estate which belongs to humanity." Other motives may have played a role—the names of men who make large gifts tend to be cut in stone—but there is no question that the doctrine of stewardship led not only to philanthropy on a vast scale but also to thousands of smaller benefactions. To this doctrine we owe Carnegie's libraries, museums, and music hall; the institutes and art galleries organized by Cooper, Peabody, and Mellon; universities endowed by Vanderbilt, Cornell, Stanford, and Rockefeller; and much else.

"Book Learning Is Something . . ."

In the conventional view of the nineteenth century, neither genius nor college education offered any advantage to the young man who sought success in business. Indeed, both were handicaps.

Geniuses were criticized for laziness and lack of discipline. "So far as my observations have ascertained the species," Henry Ward Beecher assured an audience in 1844, ". . . they are to be known by a reserved air, excessive sensitiveness, and utter indolence; by the reading of much wretched poetry, and the writing of such, yet more wretched; by being very conceited, very affected, very disagreeable, and very useless:—beings whom no man wants for friend, pupil, or companion."

William Holmes McGuffey saw things the same way:

> Thus, plain, plodding people, we shall often find,
>   Will leave hasty, confident people behind:
> Like the tortoise and hare, though together they start
>   We soon clearly see they are widely apart.
>
> While one trusts the gifts Dame Nature bestows,
>   And relying on these, calmly stops for repose,
> The other holds slowly and surely his way,
>   And thus wins the race, ere the close of the day.

No man could make himself a genius, but anyone could work hard, and thus anyone could succeed. In the words of a typical self-help adviser, "The genius which has accomplished great things in the world, as a rule, is the genius for downright hard work. . . . This is the genius that has transformed the world, and led civilization from the rude devices of the Hottentots to the glorious achievements of our own century."

The college graduate was no better a candidate than the genius for a career in business. When Cornelius Vanderbilt heard that England's Lord Palmerston had declared it a pity that a man of Vanderbilt's ability lacked the advantages of formal education, Vanderbilt replied, "You tell Lord Palmerston from me that if I had learned education I would not have had time to learn anything else." Vanderbilt's great rival, Daniel Drew, agreed: "Book learning is something, but thirteen million dollars is also something, and a mighty sight more."

"It is not book-learning young men need," Elbert Hubbard said in his well-known inspirational lecture "A Message to Garcia" (1899), "but stiffening of the vertebrae which will cause them to be loyal to a trust, to act promptly, concentrate their energies." In an article in 1894 in *Cosmopolitan*, Edward Bok noted that few men with college degrees had made their way to the top of the business community in New York. A decade earlier, Edwin T. Freedley went so far as to say that he doubted that more than half a dozen college graduates could be found among the nation's business leaders. "Directly or indirectly," Freedley declared, colleges had "ruined a greater number of their sons than they had ever benefitted."

Andrew Carnegie disagreed. "Just see," he wrote in 1893, "wherever we peer into the first tiny springs of the national life, how this true panacea . . . bubbles forth—education, education, education." But Carnegie recommended education in spite of—or, more accurately, on account of—its inappropriateness as a preparation for business: "Liberal education gives a man who really absorbs it higher tastes and aims than the acquisition of wealth . . . ; to find therefore that it is not the best training for business is to prove its claim to a higher domain." In the lower domain, where Carnegie himself had made his mark, "college education as it exists seems almost fatal to success."

Another self-made giant of the nineteenth century, John D. Rockefeller, tried to affirm the value of a liberal arts education, but his heart seems not to have been in it: "I think a college education is a splendid thing for a boy; but I would not say that it is absolutely necessary. I hadn't the advantage of a college education; but I had a good mother and an excellent father, and I like to feel that whatever I may have lost through failure to secure a college education I made up through my home training. It is in the home circle that the character of a boy is formed." In the end, Rockefeller seems to rank vocational training above the higher learning: "Better than a college education . . . is the training that a boy gets in the technical schools that have sprung up all over the country. This is an age of specialization. There is an unceasing demand on every hand . . . for men with special, technical knowledge."

Much better than a degree from any college, in the conventional view of the nineteenth century, was a degree from the college of hard knocks. Emerson lauded the "sturdy lad from New Hampshire or Vermont, who in turn tries all the professions, and *teams it, farms it, peddles*, keeps a school, preaches, edits a newspaper, goes to Congress, buys a township, and . . . always like a cat falls on his feet." Such a fellow is "worth a hundred of these city dolls," the sage of Concord declared, who fiddle away four years in college and fall utterly apart if "not installed in an office within one year afterwards in the cities or suburbs of Boston or New York."

In the competition with the college man, the great advantage of the self-made man was experience. As a method of preparing well-rounded men of business, what could surpass an old-fashioned apprenticeship in which a boy began at the bottom, sweeping the floor of the office, and then moved patiently upward on a path that took him through every job in an enterprise—messenger, file clerk, shipping clerk, salesman, buyer, bookkeeper, office manager, general manager? Andrew Carnegie had risen from such a start and delighted in reciting the names of other prominent businessmen who shared his background. How could a college man ever compete with a man trained in this way? How could he ever make up for the years wasted on the acquisition of superfluous learning? "The prize takers have too many years the start of the graduate," Carnegie declared. "They have entered for the race invariably in their teens—in the most valuable of all the years for learning—from fourteen to twenty; while the college student has been learning a little about the barbarous and petty squabbles of the past . . . the future captain of industry is hotly engaged in the school of experience, obtaining the very knowledge required for his future triumphs."

Though college education was regarded as harmful, young men were encouraged to embark upon a program of self-culture. Institutions aimed at furnishing educational opportunities for working-class Americans sprang up in pre-Civil War America. In 1826, for instance, an English immigrant named Timothy Claxton founded the Boston Mechanics' Institution, and Josiah Holbrook of Massachusetts founded the first American lyceum. The idea caught on, and by 1834 nearly three thousand local lyceums had been organized to provide adult Americans with opportunities for self-education. In the 1840s and 1850s, frequent speakers at lyceums included Ralph Waldo Emerson, Henry David Thoreau, Daniel Webster, Henry Ward Beecher, and Nathaniel Hawthorne.

Mercantile libraries, where clerks and mechanics could gather in the evenings for readings and lectures, also flourished, and businessmen often endowed or subsidized them. In the second half of the century, public libraries ranked among the favorite philanthropies of Ezra Cornell, Andrew Carnegie, and other self-made men. Peter Cooper showed his commitment to the idea of self-culture when he organized Cooper Union in New York, where poor youths could attend free lectures and study mathematics, mechanics, chemistry, electricity, drawing, and other subjects of vocational interest. In Baltimore, shortly before his death in 1869, merchant Ezra Peabody founded and endowed Peabody Institute, which provided not only classes but also a library, a program of lectures, an academy of music, and an art gallery.

For the great mass of Americans in the nineteenth century, there was no culture except self-culture. In 1900 only 6.3 percent of America's seventeen-year-olds graduated from high school, and only 2.3 percent of youths eighteen to twenty-four years old were enrolled in college degree-credit programs. Of the prominent businessmen listed in the 1900 edition of *Who's Who in America*, 84 percent had not been educated beyond high school. But times were changing. In an article titled "The College Man and the Corporate Proposition," published in 1900, corporation lawyer James B. Dill observed that "the demand today for trained minds, devoted to specific lines of work, has created a demand for college trained men." Traditional apprenticeships could not meet the needs of industrial America. "There is a great deal to be gained," one old-timer complained in 1904, "by the discipline of daily life that comes with drudgery, such as the washing of ink-stands, cleaning windows, carrying bundles, and sweeping out the store," but "unfortunately for the boy's own good, the conditions are such at the present that he is not called upon to do that work as was the custom a generation ago." A boy who began by washing out inkstands might acquire the skills to manage an office, but he was not likely to acquire the skills to manage an enterprise like Rockefeller's Standard Oil or Carnegie's U.S. Steel.

Holy Horatio

The success literature of the nineteenth century did not merely include sermons, lectures, and all manner of self-help guidebooks. It also included fiction. Of the novelists who took success as their subject, none won a larger audience, and none has been more thoroughly misunderstood, than Horatio Alger, Jr.

The son of a Unitarian minister, Alger was born in 1832 in Chelsea, Massachusetts. In his youth his piety earned him the nickname "Holy Horatio." He graduated from Harvard at twenty, and over the next dozen years he worked at a variety of teaching, writing, and editing jobs, traveled, and obtained a degree from Harvard Divinity School.

In December 1864 Alger was ordained as minister of the Unitarian Society of Brewster, Massachusetts. Less than two years later he resigned upon being confronted with the charge that he had committed, in the words of a special committee of the parish, "a crime of no less magnitude than the abominable and revolting crime of unnatural familiarity with *boys*." When presented with evidence of his guilt, Alger, the committee reported, "neither denied or attempted to extenuate but received it with apparent calmness of an old offender—and hastily left town on the very next train for parts unknown—probably Boston."

In fact, Alger fled to New York. "Friar Anselmo's Sin," a poem he wrote only a few days after his appearance before the parish committee, suggests that his "apparent calmness" masked inner turmoil:

> Friar Anselmo (God's grace may he win!)
> Committed one sad day a deadly sin;
>
> Which being done he drew back, self-abhorred,
> From the rebuking presence of the Lord,
>
> And, kneeling down, besought, with bitter cry,
> Since life was worthless grown, that he might die.

A cry of distress interrupts Anselmo's meditation, and he finds that a "wounded traveler" has "crawled for aid unto the convent door." After he nurses the traveler back to health, the friar is visited by an angel who shows him the path out of despair:

> "Courage, Anselmo, though thy sin be great,
> God grants thee life that thou may'st expiate.

"Thy guilty stains shall be washed white again,
By noble service done thy fellow-man."

The parallel with Alger's situation after his dismissal is obvious. Horatio's "noble service" would be to write fiction that would teach juveniles to love "moral beauty" and to do good. Through his pen he would earn a living, expiate his guilt, and live a life of service.

Soon after his arrival in New York, Alger became aware of the miserable conditions that afflicted the thousands of orphans and runaways who had flocked to the city during and after the Civil War. He became interested in the work of the Newsboys' Lodging House, founded by the urban reformer Charles Loring Brace, and began to spend much time there. "By his warmheartedness and sympathy," a biographer reports, "Alger won the confidence of the street gamins, made innumerable friends among them, and came to know their life in all its details."

In January 1867, in *The Student and Schoolmate* magazine, Alger published the first installment of a novel about these vagrant children. *Ragged Dick; or, Street Life in New York* was the first of more than one hundred juvenile novels that Alger wrote between 1867 and his death in 1899. Its popularity, combined with the fact that it launched Alger's remarkable career, gives it a special place in the history of American literature. In 1947 the Grolier Club of New York included *Ragged Dick* in a list of the one hundred most influential books printed in the United States before 1900. More recently, in an article in *American Heritage*, literary critic Jonathan Yardley listed it among "ten books that shaped the American character"—"books that extended their influence from the relatively small circle of regular readers into the general culture of the nation."

In a sense, Alger wrote only one book, which he published under a hundred titles. This one book included the eight volumes of the "Ragged Dick" series, the eight volumes of the "Tattered Tom" series, the eight volumes of the "Luck and Pluck" series, the four volumes of the "Brave and Bold" series, the four volumes of the "Way to Success" series, and so on. Often the title alone tells the whole story: *Do and Dare, Fame and Fortune, Sink or Swim, Slow and Sure, Strive and Succeed, Strong and Steady, Try and Trust, Wait and Hope, Wait and Win, Bound to Rise.*

In the twentieth century, the phrase "Horatio Alger hero" is commonly used to describe a person who has risen from rags to riches through personal merit. Oddly, the heroes of Alger's own novels do not fit the definition. Merit plays a role in their rise, but luck often plays an equal role. Indeed, the turning point in virtually all of Alger's novels comes in a chapter titled "————'s Luck."

Ragged Dick, for instance, leaps to the rescue when a child falls from a ferryboat. The grateful father gives him a job in his countinghouse. The hero of *Brave and Bold* wins a generous reward when he happens to be on hand to stop a train speeding toward a boulder on a railroad track. Phil the Fiddler collapses in a snowdrift on Christmas Eve, only to be found by a wealthy physician who lost his only child on Christmas four years earlier. Phil is nursed to health and adopted.

In general, success comes to Alger's heroes not through luck alone, nor through pluck alone, but through the combination of luck and pluck. The boys act promptly when the opportunity to act presents itself. Moreover, even when luck alone seems decisive—for instance, when a dead father's seemingly worthless mining stock turns out to be worth a fortune—Alger's heroes always deserve their luck. "The best way to strive for success is to deserve it," the author told his young readers, and he gave them a warning: "He who trusts wholly to luck, trusts to a will-o'-the-wisp."

The idea that the typical Alger hero rises through merit is not the only misconception that has taken hold in the twentieth century. A second misconception, probably even more widespread, is that Alger's ragged protagonists attain great wealth. In fact, as John G. Cawelti has pointed out, the rise is not from rags to riches but from rags to respectability. An adviser to Ragged Dick teaches him the crucial lesson: "If you'll try to be somebody, and grow up into a respectable member of society, you will. You may not become rich,—it isn't everybody that becomes rich, you know,—but you can obtain a good position, and be respected."

In the rise to respectability, the key events are the acquisition of a good suit and the gift of a pocket watch from the hero's patron. Most of the novels stop when the hero obtains a promising job, generally in a mercantile establishment. The goal is not great wealth, but a foothold in the middle class. "I shall feel rich earning seven dollars per week," one hero declares. The prospect of earning nine dollars a week makes another "feel like a millionaire." With five dollars in his pocket, another feels "as rich as Stewart or Vanderbilt."

Alger has been both praised and criticized as an apologist for orthodox capitalism, but neither the praise nor the criticism catches his spirit. Like most of the nineteenth-century success writers, he was a moralist. He frequently quoted the biblical declaration that "the love of money is the root of all evil," and he was not being complimentary when he said that a character "has made money his god, and serves his chosen deity faithfully." To the end, though he lost his ministry, Alger wrote as if from a pulpit. It is better to be "poor and honest," he told his readers, "than live in a fine house, surrounded by luxury, gained by grinding the faces of the poor."

Alger himself was a typical Alger hero in at least one sense: He enjoyed only modest success in his own lifetime. Of well over one hundred novels, he had only four best sellers, all published between 1868 and 1871. In 1897 he estimated that all of his books combined had sold less than a million copies. At his death in 1899, most of his bequests involved copyrights, manuscripts, and his private library. He left less than $1,000 in cash to friends and relatives.

In the two decades after Alger's death, a remarkable revival occurred. Estimates of total sales vary widely, but it seems safe to say that no less than seventeen million volumes were sold in this period. As the age of the automobile dawned, something in the novels struck a chord, perhaps their evocation of a simpler time.

The boom ended in the twenties, and in 1926 the leading publisher of Alger's books stopped publishing them. In 1932, the centenary of Alger's birth, less than 20 percent of seven thousand boys surveyed in New York City recognized his name. Fifteen years later, a poll of twenty thousand New York children found that 92 percent had never heard of Alger, and less than 1 percent had read any of his books. In that same year, the American Schools and Colleges Association, Inc., concerned about "the trend among young people toward the mind-poisoning belief that equal opportunity was a thing of the past," established a Horatio Alger Award. The award honored men who "by their own efforts had pulled themselves up by their bootstraps in the American tradition." Thus, with the virtual disappearance of an actual audience for Alger's work, the mythic Alger hero emerged, rising by pure merit, pulling himself up by his bootstraps.

Alger was not the only nineteenth-century writer who specialized in didactic fiction for juveniles. A host of forgotten predecessors—writers such as Jacob Abbott, Louisa M. Tuthill, J. H. Ingraham, and A. L. Stimson—told similar stories. In 1865, two years before the publication of *Ragged Dick*, Mark Twain parodied the conventions of the genre in a wry sketch, "The Story of a Good Little Boy."

The good little boy, Twain tells his readers with characteristic mischievousness, "had a noble ambition to be put in a Sunday-school book. He wanted to be put in, with pictures representing him gloriously declining to lie to his mother, and her weeping for joy about it; and pictures representing him standing on the doorstep giving a penny to a poor beggarwoman with six children, and telling her to spend it freely, but not to be extravagant, because extravagance is a sin."

Despite his piety, nothing goes well for the good little boy, who eventually is blown to bits by nitroglycerin while looking for bad little boys to chastise. His story, Twain observes, lends itself to no comfortable moral, for it "didn't come out according to the books." Indeed, "Every boy who ever did as he did prospered except him. His case is truly remarkable. It will probably never be accounted for."

Certainly such a story could not be accounted for in the conventional juvenile fiction of the nineteenth century. Nor was there any need to account for it. In the juvenile literature, as in the success literature that addressed itself to adults, goodness never failed. Wealth and worth went hand in hand.

CHAPTER 5

Dissenting Voices: 1850

Thoreau's Success Book

Early in 1848 James Wilson Marshall, a carpenter from New Jersey, discovered nuggets of gold at the site of a sawmill he was building for Johann Sutter in California. The discovery, announced by President Polk in his farewell address to Congress, set off a rush to the West. In 1849 about forty thousand prospectors came to California by sea, sailing around Cape Horn or trekking across the Isthmus of Panama. Another forty thousand risked cholera and Indians on the two-thousand-mile overland route across the United States.

In Massachusetts, Henry David Thoreau watched the scramble with wry detachment. "The rush to California," he wrote later, "reflect[s] the greatest disgrace on mankind. . . . The hog that gets his living by rooting, stirring up the soil so, would be ashamed of such company. . . . What a comment, what a satire, on our institutions! . . . Did God direct us so to get our living, digging where we never planted,—and He would, perchance, reward us with lumps of gold?"

The gold rush offended Thoreau chiefly on moral grounds, as a form of speculation. "The gold-digger in the ravines of the mountains is as much a gambler as his fellow in the saloons of San Francisco. What difference does it make if you shake gold or shake dice?" There was nothing virtuous, Thoreau felt, in the exertions of the prospectors. "The gold-digger is the enemy of the honest laborer, whatever checks and compensations there may be. It is not enough to tell me that you worked hard to get your gold. So does the Devil work hard."

Any conventional moralist might have gone this far. But Thoreau went farther: "With that vision of the diggings still before me, I asked myself why *I* might not be washing some gold daily, though it were only the finest particles,—why *I* might not sink a shaft down to the gold within me, and work that mine." The prospectors lost their gamble even if they won: "Men rush to California and Australia as if the true gold were to be found in that direction; but that is to go to the opposite extreme to where it lies. They go prospecting farther and farther away from the true lead, and are most unfortunate when they think themselves most successful."

What was most strange, Thoreau concluded, was that men ignored this inner wealth even though they could possess it without packing their bags or fighting off hordes of rivals. "If a digger steal away, prospecting for this true gold, into the unexplored solitudes around us, there is no danger that any will dog his steps, and endeavor to supplant him . . . no one will ever dispute his claim. . . . He may mine anywhere, and wash the whole world in his tom."

Thoreau's comments on the gold rush appear in an essay called "Life Without Principle," published posthumously in the *Atlantic Monthly* in 1863. Here, as in the rest of his work, Thoreau dissents vigorously from the usual definition of success and offers a powerful alternative vision. In his writing and in his life, Thoreau poses a permanent challenge to any thoughtless affirmation of business values and business success.

Thoreau grew up in Concord, Massachusetts, attended Harvard, worked briefly as a schoolteacher, and was twenty-four when, in 1841, Ralph Waldo Emerson invited him to join the Emerson household as a general handyman. A double tragedy in 1842—the death of Thoreau's older brother Tom early in January, followed by the death of Emerson's six-year-old son Waldo sixteen days later—deepened the friendship of the two men. Emersonian echoes often ring in Thoreau's prose. For instance, Emerson's essay "Self-Reliance," published in 1841, strikes a note that his disciple sounded again and again: "Society everywhere is in conspiracy against the manhood of every one of its members. . . . Whoso would be a man must be a nonconformist."

On land owned by Emerson on the northwestern shore of Walden

Pond, Thoreau built a cabin—"a tight shingled and plastered house, ten feet wide by fifteen long"—into which he moved on July 4, 1845. There he lived alone until September 6, 1847. His account of this "experiment," published in 1854, is the most important self-help book in American literature.

As Thornton Wilder has pointed out, *Walden* is "a manual of self-reliance"—Emerson brought firmly down to earth. But it is more than that. In *Walden*, the conventional success literature of the nineteenth century is turned upside down. The usual definitions of "success" and "failure," "wealth" and "poverty," are deliberately and defiantly reversed. *Walden* is a business book with a twist. The business that interested Thoreau was the business of living.

The subject of *Walden* is not how to succeed in business but how to succeed in life; not how to get rich by making much but how to live richly by living on little. Thoreau hopes that his book will be read not only by "the mass of men who are discontented" but also by "that seemingly wealthy, but most terribly impoverished class of all, who have accumulated dross, but know not how to use it, or get rid of it, and thus have forged their own golden or silver fetters."

A portrait of the author as a man of business—a man who *minds* his business, in the deepest sense—runs throughout *Walden*. Thoreau is aware that many of his contemporaries consider him impractical, but he insists that the opposite is true: "I have always endeavored to acquire strict business habits; they are indispensable to every man."

Strict business habits were especially important to him, Thoreau explains, because in his youth "I determined to go into business at once, and not wait to acquire the usual capital. . . . My purpose in going to Walden Pond was not to live cheaply nor to live dearly there, but to transact some private business with the fewest obstacles." To be stopped from transacting that business "for want of a little common sense, a little enterprise and business talent," seemed to Thoreau "not so sad as foolish."

The business itself, Thoreau concedes, was unusual. "How many mornings, summer and winter, before any neighbor was stirring about his business, have I been about mine! . . . It is true, I never assisted the sun materially in his rising, but doubt not, it was of the last importance only to be present at it." In addition to watching the sun rise, Thoreau served, he says, as "self-appointed inspector of snow-storms and rain-storms," and he also made a business of listening: "So many autumn, ay, and winter days, spent outside the town, trying to hear what was in the wind. . . . I have well-nigh sunk all my capital in it."

"My accounts," Thoreau boasts, "I can swear to have kept faithfully." The long first chapter of *Walden*, titled "Economy," is full of talk about revenues and expenses. Thus we learn, when Thoreau discusses his cabin, that it cost him $8.03½ for boards, $4.00 for shingles, $4.00 for one thousand old bricks, $2.40 for two casks of lime, $3.90 for nails, $0.14 for hinges and screws, and exactly one penny for chalk. And we learn that he spent on food, in one period of eight months, exactly $8.74, including $1.73½ for rice, $1.73 for molasses, $0.88 for flour, $0.25 for apples, and $0.02 for one watermelon. "My greatest skill," he declares, "has been to want but little."

Wanting little, he finds that he is rich, for "a man is rich in proportion to the number of things he can afford to let alone." The struggle to get rich makes men poor, robbing them of their lives and chaining them to their possessions: "When I consider my neighbors, the farmers of Concord, . . . I find that for the most part they have been toiling twenty, thirty, or forty years, that they may become the real owners of their farms. . . . And when the farmer has got his house, . . . it may be the house that has got him."

Our houses, Thoreau declares, "are such unwieldly property that we are often imprisoned rather than housed in them." Thus, "If one designs to construct a dwelling-house, it behooves him to exercise a little Yankee shrewdness, lest after all he find himself in a workhouse, a labyrinth without a clue, a museum, an almshouse, a prison, or a splendid mausoleum instead." As for furniture, "Pray, for what do we *move* ever but to get rid of our furniture? . . . If I have got to drag my trap, I will take care that it be a light one and do not nip me in a vital part."

"If a man own land," Emerson wrote later, "the land owns him." With the same love of paradox, Thoreau writes: "We do not ride on the railroad; it rides upon us." The nation "lives too fast. Men think that it is essential that the *Nation* have commerce, and export ice, and talk through a telegraph, and ride thirty miles an hour . . . but whether we should live like baboons or like men, is a little uncertain."

Everywhere, men stagger beneath the burden of superfluous possessions: "I see young men, my townsmen, whose misfortune it is to have inherited farms, houses, barns, cattle, and farming tools; for these are more easily acquired than got rid of. . . . Who made them serfs of the soil? . . . Why should they begin digging their graves as soon as they are born? . . . How many a poor immortal soul have I met well-nigh crushed and smothered under its load, creeping down the road of life, pushing before it a barn seventy-five feet by forty . . . and one hundred acres of land tillage, mowing, pasture, and wood-lot!"

Every possession has its cost, and "the cost of a thing is the amount of what I will call life which is required to be exchanged for it." The only true economy is simplicity. "Our life is frittered away by detail. . . . Let your affairs be as two or three, and not a hundred or a thousand; instead of a million count half a dozen, and keep your accounts on your thumb-nail. . . . Simplify, simplify. Instead of three meals a day . . . eat but one; instead of a hundred dishes, five; and reduce other things in proportion."

The secret of success is to concentrate on necessities. "When a man is warmed by the several modes which I have described, what does he want next? Surely not more warmth of the same kind, as more and richer food, larger and more splendid houses, finer and more abundant clothing. . . . When he has obtained those things which are necessary to life, there is another alternative than to obtain the superfluities; and that is, to adventure on life now."

To live now—at bottom, that is all Thoreau wants. *Walden* is a young man's book, and it burns with a young man's impatience. The idea of deferred gratification has never had a more passionate enemy than Thoreau: "This spending of the best part of one's life earning money in order to enjoy a questionable liberty during the least valuable part of it reminds me of the Englishman who went to India to make a fortune first, in order that he might return to England and live the life of a poet. He should have gone up garret at once."

To see men wasting time bothers Thoreau as much as it bothered Franklin. But, unlike Franklin, Thoreau sees work itself as a waste if its purpose is to acquire superfluous wealth: "Superfluous wealth can buy superfluities only. Money is not required to buy one necessary of the soul." The restlessness of his neighbors appalls him. "It would be glorious to see mankind at leisure for once," he declares in "Life Without Principle," and he adds, "I wish to suggest that a man may be very industrious, and yet not spend his time well. There is no more fatal blunderer than he who consumes the greater part of his life getting his living." In *Walden*, contemplating the lives of his neighbors, Thoreau comments, "The twelve labors of Hercules were trifling in comparison . . . ; for they were only twelve, and had an end."

What is idleness? he asks. What is enterprise? "If a man walk in the woods for love of them half of each day, he is in danger of being regarded as a loafer; but if he spends his whole day as a speculator, shearing off those woods and making earth bald before her time, he is esteemed an industrious and enterprising citizen. As if a town had no interest in its forests but to cut them down!"

Industry that does no positive good offends him as much as industry that does harm. "Most men would feel insulted if it were proposed to employ them in throwing stones over a wall, and then in throwing them back, merely that they might earn their wages. But many are no more worthily employed now. . . . To have done anything by which you earned money *merely* is to have been truly idle or worse."

Wanting little, Thoreau suggests, a man is rich. Working little, a man is free. Instead of the industry that wastes life, Thoreau proposes an "idleness" that savors every moment. Whereas Franklin reminds his readers that time is money, Thoreau reminds them that time is life. "Sometimes, in a summer morning, having taken my accustomed bath, I sat in my sunny doorway from sunrise to noon, rapt in a revery. . . . This was sheer idleness to my fellow-townsmen, no doubt, but if the bird and flowers had tried me by their standard, I should not have been found wanting."

Though he was only forty-five when he died, Thoreau's work does not seem unfinished. Perhaps this is because he remained unmarried, and the philosophy that he expresses with such pungent eloquence is the philosophy of an unattached man—a man responsible only for himself. To saddle himself with a family no more suited this great enemy of encumbrances than to saddle himself with a house and furniture. Thoreau appeals especially to the uncommitted young, but the renunciations that thrill many of us at twenty ring less grandly once spouses and children enter our lives. The essential case against Thoreau, as F. O. Matthiessen has pointed out, is captured in a single sentence of philosopher Alfred North Whitehead: "The self-sufficing, independent man, with his peculiar property which concerns no one else, is a concept without any validity for modern civilization."

Despite his limitations, Thoreau's rejection of business values—his rejection of "this restless, nervous, bustling, trivial Nineteenth Century"—occupies a central place in American thought. Contempt for acquisition as an end has never been more powerfully expressed. In the same essay in which he offered his thoughts on the gold rush, Thoreau made this comment on America's preoccupation with business: "What an infinite bustle! . . . If a man was tossed out of a window when an infant, and so made a cripple for life, or scared out of his wits by the Indians, it is regretted chiefly because he was thus incapacitated for—business! I think that there is nothing, not even crime, more opposed to poetry, to philosophy, ay, to life itself, than this incessant business."

Like much else in Thoreau, this taunt still stings. Thoreau, Emerson says, "did not feel himself except in opposition. He wanted a fallacy to expose, a blunder to pillory. . . . It cost him nothing to say No." In the art of saying no to business, no American has surpassed this Yankee gadfly.

Brook Farm

Having renounced commerce, Thoreau went to live alone in the woods. Others who made similar renunciations decided to live in groups. Of dozens of cooperative experiments in this period, probably the ones best remembered today are Brook Farm, organized by George Ripley in Massachusetts in 1841; Fruitlands, organized by Bronson Alcott (the father of Louisa May) in Massachusetts in 1844; and the Oneida Community, organized by John Humphrey Noyes in Oneida, New York, in 1848. The remarkable people who were involved with Brook Farm make it the most interesting of the three.

The winter of 1840–41 was a time of unusual ferment in New England. "We were all a little mad that winter," Emerson wrote later. "Not a man of us that did not have a plan for some new Utopia in his pocket." In an article about the Convention of Friends of Universal Reform that gathered in Boston in November 1840, Emerson captures the spirit of the time: "Madmen, madwomen, men with beards, Dunkers, Muggletonians, Come-outers, Groaners, Agrarians, Seventh-Day Baptists, Quakers, Abolitionists, Calvinists, Unitarians, and Philosophers—all came successively to the top, and seized their moment, if not their *hour*, wherein to chide, or pray, or preach, or protest."

In this atmosphere, Emerson's friend George Ripley made plans for an experiment in communal living. Born in 1803, Ripley had graduated first in his class from Harvard in 1823, had been ordained in the Unitarian ministry in 1826, and had served for fifteen years as minister of the Purchase Street Church in Boston. But the complacency of the comfortable Bostonians in his congregation distressed him. On October 1, 1840, in what historian Perry Miller has called "one of the great symbolic gestures of the era," Ripley resigned his ministry.

"Blame me for it if you will," Ripley wrote in his letter of resignation, "but I cannot behold the degradation, the ignorance, the poverty, the vice, the ruin of the soul, which is everywhere displayed in the very bosom of Christian society in our own city . . . without a shudder. I cannot witness the glaring inequalities of condition, the hollow pretension of pride, the scornful apathy with which many urge the prostration of man, the burning zeal with which they run the race of selfish competition, . . . without the sad conviction that the spirit of Christ has well-nigh disappeared from our churches, and that the fearful doom awaits us."

Four years earlier, on September 19, 1836, the first meeting of an informal "Transcendental Club" had been held at Ripley's home. The club included such New England luminaries as Ripley, Emerson, Bronson Alcott, Orestes A. Brownson, and, after 1837, Theodore Parker, Margaret Fuller, and Elizabeth Peabody. For a while Ripley helped Margaret Fuller edit a quarterly journal, *The Dial*, founded by the group in 1840. But in 1841 he gave up this editorial role to found a two-hundred-acre agricultural colony, the Brook Farm Institute of Agriculture and Education, in West Roxbury, nine miles from Boston.

Ripley was inspired by the idea of a Christian community, run on the principle of cooperation rather than competition. In the Constitution of the Brook Farm Association, its founding members declared that they were uniting in a voluntary association "to establish the external relations of life on a basis of wisdom and purity" and "to apply the principles of justice and love to our social organization." Their feelings about business were clear. They wanted "to substitute a system of brotherly cooperation for one of selfish competition" and "to diminish the desire of excessive accumulation by making the acquisition of individual property subservient to upright and disinterested uses."

On April 1, 1841, the great experiment began. Its first members included Ripley himself; his wife, Sophia; his sister; and eight or ten others. Brook Farm was the expression of a gentle radicalism. Though competition was abolished, private property was not. "We take human nature as it is—as God made it," one of the early Brook Farmers declared. ". . . The desire, the personal desire to acquire property is a fundamental trait of character more or less strong in every individual. If society cannot be adjusted to that trait, it will fail." Not wishing to fail, Ripley organized a cooperative community that retained private ownership.

Each member of the farm worked for sixty hours a week from May through October, and for forty-eight hours a week from November through April. A balance of labor and leisure was the goal. No one escaped some drudgery. Even Nathaniel Hawthorne played "chambermaid to a group of cows," as he reported later, and "milked the transcendental heifer."

Ripley's energy impressed everyone, and his versatility was an inspiration. "He was up before dawn," Van Wyck Brooks wrote in *The Flow-ering of New England*, "dressed in his blue tunic and cowhide boots, milking, cleaning the stalls, blacking the shoes of some member who was going to town, carting off the vegetables to market, directing the field opera-tions, writing diplomatic letters, giving a Sunday lecture on Kant or Spinoza, or, on a winter evening, gathering the members about him in the snow, while he discoursed on the constellations."

In its first year Brook Farm attracted over four thousand visitors, in-cluding such eminent figures as Emerson, Thoreau, Margaret Fuller, Horace Greeley, and Henry James, Sr. Though the experiment fasci-nated them, the best-known transcendentalists remained uncommitted. "I do not wish to remove from my present prison to a prison a little larger," Emerson wrote in his journal after a conversation with Ripley. "I wish to break all prisons." Thoreau was more vehement: "I'd rather keep bachelor's hall in hell," he wrote, "than go to heaven if that place is heaven." (As Emerson observed later, Thoreau was "in his own person a practical answer, almost a refutation, to the theories of the socialists.")

The doubts of outsiders intensified when, in 1844, Ripley began to plan a reorganization of Brook Farm along lines recommended by French socialist Charles Fourier. Fourier wanted to organize society as a series of cooperative agricultural communities called phalanxes. Each phalanx would consist of two thousand persons and occupy six thousand acres of land. The individual was subordinated to the group. Thus, as V. F. Calverton has commented, after its reorganization as a phalanx Brook Farm "was no longer the individualist co-operative venture of Ripley, but the non-individualist co-operative venture of Fourier. . . . Individ-ual initiative and independence were largely blotted out. . . . Instead of everyone making a place for himself, everyone had a place made for him."

Ripley seems to have persuaded himself that a stronger central au-thority would help Brook Farm to solve the financial problems that had troubled it almost from the start. He was influenced by a columnist for Horace Greeley's *New York Tribune*, Albert Brisbane, who was Fourier's most ardent and effective American disciple. He was also influenced by Greeley himself. "Your scheme has elements of Fourierism in it, but undeveloped," Greeley told him. "Now that many are taking it up in-eptly, why don't you turn your Farm into a phalanx and show them a real one?"

Ripley's transcendentalist friends were skeptical. Margaret Fuller commented, "The community begins to seem a mechanical attempt to reform society, instead of a poetic attempt to regenerate it." Emerson had expressed his misgivings about Fourierism in an article published in *The Dial* in July 1842: "Our feeling was, that Fourier had skipped no fact but one, namely, life. He treats man as a plastic thing, something that may be put up or down, ripened or retarded, moulded, polished, made into solid, or fluid, or gas, at the will of the leader; . . . but skips the faculty of life, which spawns and scorns systems and system-makers, which eludes all conditions, which makes or supplants a thousand phalanxes and New-Harmonies with each pulsation."

In 1845, Brook Farm borrowed heavily to finance the construction of a major new building, the phalanstery, which was intended to house most of the members and to serve as a center of activity. Then, on March 3, 1846, the nearly completed phalanstery burned to the ground. The colony never recovered. A few dozen members lingered until August 1847, when the association officially dissolved.

Even before then, George and Sophia Ripley had moved to New York, where George edited the Fourierist journal the *Harbinger* until it failed early in 1849. Later that year, George succeeded Margaret Fuller as the book reviewer on Horace Greeley's *Tribune*, a position he held until his death in 1880. It took him ten years to pay off the debts associated with Brook Farm, but he paid them at last, and he retained his taste for difficult projects. With his former pupil at Brook Farm, Charles A. Dana, he edited the first encyclopedia produced in the United States, the *New American Encyclopaedia*, published in sixteen volumes between 1858 and 1863.

American history offers no more vivid example of a particular kind of utopian impulse—the urge to substitute a system of cooperation for one of competition—than Brook Farm. Years later, in *The Blithedale Romance*, trying to explain the failure of the community, Hawthorne pointed to the tension between the individual and the group: "It was a society such as has seldom met together; nor, perhaps, could it reasonably be expected to hold together long. Persons of marked individuality—crooked sticks, as some of us might be called—are not exactly the easiest to bind up into a fagot."

A second problem was an unworldly attitude toward work. "I believe in the divinity of labor," George Ripley declared, but drudgery remained drudgery. The great danger, Hawthorne wrote, was not that the dreamers would fail to become "practical agriculturalists," but that "we should probably cease to be anything else. While our enterprise lay all in theory, we had pleased ourselves with delectable visions of the spiritualization of labor. It was to be our form of prayer and ceremonial of worship. . . . But the clods of earth . . . were never etherealized into thought. Our thoughts, on the contrary, were fast becoming cloddish."

Hawthorne himself lasted only a few months at Brook Farm, but those months were enough for him to learn one lesson that still seems important. On May 4, 1841, after a day spreading manure, he wrote to his fiancée, Sophia Peabody, in a tone of cautious affirmation: "There is nothing so unseemly and disagreeable in this sort of toil as thou wouldst think. It defiles the hands, indeed, but not the soul." Within a month, however, his mood had changed: "That abominable goldmine!" (He is speaking of the manure.) "Thank God, we anticipate getting rid of its treasures, in the course of two or three days! Of all hateful places, that is the worst; . . . It is my opinion, dearest, that a man's soul may be buried and perish under a dung-heap or in a furrow of the field, just as well as under a pile of money."

Not to perish under a pile of money or a pile of dung—that seems a modest hope, but to Americans in search of a middle way, the failure to satisfy that hope is what matters most about Brook Farm.

Herman Melville

In 1853, six years after Brook Farm shut its doors, one year after Hawthorne published *The Blithedale Romance*, and one year before Thoreau published *Walden*, a friend of Hawthorne, best known as the author of novels about sea voyages, published in *Putnam's Monthly Magazine* an extraordinary story about business. In "Bartleby, the Scrivener: A Story of Wall Street," Herman Melville took his readers on a journey to a world as exotic as the South Sea islands he had celebrated in *Typee* and *Omoo*—the world of a law firm in lower Manhattan.

In the twentieth century, literary critics and scholars have tended to emphasize meanings that lie below the surface in "Bartleby," but they have missed the surface itself. In their eagerness to explore the depths, they have missed the point that "Bartleby" is a story about business. Indeed, it is probably the subtlest and most suggestive story about business that any American has ever written. Among the dissenting voices of this period, none is more memorable than the voice of Melville's forlorn protagonist.

On the "superficial" level that most critics ignore—which is to say, on the level that immediately engages the reader—the subject of "Bartleby" is employee relations, specifically the relationship between a baffled manager and a staggeringly uncooperative subordinate. The story is narrated by Bartleby's employer. This gentleman introduces himself as "one of those unambitious lawyers who never address a jury, or in any way draw down public applause; but, in the cool tranquillity of a snug retreat, do a snug business among rich men's bonds, and mortgages, and title-deeds"—in short, a man who has based his life upon "a profound conviction that the easiest way of life is the best."

"All who know me," the attorney boasts, "consider me an eminently *safe* man. The late John Jacob Astor, a personage little given to poetic enthusiasm, had no hesitation in pronouncing my first grand point to be prudence; my next, method. I do not speak it in vanity, but simply record the fact, that I was not unemployed in my profession by the late John Jacob Astor; a name which, I admit, I love to repeat; for it hath a rounded and orbicular sound to it, and rings like unto bullion."

The attorney manages a staff of three in an office "not . . . very arduous, but very pleasantly remunerative." His troubles begin when business takes so sharp a turn for the better that he finds it necessary to enlarge his staff.

Enter Bartleby—"a motionless young man . . . pallidly neat, pitiably respectable, incurably forlorn"—exactly the job applicant who will command the interest of a manager whose deepest motive, no matter what he might claim, is to find a candidate who will not make trouble.

Bartleby begins as an exemplary employee. "As if long famishing for something to copy, he seemed to gorge himself on my documents." What more could any manager want, especially when the new employee combines such splendid productivity with a character "so singularly sedate"?

A manager may expect the rebellion of a disgruntled, immature, or hotheaded employee, but few managers ever anticipate the rebellion of a reliable employee. In Bartleby's case, the rebellion comes without warning, and it announces itself "in a singularly mild, firm voice . . . [without] the least uneasiness, anger, impatience, or impertinence." There is no provocation. On a day like any other, the attorney gives an order like any other order and receives in return the astounding reply, "I would prefer not to."

Unlike a modern executive, the boss in "Bartleby" cannot consult a guide that promises to tell "How to Handle the Problem Employee." He must rely on his own instincts and experience, but nothing in his experience has prepared him for a gentle rebel. "I was turned into a pillar of salt," he confesses, "standing at the head of my seated column of clerks."

Even in circumstances that he regards as "unprecedented and violently unreasonable," the attorney does not rush to judgment. The "wonderful mildness" of Bartleby, the utter absence of anything that resembles insolence or hostility, causes his employer to tolerate behavior that he would not accept from a subordinate who displayed the least hint of animosity.

Any manager who has wavered over the fate of a marginal employee will sympathize with Melville's narrator as he flounders in an agony of indecision and rationalization. Irritation at the challenge to his authority is softened by pity and an appreciation of Bartleby's value to the business: "Poor fellow! thought I, he means no mischief; . . . He is useful to me. I can get along with him."

But the list of tasks that Bartleby prefers not to undertake grows steadily longer, and the manager finds himself scheming to provoke the outright defiance that would justify outright dismissal. A trivial order is given, Bartleby prefers not to comply, and his employer imagines that the moment of truth has arrived:

"You *will* not."

"I *prefer* not."

Passive resistance has never been more perfect. Bartleby never refuses, but he prefers not to proofread his copy, prefers not to run errands, prefers not to say anything that might clarify or justify his rebellion. Asked to be "a little reasonable," he answers honestly that "at present I would prefer not to be a little reasonable." At last he announces that he prefers to do no more copying—prefers to do no work at all.

The bafflement of the manager in this encounter is the bafflement of a business mind brought into contact with a mind that declines to attend to business. But it is more. It is the bafflement of a good man—a reasonable, civilized, and charitable man—brought into contact with a spirit of suicidal negation. The comedy moves inexorably to a tragic conclusion.

In the end, reasoning that "since he will not quit me, I must quit him," the attorney moves his office to another location. Evicted by the new landlord, Bartleby "persists in haunting the building generally," until at last he is imprisoned as a vagrant. In jail, predictably, he prefers not to eat, although the attorney bribes a jailer to bring him food. As others might succumb to age or disease, Bartleby succumbs to his preferences.

Bartleby's rebellion is absolute. It begins as a rebellion against business and business values, but it goes much farther. The revolt against petty office responsibilities turns into a revolt against life itself. The refusal to attend to business charms almost everyone who reads the story, but Melville forces his readers to face the horror beneath the charm: The refusal to attend to business is a refusal to live.

Bartleby is a pure type—the perfect expression of what the twentieth century has come to call "a negative attitude." No guidance or counseling could save him; no modern principles of enlightened personnel management could change his fate. In the end, his employer can only say with a sigh, "Ah, Bartleby! Ah, humanity." Melville seems to sigh with him.

An examination of other sources shows that financial worries were a major cause of anguish and frustration to Melville in this period. "Dollars damn me," he complained in a letter to Hawthorne in 1851, as he struggled to complete *Moby Dick*. His early novels had sold well, but he feared that posterity would remember him only as a "man who lived among the cannibals." What he felt "most moved to write," he realized with increasing bitterness, was "banned" because it would not sell. "Yet, altogether, write the *other* way I cannot. So the product is a final hash, and all my books are botches."

The anger here contrasts strikingly with the good humor about money that permeates the early pages of *Moby Dick*. Long before Ahab limps onto the scene, Melville introduces a business perspective through his narrator, an ordinary sailor named Ishmael, who amiably acknowledges the role of monetary factors in his life: Whenever he is depressed, Ishmael tells us, he goes to sea, but "I do not mean to have it inferred that I ever go to sea as a passenger. For to go as a passenger you must needs have a purse, and a purse is but a rag unless you have something in it." No, Ishmael explains, he always goes to sea as a sailor, "because they make a point of paying me for my trouble, whereas they never pay passengers a single penny that I ever heard of."

The distinction between the sailor who is paid and the passenger who pays inspires Melville to indulge in a bit of genial philosophizing. "The act of paying," Ishmael declares, "is perhaps the most uncomfortable infliction that the two orchard thieves entailed upon us. But *being paid*, —what will compare with it? The urbane activity with which a man receives money is really marvelous, considering that we so earnestly believe money to be the root of all earthly ills. . . . Ah! how cheerfully we consign ourselves to perdition!"

An attitude of amused tolerance toward business still seems to prevail when Ishmael is interviewed by Bildad and Peleg, the owners of the whaling ship *Pequod*. The Quaker Bildad, Melville explains, had "come to the sage and sensible conclusion that a man's religion is one thing, and this practical world quite another. This world pays dividends." The tone is not cheerful, however, when, one quarter of the way through the novel, speaking to the reader in his own voice rather than Ishmael's, Melville considers the task that remains: "Oh, Time, Strength, Cash, and Patience!" he pleads. A few pages earlier, when Ahab ponders what he must do to keep his crew motivated, the word "cash" becomes a threat and an obsession: "I will not strip these men, thought Ahab, of all hopes of cash—aye, cash, they may scorn cash now; but let some months go by, and no perspective promise of it to them, and then this same quiescent cash all at once mutinying in them, this same cash would soon cashier Ahab."

It is necessary, of course, to distinguish Melville's attitudes toward money from the attitudes of the characters he invents. But there is little doubt that the business aspects of writing—the pressure to convert words into cash—were increasingly oppressive to him. After *Moby Dick*, which received mixed reviews, Melville presented the public with a novel, *Pierre*, about an author who decides to abandon the kind of fiction that has made him popular and to write instead a novel that will satisfy his own sense of truth. Unable to publish this naysaying book or to extricate himself from impossible romantic entanglements, Melville's hero suffers immensely and finally commits suicide in prison.

Pierre led reviewers to question its creator's sanity. At the age of thirty-three, Melville had written six novels in seven years—a tremendous effort. With this effort, he had exhausted the patience of his public and his publisher, made a wreck of his career, and brought his family to the brink of bankruptcy. His health showed signs of breaking down.

In the spring of 1853, Melville's publisher, Harper & Brothers, gave up on him, rejecting his new manuscript. At about the same time, a fire at Harper's destroyed the plates of Melville's previous novels. At this point, in desperate need of cash, Melville began to write stories for magazines. Over the next three years he wrote fifteen short magazine pieces and one potboiler, *Israel Potter*, in which, as we have seen, he tossed off as shrewd a portrait of Benjamin Franklin as our literature offers. When, in one of the first stories written in this period, Bartleby says that he would prefer not to do the copying that his employer requires, it is impossible not to hear Melville saying, in answer to the urgings of his family, his friends, and his publisher, that, damn it, he would prefer not to copy his early successes—which is to say, that he would prefer not to write as his friends pleased, as his family pleased, as his publisher pleased, as, indeed, anyone but he himself pleased, no matter how his work sold.

In this spirit, Melville produced, in 1857, a comedy so bleak and unsettling that it seems safe to say that it will never find a large audience. Like "Bartleby," *The Confidence-Man* exists on many levels. Also like "Bartleby," it is, from one perspective, a book about business—to be specific, a book about sales and salesmanship.

The Confidence-Man takes us on a voyage down the Mississippi on the steamboat *Fidele* (from the Latin *fides*, meaning "faith," as the word "confidence" means "with faith"). The action takes place on April 1—April Fool's Day—and every encounter in the novel is an encounter of a confidence man and a potential dupe, or an encounter of two confidence men.

Every interaction in *The Confidence-Man*, every human relationship, involves an attempted sale. Everyone on the *Fidele* is a fool or a fraud, a sucker or a salesman, a wolf, a sheep, or a wolf in sheep's clothing. The first chapter introduces a mysterious stranger who wears a hat with "a long fleecy nap" and who has a "lamb-like figure." In a later chapter, one character complains, quite justifiably, that it is hard to have confidence with "everybody fleecing me." On Melville's Mississippi—that is, at the symbolic center of midcentury America—everyone is trying to fleece someone else, or trying to avoid getting fleeced.

The "lamb-like figure" in the first chapter is a deaf-mute who holds high on a slate a series of messages: "Charity thinketh no evil," "Charity suffereth long, and is kind," "Charity endureth all things," "Charity believeth all things," and, finally, "Charity never faileth." In a society that considers itself Christian, these messages provoke "stares and jeers," not to mention a suspicion of "lunacy." No such suspicion attaches to the actions of the ship's barber, who opens his shop "with business-like dispatch" and immediately hangs over his door a sign that reads, "No Trust"—an inscription that, Melville notes, "did not, as it seemed, provoke any corresponding derision or surprise, much less indignation; and still less, to all appearances, did it gain for the inscriber the repute of being a simpleton."

Is the "lamb-like figure" with his message of charity a disciple of Christ, or Christ Himself, or is he the "mysterious impostor, supposed to have recently arrived from the East," for whom a reward is offered on a placard posted outside the captain's office? Is he as innocent as he seems, or is the innocence feigned—is it a *seeming* innocence? Melville never says. But in the chapters that follow, he introduces a series of confidence men— or, perhaps, a single confidence man in a series of disguises—who test the charity of the passengers on the good ship *Fidele*.

Every test of charity is also a test of faith. In a typical scene, a stranger who purports to be "traveling agent of the Widow and Orphan Asylum, recently founded among the Seminoles," approaches a woman who has been reading a gilt testament:

> "Madam, pardon my freedom, but . . . May I ask, are you a sister of the Church?"
>
> "Why—really—you—"
>
> ". . . It may be wrong . . . but I cannot force myself to be easy with the people of the world. I prefer the company, however silent, of a brother or sister in good standing. By the way, madam, may I ask if you have confidence?"
>
> "Really, sir—why sir—really—I—"
>
> "Could you put confidence in *me* for instance?"
>
> "Really, sir—as much—I mean, as one may wisely put in a— a—stranger, an entire stranger . . ."
>
> "No one can befriend me, who has not confidence."
>
> "But I—I have—at least to that degree—I mean that . . . Believe me, I—yes, yes—I may say—that—that—"
>
> "That you have confidence? Prove it. Let me have twenty dollars."
>
> "Twenty dollars!"
>
> "There, I told you, madam, you had no confidence."

Despite this start, a sale is made at last—that is, a gift is given. In this case, the salesman works in what he calls "the charity business." The distrust that the charity agent must overcome is matched, in later chapters, by the distrust that a herb doctor must overcome to sell his "Omni-Balsamic Reinvigorator" and his "Samaritan Pain Dissuader." In every sale, Melville shows, the salesman must sell confidence itself. As one of the novel's many smooth talkers observes, "Confidence is the indispensable basis of all sorts of business transactions. Without it, commerce between man and man, as between country and country, would, like a watch, run down and stop." This truth holds whether the product to be sold is a stock or a bond, a patent medicine, a piece of land, a philosophy, a philanthropy, a political party, or a religion.

If trust leads to being duped, where does distrust lead? In the final chapter of the novel, Melville suggests a bleak answer. Encountering a skeptical old man, the confidence man sells him, in quick succession, a lock for his door, a money belt, a counterfeit detector, and a life preserver (actually, a "brown stool with a curved tin compartment underneath"—i.e., a toilet). As the evening darkens, the old man stands with "money-belt in hand, and life-preserver under arm"—an image that captures perfectly the paradox that Melville has been exploring: "See how distrust has duped you."

In the end, Melville has no trust in distrust, no faith in faithlessness, no confidence in suspicion. On the ship *Fidele* he finds "a piebald parliament . . . of all kinds of that multiform pilgrim species, man"—"men of business and men of pleasure; parlor men and backwoodsmen; farm-hunters and fame-hunters; heiress-hunters, gold-hunters, buffalo-hunters, bee-hunters, happiness-hunters, truth-hunters, and still keener hunters after all these hunters." From all of this buying and selling, all of this business, Melville stands apart. Though the Mississippi itself pours along "in one cosmopolitan and confident tide," Melville ruefully dissents. He cannot say yes.

CHAPTER 6

John D. Rockefeller: "Bound to Be Rich!"

"Go Steady"

When the boys played ball, legend says, John D. Rockefeller kept score. One of the most striking anecdotes about him concerns his precision as a scorekeeper. In his reminiscences, publisher Frank Nelson Doubleday describes how, early in 1908, after much scheming on his part, "the great oil king took notice of the insignificant publisher and invited me to play golf with him." Rockefeller's golf, Doubleday recalls, "was the exact reverse of Mr. Carnegie's golf. Carnegie could not stand being beaten and would take the utmost liberties with the score. Rockefeller was strictness itself in counting every stroke. I remember that one tee at Augusta faced a little swamp. If Rockefeller had the misfortune to drive into this morass, he would stop and put on a pair of rubbers, go into the mud, and hammer at his ball, accounting for every stroke. . . . Considering everything, he played a remarkable game, and always in strict conformity to the rules."

"Rockefeller in his soul was a bookkeeper," an early biographer remarked. From early boyhood, the future tycoon kept track of receipts and expenditures, to the penny, in a little book that still survives—the famous Ledger A. He began his business career as an accounting clerk. Hope never skewed his calculations. "Look ahead," he advises ambitious youths in the autobiography that grew out of his meetings with Double-day. ". . . Be sure that you are not deceiving yourself at any time about actual conditions." When a business begins to fail, he notes, most people are afraid "to study the books and face the truth." The executives at Standard Oil never made this mistake: "We knew how much we made and where we gained or lost. At least, we tried not to deceive ourselves." In business and in golf, Rockefeller never counted incorrectly. He always knew the score.

John Davison Rockefeller was born on July 8, 1839, the second of six children and the eldest son, on a farm in Tioga County in western New York State. His mother was of Scottish stock—a pious, strict, strong woman. One of her favorite maxims, "Willful waste makes woeful want," made a special impression on John, whose character resembled hers much more than it resembled his father's. William Avery Rockefeller was a big, cheerful man who traveled much of the time, often to camp meetings, where he sold patent medicines and advertised himself as "Dr. William A. Rockefeller, the Celebrated Cancer Specialist." He did not spoil his sons. "I trade with the boys," he bragged to a neighbor, "and skin 'em and . . . beat 'em every time I can. I want to make 'em sharp."

After moving his family to Cleveland in 1853, "Doc" Rockefeller disappeared for longer and longer periods. Years later, his son's renown stimulated curiosity about him. In 1908, one of Joseph Pulitzer's men reported that the father of the richest man in the world had died in 1906 at the age of ninety-six, that he had spent the last forty years of his life living in South Dakota under an assumed name in a bigamous marriage with a women twenty years his junior, and that he was buried in an unmarked grave in Freeport, Illinois. No one knows for sure.

After graduating from Cleveland's Central High School in 1855, young John spent three months in a commercial college in Cleveland that taught him the rudiments of bookkeeping. On September 26, 1855, he began his first job—as a clerk at $3.50 a week in a firm of commission merchants named Hewitt & Tuttle. The job offered an old-fashioned business apprenticeship. His duties, Rockefeller declares in his autobiography, "were vastly more interesting than those of an officeboy in a large house today." The young man who had kept his own ledger for years was paid, now, to keep a ledger for his firm: "I thoroughly enjoyed the work. . . .

I had trained myself to the point of view . . . that my check on a bill was the executive act which released my employer's money from the till and was attended with more responsibility than the spending of my own funds."

In 1859, at the age of twenty, with $1,000 he had saved himself and $1,000 borrowed from his father, Rockefeller joined an Englishman, Maurice B. Clark, in establishing the firm of Clark & Rockefeller. It was a great moment in Rockefeller's life: "Mentally I swelled with pride—a partner in a firm with $4,000 in capital!" The firm dealt in grain, hay, meats, and other goods, and it prospered from the start, making a profit of $4,400 on sales of $450,000 in its first year, $17,000 in its second, and much more in the years that followed, as the Civil War brought a surge in demand.

Rockefeller did not fight. "I wanted to go in the army and do my part," he said years later. "But it was simply out of the question. There was no one to take my place. We were in a new business, and if I had not stayed it must have stopped—and with so many dependent on it." The argument might have been more persuasive if it had come from a married man.

Success brought a new kind of anxiety. In his twenties, Rockefeller did not know that he was going to be the richest man in the world, any more than Shakespeare knew he was going to be the best poet. So Rockefeller worried. "I seldom put my head upon the pillow at night without speaking a few words to myself in this wise: 'Now a little success, soon you will fall down, soon you will be overthrown. Because you have got a start, you think you are quite a merchant; look out, or you will lose your head—go steady.' "

A religious bent that testified to the influence of his mother showed itself early in Rockefeller's life. In 1854 he joined the Erie Street Baptist Church in Cleveland, and at eighteen he was elected one of its five trustees. He contributed to charity about 10 percent of his early earnings. In his autobiography, no passage has more feeling than his description of his role in raising $2,000 to pay off the mortgage on the church building.

In 1864 Rockefeller married Laura Celestia Spelman, the daughter of a Cleveland businessman. From Ledger B we know that the wedding ring cost $15.75. One of the bride's first pleasures was to attend a Bible class taught by her husband at the Erie Street Baptist Church. There would be five children: Bessie (1866–1906); Alice (1869–70); Alta (1871–1962); Edith (1872–1932); and John, Jr. (1874–1960).

"When it's raining porridge," Rockefeller's sister Lucy once said, "you'll find John's dish right side up." Now he became aware that it was raining porridge in Pennsylvania. In 1859, in Titusville, a former railway conductor named Edwin L. Drake had become the first person to drill successfully for oil. Soon a thousand gallons a day poured from Drake's well. A rush to the oil regions of western Pennsylvania followed. By the end of 1860, thanks to the spread of the drilling techniques that Drake developed but failed to patent, approximately two thousand wells and borings had been dug in Pennsylvania. A new era had begun. Annual production of crude oil rose from two thousand barrels in 1859 to 4.8 million barrels in 1869.

In 1863, Rockefeller invested $4,000 to join Maurice Clark and a friend of Clark's named Samuel Andrews in a partnership "organized . . . to refine and deal in oil." By 1865, Andrews, Clark & Company operated the largest refinery in Cleveland. But a disagreement arose among the partners; Clark did not want to expand as aggressively as Rockefeller and Andrews did. At an auction on February 2, 1865, Rockefeller, representing himself and Andrews, bid for the business against Clark. When the bidding reached $70,000, Rockefeller "almost feared for my ability to buy the business and have the money to pay for it." But he overcame his fear, and at $72,500, Clark gave up. "It was the day that determined my career," Rockefeller said later.

The new firm, Rockefeller and Andrews, grew rapidly between 1865 and 1869. Andrews, a self-taught chemist, handled the technical side of the business. Rockefeller's brother William was sent to New York to handle the export trade. Henry M. Flagler, whose "vim and push" had impressed Rockefeller in his days as a commission merchant, was brought into the firm as a partner. With Flagler came Steven V. Harkness, an uncle of Flagler's wife. Harkness, who had made a fortune in the whiskey business, did not play an active role in management, but Flagler handled many difficult negotiations and drew up most of the firm's contracts. He and Rockefeller lived a few blocks from each other on Euclid Avenue in Cleveland, walked to work together, had desks in the same office, and soon became good friends. "It was a friendship," Rockefeller wrote in his autobiography, "founded on business, which Mr. Flagler used to say was a good deal better than a business founded on friendship, and my experience leads me to agree with him."

By 1869, only ten years after the discovery of oil in Pennsylvania, Rockefeller and his partners had established in Cleveland the largest oil refining complex in the world. Gross receipts for the year ending September 30, 1869 were $2,433,689—an amount approximately equal to the combined receipts of the next three largest refineries in Cleveland. Though Rockefeller was only thirty, his oil works produced one tenth of the nation's output of refined petroleum. At about this time, one biographer reports, a bystander was astonished to see the sober young Sunday school teacher, thinking himself alone in his office, jump into the air and exclaim, "I'm bound to be rich! Bound to be rich! *Bound to be rich!*"

"The Difficult Art of Getting"

On January 10, 1870, the various Rockefeller partnerships were consolidated as the Standard Oil Company of Ohio, with capitalization of $1 million. Ten thousand shares valued at $100 each were issued. Rockefeller, the president, received 2,667; Steven V. Harkeness received 1,334; Flagler, Andrews, and William Rockefeller each received 1,333; and the Flagler-Andrews-Rockefeller partnership received 1,000.

Years later, in the third chapter of the autobiography that Frank Doubleday ghostwrote for him, Rockefeller discussed his business career under the title "The Difficult Art of Getting." What he never quite managed to say, or perhaps even to see, was that the difficulties he experienced paled next to the difficulties he posed for his competitors.

The size of Standard Oil gave it a terrific advantage. In the first place, size made possible a vertical integration of the business. To reduce costs, the firm eliminated the middleman wherever possible. It bought tracts of timber and built its own barrels, produced itself the sulfuric acid that was needed for refining, built its own wharfs and warehouses, obtained its own fleet of tankers. Rockefeller's aversion to waste—"Willful waste makes woeful want"—also led to success in the manufacture and marketing of by-products, from paraffin to machine lubricants. Most important, economies of scale sharply reduced the cost of producing kerosene itself. Unit costs dropped from six cents a gallon at a refinery with daily throughput of five hundred barrels to three cents a gallon at a refinery with daily throughput of fifteen hundred barrels. Thus Standard Oil was not merely the largest producer in the industry; it also was the low-cost producer.

Another advantage of size was that it gave Standard Oil tremendous leverage with the railroads that shipped oil to the eastern markets. The railroads needed a high volume of freight to recover their high fixed costs. In return for guaranteed shipments, many shippers received rebates—

discounts from the published rates. Since Standard produced more than any other firm, it could make the best deal with the railroads.

Rebates were a major weapon in Standard's arsenal when, in the early 1870s, it went to war against its competitors in Cleveland. Sometime in 1870, Flagler told the Lake Shore Railroad (a subsidiary of Vanderbilt's New York Central) that Standard would guarantee to ship sixty carloads of oil a day if the Lake Shore would give the company a rate of $1.30 a barrel from Cleveland to New York, compared to the published rate of $2.00 a barrel. The Lake Shore accepted. When other refiners protested, the Lake Shore replied that the same arrangement "was open to any and all parties who would secure or guarantee the like amount of traffic." Of course, no other producer could make such a guarantee.

At this point Rockefeller and his colleagues began to buy out other refiners in Cleveland. Standard's deal with the Lake Shore may have been one reason that, as Rockefeller recalled later, "most of the refiners were very desirous to get out of the business." To Rockefeller, the facts were clear: "You can never make money in my judgment," he told one competitor. "If you refuse to sell, it will end in your being crushed." By 1872 Standard controlled one quarter of the nation's total oil refining capacity.

The conquest of Cleveland was followed by the creation of a national monopoly. As he had done in Cleveland, Rockefeller used rebates as a major weapon. Early in 1875, the three railroad trunk lines that carried oil to the eastern ports agreed to give Standard and its allies a special rebate of 10 percent, on top of its standard rebate, in return for help in assuring an even flow of oil shipments. At about the same time, Standard made extensive purchases of oil pipelines. It also moved to buy or lease oil terminals in New York from the New York Central and the Erie railroads, with the result that all competitors who shipped through New York on the great northern trunk lines were compelled to use facilities owned by Standard Oil.

Thus armed, Standard sought to obtain control of its major competitors outside Cleveland. In October 1874 the largest refining companies in Philadelphia, Pittsburgh, and New York entered the Standard alliance. Other companies followed. All of this was done secretly. Each firm continued to operate under its own name; each was instructed to buy other refiners when possible. By the end of 1878 the Standard alliance controlled over 90 percent of the oil refining industry in the United States. John D. Rockefeller was thirty-nine years old.

The expansion of Standard Oil raised a thorny legal problem. Standard was incorporated in Ohio, but it had no legal right to own property in other states. In 1881 one of Rockefeller's lieutenants, Samuel Dodd, proposed a solution. The Standard Oil Trust Agreement, enacted on January 2, 1882, established a board of nine trustees to hold the securities of the forty companies in the Standard alliance. An executive committee chaired by Rockefeller ruled the new combination.

The trust was significant in two ways. It established a strong central office to administer Standard's increasingly far-flung holdings. And, because the trustees were legally agents for stockholders and not for the corporations, the arrangement helped protect the secrecy that Rockefeller prized. As David Horowitz and Peter Collier have observed, the trust's "very complexity set up a maze of legal structures that successfully rendered its workings impervious to public investigation. . . . It was never clear who owned what or who was responsible for which actions."

Despite the cloud of uncertainty that often surrounded its actions, Standard was the object of increasingly intense criticism. A pioneering investigation was conducted in 1879 by a subcommittee of the New York State legislature chaired by Alonzo Hepburn. Two years later, in the March 1881 issue of the *Atlantic Monthly*, Henry Demarest Lloyd won wide attention with an impassioned though not always accurate attack on the company. A biting style made Lloyd a formidable adversary. "The Standard," he wrote with characteristic humor, "has done everything to the Pennsylvania legislature except refine it."

In his autobiography, Rockefeller defends Standard Oil against a number of persistent criticisms. His answers are not always persuasive, but they are often reasonable, and sometimes they are powerful. In any case, they are worth noting.

In answer to critics who charged that Standard's size alone made it dangerous, Rockefeller concedes that "the power conferred by combination may be abused," but he does not concede that the potential abuse of power outweighs the economic advantages that size makes possible. "This fact is no more of an argument against combinations," he comments, "than the fact that steam may explode is an argument against steam."

In answer to critics who were disturbed or outraged by rebates, Rockefeller asserts that Standard "received no advantages for which it did not give full compensation." It shipped in large quantities; it furnished loading and discharging facilities; it provided regular traffic; it even carried its own insurance, thus exempting the railroads from liability for fire. Rebates, Rockefeller says, were a natural outcome of free competition.

Rockefeller does not answer the charge that Standard benefited not merely from rebates but also from a related device called the "draw-back"—a payment by the railroads to Standard Oil of a percentage of the shipping charges paid by non-Standard refiners. His answer, one imagines, would have been what it was in the case of rebates: Standard "made the best bargains possible. . . . Other companies sought to do the same. . . . All this was following in the natural laws of trade." (The Interstate Commerce Act of 1887, it should be noted, made both rebates and drawbacks illegal.)

Another charge that Rockefeller does not bother to answer is that Standard routinely bribed the employees of competitors. An independent refiner named John Teagle told a congressional committee that he had learned that Standard paid his bookkeeper to provide it with a daily report—what was produced, costs and revenues, where shipments were sent. This, too, perhaps, merely followed "the natural laws of trade."

To the accusation that Standard Oil forced competitors to sell out at prices it dictated, Rockefeller makes a forceful response. He answers in detail the charge that, in one celebrated case, he "personally robbed a defenseless widow of an extremely valuable property, paying her only a mere fraction of its worth." His answer is persuasive, but vindication in a single case will not satisfy anyone who knows that dozens of other cases remain unmentioned. Though its critics may have exaggerated, it would be difficult to argue that Standard Oil did nothing to deserve its reputation of ruthlessness. The *New York World* put matters in perspective when it parodied Rockefeller's public statements with a mock definition of a trust: "A philanthropic institution created by the benevolent absorption of competitors to save them from ruin, combined with the humane conservation and ingenious utilization of natural resources for the benefit of the people."

The conquest of Cleveland and the creation of a national monopoly were followed, in the 1880s, by aggressive international expansion. Nearly all the American oil exports to Asia, Africa, and South America in this period were exports of Standard Oil. When World War I arrived, Standard held more than 75 percent of the European oil market.

Also in the 1880s, Standard moved into crude oil production for the first time. Giant new oil fields in northern Ohio and Indiana—the Lima fields—were discovered in 1886, and by 1888 Ohio and Indiana produced 35 percent of all crude oil in the United States. With output declining in Pennsylvania, Standard made a major investment in the Lima fields. By 1892 it was producing 25 percent of the nation's crude oil. Standard Oil of Indiana became a major subsidiary.

Meanwhile, the Standard Trust faced new legal challenges. On March 2, 1892, the Ohio Supreme Court ruled that Standard of Ohio had violated its charter by doing business outside the state. The trustees responded by "dissolving" the Standard Trust, but this was a change in form, not in substance. In June 1899, under a law that had not existed when the original trust was established, Standard Oil of New Jersey was incorporated as a holding company for the various Standard subsidiaries. This holding company, in turn, was ruled illegal by the U.S. Supreme Court in a decision handed down on May 15, 1911. In response to that decision, the combination was divided into thirty-eight companies, with no common officers or directors.

By that time, it seems, Rockefeller did not care much. Though he retained the title of president, he had not played an active role in the management of the company since 1897. His fortune at that point was about $200 million. But something extraordinary was about to happen. At roughly the same time that Edison's electric light reduced the demand for kerosene as an illuminant, Henry Ford started to manufacture automobiles. And Standard Oil made the fuel that fired the internal-combustion engine.

"The Difficult Art of Giving"

In his autobiography and in his life, Rockefeller's interest in "The Difficult Art of Getting" was balanced by an interest in philanthropy—"The Difficult Art of Giving." What made for difficulty was the number of requests that poured in as Rockefeller's fortune increased. Rockefeller was willing to give, but he could not bear to give blindly. The discomfort he experienced in this situation comes through clearly in his reminiscences. "About the year 1890," he writes, "I was still following the haphazard fashion of giving here and there as appeals presented themselves. I investigated as I could, and worked myself almost to a nervous breakdown in groping my way, without sufficient guide or chart, through this ever-widening field of philanthropic endeavour."

What he needed, he felt, was to rationalize his philanthropy—to develop an "organized plan" of giving based on well-defined "underlying principles." To help in this effort, in March 1891 he hired an energetic Baptist minister named Frederick T. Gates, then in his middle thirties. Rockefeller had met Gates a couple of years earlier, when Gates had been involved in the discussions that led to a gift of $600,000 that helped found the University of Chicago. (In all, Rockefeller gave more than $30 million to the university, much of it for endowment.)

With Gates's assistance, Rockefeller struggled to define principles that might guide his giving. The philanthropy that mattered most, he decided, was philanthropy that struck at the root of fundamental problems. "To help the sick and distressed appeals to the kindhearted always, but to help the investigator who is striving successfully to attack the causes which bring about sickness and distress does not so strongly attract the [average] giver of money. . . . The best philanthropy is constantly in search of the finalities—a search for cause, an attempt to cure evils at their source."

The principle of attempting to "cure evils at their source" gave a focus to Rockefeller's philanthropy. As a guide, it was invaluable. We need not wonder, for instance, how Rockefeller would have responded to the problem of homelessness that emerged in many American cities in the early 1980s. "It is interesting," he writes in his memoirs, "to follow the mental processes that some excellent souls go through to cloud their consciences when they consider what their duty actually is. One man says: 'I do not believe in giving money to street beggars.' I agree with him . . . but that is not a reason why one should be exempt from doing something to help the situation represented by the street beggar."

To this philosophy, Rockefeller added a belief in the "the benevolent trust"—a corporation formed "to manage the business side of benefactions." In a speech to an audience of "rich and influential people" that he quotes at the end of his memoirs, he explained why he favored this new kind of organization: "You would not place a fortune for your children in the hands of an inexperienced person, no matter how good he might be. Let us be as careful with the money we would spend for the benefit of others as if we were laying it aside for our own family's future use. Directors carry on these affairs in your behalf. Let us erect a foundation, a trust, and engage directors who will make it a life work to manage . . . this business of benevolence."

Practicing what he preached, Rockefeller founded four major philanthropic institutions: the Rockefeller Institute for Medical Research (1901); the General Education Board (1902); the Rockefeller Foundation (1913); and the Laura Spelman Rockefeller Memorial Foundation (1918), which later merged with the Rockefeller Foundation. Gates had warned, "Your fortune is rolling up, rolling up like an avalanche! You must keep up with it! You must distribute it faster than it grows. If you do not, it will crush you and your children and your children's children." Through philanthropy, Rockefeller and his family escaped this dire fate.

A typical project—now largely forgotten—was the campaign to exterminate a disabling intestinal parasite, the hookworm, that afflicted millions of people around the world. In his autobiography, Gates describes an early meeting: "The southern guests immediately recognized the mysterious 'ground itch' of their barefoot boyhood. But their amazement knew no bounds when [Dr. Charles W.] Stiles disclosed the previous life history of the cause of the ground itch, from the egg in the soil to the minute worm in the sole of the foot, and then its after history in the blood, until at last it fastened its poisoned fangs in the lining of the intestines, where, increasing in number year by year so long as the victim went barefoot, whether child or adult, it had sometimes reached the number of 5,000 in a single victim. . . . The world had recently been appalled by the destruction of life in the sinking of the *Titanic*. But at least ten *Titanic*s full of children and youth were sunk by the fatal ravages of the hookworm every year, to say nothing of the nearly complete disablement of many times the number."

With a gift of $1 million in October 1909, Rockefeller launched a campaign aimed at wiping out hookworm disease in ten years. By 1913, half a million Southerners had been treated. But the disease was not limited to the United States. The hookworm flourished in a belt that reached for thirty degrees on each side of the equator—a belt where more than a billion people resided. Under the International Health Commission, a division of the Rockefeller Foundation, a worldwide attack began in 1913. The campaign against hookworm disease, thought Charles W. Eliot, the retired president of Harvard, was "the most effective campaign against a widespread disabling disease which medical science and philanthropy ever combined to conduct."

Public health was a primary concern of the Rockefeller Foundation, founded in 1913 "to promote the well-being of mankind throughout the world." The foundation was intended to be a permanent, self-perpetuating engine of benevolence. Rockefeller's purpose, Gates wrote, was "to incorporate a fund which, passing on from generation to generation, may do for the philanthropies of each generation, so long as organized society shall exist, what he has tried personally to do in his own life for the philanthropies of his own generation."

The activities of the foundation in the year after Rockefeller's death, as summarized by his biographer Allan Nevins, show how far it ranged in the effort to carry out its mandate:

Vaccination of more than a million people in Brazil with an effective virus against yellow fever developed by the International Health Division; work to combat a severe outbreak of malaria in North Brazil; investigations of influenza, the common cold, tropical anemia, and other ailments; maintenance of a school in the Fiji Islands to train doctors for Oceania; large grants to the State Institute of Public Health in Stockholm and the Nursing School of the University of Toronto; support of psychiatrical and neurological work in London, Montreal, St. Louis, New York, Stanford, Baltimore, and other centers; the grant of $750,000 to Yale for its Institute of Human Relations; appropriations to a number of universities, from Leeds to California, for work in developing the new field of molecular biology; a grant of $1,500,000 to the University of Chicago toward an endowment fund for research in the biological sciences; a grant to the University of Illinois for studies in nutrition; battles against malaria in Cuba, Egypt, Greece, India, and other lands; support of the medical school of the American University of Beirut, of the Peiping Medical College, and of the China Medical Board, Inc.; a long list of grants to agencies trying to promote better international relations. . . ; support of mass education in China; . . . grants to the Social Science Research Council and the American Council of Learned Societies; assistance to a long series of agencies for research and training in public administration. . . ; contributions for the development of Chinese studies in various American universities; appropriations for an annual Handbook of Latin American Studies; grants for archaeological work; assistance to the Library of Congress in microfilming; promotion of the drama by assistance to the regional dramatic work at the University of North Carolina and Western Reserve University. . . ; grants to the Museum of Modern Art in forming a library of motion picture films, and to the World Wide Broadcasting Foundation in experimenting with radio programmes of educational and cultural value.

In all, starting with gifts of $2.77 in 1855, Rockefeller gave away $550 million in his lifetime. His son John, Jr., gave away $552 million, and his grandchildren, according to *Fortune* magazine, had given away $400 million as of 1986. Yet the end was not in sight. In 1987 the Rockefeller Foundation was still the seventh-largest private foundation in the United States, with assets of $1.6 billion. There is little reason to think that it will fail in its aim of supporting "the philanthropies of each generation, so long as organized society shall exist."

Having retired in 1897, Rockefeller lived on and on. Now and then the public got a glimpse of him in a photograph. The richest man in the world peered at the camera with, in Robert Heilbroner's phrase, "the incredibly shrunken face of an animate mummy." A different image is preserved in the photographs that accompanied Rockefeller's autobiography, published in 1908–1909. To see a steely gaze, take a look at Rockefeller here—at ages thirteen, eighteen, twenty-five, twenty-six, twenty-eight, and forty-five. Not once, it seems, did any photographer say "Smile."

Golf and landscape gardening were the joys of Rockefeller's old age. Perfecting the views at his estate at Pocantico Hills on the Hudson became an obsession. Railroad tracks that spoiled a scene were relocated at a cost of $700,000. Trees were transplanted by the thousand. Hills were moved. When Rockefeller died at last, in 1937, a wisecrack by George S. Kaufman seemed as good an epitaph as any. "It was an example," Kaufman said of the old man's landscape gardening, "of what God could have done if He'd only had the money." Even a Baptist with the soul of a bookkeeper might have smiled at that.

CHAPTER 7

Andrew Carnegie: "I Could Have Slain King, Duke, or Lord . . ."

"The Gospel of Wealth"

John D. Rockefeller was not the only late-nineteenth-century industrialist who developed novel ideas about philanthropy. America's great steel magnate Andrew Carnegie was another mogul whose giving was as interesting as his getting.

An entry that Carnegie made in his journal in 1868, at the age of thirty-three, shows clearly that Mammon was not a god he could worship with perfect enthusiasm:

> Thirty-three and an income of $50,000 per annum! . . . Beyond this never earn—make no effort to increase fortune, but spend the surplus each year for benevolent purposes. Cast aside business forever, except for others.
>
> Settle in Oxford and get a thorough education, making the acquaintance of literary men—this will take three years of active work—pay especial attention to speaking in public. Settle then in London and purchase a controlling interest in some newspaper or live review and give the general management of it attention, taking part in public matters, especially those connected with education and improvement of the poorer classes.

Man must have an idol—the amassing of wealth is one of the worst species of idolatry—no idol more debasing than the worship of money. Whatever I engage in I must push inordinately, therefore should I be careful to choose that life which will be the most elevating in its character. To continue much longer overwhelmed by business cares and with most of my thoughts wholly upon the way to make more money in the shortest time, must degrade me beyond hope of permanent recovery. I will resign business at thirty-five, but during the ensuing two years I wish to spend the afternoons in receiving instruction and in reading systematically.

Carnegie did not retire at thirty-five, but the ambivalence that marks this passage persisted to the end of his life. His distrust of business had deep roots. The village of Dunfermline, Scotland, where he was born in 1835, was a center of revolutionary agitation. Carnegie's father spoke regularly at Chartist rallies, and his uncle was renowned as a fiery advocate of expanded rights for the working class. "I remember as if it were yesterday," Carnegie wrote later, "being awakened during the night by a tap at the back window by men who had come to inform my parents that my uncle, Bailie Morison, had been thrown in jail because he dared to hold a meeting which had been forbidden. . . . It is not to be wondered at that, nursed amid such surroundings, I developed into a violent young Republican whose motto was 'death to privilege.' " As a child, Carnegie recalled after he had made his fortune, "I could have slain king, duke, or lord, and considered their death a service to the state."

Carnegie immigrated to the United States with his family in 1848 and settled in Allegheny, Pennsylvania, where he took a job at $1.20 a week as a "bobbin boy" in a cotton factory. Later he worked as an engine tender and as a telegraph messenger and operator. At eighteen, in 1853, he took a job with the Pennsylvania Railroad, where he remained for twelve years, rising from position to position until he became superintendent of the Pittsburgh Division.

In 1865 Carnegie resigned from the railroad to start his own firm, the Keystone Bridge Company. Then, on a trip to England in the early 1870s, Carnegie paid a visit to a British mill that used the Bessemer process for mass-producing steel. Convinced that "The day of iron has passed!" Carnegie rushed home with a new mission: He would make steel.

The day of iron had not quite passed, but it was passing. It was the age of the railroad, and for railroad tracks alone, America's steel output rose from about thirty thousand tons in 1870 to 850,000 tons in 1880 and then to nearly 1.9 million tons in 1890. In 1880, nearly half of the nation's new rails were made of iron; in 1885, almost 99 percent were made from steel. And much of that steel was made by Andrew Carnegie. In 1885 Great Britain led the world in steel production. Fourteen years later, Carnegie Steel outproduced Britain by 695,000 tons.

Andrew Carnegie emerged as one of the richest men in the world. Yet his wealth was a source of inner strain. He was the same man who, at thirty-three, had feared that a life devoted to business "must degrade me beyond hope of permanent recovery." He was the same man who had worried about worshiping false gods—"no idol more debasing than the worship of money." Now the urge to justify his position found voice in a remarkable article—an article first published under the title "Wealth" in the *North American Review* in June 1889, and frequently reprinted later under the title "The Gospel of Wealth."

In "The Gospel of Wealth," Carnegie seeks to explain how a rich man can help society and save his soul. Under the influence of British social scientist Herbert Spencer and his philosophy of social Darwinism, Carnegie begins by making the case for huge fortunes. "We must accept and welcome," he affirms, ". . . great inequality of environment, the concentration of business . . . in the hands of the few, and the law of competition." These conditions are "not only beneficial but essential for the future progress of the race." Civilization, Carnegie argues, "took its start from the day that the capable, industrious workman said to his incompetent and lazy fellow, 'If thou dost not sow, thou shalt not reap,' and thus ended primitive Communism by separating the drones from the bees." Individualism, the "law" of competition, the "law" of accumulation of wealth, the "sacredness" of property—"these are the highest results of human experience . . . the best and most valuable of all that humanity has yet accomplished."

Having concluded that "the best interests of the race" are promoted by a condition of affairs that "inevitably gives wealth to the few," Carnegie turns his attention to a vital question: "What is the proper mode of administering wealth after the laws upon which civilization is founded have thrown it into the hands of the few?"

One possibility that the rich often have favored is to leave great fortunes to their children. This choice, Carnegie says, is the worst one. If done from affection, it is "misguided affection," for "observation teaches that . . . great sums bequeathed oftener work more for the injury than for the good of the recipients." Thus, "wise men will soon conclude that, for the best interests of the members of their families and of the state, such bequests are an improper use of their means."

A second possibility is to leave wealth at death for public purposes. Here, too, Carnegie is unenthusiastic. "Men who leave vast sums in this way may fairly be thought men who would not have left it at all had they been able to take it with them." Moreover, "Knowledge of the results of legacies bequeathed is not calculated to inspire the brightest hopes of much posthumous good being accomplished. . . . In many cases the bequests are so used as to become only monuments of his folly."

The third possibility is for the rich man "to attend to the administration of wealth during his life." This, Carnegie argues, "is the end that society should always have in view, as being by far most fruitful for the people." It is "the true gospel concerning wealth."

This gospel lights the way for the tycoon burdened with superfluous riches. The first duty of the man of wealth is "to set an example of modest, unostentatious living, shunning display or extravagance," and "to provide moderately for the legitimate wants of those dependent upon him." Having fulfilled these requirements, the man of wealth will "consider all surplus revenues which come to him simply as trust funds which he is called upon to administer, and strictly bound as a matter of duty to administer in the manner which, in his judgment, is best calculated to produce the most beneficial results for the community." In this way the man of wealth becomes "the mere agent and trustee for his poorer brethren, bringing to their service his superior wisdom, experience, and ability to administer, doing for them better than they would or could do for themselves."

A happy solution! "Thus is the problem of rich and poor to be solved. The laws of accumulation will be left free; the laws of distribution free. Individualism will continue, but the millionaire will be but a trustee for the poor; entrusted for a season with the great part of the increased wealth of the community, but administering it for the community far better than it could or would have done for itself."

For the Midas who ignores his message, Carnegie has no pity. In a conclusion that was widely quoted and approved, he warned, "The man who dies leaving behind him millions of available wealth, which was his to administer during life, will pass away 'unwept, unhonored, and unsung,' no matter to what uses he leaves the dross which he cannot take with him. Of such as these the public verdict will then be: 'The man who dies thus rich dies disgraced.' "

"My Chief Happiness"

In 1901 Carnegie retired after receiving $250 million from the sale of his steel company to a group of investors (headed by J. P. Morgan) who were organizing the U.S. Steel Company. The negotiations between Carnegie and Morgan were remarkable for their simplicity. Carnegie jotted a few figures in pencil on a slip of paper, which his associate Charles Schwab took to Morgan. Morgan glanced at the figures and said, "I accept." Years later, Carnegie said to Morgan, "I made one mistake, Pierpont, when I sold out to you." What was that? the banker asked. "I should have asked you for a hundred million more than I did," Carnegie replied. "Well," Morgan said, "you would have got it if you had."

Even before his retirement, Carnegie had begun vigorously to practice what he preached in "The Gospel of Wealth." To the dismay of many clergymen, he once published his personal ranking of causes in order of philanthropic worthiness:

1. universities
2. free libraries
3. hospitals
4. parks
5. concerts and meeting halls
6. swimming baths
7. churches

A storm of protest followed. Carnegie eventually gave 7,689 organs to churches at a cost of more than $6 million, but it seems that he classified these as gifts in support of music, not religion.

Other gifts included more than $60 million to build 2,811 free public libraries around the world; $20 million to various colleges; $29 million to the Carnegie Foundation for the Advancement of Teaching; $22 million to found the Carnegie Institute of Pittsburgh; $22 million to found the Carnegie Institution of Washington; $10 million to "Hero" Funds; $10 million to the Carnegie Endowment for International Peace; $10 million to the Scottish Universities Trust; $10 million to the United Kingdom Trust; $5 million to establish a pension and benefit fund for employees of Carnegie Steel; $50,000 to prevent the sale of Lord Acton's personal library; and annuities of $10,000 a year to President William Howard

Taft and $5,000 a year to the widows of Grover Cleveland and Theodore Roosevelt.

Carnegie's largest single gift was $125 million to establish the Carnegie Corporation of New York, which became his residuary legatee. Though John D. Rockefeller had the same idea at about the same time, the Carnegie Corporation was the first modern philanthropic foundation administered by independent trustees. The object of the corporation, founded in 1911, was, in Carnegie's words, "to promote the advancement and diffusion of knowledge and understanding among the people of the United States by aiding technical schools, institutions of higher learning, libraries, scientific research, hero funds, useful publications and by such other agencies and means as shall from time to time be found appropriate therefor."

Carnegie's giving reflected not merely his interests but also the idiosyncrasies of his strong personality. Unaware that Carnegie detested football, Woodrow Wilson, then president of Princeton, proudly showed the college's playing fields to the retired steel master when he visited in 1906. At the end of the day, Carnegie told Wilson that he knew exactly what Princeton needed. "What?" asked the eager host. "A lake!" said the philanthropist. "That will take the young men's minds off football." In this way Princeton obtained a $400,000 lake 3½ miles long.

Despite his best efforts, Carnegie was still rich when he died. But he was not disgracefully rich. He had given away, in his own lifetime, approximately $350 million. In his instructions to the trustees of the Carnegie Corporation, written in the simplified spelling he advocated as a matter of principle, Carnegie wrote his own best epitaph: "Conditions on erth inevitably change; hence; no wise man will bind Trustees forever to certain paths, causes, or institutions. I disclaim any intention of doing so. . . . My chief happiness, as I write these lines, lies in the thot that, even after I pass away, the welth that came to me to administer as a sacred trust for the good of my fellow men is to continue to benefit humanity." In the case of Carnegie as in the case of Rockefeller, the art of getting and the art of giving were well balanced in the end, though not quite so balanced as to wipe out the memory of the ruthlessness that had accompanied the getting.

CHAPTER 8

J. Pierpont Morgan: "And to Think He Was Not a Rich Man!"

A Banker's Son

If you visit the Pierpont Morgan Library in New York City, you will linger in the East Room with its priceless manuscripts; you will gaze at the gorgeous rotunda; and you will remember the Medici as your eyes wander from treasure to treasure in the magnificent West Room, which served as Morgan's study. Yet, oddly, you will leave the library without once having been reminded of the extraordinary events that took place in these rooms in late October and early November 1907, as the nation's financial markets trembled on the edge of a catastrophic collapse.

The scene is vividly re-created by Frederick Lewis Allen in his fine biography *The Great Pierpont Morgan:*

> Night after night there were conferences at the Morgan Library. On Thursday evening [October 24] the presidents of the banks and of the trust companies gathered in the lofty East Room . . . while Morgan sat in the West Room at his little card table, smoking a cigar and playing solitaire. On Friday the scene was repeated. . . . The bankers would work out a scheme, and one of them would cross the marble hallway to the West

Room and tell Morgan about it, and he would listen, and say briefly, "No, that won't work," and continue with his cards. . . .

The setting was a strange one for the discussion of a currency problem. The West Room of the Morgan Library was walled with red silk damask, patterned with the arms of the Chigi family of Rome. On the walls hung splendid Florentine masterpieces of the fifteenth and sixteenth centuries. Upon the bookshelves stood a bust by Michelangelo and a rock-crystal bowl said to have been mounted for Queen Christina of Sweden. The mantelpiece and the gilded ceiling had been made for great Italian houses. Morgan sat in a red plush armchair by the fire in this great room . . . and here—while elsewhere in the Library the other financiers who had become his lieutenants in the struggle against the panic labored at the making of battle plans—he concentrated on the cards before him, slowly puffing his black cigar. . . .

A little more than five years later, charges that Morgan headed a dangerously powerful "money trust" were the subject of sensational hearings in Washington. And only a few months after that, America's mightiest banker was gone—dead in Rome at the age of almost seventy-six.

The survivors struggled to take his measure. "In my opinion," said investment banker James Seligman, "he was the greatest man this country or the world has ever known." The rector of Trinity Parish in New York City thanked God for J. P. Morgan.

Others dissented. The *New York Call*, a socialist newspaper, lashed Morgan with rhetoric it might have borrowed from editorials written after the death of Cornelius Vanderbilt or John Jacob Astor: "He was the very typification of capitalism, in all its cruel remorselessness. He never scrupled as to the methods concerned when it was a question of crushing a competitor."

Today, few people have any clear idea why Morgan provoked so intense a response, and even fewer can place him in any historical perspective. In his monumental study of the rise of modern business enterprise in the United States, *The Visible Hand*, business historian Alfred D. Chandler, Jr., makes the distinction between "family or entrepreneurial capitalism," "financial capitalism," and "managerial capitalism." In family or entrepreneurial capitalism, the firm is dominated by the family of the founder. In financial capitalism, the firm is dominated by representatives of banks and other financial institutions. In managerial capitalism, the firm is dominated by career executives. In the past century and a half, Chandler argues, managerial capitalism has replaced family or financial capitalism in nearly every important sector of the American economy. The story of American enterprise in this period is the story of

"the managerial revolution in American business"—that is, the story of
how and why "modern American capitalism became managerial capitalism."

In this perspective, John D. Rockefeller and Andrew Carnegie were
representatives of entrepreneurial capitalism. After they retired, the em-
pires they built were dominated by anonymous executives. J. P. Morgan, by contrast, was not a man who made or built or marketed anything.
He was a money lord—the symbol and supreme example of financial
capitalism in the United States. Like Carnegie and Rockefeller, Morgan
presents a grand example of a type that has not prevailed—a dinosaur.
Dinosaurs, almost everyone agrees, are more interesting than the creatures that supplanted them.

John Pierpont Morgan was born on April 17, 1837, in Hartford, Connecticut. His grandfather, Joseph Morgan, was a prominent local merchant, and his father, Junius Spencer Morgan, was a successful merchant
in Hartford and Boston and, later, a prominent international banker.

In 1854 Junius moved his family from Boston to London, where he
had accepted a partnership in a merchant-banking firm. Whereas many
of America's nineteenth-century millionaires could boast of a rise from
rags to riches, young Pierpont was polished at the Institut Sillig on Lake
Geneva in Switzerland and the University of Göttingen in Germany,
where he excelled in mathematics.

In 1857 Morgan took a position as a junior accountant in the New
York office of Duncan, Sherman & Co., the American representative of
his father's firm. He worked hard, prospered, and enjoyed the pleasures
that polite society traditionally makes available to a banker in his bachelor years.

Tragedy struck in 1861. Morgan had fallen in love with Amelia Sturges,
a young woman from a well-to-do New York family. In March, Mimi
grew ill with tuberculosis. When her condition worsened, Morgan decided that he would marry her at once and take her abroad. In the biography written many years later by Morgan's son-in-law Herbert L.
Satterlee, the most moving episode in the life of a man often described
as heartless is vividly recounted:

> The marriage took place in the Sturges town house, No. 5 East Four-
> teenth Street, on October 7. Only the family and intimate friends were
> present. . . . Pierpont carried Mimi downstairs into the back parlor. . . .
> The folding doors were opened and the wedding party in the front parlor

saw the little bride, held on her feet by the strong young bridegroom while the short ceremony was being performed. At the conclusion of the service the doors were closed again so that the newly made Mrs. Morgan might be spared the fatigue of greeting her relatives and friends.

In search of sun, Morgan took Mimi to Algiers and then to Nice, but she died on February 17, 1862, a little over four months after their marriage. Morgan returned to New York in June, plunged back into his work, and, on September 1, with his cousin Jim Goodwin, formed a partnership under the name J. Pierpont Morgan & Co. The chief business of the firm was to act as the American agent for the firm of Pierpont's father.

Like many young men, Morgan paid $300 for a substitute to take his place in the Union Army. Along with the evasion of service, two business episodes during the Civil War have cast a shadow on his reputation. One, the Hall Carbine Affair, occurred in the summer of 1861. Morgan lent $20,000 to a New York politician named Simon Stevens, who had contracted to sell to General Frémont, for $22 each, outmoded carbines that an enterprising gun dealer had purchased from the War Department itself for $3.50 each. Morgan's role in this transaction may have been less central than early muckrakers charged, but it seems fair to conclude that, as the *Dictionary of American Biography* puts it, the affair did not "redound to his credit."

The second episode involved a speculation that took advantage of the increased sensitivity of gold prices after the federal government suspended the redemption of its bank notes in gold late in 1861. In 1863 Morgan and a young man named Edward Ketchum acquired about $1.15 million in gold, shipped half of their hoard abroad, and sold the rest at a profit of $132,000 when the price rose in response to the shortage they had helped to create. *The New York Times* attacked the speculation as the work of "a knot of unscrupulous gamblers who care nothing for the credit of the country"—a comment that Morgan probably considered an outrageous assault on the honor of men engaged in legitimate enterprise.

In 1865 Morgan married for the second and last time, and over the next eight years a son and three daughters were born. As a partner in Dabney, Morgan & Co., Morgan prospered. Yet he did not quite flourish. Mysterious ailments afflicted him—persistent fatigue and insomnia, headaches, dizzy spells, fainting spells, and a hereditary skin condition that erupted periodically all his life. At the age of thirty-three, he informed his father that he was considering retirement!

Though the hazards of psychobiography are well known, the possibility that these symptoms point to some inner turmoil has to be acknowledged. Perhaps Morgan doubted he could ever emerge from the shadow of a strong-willed father. Perhaps he resented the demands of a career he felt he had not quite chosen. We can speculate, but probably we will never know.

We do know that from about 1857 until his father's death in 1890, Morgan regularly wrote letters to him—letters that Morgan's son-in-law describes as "perfectly frank and absolutely confidential." The letters were saved by Junius Morgan, bound in annual volumes, and locked on a shelf in his library. Pierpont burned the whole collection in 1911.

Railroad Finance

Instead of retiring, Morgan accepted an offer from the Drexels, the powerful Philadelphia banking family, and in 1871 Drexel, Morgan & Co. of New York was established. Morgan insisted upon, and was granted, a year's leave for his health before he set foot in the office.

In the 1870s Morgan began to emerge as a major figure in railroad finance. His involvement had started in 1869, when, as an ally of the Albany & Susquehanna Railroad, Morgan had participated in a successful effort to thwart a takeover attempt masterminded by Jay Gould and supported, at a crucial meeting of stockholders, by a gang of hired ruffians led by Jim Fisk. This contest, *The New York Times* reported in 1873, "made Mr. Morgan universally respected as an able financier."

The savage competition among American railroads worried the foreign investors whom Morgan represented. It also worried Morgan. Out of the anxiety precipitated by competition came, in 1885, one of the most dramatic triumphs of Morgan's career.

In this episode Morgan acted as peacemaker in a battle between the two largest railroad systems in the United States, the Pennsylvania and the New York Central. In 1883 William H. Vanderbilt, still the dominant figure in the New York Central, had invaded the territory of the Pennsylvania by joining forces with Andrew Carnegie to finance the construction of the South Pennsylvania Railroad from Reading to Pittsburgh. The Pennsylvania retaliated by buying shares in the West Shore Railroad, which ran from New York to Buffalo parallel to the New York Central. A clash that would wound both titans seemed inevitable.

At this point Morgan arranged an extraordinary meeting. It took place in July 1885 on Morgan's 165-foot steam yacht *Corsair*. George B. Roberts, president of the Pennsylvania, was there, along with Frank Thomson, a key vice president; Chauncey Depew, president of the New York Central; and Morgan himself, with authority to act on behalf of William Vanderbilt.

The gorgeous black yacht left from Jersey City at ten on a sunny morning, steamed slowly up the Hudson to West Point, turned around and steamed down the Hudson to the Atlantic and down to Sandy Hook, then turned again and, as the light waned and the heat relented, steamed back to Jersey City. All the while, Roberts would not compromise. At last, as he shook hands with Morgan at the gangway, the man who ran the giant Pennsylvania said, "I will agree to your plan and do my part." The railroad war was averted.

The compromise that Morgan worked out between the Pennsylvania and the New York Central was, it is clear, an agreement that restrained competition. As such, it was not unusual. In the 1870s and early 1880s, American railroad managers tried to control competition through cooperation—first through informal alliances, then through formal cartels. But speculators like Jay Gould undermined these efforts. In response, railroad managers and the financiers who backed them began to build giant systems that would assure a constant flow of freight and passengers.

More than any other financier, Morgan dominated this process. As railroads began to develop giant systems encompassing from five thousand to ten thousand miles of track, they were forced to rely on investment bankers with close ties to British and European sources of capital. No one had closer ties than J. P. Morgan. In addition, when bankruptcy led to reorganization, as it often did, railroad managers were forced to yield a measure of control to the financiers who bailed out their floundering enterprises. No one played a larger role in railroad reorganizations than J. P. Morgan.

As his role in railroad finance grew, Morgan stepped up his efforts to limit competition. Late in 1888, for instance, he brought the presidents of nearly all railroads west of St. Louis and Chicago to a series of conferences at his mansion in New York City. Through a "gentleman's agreement" signed early in 1889, a western association was formed with authority to set rates and to allocate traffic among the participants. After a similar meeting in 1890, Morgan's enthusiasm overflowed in a remarkable statement to the press: "I am thoroughly satisfied with the results accomplished. The public has not yet appreciated the magnitude of the work. Think of it—all the competitive traffic of the roads west of Chicago and St. Louis placed in the control of about thirty men! It is the most important agreement made by the railroads in a long time, and it is as strong as could be desired."

In 1897, federal courts ruled that associations of this kind violated the Sherman Antitrust Act of 1890. Even before then, however, it had become clear that associations were not as effective an obstacle to competition as Morgan had hoped. The next step, which Morgan pursued vigorously through the 1890s, was to defuse competition through consolidation. By 1906, seven huge systems dominated American railroad transportation. Of the seven, one system was headed by Morgan, and three others were strongly subject to his influence.

The consolidation of railroad systems under the influence of America's great banking houses, especially the House of Morgan, is one of the major stories of American business history. In the process of consolidation, business historian Alfred D. Chandler, Jr., tells us, the railroads "became and remained the private business enterprises that most closely exemplified financial capitalism in the United States. . . . In few other types of American business enterprise did investment bankers and other financiers have such influence."

Morgan the Collector

In person Morgan was formidable—a powerful, broad-shouldered man with eyes that blazed and an awful nose, reddened and swollen by a skin condition that worsened as he aged. His manner often struck outsiders as brusque. Photographer Edward Steichen said that meeting his gaze was like facing the headlights of an express train bearing down on you— a description that comes frighteningly to life in the famous photograph taken by Steichen in 1903.

Morgan lived well, though not as lavishly as some of the more exuberant millionaires of his time. His residences included a brownstone mansion at the corner of Thirty-sixth Street and Madison Avenue in New York City (now occupied by the white marble annex of the Morgan Library); his country house, Cragston, at Highland Falls on the Hudson; a thousand-acre hideaway in the Adirondacks; a big house inherited from his father at Prince's Gate in London, with paintings by Rubens and Rembrandt and a special room designed to display a splendid collection by eighteenth-century French master Fragonard; and Dover House, a big country place outside of London, also inherited from his father, with gardens and orchards and a dairy farm.

His favorite residence was his yacht. *Corsair III*, completed in 1898, was 302 feet long on the waterline, compared to 204 feet for *Corsair II*, completed in 1891, and 165 for the original *Corsair*, purchased in 1882. (By comparison, it might be noted that Malcolm Forbes made headlines when, in 1985, he ordered a 151-foot yacht to replace his 126-footer.)

On weekday nights in spring and summer, Morgan often dined and slept on his yacht. He was commodore of the New York Yacht Club from 1897 to 1899, and headed the syndicate that built the yacht *Columbia*, which successfully defended the America's Cup in 1899 and 1901. When a prospective yachtsman asked him about maintenance costs, Morgan made a reply that has become famous: "Anybody who even has to think about the cost had better not get one."

Another famous remark was that he could do a year's work in nine months but not in twelve. After the age of sixty, Morgan routinely left in March for three or four months abroad. He traveled in splendor—a habit that had begun early. A photograph taken at the Temple of Karnak at Luxor in Egypt, in 1877, shows the forty-year-old banker looking remarkably like Theodore Roosevelt, with a bushy moustache, a pith helmet, a three-piece knickerbocker suit, and an escort of exotic-looking natives (not to mention his wife, the nurse, the maid, and several other women, all dressed so uncomfortably one wants to weep for them).

His wife did not usually accompany Morgan on his vacations. Pierpont treated her with respectful affection, and the marriage lasted, but there is little reason to think that its stability was based on fidelity. Attractive women often traveled with him, and actress Maxine Elliott is said to have been the mistress of both Morgan and King Edward VII of England. In the legends and comments that have come down to us, it is difficult to disentangle rumor, innuendo, and a kind of leering envy. Art dealer James Henry Duveen probably went too far when he wrote that Morgan's "*adventures galantes* partook of the splendor and ostentation of King Solomon."

Philanthropy interested Morgan from an early age. Unlike John D. Rockefeller and Andrew Carnegie, he did not develop a philosophy of giving, but simply gave to the causes and institutions that pleased him— the Wadsworth Athenaeum in Hartford; the Harvard Medical School; St. Paul's Cathedral in London; a hospital in Aix-les-Bains; and, in New York City, St. George's Church in Stuyvesant Square, the Lying-in Hospital, St. Luke's Hospital, the American Museum of Natural History, the YMCA, the Cathedral of St. John the Divine, the Metropolitan Opera, and the Metropolitan Museum of Art.

Above all, he took an interest in the Metropolitan Museum of Art, which he had helped to organize in 1871 and where he served as president from 1904 until his death in 1913. In his relations with the Metropolitan, Morgan's philanthropic impulses merged with the great passion of his private life—his interest in collecting.

His collecting began in earnest in 1888, when he purchased an original manuscript by Thackeray. Soon Morgan was buying whole libraries. Medieval and Renaissance illuminated manuscripts especially appealed to him. He also liked to own what no one else could own—manuscripts by Dickens, the original draft of Keats's *Endymion*, love letters from Napoleon to Josephine, the only surviving fragment of *Paradise Lost*.

In 1900 he began to plan a separate building to house his manuscripts and books. As his architect he chose Charles F. McKim, a leader in the American neoclassical revival who is remembered today not only for the Morgan Library but also for the Boston Public Library and, in New York City, the Columbia University Library, the University Club, and the original Pennsylvania Railroad Station. McKim designed for Morgan an exquisite one-story white marble building in the style of an early-sixteenth-century Italian Renaissance palazzo. The Library was completed in 1906 and was donated to the public by Morgan's son in 1924.

When Morgan was in his sixties, his collecting expanded to include an immense variety of *objets d'art*. A collection worth more than $50 million was amassed in less than two decades. Morgan was, according to art historian Aline Saarinen, "the most prodigious private collector of all time."

At the Metropolitan Museum, Morgan ruled without challenge. Inevitably, his regal manner provoked some conflict with the aesthetes who served him. From England in 1906 he summoned art critic and connoisseur Roger Fry to be second-in-command at the museum. "He likes to be in a position of being surrounded by people he has in his power to make or unmake," Fry wrote in a confidential letter. ". . . He's much too much a God Almighty." After his dismissal in 1910, Fry flung a final dart: "A crude historical imagination was the only flaw in his otherwise perfect insensibility toward art."

In the last years of his life, Morgan made annual trips up the Nile to see the Metropolitan's excavations in Egypt—excavations that he financed and that culminated in the opening of the great Egyptian galleries at the Metropolitan on November 11, 1912.

By that time Morgan was making plans for the disposition of his own vast holdings. In a grand miscalculation, the New York City Board of Estimate hesitated to appropriate funds for a Morgan Wing of the Metropolitan. Miffed by the city's hesitation, he left his collections to his son, with a declaration that he still hoped for some arrangement "which would render them permanently available for the instruction and pleasure of the American people."

At the Metropolitan in June 1914, the Morgan collection was displayed in its entirety for the only time. Then, for reasons it is difficult to comprehend, Pierpont, Jr., decided to sell some assets to raise cash for estate taxes. Five splendid Fragonards went to steel magnate Henry Frick. A Vermeer went to sugar tycoon Henry O. Havemeyer. Major collections of tapestries, Chinese porcelains, and Bourbon decorative arts went to English dealers. The dazzling miscellany that remains at the Metropolitan—more than six thousand objects—is only two fifths of the treasure it might have had.

Morgan the Consolidator

Morgan did not merely play a leading role in railroad finance and government finance. As his career progressed, he also played an increasingly active role in industrial finance.

One area that especially interested him was steel. In 1898–99 Morgan sponsored the consolidation of several smaller companies into the Federal Steel Company, headed by the Chicago lawyer Elbert H. Gary. But even that consolidation did not bring to the industry the degree of order that Morgan always preferred. Negotiations with Andrew Carnegie ensued, and in 1901 a new colossus was formed. With a total capitalization of $1.4 billion at a time when the annual appropriations of the U.S. government had not yet reached $1 billion, U.S. Steel was the largest corporation in the world. It controlled about 60 percent of the American steel industry.

Morgan's efforts as a consolidator of giant industrial enterprises did not stop with the creation of U.S. Steel. In 1902 he arranged both the consolidation of transatlantic shipping lines to form the International Merchant Marine and the consolidation to leading farm machinery companies to form International Harvester. Later he backed the unsuccessful attempt by Theodore Vail of AT&T to unite the telephone and telegraph industries.

One effort misfired. In 1901 Morgan organized the Northern Securities Company, combining three major railroad lines of James J. Hill and E. H. Harriman—the Great Northern, the Northern Pacific, and the Burlington—under the umbrella of a single holding company. But in February 1902, the attorney general filed suit against the new company under the Sherman Antitrust Act. Morgan was shocked. "If we have done anything wrong," he said in a meeting with President Roosevelt, "send your man to my man and they can fix it up." But Roosevelt refused to accept this gentlemanly offer, and in 1904, in an important reversal of previous decisions, the U.S. Supreme Court ruled that the consolidation was illegal.

"A One-Man Federal Reserve"

Morgan's dominance was never demonstrated more dramatically than in the Panic of October and November 1907. The crisis began with the failure of a copper speculator named F. Augustus Heinze, who controlled a chain of banks. Then the Knickerbocker Trust Company failed, and other institutions trembled in anticipation of an assault by frightened depositors.

At the time there was no Federal Reserve Bank to serve as a lender of last resort for the institutions in trouble. Moreover, although the law required ordinary banks to maintain large cash reserves, it permitted a new kind of bank, the trust company, to operate with low reserves. If their depositors panicked, many trusts would fail. Thousands of individuals would lose their savings, buying power would evaporate, businesses would go under, and unemployment would soar—all at a time when government programs supplied no cushion against disaster.

In the absence of a central banking power, Morgan himself organized the presidents of the solvent institutions to meet the threat. For two terrifying weeks, while crisis after crisis flared, sleepless financiers wrangled in the rooms of the Morgan Library. For two weeks, on the basis of the prestige that Morgan alone commanded, capital was raised to save now one trust company, now another, now the stock exchange, now the city of New York.

In an emergency that threatened the national economy, the crucial leadership did not come from the president of the United States or from the secretary of the Treasury. It came from Morgan. Morgan served, as Frederick Lewis Allen comments, as "a one-man Federal Reserve Bank."

*   *   *

On April 27, 1912, a subcommittee of the House Committee on Banking and Currency chaired by Louisiana congressman Arsene Pujo began an investigation of America's leading bankers and the institutions they controlled. As the nation's most powerful banker, J. P. Morgan became the main target of Pujo's "money trust" hearings.

The investigating subcommittee concluded that "a few leaders of finance," working together, had achieved a "great and rapidly growing concentration of the control of money and credit" in the United States. This control has been established, the subcommittee charged, through "stock ownership, interlocking directorates, partnership and joint account transactions, and other forms of domination over banks, trust companies, railroads, and public service and industrial corporations."

The subcommittee focused especially on an "inner group" consisting of "J. P. Morgan & Co., the recognized leaders"; George F. Baker, the head of the First National Bank; and James Stillman, the head of the National City Bank. The Morgan-Baker-Stillman group controlled or strongly influenced the Bankers Trust Company, the Guaranty Trust Company, the Astor Trust Company, the Liberty National Bank, the Chemical Bank, and the National Bank of Commerce, among others.

But banks were just the beginning. According to the final report of the Pujo subcommittee, a small group of financiers linked to Morgan, Baker, or Stillman held 118 directorships in thirty-four banks and trust companies, 105 directorships in thirty-two transportation companies, thirty directorships in ten insurance companies, twenty-five directorships in twelve public utility corporations, and sixty-three directorships in twenty-four manufacturing and trading corporations. In all, associates of the "inner group" held 341 directorships in 112 corporations with total resources or capitalization of over $22 billion.

In its response to the subcommittee's charges, J. P. Morgan & Co. pointed out, quite reasonably, that "It is preposterous to suppose that every 'interlocking' director has full control in every organization with which he is connected." But the subcommittee was not interested in subtleties.

Morgan's two days of testimony in December 1912 was the high point of the hearings. It was a grand spectacle—"Morgan, Morgan, the Great Financial Gorgon," come to face his critics. The seventy-five-year-old banker denied the existence of an organized money trust, but he could not convincingly deny that a vast amount of financial power had come to rest in the hands of a few men. At bottom, Morgan's answer to the subcommittee's insinuations was simply that he had faith in the character of those few men. In a much-quoted exchange with Samuel Untermyer, the subcommittee counsel, Morgan declared that in business, "the first thing is character." "Before money or property?" Untermyer asked. With obvious sincerity Morgan answered, "Before anything else. Money cannot buy it. . . . Because a man I do not trust could not get money from me on all the bonds of Christendom."

The Pujo hearings helped pave the way for the Federal Reserve Act of 1913, which addressed some of the deficiencies so glaringly exposed in the Panic of 1907, and for the Clayton Antitrust Act of 1914, which barred interlocking directorates and prohibited various other practices tending to create monopoly or lessen competition. Morgan did not live to see these changes, but he knew that changes were coming. "American business," he lamented, "must henceforth be done in glass pockets."

The Last of His Kind

With a small party including his daughter Louisa, Morgan sailed for Europe early in 1913. His doctors had put him on a diet of barley soup and chopped meat and ordered him to limit his consumption of cigars. After a last trip up the Nile, he made his way to Rome, where his health failed completely. His entourage rebuffed the advances of art dealers and antiquaries who, the *London Daily Mail* reported, made "desperate efforts" to approach the dying banker with the offer of some final bargain.

Herbert Satterlee, who was there, has left a full account of Morgan's final days. At times, on his bed in Rome's Grand Hotel, the financier imagined that he was a boy in Hartford or at school in Switzerland. Just after midnight on Monday, March 31, he pointed upward and said, "I've got to go up the hill." He did not speak again.

Not counting art collections conservatively valued at $50 million, Morgan left an estate worth $68 million. The figure came as something of a disappointment to Americans who had grown accustomed to thinking that he commanded kingly resources. "And to think he was not a rich man!" Andrew Carnegie commented.

How important was J. P. Morgan in the long run? The best work of contemporary business historians suggests a surprising answer. Alfred D. Chandler, Jr., argues that for much of the twentieth century, historians have been unduly "fascinated by the financiers who for brief periods allocated funds to transportation, communication, and some industrial enterprises." As a result, those same historians have underestimated the importance of the operating executives who, through the knowledge that came from their immersion in the daily activities of the firm, positioned themselves to play in time "a far more central role than did the robber barons, industrial statesmen, or financiers."

With rare exceptions, Chandler concludes, salaried managers "soon came to command those enterprises where financiers were originally influential. Financial capitalism in the United States was a narrowly located, short-lived phenomenon." J. P. Morgan was the most powerful financier of his time, but, at the very moment when the outcry against the "money trust" reached its peak, power was passing in a new direction. "There will be no successor to Morgan," *The Wall Street Journal* said after his death. Three quarters of a century later, there is no reason to challenge that judgment.

CHAPTER 9

Opulence

A memorable event in the social history of the United States took place on February 6, 1897. On that day Mr. and Mrs. Bradley-Martin threw a ball that historians have cited ever since as a supreme example of vulgar expenditure.

Mr. and Mrs. Martin had moved to Manhattan from Troy, New York, and, after what has been described as "the slow growth of an imaginary hyphen," had become *the* Bradley-Martins. In the winter of 1896–97, a miserable period for many Americans, the Bradley-Martins decided that the time had come to "put money in circulation" by throwing a gigantic party, on the theory that the cash expended must trickle down to help at least a few of New York's neediest.

The "fancy dress fete" of the Bradley-Martins was held at the Waldorf-Astoria Hotel, which was transformed for the night into a replica of Versailles. Several hundred guests dressed as figures from the famous courts of England and France. "I do not think there was ever so great a display of jewels before," one attendee gushed. ". . . Bradley, as Louis XV, wore a court suit of brocade. The suit of gold inlaid armor worn by Mr. Belmont was valued at ten thousand dollars. The value of the historic gems worn by the ladies simply baffles description."

Altogether, the ball and the costumes were estimated to cost more than $300,000. The Bradley-Martins got the publicity they craved, but not the applause they craved equally. The rector of St. George's Church in New York, the parish of J. P. Morgan, warned that the affair would "draw attention to the growing gulf which separates the rich and the poor." Mark Hanna, never an enemy of privilege, thought the Bradley-Martins were fortunate that no terrorist had tossed a bomb to blow "the dancing fops and their ladies to spangles and red paste." Chastened, Mr. and Mrs. Bradley-Martin moved to England, never to return.

The Gilded Age, a novel published by Mark Twain and Charles Dudley Warner in 1873, gave the period later graced by the Bradley-Martins a name it has not outlived. It was an age when the rich, and especially the vulgar rich, were more visible than ever before in American history. Everything about the new Midases—where they lived, where they played, how they partied—seemed suddenly to command the nation's dazzled attention. Splendor had arrived in the United States, with its semicivilized attendants, Gaudiness and Ostentation. In every way, the age was the fulfillment of an observation Emerson had made much earlier: "Things are in the saddle, and ride mankind."

Mansions of the Mighty

In cities all over the country, the rich staked out their territory. In Cleveland, John D. Rockefeller and Henry Flagler built homes a few minutes' walk apart on Euclid Avenue. In Chicago, the residence of merchant Potter Palmer, on Lake Shore Drive north of the Michigan River, was hailed as "a mansion to end all mansions"—"an American architect's best thought of what a baronial castle could be." On Nob Hill in San Francisco, three of California's Big Four railroad men—Mark Hopkins, Charles Crocker, and Leland Stanford—built homes that showed that the wealth of the West Coast might yet challenge the wealth of the East.

Neither originality nor restraint distinguished the architecture of the period. America's millionaires, historian Charles A. Beard commented in *The Rise of American Civilization*, built themselves "châteaux of French design, mansions of the Italian renaissance, English castles of authoritative mien—a riot of periods and tastes, with occasionally a noble monument to the derivative genius of some American architect trained in Europe and given freedom to create."

Nowhere was the acquisitive success of America's moguls more proudly displayed than on Fifth Avenue in New York City. In 1879 William H. Vanderbilt, son of the commodore, purchased the entire block facing west between Fifty-first and Fifty-second streets. Sixty foreign sculptors and seven hundred laborers went to work, and late in 1881 a block-long brownstone palace was completed—the southern half for Vanderbilt, the northern half for two of his daughters.

Vanderbilt's mansion, says Stewart Holbrook, "turned out to be a glorious hash of styles and periods from much of the known world— French tapestries, Florentine doors, African marbles, English china, Dutch old masters," not to mention "a Japanese parlor lined with bamboo and fairly a-crawl with jeweled crickets and dragonflies." Vanderbilt modestly published an album, *Mr. Vanderbilt's House and Collection*, which assured its readers that for all its magnificence, the mansion contained nothing that was not "elegant . . . refined . . . artistic . . . choice . . . exquisite . . . delicate . . . fresh." Special praise was reserved for Mrs. Vanderbilt's bedroom: "The furniture is the most choice, the most elegant, that the mansion contains. . . . Among the fragile glitter of the upholsterer . . . there is one worn-looking object, and only one: it is the little Bible."

In the last years of the nineteenth century and the early years of the twentieth, a long stretch of Fifth Avenue facing Central Park became known as "Millionaires' Row." Here lived not only the Astors and the Vanderbilts but also the families of such well-known magnates as Sir Roderick Cameron (shipping), Senator William A. Clark (copper), James B. Duke (tobacco), Edward S. Harkness (oil), O. H. Havemeyer (sugar), Henry Phipps (iron), Daniel G. Reid (tinplate), F. W. Woolworth (merchandising), and Charles T. Yerkes (rapid transit). Upper Fifth Avenue, the *New York Herald* reported in 1898, "is a solid mile and a half of millionaires' residences, practically without a break, except where a vacant spot awaits the coming of still another Croesus."

Several of the great mansions built in this period survive today. The four-story, red-brick Georgian mansion of Andrew Carnegie, at Ninety-first Street and Fifth Avenue, has become the home of the Cooper-Hewitt Museum of Design and Decorative Arts. One block to the north, at Ninety-second and Fifth, the former home of banker Felix M. Warburg, a French Renaissance mansion completed in 1908, now houses the Jewish Museum. The Museum of the City of New York, on Fifth between 103rd and 104th streets, contains a bedroom and a dressing room from the house of John D. Rockefeller that stood until 1938 at 4 West 54th Street, just west of Fifth Avenue, on the site now occupied by the garden of the Museum of Modern Art.

Among the mansions now open to the public, nowhere does the sense of magnificence make a keener impression than in the mansion of steel magnate Henry Clay Frick, on Fifth Avenue and Seventieth Street. The paintings on display include masterpieces by Rembrandt, Titian, Hals, Goya, El Greco, Veronese, Ingres, Vermeer, Tintoretto, and Velasquez. The Fragonard Room contains the famous panels representing the Progress of Love that Madame du Barry commissioned for her pavilion at Louveciennes and that Frick eventually purchased from the estate of J. P. Morgan. The garden courtyard, with an arched glass roof put on after Frick's death, may be the most serene spot in modern Manhattan.

In glamor and influence, Fifth Avenue reached its peak in the decade before World War I. "The dominant note" of that period, writes architectural historian Henry Hope Reed, ". . . was opulence: opulence in the mansions filled with gilded Louis Seize furniture, opulence in the hotels with their marble oyster bars and rococo dining rooms, opulence in the shops selling rosepoint lace and crepe de Chine, opulence in the Brewster-built carriages and in the newfangled motorcars with names such as Simplex and Pierce Arrow . . . [and] opulence in dress, too; women in high-waisted flaring skirts of silk, with flowered and feathered hats; men in gray toppers and Prince Alberts and spats; servants in brass-buttoned, multi-colored liveries."

But the splendor did not last. The Vanderbilts owned ten mansions on Fifth Avenue in 1911. By the end of World War II, all ten had come down. With the demolition of Delmonico's Restaurant in 1925, it seemed clear that, as S. C. Burchell has written, "The diamond and lobster and champagne world of old New York . . . was coming to an end." The glitter of the Gilded Age gave way to the glitter of the twenties, and then came a decade without any glitter at all. With "hunger marchers" in Washington and thirteen million Americans unemployed, displays of lavish living passed temporarily from the scene.

Newport

In 1886, Charles Dudley Warner traced the evolution of the successful businessman "into the full-blown existence of a man of fashion." The process, he wrote, "is perfectly charted. Success in business, member-ship in a good club, tandem in the Park, introduction to a good house, marriage to a pretty girl of family and not much money, a yacht, a four-in-hand, a Newport villa. His name had undergone a like evolution. It used to be written on his business card, John B. Glow. It was entered at the club as J. Bartlett Glow. On the wedding invitations it was Mr. Bartlett Glow, and the dashing pair were always spoken of at Newport as the Bartlett-Glows."

Anyone could build a mansion in Manhattan. To attain the top rung of the social ladder, it was also necessary to have a "cottage"—that is, a mansion—at Newport. One wit described the Rhode Island resort as "New York Society's best dish, garnished with a little cold Boston celery and a fringe of Philadelphia and Baltimore parsley." The infallible sign that one had arrived, socially, was that one no longer sought to arrive. In the words of one old-line Newport spinster quoted in Cleveland Amory's *The Last Resorts*, "I want to know people who don't want to know me, they want to know people who don't want to know them, and so on ad infinitum." Another commented, "Newport consists of two kinds of people—those who know you and don't speak to you and those who don't know you and do speak to you."

At Newport Harbor between 1890 and 1914, a visitor might have seen the most magnificent yachts in the United States—J. P. Morgan's *Corsair*, William Backhouse Astor's *Nourmahal*, James Gordon Bennett's *Lysistrata*, the Drexel family's *Sultana*, and Peter A. B. Widener's *Josephine*, to name a few. It was at Newport that William R. Travers made a comment that thoughtful investors have never forgotten: "Wh-wh-where," he stammered, "are the c-c-customers' yachts?"

Newport's "cottages" have to be seen to be believed, and today, as if in permanent testimony to the extravagances of the Gilded Age, many of them are open to the public. Three of the most impressive—the Breakers, Marble House, and Belcourt—were designed by Richard Morris Hunt in the early 1890s.

Born in Vermont in 1827, the younger brother of painter William Morris Hunt, Richard Hunt was the first American architect to study at the École des Beaux Arts in Paris. After he returned to the United States in 1855, Richard's first job was helping the architect in charge of placing the dome on the Capitol in Washington, D.C. In the "battle of styles" then raging among American architects, Hunt sided with the classicists against the proponents of the Gothic revival. The mansion of William K. Vanderbilt at Fifty-second Street and Fifth Avenue in New York established him as the preeminent society architect of his time. He also designed the mansion of Mrs. William Backhouse Astor at Sixty-fifth Street and Fifth Avenue; the $300,000 Vanderbilt mausoleum at New Dorp on Staten Island; and, for George Washington Vanderbilt II, the spectacular limestone castle, Biltmore, on a plot of 130,000 acres in North Carolina. His contributions to institutional architecture included the Lenox Library, the Tribune Building, and the facade of the Metropolitan Museum of Art in New York City; the theological library and the Marquand Chapel at Princeton; the Divinity College and the Scroll and Key Club at Yale; the Fogg Art Museum at Harvard; and the National Observatory in Washington, D.C.

For Cornelius Vanderbilt II, Hunt built at Newport a $3 million "cottage" called the Breakers. There were seventy rooms, thirty-three of them for servants. Mrs. Vanderbilt, it was said, could give a party for two hundred without calling in extra help. The dominant materials are Caen stone from France on the outside and, inside, blue and green marbles and tawny alabasters. The library is paneled with Circassian walnut stamped in gold. Even the stables are overwhelming. They contain a room full of coaches, carriages, and surreys; a room with twenty-six open stalls and two box stalls; a harness room; a trophy room; workrooms; offices; and, on the second floor, a five-room apartment for the head coachman, plus a kitchen, a dining room, a library, a sitting room, and twelve bedrooms for grooms and other servants. Here, at least, the scale is human. The Breakers itself, as Richard O'Connor has remarked, "seems no more likely a place for human habitation than the interior of the Great Pyramid."

For the brother of Cornelius II, William K. Vanderbilt, Hunt designed Marble House, a "cottage" that incorporated many features of the Grand and Petit Trianons at Versailles. Marble House cost $2 million to build and $9 million to decorate. Vanderbilt's wife, Alva, was a southern belle whose social aspirations did not stop with her marriage to a Vanderbilt. In 1895, with the help of a $10 million dowry, she married her daughter Consuelo to His Grace the Ninth Duke of Marlborough—an unhappy story recounted by Consuelo in her aptly titled memoir *The Glitter and the Gold*. At Marble House, one of Alva's most brilliant touches was a splendid red-and-gold Chinese teahouse, built by an army of imported workmen. Overlooking the Cliff Walk and the sea, the teahouse was perfect in every way, except that it lacked facilities for making tea. To solve that problem, a miniature railway was installed, connecting the pantry of Marble House to the teahouse. At Mrs. Vanderbilt's tea parties, her footmen would squat on the little cars as they rode to the tea-house, with the silver trays that they balanced above their heads glittering in the sun.

For all its opulence, Marble House did not please everyone. To Consuelo, it seemed a cage. She recalled:

> It stood on restricted grounds, and, like a prison, was surrounded by high walls. Even the gates were lined with sheet iron. . . . Upstairs my own room was austere. It was paneled in a dark Renaissance boiserie. There were six windows but at best one could only glimpse the sky through their high and narrow casements. An unadorned stone mantel opposite my bed greeted my waking eyes. To the right on an antique table were aligned a mirror and various silver brushes and combs. On another table writing utensils were disposed in such perfect order that I never ventured to use them.

Alva Vanderbilt's career took a dramatic turn when, in 1895–96, she sued for divorce on the ground that Mr. Vanderbilt had had a fling with one Nellie Neustretter of Eureka, Nevada. Willie K. did not contest the charge. It was the first widely publicized divorce case in the history of American high society. When she was free, Alva promptly married Oliver Hazard Perry Belmont, an heir of New York banker August Belmont.

At Newport, Alva moved from Marble House to Belcourt, the fifty-two-room mansion that Hunt had built for Belmont in 1894. The Belmonts loved horses, and Belcourt reflected their passion. "It is a most singular house," Julia Ward Howe wrote to her daughter after one luncheon there. "The first floor is all stable, with stalls for some thirteen or more horses, all filled, and everything elaborate and elegant. Oh! to lodge horses so, and be content that men and women should lodge in sheds and cellars!"

At opposite ends of one salon at Belcourt, visitors could admire two favorite horses, stuffed, with figures of men in armor atop them. In her memoir *This Was My Newport*, Mrs. Howe's daughter recalls how the host doted on his horses:

> Belmont was very popular with men, but his great love seemed to be for animals rather than humans. . . . In the stables at "Belcourt" was every conceivable kind of turnout, and Belmont's horses were provided with the finest equine clothing ever seen. The horses had morning clothes, after-noon clothes, and evening clothes—the most elaborate being made of pure white linen with the Belmont crest, a helmet and the motto *Sans Crainte*, embroidered as large as a man's hand.

While her husband lavished attention on his horses, Alva Smith Vanderbilt Belmont became involved in various social causes—soup kitchens; clinics for the poor; model houses; antidrug campaigns; birth control; and, at last, suffrage for women. Today she is best remembered for the encouragement she offered a disheartened suffragette: "Brace up, my dear. Just pray to God. *She* will help you." Having survived her husband by a quarter century, she died in Paris in 1933, at eighty.

By that time, Newport was in decline. The ten largest cottages, Cleveland Amory informs us, were assessed for $2,773,000 in property taxes in 1925. By 1950, only four of the ten were still privately owned, and they were assessed for $823,150. "It all stopped at once," lamented one Newporter whom Amory interviewed at about that time. "I can't remember when I had a white tie on last." "It's not so bad for us," another commented. "It's awful for the servants."

Even in its golden age, Newport had its detractors. When Henry James paid a visit in the fall of 1904, the villas and palaces reminded him of "white elephants . . . all cry and no wool, all house and no garden." They had been built, he felt sure, "with the best faith in the world—though not altogether with the best light, which is always so different a matter." What troubled James in "these monuments of pecuniary power" was a failure of taste, a failure of proportion, which he exposed in prose that was elegant and deadly:

> They look queer and conscious and lumpish—some of them, as with an air of the brandished probiscus, really grotesque—while their averted owners, roused from a witless dream, wonder what in the world is to be done with them. The answer to which, I think, can only be that there is absolutely nothing to be done; nothing but to let them stand there always, vast and blank, for reminder to those concerned of the prohibited degrees of witlessness, and of the peculiarly awkward vengeances of affronted proportion and discretion.

Less scathing, but still on target, were the comments of Finley Peter Dunne's "Mr. Dooley":

> Now, don't go gettin' cross about th' rich, Hinnissy. Put up that dinnymite. Don't excite ye'ersilf about us folks in Newport. It's always been th' same way, Father Kelly tells me. Says he: ". . . F'river an' iver people have been growin' rich, goin' down to some kind iv a Newport, makin' monkeys iv thimsilves an' goin' back to the jungle. 'Tis a steady procission. . . . Ye read about th' union iv two gr'reat fortunes. A dollar meets another dollar, they are congenial, have sim'lar tastes, an' many mutual frinds.

They are married an' bring up a fam'ly iv pennies, dimes, thirty-cintses an' countherfeits. An' afther awhile, th' fam'ly passes out iv circylation. That's th' histhry iv it," says Father Kelly. "An,' " says he, "I'm glad there is a Newport." . . . "It's th' exhaust pipe," he says. "Without it we might blow up," he says. "It's the hole in th' top iv th' kettle," he says. "I wish it was bigger."

Mr. Make-a-Lister

Society must have an arbiter, someone who decides who belongs and who does not. For much of the Gilded Age, this position was filled by Ward McAllister, a foolish man with a Van Dyke beard who invented the famous "Four Hundred."

"Mr. Make-a-Lister," as he was sometimes called, was born in Savannah, Georgia, in 1827, a cousin of Julia Ward Howe and a descendant of both Richard Ward, the royal governor of Rhode Island, and Samuel Ward, the Revolutionary governor. A couple of years as an attorney in San Francisco in the days when legal fees were paid with newly panned gold, followed by marriage to a self-effacing Washington, D.C., heiress in 1853, freed him to devote the rest of his life to the hard work of having a good time.

He began with a sojourn in Europe. In *Society as I Have Found It*, a volume of reminiscences published in 1890, McAllister shares with his readers some of the highlights of the period: "My Host gets Gloriously Drunk . . . Dinner with the Chef of Windsor Castle . . . I taste Montilla Sherry for the First Time . . A Winter in Florence and Rome . . . The Grand Duke of Tuscany's Ball . . . Summer in Baden-Baden . . . Winter in Pau . . . I Learn how to give Dinners."

Back in the United States, McAllister divided his time among households in Newport, New York, and Savannah. When the son of the Duke of Devonshire and the son of the Earl of Shaftesbury paid a visit to Georgia, the stage was set for McAllister's first social triumph: "My *filets de boeuf aux truffes et champignons*, and the scions of noble English houses, placed me in the front social rank in that little, aristocratic town, and brought forth from one of its oldest inhabitants the exclamation, 'My dear boy, your aunts, the Telfairs, could give breakfasts, but you, you can give dinners.' "

The conquest of Savannah was followed by the conquest of New York.

It is not clear why anyone in Manhattan took McAllister seriously. Perhaps, in an age when new millionaires kept pushing to be admitted to society, someone was needed to shut the door. Or perhaps, as he claimed, McAllister did have a kind of talent—"the talent of and for society." No doubt, too, his snobbery helped him in some circles. The thing he disliked most about America, he declared, was the custom of shaking hands.

In New York in 1872, McAllister met the woman he later called his "one and only," his "Mystic Rose"—Mrs. William Backhouse Astor, Jr. This was *the* Mrs. Astor, the wife of the grandson of John Jacob Astor, a large, plain-featured woman who emerged in this period as the undisputed queen of New York society. At her *intime* evenings at Newport, Mrs. Astor would limit herself to one hundred guests and wear, Cleveland Amory reports, "a three-strand diamond necklace, a dazzling diamond stomacher and several chains of diamonds in lesser spots." One wit introduced himself to her with the comment, "You look like a walking chandelier."

It was McAllister's association with Mrs. Astor that led to the invention of the "Four Hundred." Since Mrs. Astor's ballroom held only four hundred people, it followed, McAllister announced in 1888, that there were only four hundred people in society. "If you go outside that number," he observed, "you strike people who are either not at ease in a ballroom or else make other people not at ease." After several years of feverish public speculation, McAllister released the names of the Four Hundred to *The New York Times*, which published the list on February 1, 1892. For reasons never explained, the list contained only a little more than three hundred names. The absence of artistic talent was striking. "The Four Hundred," one woman who appeared on the list commented, "would have fled in a body from a poet, a painter, a musician or a clever Frenchman."

Not long after his list was published, McAllister made a fatal blunder. When, in 1893, the mayor of Chicago announced that his city would give a "genuine" Chicago welcome to everyone who attended the World's Columbian Exposition there, McAllister remarked characteristically that "Hospitality which includes the whole human race is not desirable." He added that Midwesterners would do well to learn "not to frappé their wines too much." Responding in kind, Chicagoans wondered why anyone should value the opinions of a man who was nothing more than a "Head Butler," a "New York Flunky," a "Mouse Colored Ass."

In this moment of crisis, Mr. Make-a-Lister's friends decided they had had enough of him. In the highest circles of society, ridicule meant ruin.

"McAllister is a discharged servant. That is all," Stuyvesant Fish coldly informed a reporter. When the former "Autocrat of Drawing-Rooms" died in 1895, less than two dozen of the "Four Hundred" found time to attend his funeral.

Famous and Infamous Parties

The extravagance that distinguished the Gilded Age was nowhere more conspicuously displayed than in its parties. McAllister himself commented, in *Society as I Have Found It,* on the change that occurred when New York's definition of wealth "leaped boldly up to ten millions, fifty millions, one hundred millions, and the necessities and luxuries followed suit." The new standards were not easy to meet: "One was no longer content with a dinner of a dozen or more, to be served by a couple of servants. Fashion demanded that you be received in the hall of the house in which you were to dine, by five to six servants who, with the butler, were to serve the repast. . . . Soft strains of music were introduced between the courses, and in some houses gold replaced silver in the way of plate, and everything that skill and art could suggest was added to make the dinners not a vulgar display, but a great gastronomic effort, evidencing the possession by the host of both money and taste."

In her entertaining history of the Astor family, Virginia Cowles gives us an idea of what McAllister meant by "great gastronomic effort." A cousin of McAllister, Sam Ward, had married Emily Astor, the elder sister of John Jacob Astor III and William Backhouse Astor, Jr. Emily had died young, but Sam Ward lived on to become the most famous gourmet in New York. According to Cowles, the dinner whose menu is reprinted here took only three hours to consume:

Little neck clams
Montracher
Potage tortue verte à l'Anglaise
Potage crême d'artichaut
Amontillado
Whitebait
Filets de bass, sauce crevettes
Rauenthaler
Concombres
Timbales à la Milanaise
Filet de boeuf au madère

Pommery sec
Selle d'agneau de Central Park, sauce menthe
Moet & Chandon Grand Cremant Imperial Magnums
Petits pois, Tomates farcies, Pommes croquettes
Côtelettes de ris de veau à la Parisienne
Cèpes à la Bordelaise
Asperge froide en mayonnaise
Sorbet au Marasquin
Pluvier rôti au cresson
Château Margot
Salade de laitue
Fromages varies
Old Madeira Charleston and Savannah
Bombe de glace
Fraises
Pêches
Gâteaux
Raisins de serre
Café
Cognac & Liqueurs

The great parties of the Gilded Age were not distinguished merely by the quantity of the food. Sometimes higher issues were at stake. For years, in her role as guardian of social standards, *the* Mrs. Astor refused to invite any of the upstart Vanderbilts to her parties. At last Alva Vanderbilt (later Mrs. Belmont) broke down the barrier. Her weapon was a dress ball that, as the *New York Sun* reported, "In lavishness of expenditure and brilliancy of dress . . . far outdid any ball ever given before in this city."

The ball celebrated the completion of the $3 million palace that Richard Morris Hunt had built for the Vanderbilts at 660 Fifth Avenue. As soon as the party was announced, Mrs. Astor's daughter Caroline, never imagining that she might not be invited, began to rehearse a "star quadrille" for the ball. At this point Alva dropped her bombshell. Since Mrs. Astor had never paid a call on her, it simply would not be possible for her to invite young Caroline. Seeing that she had been outmaneuvered, and not wishing to disappoint her daughter, Mrs. Astor yielded. Alva's $250,000 ball, on March 6, 1883, opened high society to the Vanderbilts.

Other parties became famous because they were outrageous, idiotic, or both. A monkey in full evening dress was the guest of honor at a dinner given by Mrs. Stuyvesant Fish in Newport. At the "Horseback Dinner" given by C.K.G. Billings at Sherry's in New York City, the cream of Manhattan society dined in the saddle. At the debut of his daughter in Philadelphia in 1906, James Paul arranged for ten thousand butterflies from Brazil to be concealed in a giant bag hung close to the ceiling. When the bag was broken, the butterflies were supposed to fly into the night, but the heat had killed them, and instead of a gorgeous fluttering off, ten thousand butterflies fell to the floor like stones. Worst of all, perhaps, was an expensive dinner that Newporters arranged for their pet dogs. "In this," Cleveland Amory reports, "a regular Newport dinner table was taken off its foundations and placed on a veranda—on trestles a foot high. A hundred dogs participated, most of them in fancy dress; the menu was stewed liver and rice, fricassee of bones and shredded dog biscuit."

The opulence of the Gilded Age did not merely show off the wealth of moneyed Americans; it also exposed the wealthy to fierce criticism. In a sense, the rich could not win. If they built castles, someone was sure to note that many people still lived in hovels. If they lived more modestly, the failure to live like a lord might be held against them. In an article about John D. Rockefeller published in *McClure's Magazine* in 1905, Ida M. Tarbell complained that "No one of the three houses he occupies has any claims to rank among the notable homes of the country. . . . They show him to have no pleasure in noble architecture, to appreciate nothing of the beauty of fine lines and decorations. Mr. Rockefeller's favorite home, the house at Forest Hill, is a monument of cheap ugliness." If Rockefeller had shown a keener interest in "noble architecture," would Tarbell have approved? One doubts it. In the eyes of their critics, the rich were damned whether they lived lavishly or pinched pennies. Those who chose splendor did not merely build castles that made everyone gape. They also built targets that no one could miss.

CHAPTER 10

Dissenting Voices: 1865–1915

Thorstein Veblen: The Anatomist of Opulence

The man who thought and wrote most profoundly about the extravagances of the Gilded Age was a man who wore no jewelry of any kind, who carried his watch on a shred of black ribbon hooked to his vest by a safety pin, and who generally wore a rumpled suit and baggy trousers, with thick woolen socks held up by pins clipped to his pants legs.

Thorstein Bunde Veblen was born on a rural farm in Wisconsin in 1857, the fourth son and sixth of twelve children of Norwegian immigrants. After graduating from Carleton College in Minnesota, he studied at Johns Hopkins for a semester, failed to obtain a fellowship, and went on to Yale, where he received a Ph.D. in philosophy in 1884.

Unable to land a teaching job, Veblen returned to the family farm in Minnesota. The next seven years of his life were devoted to intensive and eccentric reading—an activity that struck his more wordly neighbors as pure idleness. One of his brothers commented later, "Thorstein was the only loafer in a highly respectable community. . . . He read and loafed, and the next day he loafed and read."

In 1891, at the age of thirty-four, Veblen appeared without invitation at Cornell University. A conservative professor of economics, J. Laurence Laughlin, was impressed by the unkempt stranger in corduroy trousers and coonskin cap, and obtained a special fellowship for him. In 1892, when Laughlin was named head of the Department of Economics at the University of Chicago, he brought Veblen as a teaching fellow.

Now that he had secured a foothold in the academy, Veblen began to publish essays with odd titles in scholarly journals: "The Economic Theory of Woman's Dress," "The Instinct of Workmanship and the Irksomeness of Labor," "The Beginnings of Ownership," "The Barbarian Status of Women." Then, in 1899, he published a book that, quite to his own astonishment, made him famous.

The title of the book was *The Theory of the Leisure Class: An Economic Study of Institutions*. In it Veblen emerged as, in the words of John Kenneth Galbraith, "the most penetrating, original, and uninhibited . . . source of social thought in his time." He also emerged as the master of a wholly original style, a style of savage circumlocution and biting, deadpan solemnity—"a kind of surgical style," writes economic historian Robert Heilbroner, "that left the world raw and exposed but perfectly bloodless, so fine-edged was his blade."

Veblen's prose takes some getting used to. For instance, after noting that the possession of property permits an "invidious comparison" with one's less prosperous neighbors, he adds a characteristic disclaimer: "In making use of the term 'invidious' . . . there is no intention to extol or depreciate . . . any of the phenomena which the word is used to characterize. The word is used in a technical sense. . . ." Similarly, after a fierce passage that discusses "the ignominy which attached to useful effort" and concludes with the declaration that "conspicuous expenditure must be an expenditure of superfluities," the reader is told: "The term 'waste' . . . is here used for want of a better term . . . and is not to be taken in an odious manner, as implying an illegitimate expenditure." Veblen is never more deadly than at the moment when he declares that he does not intend to wound.

What is most striking about Veblen is that he brings an anthropologist's eye—which is to say, the eye of an outsider—to his own time and place. No one but Veblen, looking at the rituals that accompany graduation ceremonies in modern universities, would have commented that "these usages and the conceptions on which they rest belong to a stage in cultural development no later than that of the angekok and the rainmaker." No one but Veblen would have commented that the gentleman's walking stick does not merely serve "the purpose of an advertisement that the bearer's hands are employed otherwise than in useful effort" but also "meets a felt need of barbarian man" as a weapon, and that, indeed, "The handling of so tangible and primitive a means of offense is very comforting to any one who is gifted with even a moderate share of ferocity." Sentences like these show what literary critic Alfred Kazin meant when he called Veblen "an anthropologist of the contemporary."

The Theory of the Leisure Class begins with an examination of the motives that inspire accumulation and display. The great classical economists had written about human beings as if rational calculation guided every action. Nonsense, Veblen says. Human beings are driven by vanity—the desire to impress. The end of acquisition and accumulation is not "the consumption of the goods accumulated." On the contrary, "The motive that lies at the root of ownership is emulation. . . . The possession of wealth confers honor; it is an invidious distinction." Once the ownership of property emerges as a fact in human history, "Purposeful effort comes to mean, primarily, effort directed to or resulting in a more creditable showing of accumulated wealth." This is "pecuniary emulation."

In the middle class, "the struggle for pecuniary reputability" makes men industrious and thrifty. But in the case of "the superior pecuniary class," this effect is modified. This class does not have to work, but it must find a way to show off its wealth and power. Leisure itself furnishes the evidence that wins esteem. "Conspicuous abstention from labor . . . becomes the conventional mark of superior pecuniary achievement and the conventional index of reputability." Thus the defining feature of upper-class life is "conspicuous leisure"—"a conspicuous exemption from all useful employment." Recognizing "the utility of leisure as a means of gaining the respect of others," the gentleman of leisure avoids "vulgarly productive occupations" and so avoids "the dishonor attaching to productive employments."

Nonproductive dependents add to the repute of the master. "The wife, or chief wife, consumes for him in conspicuous leisure, thereby putting in evidence his ability to sustain large pecuniary damage without impairing his superior opulence." As with the wife, so with servants: "The chief use of servants is the evidence they afford of the master's ability to pay." Under the principle of conspicuous leisure, "there arises a class of servants . . . whose sole office is fatuously to wait upon the person of their owner, and so to put in evidence his ability unproductively to consume a large amount of service."

The honor that attaches to conspicuous leisure is rivaled, Veblen suggests, by the honor that attaches to conspicuous consumption. The gentleman of leisure "consumes freely and of the best, in food, drink, narcotics, shelter, services, ornaments, apparel, weapons and accoutrements, amusements, amulets, and idols or divinities." Since consumption is evidence of wealth, "it becomes honorific; and conversely, the failure to consume in due quantity and quality becomes a mark of inferiority and demerit."

In the case of consumption, as in the case of leisure, the head of the household must overcome obstacles. "As wealth accumulates on his hands, his own unaided effort will not avail to sufficiently put his opulence in evidence." Hence he resorts to "the giving of valuable presents and expensive feasts and entertainments." Hence also "the exhibition of difficult and costly achievements in etiquette."

Consumption by dependents adds greatly to the repute of the master. The wife is required "to consume some goods conspicuously for the reputability of the household and its head." Though in ancient times she was "the drudge and chattel of the man," now the wife has become "the ceremonial consumer of goods which he produces. But she still quite unmistakably remains his chattel in theory." Servants, too, provide evidence of the master's ability to pay. The wearing of liveries and the occupation of spacious servants' quarters are examples of "vicarious consumption" that promote the honor of the master.

What unites conspicuous leisure and conspicuous consumption is "the element of waste that is common to them both." In the case of leisure, it is a waste of time and effort. In the case of consumption, it is a waste of goods. In the effort to gain the esteem that depends on pecuniary prowess, nothing is more effective than "an unremitting demonstration of ability to pay." Benjamin Franklin's advice to ambitious youths—"Waste neither time nor money"—may point the way to wealth, but it ceases to apply once wealth is attained. At that point the rule is reversed. In the game of "pecuniary emulation," victory goes to those who can most visibly and shamelessly afford to waste both time and money.

Ideals of feminine beauty, like ideals of beauty in dress, are shaped by "canons of pecuniary reputability." In the leisure class, women must be "scrupulously exempt from all useful work," so "the waist is attenuated to a degree that implies extreme debility." A delicate physique suggests "that the person so affected is incapable of useful effort and must therefore be supported in idleness by her owner." Even her undergarments declare her status: "The corset is, in economic theory, substantially a mutilation, undergone for the purpose of lowering the subject's vitality and rendering her permanently and obviously unfit for work." The discomfort is justified "by the gain in reputability which comes of her visibly increased expensiveness and infirmity."

Veblen gives his readers both a new vocabulary and a new way of seeing. Reading him is like putting on special eyeglasses. Everything is familiar; everything is strange. Have you ever seen that common phenomenon, "a circuitous drive laid across level ground"? What else can account for it except "the canon of reputable futility," expressing itself "at what is perhaps its widest divergence from the first promptings of the sense of economic beauty." Have you ever heard the ponderous circumlocutions of a leisure-class representative like William F. Buckley, Jr.? What else can account for the showy diction except the fact that elaborate locutions "are cumbrous and out of date, and therefore argue waste of time and exemption from the use and the need of direct and forcible speech"?

Even when he goes farther than we may wish to follow, Veblen displays powers of observation and analysis that make other writers seem tame. "The dog," he writes in a characteristic passage, "has advantages in the way of uselessness as well as in special gifts of temperament. . . . He has the gift of unquestioning subservience and a slave's quickness in guessing his master's mood. . . . He is the filthiest of the domestic animals in his person and the nastiest in his habits. For this he makes up in a servile, fawning attitude towards his master, and a readiness to inflict damage and discomfort on all else. The dog, then, commends himself to our favour by affording play to our propensity to mastery. . . . The dog is at the same time associated in our imagination with the chase—a meritorious employment and an expression of the honourable predatory impulse."

None of the ten books that Veblen published after *The Theory of the Leisure Class* achieved the same renown, but the books contain much that clarifies and extends his critique of the business civilization that surrounded him. The two dominant forces in modern culture, he argued in *The Theory of Business Enterprise* (1904), are business enterprise and the machine process. Business is guided by financiers; the machine process is guided by engineers. But there is a crucial gap between business objectives and industrial objectives: "The pecuniary interests of the business men . . . are not necessarily best served by an unbroken maintenance of the industrial balance."

Veblen draws a sharp distinction between industrial and pecuniary pursuits—between men who make goods and men who make money. Engineers serve the god of efficiency; financiers serve the god of profit. In the clash of these competing divinities, finance generally prevails. The men who make money give orders to the men who make goods.

How is it possible to make money without making goods? It is possible, Veblen explains, through stock market manipulations based on the discrepancy between the actual and the perceived value of an enterprise. The careers of men like Daniel Drew and Jay Gould furnished ample evidence that industrial leaders "will aim to manage the affairs of the concern with a view to an advantageous purchase and sale of its capital rather than with a view to . . . the permanent efficiency of the concern."

In many ways Veblen writes from the perspective of an old-fashioned moralist. His contempt for ostentation, waste, and inefficiency is as complete as any Puritan's. He likes engineers and mechanics; he dislikes bankers. He likes people who do useful work; he dislikes people who live off the labor of others. The right of absentee owners, he complains, is "the right to get something for nothing."

More than anything else, Veblen likes "the instinct of workmanship," with its emphasis on "efficient use of the means at hand" and "serviceability for the ends of life." The instinct of workmanship "disposes men to look with favor upon productive efficiency," and it "disposes them to deprecate waste of substance or effort." What Veblen especially dislikes about the men who run American industry is that they are "remarkably incompetent in the way of anything that can properly be called 'industrial enterprise.' " Other men produce goods and services, but the captain of industry produces nothing. To Veblen, a business consolidator like J. P. Morgan seems "a toad who has reached years of discretion and has found his appointed place along some frequented run where many flies and spiders pass and repass. . . . There is a certain bland sufficiency spread across the face of such a toad so circumstanced, while his comely personal bulk gives assurance of a pyramidal stability of principles."

In his personal life, Veblen conducted himself in a manner so thoroughly and frankly scandalous that intellectual historian Morton White later dubbed him "The Amoral Moralist." Despite his lackluster appearance, Veblen appealed enormously to women, and women appealed to him, even after he married. Unconcealed adulteries contributed to the loss of teaching positions first at the University of Chicago and later at Stanford.

As a teacher, Veblen drove his students wild with his habit of giving everyone a "C" and his mumbled, rambling lectures. One student gives us this glimpse of him: "In a low creaking tone, he began a recital of village economy among the early Germans. Presently he came upon some unjust legal fiction imposed by rising nobles and sanctioned by the clergy. A sardonic smile twisted his lips; blue devils leaped to his eyes. With mordant sarcasm, he dissected the torturous assumption that the wish of the aristocrats is the will of God. He showed similar implications in modern institutions. He chuckled quietly. Then returning to history, he continued the exposition." These displays of droning erudition earned him a reputation as "the last man who knew everything," but they did not persuade students to stay in his classes.

In 1926, three years after he published his last book, Veblen returned to the cabin near Palo Alto where he had lived when he taught at Stanford. For the last three years of his life he lived in a shack on the edge of town, in an isolation that was rarely disturbed except by skunks and wood rats. His distaste for ostentation survived to the end. A neighbor describes him wearing clothes "so coarse they would almost stand alone" and "the heaviest of work-shoes, purchased from Sears, Roebuck." He died at the age of seventy-two on August 3, 1929, leaving instructions that he be cremated "as expeditiously and inexpensively as may be, without ritual or ceremony of any kind."

The most famous attack ever made on Veblen was made in his own lifetime by H. L. Mencken. Both men were, in Veblen's phrase, "disturbers of the intellectual peace," but Mencken felt no affinity with his fellow iconoclast. What seems especially to have offended him was Veblen's style. In an essay published in *Prejudices* in 1919, Mencken lashed out: "Words are flung upon words until all recollection that there must be a meaning in them, a ground and excuse for them, is lost. . . . It is difficult to imagine worse English, within the limits of intelligible grammar. It is clumsy, affected, opaque, bombastic, windy, empty. . . . The learned professor gets himself enmeshed in his gnarled sentences like a bull trapped by barbed wire, and his efforts to extricate himself are quite as furious and quite as spectacular."

In the view of many other readers and writers, Veblen's perceptions were well worth the effort required to penetrate his prose. Literary critic Harry Levin considered him "the Balzac of sociology." Max Lerner called him "America's greatest social scientist." And C. Wright Mills called him "the best critic of America that America has produced." Novelist John Dos Passos captured Veblen's essential quality when he described him as a misfit who "couldn't get his mouth around the essential yes."

Orthodox economists never accepted him, but Veblen never accepted them. Of all the voices that have challenged the American business creed, no voice cuts more keenly than the voice that sounds in Veblen's droll and bitter commentary.

Henry George: The Man Who Raised Hell

Veblen was not the only man of his time who disturbed the peace with his pen. Another eloquent outsider, Henry George, found the extravagances of the age as outrageous as Veblen did, and he launched as fierce an attack upon them, though from a different direction.

Born in Philadelphia in 1839, the second of ten children, George dropped out of school at thirteen and survived a hard youth that included stints as an errand boy, a seaman, and a gold prospector. He had established himself as a journalist and editor in San Francisco when, on a trip to New York City in the winter of 1868–69, he "saw and recognised for the first time the shocking contrast between monstrous wealth and debasing want." That contrast became the subject of the book that made him famous, *Progress and Poverty*, published in 1879.

New York shook George deeply. "In the progress of new settlements to the conditions of older communities," he wrote a decade after his visit, "it may clearly be seen that material progress does not merely fail to relieve poverty; it actually produces it. In the United States it is clear that squalor and misery, and the vices and crimes that spring from them, everywhere increase as the village grows to the city. . . . It is in the older and richer sections of the Union that pauperism and distress among the working classes are becoming more painfully apparent."

But what caused squalor and splendor to exist side by side in a city like New York? George had not known in 1869, but a year later, riding in the hills near San Francisco, he thought he found the answer. The population in the area was growing; a railroad was coming; and speculation had caused the price of land to soar: "Like a flash it came upon me that there was the reason of advancing poverty with advancing wealth. With the growth of population, land grows in value, and the men who work it must pay more for the privilege. I turned back, amidst quiet thought, to the perception that . . . has been with me ever since."

Out of that moment of quiet thought came, nine years later, one of the most fiery books in American literature. No one who read *Progress and Poverty* could doubt where the author stood on the subject of social change: "This association of poverty with progress is the great enigma of our times. . . . So long as all the increased wealth which modern progress brings goes but to build up great fortunes, to increase luxury, and make sharper the contrast between the House of Have and the House of Want, progress is not real and cannot be permanent. The reaction must come. The tower leans from its foundations, and every new story but hastens the final catastrophe."

Powerful rhetoric is not all that George offers his readers. *Progress and Poverty* is a serious work of economic analysis. Though George's conclusions are relatively simple, the arguments that support them are not. Few readers are likely to grasp every step in his reasoning. Many give up in frustration.

The reader who persists will be rewarded. George is not a thinker who never gets down to earth. Indeed, the earth, land, is where his thinking is rooted. In Book V, Chapter 2 of *Progress and Poverty* he presents the core of his thought in a passage anyone can grasp—a passage that depends, moreover, not on sophisticated reasoning but on common sense and everyday experience:

> Take . . . some hard-headed business man, who has no theories, but knows how to make money. Say to him: "Here is a little village; in ten years it will be a great city—in ten years the railroad will have taken the place of the stage coach, the electric light of the candle; it will abound with all the machinery and improvements that so enormously multiply the effective power of labor. Will, in ten years, interest be any higher?"
>
> He will tell you, "No!"
>
> "Will the wages of common labor be any higher; will it be easier for a man who has nothing but his labor to make an independent living?"
>
> He will tell you, "No; the wages of common labor will not be any higher; . . . it will not be easier for the mere laborer to make an independent living. . . ."
>
> "What, then will be higher?"
>
> "Rent; the value of land. Go, get yourself a piece of ground, and hold possession."
>
> And, if, under such circumstances, you take his advice, you need do nothing more. You may sit down and smoke your pipe; you may lie around like the lazzaroni of Naples or the leperos of Mexico; you may go up in a balloon, or down a hole in the ground; and without doing one stroke of work, without adding one iota to the wealth of the community, in ten years you will be rich! In the new city you may build a luxurious mansion; but among its public buildings will be an almshouse.

Here is *Progress and Poverty* in a nutshell. George felt that he had found the key that explains the persistence of poverty amid advancing wealth. The problem was not the conflict between capital and labor, as Karl Marx had suggested. The problem was not the pressure of population, as Thomas Malthus had suggested. The problem was the private ownership of land. "When nonproducers can claim as rent a portion of the wealth created by producers, the right of the producers to the fruits of their labor is to that extent denied. . . . The one receives without producing; the others produce without receiving."

The solution is clear: Abolish the private ownership of land. But would that solution be just? Yes, George says. "The equal right of all men to the use of land is as clear as their equal right to breathe the air—it is a right proclaimed by the fact of their existence. . . . If we are all here by the equal permission of the Creator, we are all here with an equal title to the enjoyment of his bounty—with an equal right to the use of all that nature so impartially offers."

Moreover, George argues, the private ownership of land can be abolished without "a needless shock," through taxation: "I do not propose either to purchase or to confiscate private property in land. . . . Let the individuals who now hold it still retain, if they want to, the possession of what they are pleased to call *their* land. Let them continue to call it *their* land. Let them buy and sell, and bequeath and devise it. We may safely leave them the shell, if we take the kernel. *It is not necessary to confiscate land; it is only necessary to confiscate rent.*"

A full tax on the value of land would make other taxes unnecessary, George argues, because a tax on land would suffice "to bear the entire expenses of government." George proposes to abolish all taxes that check production—"All taxes upon manufactures, all taxes upon commerce, all taxes upon capital, all taxes upon improvements." He would depend entirely on a single tax—a tax on unimproved land. His system would reward the landowner who has worked to improve his property, but it would not reward the speculator: "If land were taxed to anything near its rental value, no one could afford to hold land that he was not using."

Progress and Poverty was a tremendous popular success, and Henry George ran a strong second as the candidate of the Labor Party in the New York City mayoral race of 1886, finishing well ahead of the Republican nominee, a twenty-eight-year-old dynamo named Theodore Roosevelt. In the years that followed, George lectured frequently in England and Ireland, and he made a long trip to Australia that laid the groundwork for later experiments with land use taxation there. Despite ill health, he campaigned again for mayor of New York in 1897, but died of a stroke on October 29 of that year, shortly after a speech at the Central

Opera House. More than one hundred thousand persons passed before his bier in Grand Central Palace, where he lay in state.

As an economic thinker, George has been underestimated, in large part because he overestimated the benefits likely to result from the single tax. Gush rarely persuades, and George could gush. Yet it is wrong to dismiss him as a crackpot. In his *History of Economic Analysis*, the great twentieth-century economist Joseph A. Schumpeter offers this respectful judgment:

> He was a self-taught economist, but he *was* an economist. In the course of his life, he acquired most of the knowledge . . . that he could have acquired by academic training, as it then was. In this he differed to his advantage from most men who proffered panaceas. Barring his panacea (The Single Tax) and the phraseology connected with it, he was a very orthodox economist and extremely conservative as to methods. . . . Even the panacea—nationalisation not of land but of the rent of land by a confiscatory tax—benefited by his competence as an economist, for he was careful to frame his "remedy" in such a manner as to cause the minimum injury to the efficiency of the private-enterprise economy.

The treatment of George in the most influential economics textbook of the twentieth century, the textbook of Nobel Prize–winner Paul A. Samuelson, is also respectful, though brief. It is not likely, write Samuelson and his coauthor, Yale professor William D. Nordhaus, that anyone will soon "write so persuasive a bible" for the single-tax movement as *Progress and Poverty*. The idea of a single tax has "merits and demerits," but the "central tenet" of George's theory is true: "Pure land rent is in the nature of a 'surplus' that can be taxed heavily without distorting production incentives or impairing productive efficiency."

George's theory of poverty does not have many defenders among twentieth-century economists. George thought that under a system of private ownership, land rent would absorb an increasing share of the national income, while wages would fall to the subsistence level. In fact, rent as a share of national income has decreased in the twentieth century. This decline has led many economists to conclude that George's program could not possibly bring all the blessings he had promised.

Moreover, George's belief that a single tax could support the entire cost of government was based on the assumption that government would continue to play a very limited role in national life. George did not foresee either the welfare or the warfare programs of the twentieth century, and it is not likely that he would have believed that a single tax could pay for them.

This caveat does not invalidate the idea of a land value tax as one tax among many. Experiments that owe much to George have taken place in Australia, New Zealand, the city of Pittsburgh, and elsewhere. Economists often recommend "a dose of Henry George" for underdeveloped countries in need of land reform. In the opinion of economic historian Steven Cord, George's views on land value taxation are what give him special relevance today. Take away those views, and George "becomes just one of many agitators of America's social conscience, to be classed with Edward Bellamy and Henry Demarest Lloyd."

Though he was certainly an agitator, George was not a socialist. He considered Karl Marx "the prince of muddleheads," and he rejected socialism because it required "the substitution of government direction for the play of individual action, and the attempt to secure by restriction what can better be secured by freedom." It is evident, he went on in a passage that clearly shows why socialists find it difficult to embrace him, "that whatever savors of regulation and restriction is in itself bad," and if elaborate schemes of regulation were carried out, "we should have a state of society resembling that of ancient Peru," without any means of achieving "an intelligent award of duties and earnings."

Here, as in several other respects, George transcends the conventional opposition of liberal and conservative. He opposed a graduated income tax on the ground that it "involves the employment of a large number of officials clothed with inquisitorial powers" and on the ground that "in proportion as the tax accomplishes its effect," it also accomplishes "a lessening in the incentive to the accumulation of wealth." Moreover, his single-tax philosophy could be interpreted as a way of setting a limit on government spending. During the New Deal, Steven Cord points out, many followers of George "were forced to take an increasingly right of center position because they could not countenance the taxation required to finance a welfare state."

In the end, however, any effort to argue that George was essentially a conservative breaks on the rock of his indignation. His moral passion is what is most memorable about him. At a time when social Darwinists like Herbert Spencer opposed all aid to the poor and the disabled on the ground that "The whole effort of nature is to get rid of such, to clear the world of them, and make room for better," George wrote that Spencer was "like one who might insist that each should swim for himself in crossing a river, ignoring the fact that some had been artificially provided with corks and others artificially loaded with lead." At a time when inventions like Alexander Graham Bell's telephone and Thomas Alva Edison's electric light appeared to promise a transformation of daily life,

George wrote, "The march of invention has clothed mankind with powers of which a century ago the boldest imagination could not have dreamed. But . . . wherever the new forces are anything like fully utilized, large classes are maintained by charity or live on the verge of recourse to it; amid the greatest accumulations of wealth, men die of starvation and puny infants suckle dry breasts. . . . The promised land flies before us like the mirage. The fruits of the tree of knowledge turn, as we grasp them, to apples of Sodom that crumble at the touch."

The religious imagery came naturally to George. He was a radical, but not a godless one. Indeed, his radicalism draws much of its energy from the conviction that God did not intend mankind to be miserable: "If an architect were to build a theater so that not more than one-tenth of the audience could see and hear, we would call him a bungler and a botch. . . . Yet so accustomed are we to poverty that even the preachers of what passes for Christianity tell us that the great Architect of the universe . . . has made such a botch job of this world that the vast majority of the human creatures whom He had called into it are condemned by the conditions He has imposed to want, suffering, and brutalizing toil."

It is impossible to imagine Thorstein Veblen making a statement like that. Veblen was a man of anger and spleen; George was a man of anger and love. Yet there was steel in him—a fighting spirit that made him a man of action as well as a man of ideas. When he was considering whether to run for mayor of New York in 1886, representatives of Tammany Hall tried to talk him out of it on the ground that "you cannot be elected, but your running will raise hell." George replied: "You have relieved me of embarrassment. I do not want the responsibility and the work of the office of the Mayor of New York, but I do want to raise hell!"

George lost the election, but he succeeded in his second objective. Perhaps the most telling tribute to George, moreover, was made by Tammany boss Richard Croker, in response to charges that fraud at the polls had robbed George of victory. "Of course," Croker said, Tammany's leaders "could not allow a man like Henry George to be Mayor of New York. It would upset all their arrangements."

Aristocrats of Intellect: The Adams Brothers

Veblen and George were outsiders—men who seem to have been born to challenge the status quo. But outsiders were not the only people who worried about the dominance of business values late in the nineteenth century. America did not have the equivalent of Europe's aristocracies, but it did have an aristocracy of intellect, and the members of that aristocracy felt increasingly alienated in a nation that seemed to have little use for their talents. Two eminent families, the Adams and James families, provide striking examples.

Henry Adams, great-grandson of John Adams and grandson of John Quincy Adams, is, as the Jews whom he hated might have said, the great *kvetcher* of American literature. To be an Adams in the United States in the second half of the nineteenth century was a destiny he could barely abide. Writing about himself in the third person in *The Education of Henry Adams*, he could not repress his resentment: "Not a Polish Jew fresh from Warsaw or Cracow—not a furtive Yacoob or Ysaac still reeking of the Ghetto, snarling a weird Yiddish to the officers of the customs—but had a keener instinct, an intenser energy, and a freer hand than he—American of Americans, with Heaven knew how many Puritans and Patriots behind him."

Adams was not merely a descendant of presidents and the son of Charles Francis Adams, Lincoln's ambassador to Great Britain during the Civil War. His mother, Abigail Brown Brooks, was the youngest daughter of Peter Chardon Brooks, a Massachusetts businessman who made a fortune in shipping ventures, insurance, and banking. At his death in 1849, Brooks left an estate of $2.5 million, which is said to have made him the richest man in New England.

Inherited wealth can be a blessing and a curse. An Adams of Henry's generation could not rise from rags to riches, could not be self-made. Worse, an Adams could not compete—not against men like Cornelius Vanderbilt or Jay Gould in business, nor against the kind of men who dominated the nation's political life in the greedy years after the Civil War.

In business and in politics, Adams felt, his ideals made him unfit—an anachronism. A brilliant article published in the *Westminster Review* in 1870, when he was only thirty-two, shows clearly how little Adams respected America's best-known businessmen. The subject of the article was "The New York Gold Conspiracy," the effort of Jim Fisk and Jay Gould to corner the gold market in 1869. Cornelius Vanderbilt, Adams writes, "at least acted in the interests of his corporations," whereas Daniel Drew "cheated equally his corporation and the public." Jay Gould "seemed never to be satisfied except when deceiving every one as to his intentions. . . . He spun huge webs, in corners and in the dark." Jim

Fisk "was coarse, noisy, boastful, ignorant; the type of a young butcher in appearance and mind."

But the differences among the actors in his drama mattered less to the young Brahmin than the one point that united them: "In speaking of this class of men it must be fairly assumed at the outset that they do not and cannot understand how there can be a distinction between right and wrong in matters of speculation."

America, Adams felt, had no place for him. Whereas his ancestors had made history, he could only watch it being made. Yet it is hard to feel sorry for him. His disdain for business is the disdain of a man who believed that no position below the presidency suited him. Even the presidency was not a prize he would run for. In the words of his friend Oliver Wendell Holmes, Jr., "He wanted it handed to him on a silver plate."

In *The Education of Henry Adams*, privately printed for one hundred friends in 1907, Adams tells the story of his life—a story, as D. W. Brogan has remarked, that might have been subtitled *The Unimportance of Being an Adams*. Failure is the theme—the failure of an education that did not prepare Adams for life in a nation dominated by business and industry. "He was not fit," old Henry says flatly of young Henry, and he never tires of that note: "Thus, at the outset, he was condemned to failure more or less complete in the life awaiting him. . . . Thus, before he was fifteen years old, he had managed to get himself into a state of moral confusion from which he never escaped." The tone differs sharply from the good-humored, easygoing tone of Benjamin Franklin's autobiography. His story, Adams says, is a story of "misdirected energy and lost opportunity"—the story of "a total misconception of life." He writes about his deficiencies with fierce irony, yet the irony he directs against himself often seems intended to demonstrate his superiority. Only a superior intellect could sustain the prose that Adams sustains for five hundred pages. Thus, even though Adams talks much about failure, the unstated point often seems to be that he was too good to succeed—too good for a tawdry world.

Like Veblen, Adams sees clearly that technology—the Dynamo—has transformed America. Unlike Veblen, he profoundly distrusts the transformation. Veblen's faith in the efficiency of engineers and the rationality of the machine process finds no echo in Adams. Technology—the railroad, the steamship, the telegraph—tore Adams's world apart and tossed him on the wrong side of the divide. He even tells us the exact month when it happened. In 1844, he writes, "the old universe was thrown into the ash-heap and a new one created. He and his eighteenth-century, troglodytic Boston were suddenly cut apart—separated forever— . . . by the opening of the Boston and Albany Railroad; the appearance of the first Cunard steamers in the bay; and the telegraphic messages which carried from Baltimore to Washington the news that Henry Clay and James K. Polk were nominated for the Presidency. This was in May, 1844; he was six years old."

This passage early in *The Education* sets the stage for the famous chapter near the end, titled "The Dynamo and the Virgin." At the Great Exposition of 1900 in Paris, Adams visited "the great hall of dynamos" and pondered the force that now dominated Western civilization: "As he grew accustomed to the great gallery of machines, he began to feel the forty-foot dynamos as a moral force, much as the early Christians felt the Cross. . . . Before the end, one began to pray to it."

Adams was stunned. "After ten years' pursuit, he found himself lying in the Gallery of Machines at the Great Exposition of 1900, his historical neck broken by the sudden irruption of forces totally new." His own education, Adams realized, had prepared him for a world driven by a different force, a force that was not mechanical, the force of the fertile Virgin: "She was the animated dynamo; she was reproduction—the greatest and most mysterious of all energies; all she needed was to be fecund."

In the clash between the old world and the new, nature and the machine, the Virgin and the Dynamo, Adams could not help preferring the former: "On one side, at the Louvre and at Chartres . . . was the highest energy ever known to man, the creator of four-fifths of his noblest art. . . . All the steam in the world could not, like the Virgin, build Chartres."

What could the Dynamo build? As his steamship carried him into New York Harbor in 1904, Adams tells us, he found the approach striking—"unlike anything man had ever seen—and like nothing he had ever much cared to see." New York was the newest of the world's great cities, the flagship city of the United States, the city of money and the machine:

> The city had the air and movement of hysteria, and the citizens were crying, in every accent of anger and alarm, that the new forces must at any cost be brought under control. Prosperity never before imagined, power never yet wielded by man, speed never reached by anything but a meteor, had made the world irritable, nervous, querulous, unreasonable and afraid. . . . Everyone saw it, and every municipal election shrieked chaos. A traveller in the highways of history looked out of the club window on the

turmoil of Fifth Avenue, and felt himself in Rome, under Diocletian, wit-
nessing the anarchy, conscious of the compulsion, eager for the solution,
but unable to conceive whence the next impulse was to come or how it
was to act. The two-thousand-years failure of Christianity roared upward
from Broadway, and no Constantine the Great was in sight.

America's trusts, however, were very much in sight. Adams was not
certain whether they controlled the Dynamo or the Dynamo controlled
them, but that uncertainty did not affect his judgment of them: "The
Trusts and Corporations stood for the larger part of the new power that
had been created since 1840, and were obnoxious because of their vigorous and unscrupulous energy. They were revolutionary, troubling all
the old conventions and values, as the screws of ocean steamers must
trouble a school of herring. They tore society to pieces and trampled it
under foot."

For years Adams had worried that the trusts might corrupt politics
and dominate the state. "We know," he had written, "what aristocracy,
autocracy, democracy are, but we have no word to express government
by moneyed corporations." Now Adams watched with interest as Theodore Roosevelt tried to tame the trusts. Adams approved the effort, but
he was not optimistic about the outcome. He suspected that "the law of
mass" was on the side of the trusts.

If he were allowed to return to earth on his one hundredth birthday
in 1938, Adams wrote in the last paragraph of his autobiography, he
doubted that he would find "a world that sensitive and timid natures
could regard without a shudder." One of his most famous witticisms was
a remark that might have been made by Veblen: The United States,
Adams said, was the first nation in history to go from barbarism to dec-
adence without passing through an intermediate stage of civilization. It
is a patrician wisecrack—the wisecrack of a man who could see the corruption of Rome when he looked at Broadway. *Mont-Saint-Michel and
Chartres*, the masterpiece he published in 1904, established Adams as a
man whose judgment of a culture mattered. He died in 1918, after a war
that did much to demolish the remnants of the civilization he cherished.

Charles Francis Adams, Jr., Henry's older brother, was less formidable an intellectual, but much more intimately involved with business.
Born in 1835, the same year as Mark Twain and Andrew Carnegie, Charles
became first an expert on railroads, then a regulator of railroads, and
finally the president of the Union Pacific Railroad. Of the four Adams
brothers in his generation, business historian Thomas McCraw asserts,

"it was Charles who made the most interesting attempt to weave the Adams tradition of public service into the harsh realities of the Gilded Age."

As a young man, Charles tells us in his autobiography, published posthumously in 1916, he "fixed on the railroad system as the most developing force and largest field of the day, and determined to attach myself to it." To break into the field, he used the one weapon every Adams commanded: the pen. In a series of masterful articles published in the *North American Review*, he demonstrated a grasp of the economics of railroading that none of his contemporaries came close to matching. An article titled "A Chapter of Erie," a dazzling account of the battle for control of the Erie Railroad that raged among Daniel Drew, Jay Gould, Jim Fisk, and Cornelius Vanderbilt in 1867, was one of the first and most brilliant examples of the genre later known as "muckraking."

But Adams was not satisfied to observe and chronicle. He wanted an active role, and his articles were shots in a campaign to win a role for himself. In 1869, at the age of thirty-four, Adams was appointed to the new Massachusetts Board of Railroad Commissioners. There, as head of the railroad commission from 1872 to 1879, Adams virtually invented what is now called the "sunshine" approach to regulation. In the opinion of Thomas McCraw, the foremost contemporary authority on the subject, Adams was one of the most effective business regulators in American history—"the first modern regulator, and one of the best ever to serve on a state commission."

To regulate a business was not the same thing as to run one, however. Having left the Massachusetts board in 1879, Adams became president of the Union Pacific Railroad in 1884, only to be forced out in 1890 by one of the men he had flayed in "A Chapter of Erie," Jay Gould. As a business executive, Adams admitted later, he "just didn't do it. The last little thing was wanting."

He took his revenge with his pen. He wrote in his autobiography:

I have known, and known tolerably well, a good many "successful" men—"big" financially—men famous during the last half-century; and a less interesting crowd I do not care to encounter. Not one that I have ever known would I care to meet again, either in this world or the next; nor is one of them associated in my mind with the idea of humor, thought, or refinement. A set of mere money-getters and traders, they were essentially unattractive and uninteresting.

They may have been unattractive and uninteresting, but the money-getters had driven Adams out of the business world, back to the life of a literary gentleman. Of the Gilded Age, he wrote: "Failure seems to be regarded as the one unpardonable crime, success as the all-redeeming virtue, the acquisition of wealth as the single worthy aim in life." An Adams could not accept so simple a measure. Yet failure rankled: "In railroads I was the typical college man,—my success would have been the success of my class, my failure is now regarded as the failure of my class. . . . Today so far as the management of railroads is concerned, I am the most discredited man in America, and my class is discredited through me, and that hurts."

Aristocrats of Intellect: The James Brothers

On July 24, 1832, a sixty-year-old businessman in Albany, New York, drew up an explosive will. The businessman was named William James, but historians call him William of Albany, to distinguish him from the elder of his two famous grandsons.

As the commercial success of Peter Brooks helped set the stage for the noncommercial achievements of his descendants, so the success of William of Albany set the stage for the dazzling literary and intellectual triumphs that followed in his family. Beyond that, the story of the James family vividly illustrates the range of attitudes toward business that often results from shifting family fortunes in America.

William was born in Ireland in 1771, the second son of a Scotch-Irish farmer who wanted him to become a minister. He resisted, choosing instead to seek his fortune in the United States, where he became a successful merchant and an early advocate of the plan to build a canal that would link the Hudson River to Lake Erie. After the canal opened, the value of William's property soared. When cholera broke out in Albany in 1832, and William sat down to think about his will, he had much to think about: eleven children, his wife, and an estate worth $3 million.

Two of his sons especially troubled him. One, named William, had rejected a career in business, become a minister, and deliberately settled far from Albany. Another, Henry (the eventual father of the famous William and Henry), had firmly resisted his father's efforts to push him into a career as a lawyer. Not only had he resisted, but at one point, after lavishing $100 on "segars and oysters and cloth from taylors," he had run off from Union College in Schenectady, leaving his father to complain that the young man had "so debased himself as to leave his parents' house in the character of a swindler." Henry himself later admitted that in this period he "scarcely ever went to bed sober, and lost my self-respect almost utterly."

In his will, as Howard M. Feinstein has pointed out in *Becoming William James*, William of Albany "was torn between a desire to protect his capital from his heirs and the wish to protect his heirs from the evils of capital." Aside from a few minor bequests, he instructed that his estate was to be held in trust for twenty-one years—the legal limit.

By placing the estate in trust, William sought to achieve the control over his children (especially the defiant Henry) that had eluded him in life. His aim, William reminded the trustees, was "to discourage prodigality and vice, and to furnish an incentive to economy and usefulness." The trustees were authorized to provide funds to prepare his sons for "any reputable profession or trade," and they were authorized to cut off any heir who led a "grossly immoral, idle or dishonorable life."

In short, the idleness and extravagance that tempted Henry would not be tolerated. Henry was left an annuity of $1,250, but not a cent more unless he straightened out.

William of Albany died (of a stroke, not cholera) in December 1832. His widow, to whom he had left the house in Albany and an annuity of $3,000 to care for herself and six minor children, sued for more and won. Young Henry also sued. A preliminary victory in 1837 enabled him to drop out of Princeton Theological Seminary and to indulge his desire for a trip to Europe. A larger victory in 1843 allowed him to take his wife and two infant sons to Europe for two years. As his father had feared, he never embraced a trade or profession. A nervous breakdown in 1844 was followed by a conversion to the philosophy of Swedish mystic Emanuel Swedenborg. With the help of his share of what his novelist son later described as "the admirable three millions," he lived as purely spiritual a life as money can buy and wrote books with titles such as *The Secret of Swedenborg, Christianity the Logic of Creation*, and *Society the Redeemed Form of Man*.

The attitude of the elder Henry toward men like his self-made father was not generous. "A man of very large possessions," he wrote, "unless he has come into them by inheritance, is almost wholly absorbed by them. Instead of being rendered free and careless, his life is a perpetual servitude. His whole energy becomes demanded by the care of his property, while he himself gradually lapses from unqualified manhood into the mere man of money. . . . As a general thing therefore we may say, the larger the possessions the smaller the man." Note the self-exemption implicit in the qualifying phrase: "unless he has come into them by inheritance."

He was determined, Henry told a friend at the age of forty-one, "to take holiday for the rest of my life, and make all my work sabbatical." His tone was not always so lighthearted, however. Sometimes he sounded remarkably like his father: "Everyone respects labor; everyone respects the man who does something more to vindicate his human quality, than just live upon his ancestral fat." When these words were written, Henry was still living on the legacy from his father.

The aversion to business persisted in the next generation. But whereas Henry, Sr., had indulged, as he himself conceded, in "a life-long career of luxury and self-indulgence," his children did not have that option. The ancestral fat was running out.

Thus we have the spectacle of young William, the future philosopher, desperately trying to balance his accounts in his sophomore year at Harvard: "Theoretically in hand fifty-four cents, actually in hand eight-two [sic] cents. Gained somehow twenty-eight cents. Hallelujah!"

Two years later, in a letter to his cousin Katharine, William revealed that he was considering a career in medicine, but not because the work inspired him. "After all," he wrote, "the great problem of life seems to be how to keep body and soul together, and I *have* to consider lucre."

Earlier, William had hoped to be a painter. In 1866, as he neared the end of his medical studies, he felt no joy at the thought of the work that awaited him. He would earn his living, he wrote to a friend, by plying "the physicking trade like any other tenth-rate man." Instead of practicing medicine, William got sick—so sick that his father gave him money to go to Europe for eighteen months. It was the sickness, Feinstein argues, of a "young man frantically running from inauthentic labor and premature responsibility."

After much anguish, William found a career he could embrace, in psychology and philosophy. Commerce was beneath him, of course, as it had been beneath his father. In 1906, in a letter to H. G. Wells, this grandson of a self-made millionaire made his most famous comment on the role of business in American life (a comment that is often quoted, but almost never in its entirety): "The moral flabbiness born of the exclusive worship of the bitch-goddess SUCCESS. That—with the squalid cash interpretation put on the word success—is our national disease."

William's brother Henry was no more attracted to the world of business than his brother or father. In *The American*, published in 1877, when he was thirty-four, Henry took as his central character an American businessman in his thirties who has made his fortune and who now seeks, in Europe, a different kind of fortune:

> Throughout these rather formless meditations he sometimes thought of his past life and the long array of years . . . during which he had had nothing in his head but "enterprise." . . . It struck him that if he had never done anything very ugly, he had never, on the other hand, done anything particularly beautiful. He had spent his years in the unremitting effort to add thousands to thousands, and now that he stood well outside of it, the business of money-getting appeared extremely dry and sterile. . . . It had come back to him simply that what he had been looking at all the summer was a very rich and beautiful world, and that it had not all been made by sharp railroad men and stock-brokers.

The American throws some light on Henry's decision to live most of his life in Europe. "I cared for money-making," his businessman hero Christopher Newman says, "but I never cared particularly for the money. There was nothing else to do, and it was impossible to be idle." A country that offered nothing to do except make money was not a country that could inspire Henry. Not money as an end, but money as a means, fascinated him. He saw money as the base that made life and adventure possible: "Upon the uses of money, upon what one might do with a life into which one had succeeded in injecting the golden stream, [Newman] had up to his thirty-fifth year, very scantily reflected."

Nearly eighty years after its publication, poet John Berryman thought that *The American* remained "the most important American novel yet written about a businessman." Henry James wrote many novels and stories in which money figures as an essential fact, but none that show much interest in business. Business seemed to Henry, as to Christopher Newman, "extremely dry and sterile." In *A Small Boy and Others*, a volume of autobiography published near the end of his life, Henry reflected on the history of his family in the decades that followed his father's rejection of a worldly career. "The rupture with my grandfather's tradition and attitude was complete; we were never in a single case, I think, for two generations, guilty of a stroke of business."

But Henry's memory was not quite accurate. His younger brother Robertson had failed not only in business but also in farming, journalism, painting, and poetry. Robertson did not share the contempt of his brilliant brothers for commerce. "I wish," he wrote at the age of fifty-two, looking back on a life of complete frustration, "our own father had steered his sons into the soap or Baking Powder line."

Unions

Another kind of dissent was heard in the years when Henry Adams, Henry James, and William James were making their reputations. This was the dissent of labor. Trade unions existed in the United States before the Civil War, but labor did not organize on a grand scale until capital organized on a grand scale, in the giant enterprises that transformed the economic landscape after 1865.

The first national labor organization in the United States was the Noble Order of the Knights of Labor, which began as a union of Philadelphia garment workers in 1869. The Knights became a national organization in 1878, with its membership rising from nine thousand in 1879 to 104,000 in 1885. The next year, after a strike won concessions from three railroads controlled by Jay Gould, membership soared to 703,000.

In the years that followed, the Knights declined swiftly. The organization was unjustly accused of being involved in the Haymarket Affair, in which a bomb killed seven police officers breaking up a labor rally at Haymarket Square, Chicago, on May 4, 1886. The organization also was weakened by the fact that it attempted to unite both skilled and unskilled workers and by the fact that its leadership was generally opposed to strikes and boycotts.

Unlike the Knights, the American Federation of Labor did not welcome unskilled workers. Founded in 1886, the AFL was a federation of trade unions that focused entirely on the interests of skilled labor. Under the leadership of Samuel Gompers, a cigarmaker who had been born in London in 1850 and whose family had immigrated to the United States in 1863, the membership of the AFL rose steadily, from 138,000 in 1886 to 225,000 in 1890, 548,000 in 1900, 1,562,000 in 1910, and 4,078,000 in 1920.

Gompers was a pragmatist who distrusted radical theories and focused on concrete issues involving wages, hours, and working conditions. While others sought "a perfect millennium," Gompers said, he was content "to fight the battles of today." While others hungered for "a world cataclysm," Gompers argued that "25 cents a day . . . brings us nearer the time when a greater degree of justice and fair dealing will obtain among men." He exercised enormous influence, serving as president of the AFL every year but one from 1886 until his death in 1924.

Little was given to labor merely because it asked. Two of the most famous strikes in American history occurred in the 1890s. One was the strike of the Amalgamated Association of Iron and Steel Workers at Andrew Carnegie's huge ironworks in Homestead, Pennsylvania, in 1892. The second was the strike of the American Railway Union against the Pullman Palace Car Company in 1894. Both strikes were crushed.

Andrew Carnegie was in England when the union contract at Homestead expired in 1892. In his absence, the negotiations were handled by the company's general manager, Henry Clay Frick. When the union refused to accept lower pay, Frick cut off negotiations and shut down the plant. He then sent two barges carrying three hundred Pinkerton agents, armed with Winchester rifles, up the Monongahela River toward Homestead. At four in the morning on July 6, 1892, strikers fired upon the barges. In the tumultuous battle that followed, half a dozen men on both sides were killed.

Six days later, eight thousand members of the Pennsylvania state militia, mobilized by the governor of Pennsylvania at Frick's request, put Homestead under martial law. Under the protection of the troops, Carnegie's company reopened the plant with nonunion workers. Enraged, a Russian-born anarchist named Alexander Berkman tried to assassinate Frick in his office in Pittsburgh on July 23. Frick was badly wounded, but survived. Berkman was sentenced to twenty-one years in jail, served thirteen years, and later was deported to the Soviet Union, along with the anarchist colleague who had helped him plan the attack on Frick, Emma Goldman. America's steelworkers were not successfully organized until the 1930s.

Employees of the Pullman Palace Car Company were required to live in the company town, Pullman, Illinois; to rent their homes and apartments from the company at prices that often ran some 25 percent higher than prices in nearby communities; to buy water and gas from the company; to subscribe to the company rental library; and to buy supplies from the company store. When a committee of employees presented a list of grievances in May 1894, the company promptly fired three members of the committee, thus precipitating what the *New York Tribune* would soon describe as "the greatest battle between labor and capital that has ever been inaugurated in the United States."

By July, the American Railway Union had ordered a boycott that affected not only the Pullman Company but also any railroad using Pullman cars. Railroad traffic in and out of Chicago was all but paralyzed. The General Managers' Association, a group of executives representing twenty-four railroads, secretly imported strikebreakers from Canada and ordered them to attach mail cars to Pullman cars so that the strikers could be accused of interfering with the mails. When violence broke out, President Grover Cleveland sent four companies of the 15th Infantry to Chicago to safeguard the mails, despite the vigorous objections of Illinois Governor John Peter Altgeld. The final blow against the strike was a federal injunction that, in effect, threw the whole force of the court against the strikers, again on the ground that the strike obstructed the mails. (The use of injunctions to break strikes remained a matter of bitter controversy until 1932, when Congress passed the Norris-La Guardia Act, prohibiting federal courts from intervening in labor disputes except in cases that threatened the national security.)

After the Pullman strike the head of the American Railway Union, Eugene V. Debs, wound up in jail for six months on charges that he had violated the court's injunction. Debs went on to have a remarkable career. After campaigning for William Jennings Bryan in 1896, Debs announced in 1897 that he had become a Socialist, and in 1898 he helped found the Socialist Party of America. He was its candidate for president in 1900, 1904, 1908, 1912, and 1920.

To hear Debs, one admirer later wrote, "was to listen to a hammer riveting a chamber in Hell for the oppressors of the poor." His persistence had some effect. In the election of 1920 Debs won nearly 920,000 votes, the most ever by a Socialist candidate, even though he ran while in jail for criticizing government prosecutions under the 1917 Espionage Act. In the same election the Republican and Democratic candidates combined to win over twenty-five million votes. Even at the peak of its popularity, socialism was not a doctrine that appealed to more than 4 or 5 percent of the American electorate.

The Industrial Workers of the World (IWW), known as the "Wobblies," was organized in 1905 by the most radical elements in the labor movement, including Communists, Socialists, militant western miners, and supporters of industrial unionism who deplored the indifference of the AFL to the interests of unskilled workers. The aim of the IWW was the abolition of the wage system and the overthrow of capitalism. "Instead of the conservative motto, 'A fair day's wage for a fair day's work,'" the Wobblies declared, "we must inscribe on our banner the revolutionary watchword, 'Abolition of the wage system.' It is the historic mission of the working class to do away with capitalism."

The most prominent leaders of the IWW were Daniel De Leon, the head of the Socialist Labor Party, and William D. Haywood, known as "Big Bill," the head of the Western Federation of Miners. Both men scorned the AFL. De Leon denounced Gompers as a "labor faker," an "entrapped swindler," and a "greasy tool of Wall Street," while Haywood proclaimed himself a friend of the "bums" and "red-blooded working stiffs" the AFL had forgotten: "We are going down in the gutter," he declared, "to get at the mass of workers and bring them up to a decent plane of living." Gompers replied that the IWW's dream of "one big union" was "fallacious, injurious, reactionary."

During World War I the IWW enraged the public by supporting strikes by metal miners at Butte, Montana, and lumber workers in the Northwest and by declaring that "We, as members of the industrial army, will refuse to fight for any purpose except for the realization of industrial freedom." At a trial in Chicago in 1918, Haywood and ninety-four others were prosecuted under the Sedition and Espionage acts. After his conviction, Haywood jumped bail and fled to the Soviet Union, where he died in 1928. By that time the IWW, or what was left of it, had ceased to be a significant force in the United States.

Even at its peak, before it took its stand against the war, the IWW never had more than sixty thousand to seventy thousand members. By comparison, membership in the AFL rose from 1.5 million in 1910 to almost 4.1 million in 1920. "The overwhelming bulk of American workingmen," writes labor historian Foster Rhea Dulles, "remained . . . fundamentally opposed to I.W.W. philosophy. . . . American labor could not be convinced that the historic role of the working class was to do away with capitalism." Though Debs and Haywood lived more dramatic lives, it was Samuel Gompers who grasped the key point: American workers wanted to join the middle class, not destroy it.

The Muckrakers

While workers in the late nineteenth and early twentieth centuries often fought with fists and guns, the journalists who called themselves "muckrakers" fought with their pens. The muckrakers themselves dispute who wrote the first muckraking article. Lincoln Steffens claimed the honor for his "Tweed Days in St. Louis," which appeared in *McClure's Magazine* in October 1902. Ray Stannard Baker pointed to two articles of his that appeared in November 1901. Mark Sullivan declared that "Actually the first article of political muckraking was the one I wrote, 'The Ills of Pennsylvania,' for the *Atlantic Monthly* . . . in October 1901."

In fact, isolated examples of muckraking (here defined as the literature of exposure) appeared before any of these. In addition to Charles Francis Adams, Jr.'s, "A Chapter of Erie" and "An Erie Raid" and Henry Adams's "The New York Gold Conspiracy," which appeared in 1869–71, there was the work of Henry Demarest Lloyd, especially his "Story of a Great Monopoly," an exposé of Standard Oil published in the *Atlantic Monthly* in 1881, and *Wealth Against Commonwealth*, a more sweeping attack on Standard Oil published in 1894.

Lloyd was eloquent but not always reliable. "As a polemic for the times," historian Allan Nevins writes, *Wealth Against Commonwealth* "was magnificent; as a piece of industrial history . . . it was almost utterly worthless." Yet Lloyd's assault had enormous influence. One reviewer called *Wealth Against Commonwealth* "the most powerful book on economics" since *Progress and Poverty*, and novelist William Dean Howells pronounced the book "Astounding, infuriating!" More than any other work, Nevins says, *Wealth Against Commonwealth* "fixed upon the public mind of America that stereotype of Rockefeller and the Standard Oil [Company] as indescribably cruel, greedy, and wicked. . . . It created a stage Rockefeller as unreal as the stage Irishman or stage Jew or stage Mark Hanna."

What was new about about muckraking in the early 1900s, in the view of historian Richard Hofstadter, was its reach—"its nationwide character and its capacity to draw nationwide attention." The era of the cheap, mass-market magazine began when S. S. McClure founded *McClure's Magazine* in 1893. At a time when most magazines sold for a quarter or more, McClure took advantage of cheaper paper made from wood pulp and of the introduction of inexpensive photoengraving techniques to offer his magazine first for fifteen cents and later for a dime. Prices that low could yield a profit only if circulation was large. "Neither the muckraking publishers and editors nor the muckraking reporters set out to expose evils or to reform society," Hofstadter writes. ". . . Muckraking was a by-product, perhaps an inevitable one, of the development of mass magazines. Even *McClure's*, the magazine that touched off the movement, had already built a large circulation upon an enterprising use of popular fiction and upon Ida Tarbell's series on the lives of Napoleon and Lincoln."

Muckraking as a movement is usually said to have begun in 1902. The first recognition of it was an editorial in *McClure's Magazine* in January 1903. As the editors prepared the issue, they noticed that it contained three exposés: Lincoln Steffens's "The Shame of Minneapolis"; the second installment in Ida Tarbell's series on Standard Oil; and Ray Stannard Baker's article on the strike of anthracite coal miners in 1902, "The Right to Work." The editors promptly wrote an editorial pointing out that all three articles might have been titled "The American Contempt for Law." The picture of the American character that emerged in the three articles was not pretty: "Capitalists, workingmen, politicians, citizens—all breaking the law, or letting it be broken. Who is left to uphold it?"

For journalists in search of secrets to expose, business was a natural object of scrutiny. Since the Civil War, nothing in American life had changed more dramatically than the scale of business; no men had made themselves felt more powerfully than Rockefeller, Carnegie, and Morgan; no institutions were more visible than the new leviathans like Standard Oil and U.S. Steel. Yet, in a sense, the leviathans were invisible. No one knew for sure how they had been put together, how they operated, what they portended. The muckrakers did not merely rake up dirt; they also satisfied a legitimate curiosity.

Though she disliked the label, one muckraker whose reputation remains high to this day was Ida M. Tarbell. Born in 1857 in a log farmhouse in Hatch Hollow, Pennsylvania, Tarbell studied biology at Allegheny College, only to discover when she graduated that a career in science was almost impossible for a woman. She was living in Paris, studying the role of women in the French Revolution and supporting herself with occasional contributions to periodicals such as *Scribner's*, when she met S. S. McClure, who persuaded her to join the staff of his young magazine in 1894.

In 1900, McClure related later in his autobiography, having already published a series of articles by other writers devoted to "the greatest American business achievements," and knowing that Tarbell "had lived for years in the heart of the oil region of Pennsylvania, and had seen the marvelous development of the Standard Oil Trust at first hand," McClure asked Tarbell to write a series on Standard Oil.

Tarbell devoted two full years to research. The history of Standard was not a subject she could approach with the detachment of a disinterested observer. After the discovery of oil near Titusville, Pennsylvania, in 1859, her father had become a manufacturer of wooden tanks for oil and, later, one of the independent oil producers who struggled not to be gobbled up by Rockefeller's voracious colossus. As a girl, Tarbell had breathed in resentment of Standard Oil as she breathed air.

Yet she produced a study that was, in the words of historian Geoffrey

Blodgett, "scrupulous, thorough, attentive to human detail, earnest for balanced truth, moderately reformist." She made an honest effort to get the facts right, in the belief that the facts made the case against Standard more eloquently than rhetoric. Though he challenged her accuracy in some points, even Allan Nevins conceded that much of her indictment of Standard was "absolutely irrefutable." Her book, he added, was "easily the best piece of business history that America had yet produced"— "the most spectacular success of the muckraking school of journalism, and its most enduring achievement." Rockefeller himself was less enthusiastic. He called Tarbell "Miss Tarbarrel."

Although she hoped that her work "might be received as a legitimate historical study," Tarbell wrote years later in her autobiography, ". . . to my chagrin I found myself included in a new school, that of the muckrakers." Her readers wanted her to do more muckraking, but "I soon found that most of them wanted attacks. They had little interest in balanced findings." Tarbell steadfastly refused to say what she did not think. She hated the methods of Standard Oil, but she did not hate business. In *New Ideals in Business* (1916), she praised Frederick W. Taylor's techniques of "scientific management" and Henry Ford's experiments in corporate paternalism. Later she wrote laudatory biographies of steel magnate Elbert H. Gary and the chairman of General Electric, Owen D. Young.

Not all of the muckrakers shared Tarbell's respect for fact or her interest in "balanced findings." One who did not was Thomas W. Lawson, whose series titled "Frenzied Finance" appeared in *Everybody's* magazine in 1904–5. Lawson was a stock-market operator who, in association with H. H. Rogers and William Rockefeller of Standard Oil, had developed a scheme that resulted in the creation of a copper trust, Amalgamated Copper, in 1899. Later Lawson's association with Rogers and Rockefeller was broken, and a grudge may have contributed to Lawson's decision to tell the story of Amalgamated Copper in "Frenzied Finance." Lawson sought to be sensational, and he succeeded, in part by permitting his readers to take away the false impression that John D. Rockefeller had played a role in the affair. In fact, Rockefeller had condemned it. Nevertheless, Nevins writes, Lawson's indictment of the "organized speculation and thimble-rigging which made Amalgamated Copper possible was perfectly sound."

Today Lawson is chiefly remembered for a single phrase: "the 'System.' " The evils he was exposing, Lawson wrote, were not the creation of evil men: "The men are merely individuals; the 'System' is the thing at fault, and it is the 'System' that must be rectified."

Another muckraker who sometimes got careless about facts was David Graham Phillips, whose series "The Treason of the Senate" stirred up a storm of controversy when it appeared in William Randolph Hearst's *Cosmopolitan* in 1906. Whereas Lawson had spoken of "the 'System,' " Phillips spoke of "the 'interests.' " In the first article in the series he declared his theme: "The treason of the Senate! Treason is a strong word, but not too strong . . . to charactize the situation in which the Senate is [the] eager, resourceful, indefatigable agent of interests as hostile to the American people as any invading army could be, and vastly more dangerous; interests that manipulate the prosperity produced by all, so that it heaps up riches for the few; interests whose growth and power can only mean the degradation of the people. . . . The Senators are not elected by the people; they are elected by the 'interests.' "

Phillips called William B. Allison of Iowa the "craftiest agent" of the interests; Joseph Benson Foraker of Ohio the "best stump speaker" for the interests; and Henry Cabot Lodge of Massachusetts "the familiar coarse type of machine politician disguised by the robe of the 'Gentleman Scholar.' " He pointed out that the former attorney for the Vanderbilts and president of the New York Central Railroad, Senator Chauncey M. Depew of New York, sat on the boards of seventy corporations and received more than $50,000 annually in fees from these firms.

"The head of it all," Phillips charged, was Nelson W. Aldrich, the senior senator from Rhode Island and the man whose daughter Abby had married, in 1901, the son of John D. Rockefeller. In Rhode Island, Phillips showed, and here without bending the facts, "The Aldrich machine controls the legislature, the election boards, the courts—the entire machinery of the 'republican form of government.' " In all, Aldrich served in the Senate for thirty years, from 1881 to 1911. But Phillips was not impressed by his record as a legislator. "No railway legislation that [harmed] the 'interests'; no legislation on the subject of corporations that would interfere with the 'interests' . . .; no legislation on the tariff question unless it secured to the 'interests' full and free license to loot; no investigations of wholesale robbery or of any of the evils resulting from it—there you have in a few words the whole story of the Senate's treason under Aldrich's leadership."

Phillips had gone too far for many people. The editors of *Collier's* magazine commented: " 'The Treason of the Senate' has come to a close. These articles made reform odious. They represented sensational and money-making preying on the vogue of the 'literature of exposure,' which had been built up by truthful and conscientious work of writers like Miss Tarbell, Lincoln Steffens and Ray Stannard Baker. . . . Mr. Phillips' articles were one shriek of accusations based on the distortion of such facts as were printed, and on the suppression of facts which were essential."

Even President Theodore Roosevelt protested. In a letter to George H. Lorimer, editor in chief of *The Saturday Evening Post*, Roosevelt wrote, "I do not believe that the articles that Mr. Phillips has written, and notably these articles on the Senate, do anything but harm. They contain so much more falsehood than truth that they give no accurate guide for those who are really anxious to war against corruption, and they do excite a hysterical and ignorant feeling against everything existing, good or bad."

Phillips and Lawson, John Chamberlain wrote later, were "dealers in pyrotechnics," whereas Steffens and Tarbell were "the scholars of the movement." The excesses that bothered Theodore Roosevelt even troubled some editors. Ellery Sedgwick, an editor of *McClure's* who later headed *The Atlantic Monthly*, charged that "men are tried and found guilty in magazine counting-rooms before the investigation is begun." *Collier's* asked ironically, "Why listen to facts when diatribes are at hand?"

In a speech on April 14, 1906, that was prompted in part by Phillips's "The Treason of the Senate," Roosevelt gave the journalism of exposure a name it never shook off. At the laying of the cornerstone of the U.S. House of Representatives office building in Washington, speaking to an audience that included members of the Senate and the House, cabinet members, and Supreme Court justices, Roosevelt said, "In Bunyan's *Pilgrim's Progress* you may recall the description of the Man with the Muckrake, the man who could look no way but downward, with a muckrake in his hands; who was offered a celestial crown for his muckrake, but who would neither look up nor regard the crown he was offered, but continued to rake to himself the filth of the floor."

The Man with the Muckrake, Roosevelt went on, "typifies the man who in this life consistently refuses to see aught that is lofty, and fixes his eyes with solemn intentness only on that which is vile and debasing. Now, it is very necessary that we should not flinch from seeing what is vile and debasing. There is filth on the floor, and it must be scraped up with the muckrake; and there are times and places where this service is the most needed of all the services that can be performed. But the man who never does anything else . . . speedily becomes, not a help to society, not an incitement to good, but one of the most potent forces of evil."

In general, the aim of the muckrakers was to expose problems, not to offer solutions. They believed in what S. S. McClure called "the tonic effect of the inquiry." They also believed in exhortation—in what Richard Hofstadter later described as "the efficacy of continued exhortation." Most of the muckrakers were middle-class, Protestant, and moderate. When Baker, Tarbell, and others left *McClure's* in 1906 to start their own magazine, they announced: "Our magazine will be wholesome, hopeful, stimulating, uplifting. . . ."

Though they did not generally promote specific reforms, one area where the muckrakers could take credit for new legislation was the regulation of food and drugs. Edward Bok, Mark Sullivan, and Samuel Hopkins Adams led the crusade against patent medicine fraud. Adams's series in *Collier's* in 1905–6 was devastating. "Gullible America," he wrote in his first article, "will spend this year some seventy-five millions of dollars in the purchase of patent medicines. In consideration of this sum it will swallow huge quantities of alcohol, an appalling amount of opiates and narcotics, a wide assortment of varied drugs ranging from powerful and dangerous heart depressants to insidious liver stimulants; and, far in excess of all other ingredients, undiluted fraud. For fraud . . . is the basis of the trade."

Another area of concern was the food Americans were eating. The issue was not new. After the Spanish-American War, at a hearing on what came to be called the "embalmed beef" scandal, Theodore Roosevelt had told an investigating committee that he would as happily eat his old hat as the canned meat that had been shipped to American soldiers in Cuba during the war. Later, charges that the great meat packers of Chicago engaged in unfair business practices had led to the dissolution of the National Packing Company that Gustavus Swift had formed with J. O. Armour and Edward Morris in 1902. Most damaging of all, in the eyes of the public, was the publication of Upton Sinclair's muckraking novel *The Jungle* in 1905.

"There was never the least attention paid to what was cut up for sausage," Sinclair wrote in a typical passage. ". . . There would be meat that had tumbled out on the floor, in the dirt and sawdust, where the workers had tramped and spit uncounted billions of consumption germs. There would be meat stored in great piles and thousands of rats would race about on it. . . . A man could run his hand over these piles of meat and sweep off handfuls of the dried dung of rats. These rats were nuisances, and the packers would put poisoned bread out for them; they would die, and then rats, bread, and meat would go into the hoppers together."

In 1906, meat from Chicago was shipped all over the world, and *The Jungle* caused a tremendous stir. In a review published in England, young Winston Churchill declared that the book had "disturbed . . . the digestions and perhaps the consciences of mankind." Sinclair himself commented, "I aimed at the public's heart, and by accident I hit it in the stomach." The uproar led to the passage of the Pure Food and Drug Act in 1906.

As the example of Sinclair suggests, muckraking was not limited to nonfiction. In a long career, Sinclair himself wrote *The Money Changers* about Wall Street, *The Metropolis* about the rich in New York, *The Flivver King* about the automobile industry, *King Coal*, *Oil!*, and many other novels. Robert Herrick told the story of an unscrupulous industrialist in *The Memoirs of an American Citizen*. Frank Norris examined California railroad interests in *The Octopus* and showed how grain speculators controlled the wheat market in *The Pit*. In his Cowperwood trilogy, a writer whom Norris helped to discover, Theodore Dreiser, told the story of a tycoon whose career was based on the career of Philadelphia and Chicago streetcar magnate Charles T. Yerkes. Dreiser's achievement transcended muckraking but still owed much to it.

Though most of the muckrakers were moderate in temper and aim, a few of them were Socialists. Upton Sinclair ran unsuccessfully for office several times as a Socialist, and he nearly was elected governor of California in 1934, when he managed to win the Democratic nomination. Other Socialist muckrakers include Charles Edward Russell, who ran for mayor of New York City on the Socialist ticket in 1913, and Gustavus Myers, who did the research for Lawson's "The Treason of the Senate" and who needed three volumes for his comprehensive *History of the Great American Fortunes*, published in 1909–10. Myers felt that many of the muckrakers were shallow, and he did not consider himself one of them. His work is rarely read today, but his blistering judgments still affect students through his influence on Matthew Josephson's widely read *The Robber Barons*.

The decline of muckraking as a movement began with the speech by Roosevelt that gave it its name. Many factors contributed to the decline: retaliation by advertisers, especially food and patent medicine advertisers; the refusal by some banks to extend credit to magazines that might blast them; the inevitable fatigue of a scandal-satiated public. In a sense, too, the government began to do its own muckraking, as in the Pujo hearings, which required J. P. Morgan to face government investigators.

Muckraking as a movement is generally thought to have ended between 1910 and 1912. War in Europe killed off any life that remained in it. Isolated examples followed, as isolated examples had preceded 1900. But the essential feature—the critical mass of magazines, editors, and writers devoted to muckraking—was gone. The magazines had made the movement, as was suggested in a story the muckrakers loved to tell. An Alaskan miner, it was said, had walked into an editor's office and demanded that he launch a crusade.

"Well!" the editor said, "you certainly are a progressive, aren't you?"

"Progressive!" the miner bellowed. "Progressive! I tell you I'm a full-fledged insurgent. Why, man, I subscribe to thirteen magazines."

Only fifty years separated the Civil War from World War I, yet in those fifty years the scale of business in the United States was utterly transformed. The many voices of dissent in that period bear witness to the profundity of the change. The rise of giant enterprise was an earthquake that shook the nation to its foundations. America, the dissenters suggested, was losing control of its destiny. Or, rather, control had been wrested from it, and the nation's destiny was in doubt. History was a hijacked train with "the 'interests' " in command.

CHAPTER 11

Henry Ford:
The Consummate Crank

The Machine That Changed America

In 1900 the total population of the United States stood at seventy-six million, well over the population of 5.3 million in 1800 and 23.2 million in 1850. More than half of the seventy-six million lived in places that the census bureau classified as "rural territory." New York led American cities with 3.4 million people, followed by Chicago with 1.7 million and Philadelphia with 1.3 million. Atlanta had not yet reached one hundred thousand, Dallas had not yet reached fifty thousand, Phoenix had not yet reached ten thousand, and Miami was a village that had not yet reached two thousand. The population of Detroit, not yet dubbed the "Motor City," was 286,000, over thirteen times its population of 21,000 in 1850 but far below the 1.8 million it would reach in 1950.

The dominant form of transportation in rural areas was the horse and buggy. In cities people walked, rode the new streetcar systems, or drove in horse-drawn carriages. The stench of horse manure could be overpowering.

Most buildings were modest in scale. In Chicago, the first skeleton-frame skyscraper, William Le Baron Jenney's ten-story Home Insurance Building, had gone up in 1883–85; and in New York, Otis Brothers & Company had installed the first electric elevator in the Demarest Building in 1889. But few people could imagine that skyscrapers of seventy stories and more would transform the city's skyline in the next thirty years.

Indoors, private bathrooms were still a luxury. Flush-valve toilets, cast-iron radiators, and cast-iron enameled bathtubs were not yet invented or not yet widely available. Also absent were the electrical marvels that would revolutionize domestic life in the twentieth century—washing machines and dryers, refrigerators, dishwashers, garbage disposals, air conditioners.

More than 1.5 million telephones had been installed in the United States since 1876—one telephone for every fifty people. Alexander Graham Bell's "electrical toy" was transforming life in American offices, along with the adding machine invented by William S. Burroughs in 1888, Lewis Waterman's fountain pen, and the newfangled typewriting contraptions. Despite these advances, the most common copying machine was still a clerk with neat handwriting.

Meanwhile, an invention that would change everything was taking shape. The first two-cycle gasoline engine had been built in Paris in 1860 by Étienne Lenoir. An American, George Brayton, had exhibited his own version at the Centennial Exposition in 1876—the same year that German inventor Nickolaus Otto built the first reliable four-stroke, internal-combustion engine. In 1879, an American patent lawyer, George Selden, applied for a patent for a road vehicle based on a rudimentary internal-combustion engine, though he did not bother to build the vehicle. A crude gasoline-operated automobile was demonstrated in Paris in 1886. In the United States, Charles and Frank Duryea drove the first gas car, a one-cylinder job, in Springfield, Massachusetts, in 1889. In 1896, when Henry Ford drove his first "quadricycle," the Duryea brothers sold thirteen cars. Three years later, automobiles garlanded with flowers were paraded at an "Automobile Festival" in Newport, Rhode Island. By 1900, four thousand automobiles had been manufactured in the United States, three quarters of them powered by steam or electricity. That same year, thirty-eight new automobile companies were founded, and Henry Ford's Detroit Automobile Company folded.

Henry Ford was thirty-seven years old in 1900. His grandparents and their seven children had emigrated from Ireland in 1847, settling near

Detroit, in Dearborn, where their eldest son, William, eventually became a prosperous farmer and where William's son Henry was born in 1863. In his teens Henry loved to tinker and spent endless hours taking apart watches and putting them back together. His mother instilled discipline with maxims that might have come out of Poor Richard: "You must earn the right to play." "The best fun follows a duty done." "You may have pity on others, but you must not pity yourself." She died in 1876 after giving birth to a stillborn child in her ninth pregnancy. Without her, Henry said later, the Ford household was "like a watch without a mainspring."

Hating the drudgery of farm life, in 1880 Henry ran away to Detroit, where he took a job as an apprentice in a machine shop at $2.50 a week and moonlighted repairing watches in a jewelry shop. After a few months he joined the Detroit Drydock Company, the city's largest shipbuilding firm, which gave him the opportunity to learn about engines of all kinds.

Henry returned to his father's farm in 1882, but not with the intention of becoming a farmer. For the next six years his life was oddly unfocused. After marrying Clara Bryant in April 1888, he built a house on a tract of land given to him by his father on condition that he abandon his tinkering. Henry made a little money selling lumber and firewood, but continued to devote all his spare time to experiments with steam and gas engines.

In September 1888 Henry and Clara moved to Detroit, where Henry had been offered a job with the Detroit Edison Company. Henry rose rapidly, becoming chief engineer at $1,000 a year in 1893. Also in 1893, Clara gave birth to a son, their only child, whom they named Edsel after an old friend of Henry's.

In a workshop he had set up in a small brick shed in his backyard, Henry fiddled with gasoline engines in an effort to come up with a workable motor for a self-propelled gasoline vehicle. Neighbors called him "Crazy Henry!" Nevertheless, he developed a "quadricycle" by mounting a four-cycle, air-cooled gasoline motor that delivered three or four horsepower on a five-hundred-pound chassis and body made mostly of wood. Early in the morning of June 4, 1896, the first Ford automobile rattled onto the road.

For the next three years Henry worked on a second car. This one cemented his reputation as a man to reckon with in the emerging automobile business. It weighed 875 pounds and featured fully enclosed mechanical elements, electric spark ignition, and chain-and-sprocket transmission. On August 5, 1899, Mayor William C. Maybury of Detroit and a few friends put up $15,000 to found the Detroit Automobile Company, with Henry as "chief engineer" and partner. In response, Henry's boss at Detroit Edison offered him the position of general superintendent on the condition that he abandon his crazy experiments. Henry did not merely turn down the offer; he quit. At the age of thirty-six, after nine years at Detroit Edison, he was on his own.

A prototype vehicle was ready on January 12, 1900. Henry gave a ride to a reporter from the *Detroit News Tribune*, who preserved the moment for posterity: "There has always been at each decisive period in the world's history some voice, some note, that represents the prevailing power," he wrote. Once the voice of power had been the lion's roar; later it had been "the shriek of the steam whistle. . . . And now, finally, there was heard in the streets of Detroit the murmur of this newest and most perfect of forces, the automobile rushing along at the rate of 25 miles an hour. What kind of noise is it? It is not like any other sound in the world . . . a long, mellow gurgling sound, not harsh, not unrhythmical, a note that falls with pleasure on the ear. . . . And the sooner you hear its chuck! chuck! the sooner you will be in touch with civilization's newest voice."

Despite the success of the prototype, Ford resigned from the Detroit Automobile Company in November 1900, largely because his backers wanted him to focus on sales while he wanted to focus on improving the production process. For the next year, recognizing that, as he put it in his autobiography, "the public refused to consider the automobile in any light other than as a fast toy," Henry reluctantly turned his attention to automobile racing. On October 10, 1901, in a race at the Detroit Fairgrounds against world speed record holder Alexander Winton, Henry won a victory that rekindled the interest of investors, who put up a stake of $30,500 to establish the Henry Ford Company on November 30, 1901.

This venture lasted until March of the next year. Commenting on his decision to leave, Henry wrote in his autobiography:

I could get no support at all toward making better cars to be sold to the public at large. The whole thought was to make to order and to get the largest price possible for each car. And being without authority other than my engineering position gave me, I found that the new company was not a vehicle for realizing my ideas but merely a money-making concern—that did not make much money. In March, 1902, I resigned, determined never again to put myself under orders.

Backed by Detroit coal dealer Alexander Y. Malcomson, Ford spent
the next year developing a new car, which he called the Model A. Ford's
third and last company, the Ford Motor Company, was founded on
June 16, 1903. One thousand shares of stock valued at $100 each were
divided among twelve original stockholders. Ford and Malcomson each
held 255 shares, so that together they owned 51 percent of the company. The total capital paid into the company at this time—$28,000—
remained for more than half a century the only capital paid in from any
source other than operations.

The Model A was, as an early ad put it, "a thoroughly practical car
at a moderate price." Over the next five years Henry marched through
the alphabet—developing and selling Models A, B, C, F, K, N, R, and
S. But he continued to have trouble sharing authority. Ford wanted to
make a cheap car suitable for mass production, whereas Malcomson and
some of the other investors thought that the automobile would remain a
luxury. The disputes among the investors sometimes got nasty. When a
six-cylinder model was proposed, Henry resisted with the comment,
"A car should not have any more cylinders than a cow has teats."

At last Henry decided that he "had to have control." In 1906 he bought
out Malcomson for $175,000. That gave Henry 51 percent of the com-
pany. Additional purchases at about the same time increased his holdings to 585 shares, or 58.5 percent.

Henry was a man with a mission. "I will build a car for the multitude," he declared. "It will be large enough for the family but small
enough for the individual to run and care for. It will be constructed of
the best materials, by the best men to be hired, after the simplest designs
that modern engineering can devise. But it will be so low in price that
no man making a good salary will be unable to own one—and enjoy with
his family the blessings of hours of pleasure in God's great open spaces."

The car that would fulfill the mission was ready in 1908. It was plain,
cheap, light, and durable. It weighed twelve hundred pounds, had a
four-cylinder, twenty-horsepower, water-cooled engine, and cost $850.
It was black. On October 1, 1908, the first of fifteen million Model T's
rolled out of the Ford factory on Piquette Avenue in Detroit.

The Model T was an immediate success. Henry had built what he
promised: a car for the masses. City folk liked it. Farmers liked it. After
it had been around a while, the Model T even got a nickname, like the
teasing nickname a wife may get in a good marriage: "Tin Lizzie."

There was one fly in Henry's ointment—a big one. Back in 1879,
George Selden had applied for a patent for a road vehicle based on an

internal-combustion engine. The patent had been granted in 1895. Two years later, a group led by former secretary of the Navy William C. Whitney had bought the rights to the patent for $10,000 and one fifth of any future royalties.

Only a few weeks after it was organized in 1903, the Ford Motor Company had received a warning notice: "United States patent no. 549,160 granted to George B. Selden November 5, 1895, controls broadly all gasoline automobiles which are accepted as commercially practical. Licenses under this patent have been secured from the owner by the following named manufacturers. . . ." Ford responded with a notice that ran in the *Detroit News* on July 28, 1903: "The Selden patent does not cover any practicable machine, no practicable machine can be made from it, and never was so far as we can ascertain." The Association of Licensed Automotive Manufacturers sued.

The lawyers maneuvered for six years, until at last, on May 28, 1909, the case went to trial in New York. Henry's team tried to show that the automobile was the product of technological innovations that went back well beyond 1879. Henry himself testified, "I invented nothing new. I simply assembled into a car the discoveries of other men behind whom were centuries of work. . . . Had I worked fifty or ten or even five years before, I would have failed. So it is with every new thing. Progress happens when all the factors that make for it are ready, and then it is inevitable."

The court ruled against Ford on September 15, 1909. But in a decision handed down on January 9, 1911, the appellate judge ruled that the Selden patent applied only to two-cylinder vehicles. That ruling meant that Henry Ford did not need a license to go on doing what he did best: making automobiles.

"The Way to Make Automobiles"

Now that he had designed the Model T, making it was Henry's obsession. He decided to freeze the design and concentrate on the production process. He felt about the Model T the way an artist might feel about a masterwork. In Henry's eyes, one employee said later, "The Model T was God and we were to put away false images."

As early as 1903, Henry had articulated his philosophy of production. "The way to make automobiles," he said, "is to make one automobile like another automobile, to make them all alike, to make them come through the factory just alike, just as one pin is like another pin when it comes from a pin factory."

This was easier said than done. How exactly could automobiles be made "all alike"? Part of the answer, Henry realized, was to use machine tools to make interchangeable parts. If machines are used to make parts so nearly identical that they can be exchanged without special fitting, the parts are said to be interchangeable. Precision manufacture of this kind is often wrongly thought to go back to Eli Whitney's work manufacturing muskets in the early 1800s. In fact, Whitney never produced firearms whose parts were even close to being interchangeable. But pioneering work in arms manufacture using interchangeable parts was done before the Civil War by men such as John H. Hall of the Harpers Ferry Armory, Simeon North of the Staddle Hill factory in Middletown, and Roswell Lee of the Springfield Armory.

Producing parts was not Henry's only problem. The parts had to be assembled. All the parts in the world would not yield a large number of cars unless the company figured out an efficient way of putting them together. "In our first assembling," Henry wrote in his autobiography, "we simply started to put a car together at a spot on the floor and workmen brought to it the parts as they were needed in exactly the same way that one builds a house. . . . The undirected worker spends more of his time walking about for materials and tools than he does in working; he gets small pay because pedestrianism is not a highly paid line."

On New Year's Day in 1910, Henry opened a gigantic new plant in Highland Park, a Detroit suburb. It contained fifteen thousand machines. More than fifty thousand square feet of glass were in its roof and walls, which led to its nickname, "The Crystal Palace." Eventually the Highland Park complex covered 229 acres, including 52 acres of floor space.

Henry and his engineers continued to develop more efficient manufacturing techniques. It was an evolutionary process. One of Henry's key executives, Charles Sorensen, wrote years later:

Henry Ford had no ideas on mass production. He wanted to build a lot of autos. He was determined but, like everyone else at that time, he didn't know how. In later years he was glorified as the originator of the mass production idea. Far from it; he just grew into it, like the rest of us. The essential tools and the final assembly line with its many integrated feeders resulted from an organization which was continually experimenting and improvising to get better production.

This understates Henry's contribution. If the organization "was continually experimenting and improvising to get better production," it was because Henry pushed it to experiment and improvise. Production at Highland Park soared: 20,727 cars were produced in 1910; 53,488 in 1911; and 82,388 in 1912. Then came the great breakthrough.

"The idea," Henry wrote in his autobiography, "came in a general way from the overhead trolley that the Chicago packers use in dressing beef." But instead of the "disassembly" line found in the slaughterhouses, Henry and his associates developed an assembly line. The manufacturing system that evolved at Highland Park has been well described by historian William Greenleaf:

> After the company moved its operations to Highland Park early in 1910, Ford . . . arranged machines, materials, and men in patterns that systematized "line" or sequential production, eliminated unnecessary motion, and cut factory costs. . . . materials were transported from one work station to another by overhead conveyors, gravity slides and tubes, endless belts, and other mechanical handling devices according to predetermined plan and without interrupting the progressive movement of parts, subassemblies, and assemblies into the feeder lines; the work was brought to the man, not the man to the work, in a manner that kept the moving lines of materials waist-high at all times, so that the workers . . . would not have to bend, stoop, or engage in any other movement interfering with his maximum efficiency and productivity.

The first continuously moving line was tested on about April 1, 1913. In 1913–14, the change from stationary to moving assembly reduced the average assembly time for a Model T from 12.5 hours to 1.5 hours. Production rose from 82,388 cars in 1912 to 189,088 in 1913, 230,788 in 1914, 394,788 in 1915, and 585,388 in 1916.

The gains in production in this period were accompanied by gains in productive efficiency, made possible by standardized design, the use of machine tools to produce interchangeable parts, and the continuously moving assembly line. Gains in productive efficiency meant that Ford could charge less for its cars. The retail price of the Model T dropped from $850 in 1908 to $360 in 1916. Profits per car also went down, but sales skyrocketed. Ford sold 5,986 Model T's in 1908, 19,293 in 1910, 78,611 in 1912, 260,720 in 1914, and 577,036 in 1916. "Every time I reduce the charge for our car by one dollar," Henry crowed, "I get a thousand new customers." Whereas in 1908 the Ford Motor Company had built about 10 percent of the nation's cars, in 1914 it built almost half.

The only trouble with the moving assembly line was that workers hated it. In 1913 the company estimated that it hired 9.63 new workers for every one it retained. Absenteeism among factory employees averaged 10 percent a day. To address these problems, Henry made a bold move. At a time when other automobile factories in Detroit paid $1.80 a day for unskilled labor and $2.50 a day for skilled labor, Henry announced that he would pay $5.00 a day to most employees and that he would reduce shift time from nine to eight hours.

The $5.00 day achieved its immediate business purpose: employee turnover plunged, and absenteeism declined from 10 percent a day to less than half of 1 percent. But the $5.00 wage also had consequences that were not foreseen. It made Henry a national celebrity, and it helped create a big new group of customers for his cars. As Henry wrote once he understood what had happened, "Our own sales depend in a measure upon the wages we pay. If we can distribute high wages, then that money is going to be spent and it will serve to make storekeepers and distributors and manufacturers and workers in other lines more prosperous and their prosperity will be reflected in our sales."

There was a negative side to Ford's wage scheme. To be eligible, Henry notes in his autobiography, "The man and his home had to come up to certain standards of cleanliness and citizenship." The plan applied to "married men living with and taking good care of their families" and to single men "who lived wholesomely." To make sure that no one benefited who was not wholesome, Ford established a Sociological Department. Investigators visited employees in their homes, made sure that standards of cleanliness were being met, demanded to see bankbooks and marriage certificates. A pamphlet titled *Rules of Living* instructed employees to use plenty of soap and water at home, not to spit on the floor, and not to make purchases on the installment plan. In his autobiography Henry acknowledges that errors were made: "Nothing paternal was intended!—a certain amount of paternalism did develop."

The $5.00 wage made Henry a hero to many working Americans, but his reputation did not remain untarnished for long. In 1915, fearing that the "absentee owners and parasites" of Wall Street might draw the United States into a conflict in which it had no stake, he spoke out against American involvement in the European war. Then, in November 1915, Hungarian-American feminist Rosika Schwimmer and American pacifist Louis P. Lochner persuaded Henry that the war might be ended through a "Neutral Conference for Continuous Mediation." Captivated by the idea, Henry decided to charter the Scandinavian-American liner *Oskar II* to take an American delegation to Europe.

In a personal meeting with Woodrow Wilson, Henry tried to enlist the president's support, but Wilson was lukewarm to the idea. At last Henry lost his patience. "Tomorrow at ten in New York," he warned, according to Lochner's account, "representatives of every big newspaper will come to my apartment for a story. I have today chartered a steamship. I offer it to you to send delegates to Europe. If you feel you can't act, I will. I will then tell the newspapermen that I will take a ship of American delegates to Europe."

The newspapers reported Henry's plans, but the response was not encouraging. Theodore Roosevelt said that "Mr. Ford's visit abroad will not be mischievous only because it is ridiculous." Cartoonists pictured the lanky industrialist as a midwestern Don Quixote tilting at windmills from the seat of his Tin Lizzie.

Magazine publisher S. S. McClure and the governor of North Dakota, Louis Hanna, joined Henry on the Peace Ship, but Thomas Edison, naturalist John Burroughs, William Howard Taft, William Jennings Bryan, Ida Tarbell, Lincoln Steffens, and many others declined. The ship sailed from Hoboken, New Jersey, on December 2, 1915, and docked at Christiana (now Oslo), Norway, on December 18. By that time Henry's enthusiasm had cooled. Telling Lochner, "You've got this thing started and can get along without me," he sailed back on December 23. When the United States entered the war, the Ford Motor Company filled government contracts for ambulances, trucks, tanks, Eagle boats, Liberty aircraft motors, shells, helmets, armor plate, and gun caissons.

The Peace Ship was generally considered a fiasco, but Henry never renounced it. In his autobiography he commented, "The mere fact that it failed is not, to me, conclusive proof that it was not worth trying. . . . I think everyone will agree that if it had been possible to end the war in 1916 the world would be better off than it is to-day."

His promotion of the Peace Ship was not the only episode that raised doubts about Henry. On June 22, 1916, after President Wilson had called out the National Guard in response to Pancho Villa's raids near the Mexican border, a Ford press agent told a reporter for the *Chicago Tribune* that the company would dismiss employees who fought against Villa. The next day the *Tribune* commented in an editorial, "If Ford allows the rule of his shops to stand he will reveal himself not as merely an ignorant idealist but as an anarchistic enemy of the nation which protects his wealth. A man so ignorant as Henry Ford may not understand the fundamentals of the government under which he lives."

Henry filed a libel suit demanding $1 million in compensation for damages. When the trial finally took place in May 1919, the *Tribune*'s attorney, Elliott Stevenson, initiated a line of questioning that proved highly embarrassing to Ford:

> STEVENSON: Now I shall inquire whether you were a well-informed man, competent to educate people. . . . Have there been any revolutions in this country?
> FORD: There was, I understand.
> STEVENSON: When?
> FORD: In 1812.
> STEVENSON: When?
> FORD: In 1812.
> STEVENSON: In 1812, the Revolution?
> FORD: Yes.
> STEVENSON: Any other times?
> FORD: I don't know.
> STEVENSON: You don't know of any other?
> FORD: No.
> STEVENSON: Don't you know there wasn't any revolution in 1812?
> FORD: I didn't know that. I didn't pay much attention to it. . . .
> STEVENSON: Did you hear of Benedict Arnold?
> FORD: I have heard the name.
> STEVENSON: Who was he?
> FORD: I have forgotten who he was. A writer, I think.

In his summation to the jury, Stevenson was devastating: Ford's suit, he said, "forced us to open the mind of Henry Ford and expose it to you bare . . . to disclose the pitiable condition he had succeeded in keeping from the view of the public." Now the public knew. Henry Ford was a mechanical genius with a grade-school education. He was a man who believed, as he had said not long before in a newspaper interview, that "History is more or less bunk." But he was not a deep thinker whose beliefs deserved to be taken seriously. The jury found the *Tribune* guilty of libel and awarded Henry six cents in damages.

Total Control

Henry owned 58.5 percent of the company, but majority control was not the same thing as total control. He found that out in 1916. The year before, the company had made a net profit of $60 million, of which $25 million would have been paid out in dividends in normal circumstances. But Henry wanted to use those profits to build a huge new plant. He announced that he intended to limit annual dividends to a total of $1.2 million.

The Dodge brothers, John and Horace, had different ideas. They had been among the original investors when the Ford Motor Company was organized in 1903. On the basis of an investment of $3,000 in cash and $7,000 in work and materials, they owned 10 percent of the company. They had started their own automobile company in 1913, financed in part by dividends they received from Ford. Those dividends had been about $1.2 million in 1915. Now Henry was saying they would get $120,000 a year, not merely for one year but for the indefinite future.

On November 2, 1916, the Dodge brothers filed suit, asking the court for an injunction to halt work on the new plant and for an order to compel Ford to distribute 75 percent of its cash surplus, or about $39 million, as dividends. That same day, the court issued a restraining order that prohibited the use of company funds for plant expansion.

In a decision handed down in October 1917, the Michigan Circuit Court ordered Ford to pay a special dividend of $19.275 million, half the amount the Dodges had asked for. Henry not only appealed but also resigned as president of the Ford Motor Company effective December 30, 1918. In February 1919 the Michigan Superior Court sustained the earlier ruling and ordered Ford to pay interest on the withheld dividends, bringing the total judgment to more than $20 million. The next month, Henry announced that he planned to organize a new company to produce a car that would sell for less than the Model T.

"Mr. Ford never threatens," a spokesman said when asked if this statement was a threat. Nevertheless, the minority stockholders knew that the Ford Motor Company without Henry Ford was not the world's most attractive investment. When Henry initiated confidential negotiations to see if they wanted to sell, they sold. The Dodge brothers received $25 million for their 2,000 shares. In all, Henry paid $105,820,894.57 for the full minority interest of 41.5 percent. He was now the sole owner of the Ford Motor Company. "Of course," his son Edsel told *The New York Times*, "there will be no need of a new company now."

In the reorganization of Ford enterprises that followed, Henry Ford received 55.2 percent of the reissued shares; his wife, Clara, received 3.1 percent; and Edsel received 41.7 percent. "All of the Ford properties," writes William Greenleaf, "were thus combined in a single unit under the centralized control of Henry Ford, who wielded greater power over his corporate domain than either John D. Rockefeller, Sr., or Andrew Carnegie ever exercised over their own."

Having secured absolute control, Henry was free to push ahead with his new plant on a two-thousand-acre tract of land near the Rouge River. He had purchased the tract in 1915. Occasional difficulties in obtaining supplies during the war had sharpened his determination to assure his sources of supply. At Highland Park he had achieved a continuous flow of materials *inside* his factory. At the Rouge complex he wanted to achieve a continuous flow of raw materials *into* his factory.

At the Rouge, Henry built an industrial colossus that contained blast furnaces, coke ovens, dock facilities, the world's largest foundry, and other facilities. The Rouge River itself was deepened and widened so that ships could carry ore from the Great Lakes. In the 1920s Henry's purchases included forests and iron mines in upper Michigan, coal mines in Kentucky and West Virginia, glass plants in Pennsylvania and Minnesota, and a rubber plantation in Brazil. Through this "vertical integration" backward to the sources of supply, he gained control of all the raw materials he needed to make automobiles—iron and steel, lumber, coal, limestone, silica sand for glass, rubber for tires.

"The Rouge," write historians Allan Nevins and Frank Ernest Hill, "was an industrial city, immense, concentrated, packed with power." Its ninety-three buildings contained 159.62 acres of floor space—more than three times the floor space at Highland Park. By 1927, when the last assembly line was transferred from Highland Park, seventy-five thousand men worked at the Rouge. Five thousand janitors used up five thousand mops and three thousand brooms a month, plus eighty-six tons of soap to wash the floors, walls, and 330 acres of windows. Ninety-three miles of railroad trackage and twenty-seven miles of conveyors facilitated the movement of materials through the giant complex.

At the same time as he was building the Rouge, Henry got rid of many executives who had played key roles in the company's early years. Paranoia and ruthlessness were the distinctive marks of Henry's regime in these years. Peter Collier and David Horowitz have compared this period at Ford to the time in a nation's history when a totalitarian state emerges: "First came the elimination of constitutional checks and balances . . . in the putsch by which Henry got rid of all minority stockholders; next there were purges of those who had helped make the company; and finally a dictator emerged, supported by a few tough lieutenants and a cult of personality."

Ford later denied that he had fired anyone, though he conceded that "every now and then we did drag a dead skunk across somebody's trail." The cruelty in this joke was typical. Ford always had had a mean streak, and now it seemed to get out of hand. One executive who was fired, the head of the Sociology Department, said as he departed, "If only Mr. Ford was properly assembled! He has in him the makings of a great man but the parts are laying about him in disorder."

The most powerful lieutenants who emerged in this period were Charles Sorensen, who took command at the Rouge, and Ernest G. Liebold, Henry's private secretary and personal fixer. One manager said of them, "They were always thinking of themselves as little gods who were to be feared." Sorensen's strong-arm tactics and frequent tirades created an atmosphere of intimidation. People who made the transition from Highland Park to the Rouge were shocked. At Highland Park, one manager recalled, "There was an internal desire in the man to do a good job. . . . When he came to the Rouge plant, he had to do a good job or get his head chopped off." Walter Reuther, a Ford tool- and diemaker who later became famous as a leader of the United Auto Workers, said, "Highland Park was civilized, but the Rouge was a jungle."

The Power to Destroy

The brutality that marred Henry's rule of Ford in the 1920s was not the only ugliness associated with him. In his testimony in the libel suit against the *Chicago Tribune*, Henry had shown himself to be ignorant. In the years that followed, he showed that his ignorance could be vicious.

Henry was a man who combined high mechanical aptitude with a remarkable susceptibility to prejudices and superstitions—a man who worried about black cats and walking under ladders, who disliked going out on Friday the thirteenth, who would spend the day with his sock inside out if he happened to put it on the wrong way in the morning.

Like many people in the Midwest, Henry also disliked the bankers and financiers of Wall Street. And he especially disliked "international bankers" who were Jewish, like the Rothschilds and the Warburgs. His colleague on the Peace Ship, Rosika Schwimmer, recalled that once during a luncheon he astonished her by declaring, "I know who started the war—the German Jewish bankers. I have the evidence here. Facts. The German Jewish bankers caused the war."

In November 1918 Henry bought a small country newspaper, the *Dearborn Independent*, with the intention of expressing his opinions on, issues that concerned him. The issue that most concerned him, as it turned out, was "the Jewish question." For ninety-one consecutive weeks, starting with a tirade titled "The International Jew: The World's Problem," the *Dearborn Independent* devoted itself almost entirely to anti-Semitic propaganda.

Henry blamed the Jews for everything that bothered him in modern life. Intemperance was rising because "the profits of spirituous liquors flow in large amounts to Jewish pockets." Rents were rising because of "Jewish landlords." Hemlines were rising because of the influence of "Jewish clothing concerns." Morals were falling because Jewish interests sought "to render them loose in the first place and keep them loose." Gambling, movies, jazz, jewelry—"every such activity has been under the mastery of the Jews."

No "evidence" against the Jews was too unreliable to publish. In 1905, a Czarist agent in Russia had concocted a forgery, *The Protocols of the Elders of Zion*, in an effort to divert revolutionary activity into a safe channel of anti-Semitism. *The Protocols* interpreted much of the world's history as the history of an international Jewish conspiracy against Christian civilization. They charged, for instance, that Queen Isabella of Spain had been "a Jewish front." Henry used *The Protocols* as the source of numerous articles in the *Independent*, but added some imaginative new touches of his own. He believed, for instance, that Jewish bankers had hired John Wilkes Booth to assassinate Abraham Lincoln and that Booth had not died in 1865 but had been whisked off to the West Coast and given a new identity. Henry expressed some interest in buying the embalmed body of this California Booth, but was dissuaded.

Henry organized the Dearborn Publishing Company to publish a series of anti-Semitic pamphlets, which later were reprinted in a single volume under the title *The International Jew*. The book did not sell well in the United States, but it became a best seller in Germany in the early 1920s. In 1922 a reporter for *The New York Times* saw a copy conspicuously displayed on the desk of Adolf Hitler, along with a photograph of Ford.

The threat of legal action put an end to this inglorious phase of Henry's public career. In 1924–25, under the title "Jewish Exploitation of Farmers' Organizations," the *Independent* published a series of attacks on Aaron Sapiro, a well-known Chicago attorney who was involved in organizing agricultural cooperatives. Sapiro filed suit for defamation of character, asking for $1 million in damages. Henry settled out of court and, on July 7, 1927, issued a less than completely honest apology:

To my great regret I have learned that Jews generally, and particularly those of this country, not only resent these publications as promoting anti-Semitism, but regard me as their enemy. . . . This has led me to direct my personal attention to this subject in order to ascertain the exact nature of these articles. As a result of this survey I confess I am deeply mortified that this journal, which is intended to be constructive and not destructive, has been made the medium for resurrecting exploded fictions, for giving currency to the so-called protocols of the wise men of Zion which have been demonstrated, as I learn, to be gross forgeries, and for contending that the Jews have been engaged in conspiracy to control the capital and industries of the world. . . .

Had I appreciated even the general nature, to say nothing of the details, of these utterances, I would have forbidden their circulation, without a moment's hesitation.

In fact, according to Henry's personal secretary, Ernest Liebold, the articles "were prompted largely by Mr. Ford," who "kept in touch with every phase." Having issued his apology, Henry stopped publishing the *Independent* at the end of 1927. But the episode did not prevent him from accepting the Grand Cross of the German Eagle from Hitler's government in 1938.

The Ford Motor Company was the world's largest family enterprise. Henry's son Edsel had been named president of the company on December 31, 1918. Edsel soon realized, however, that, as he sadly put it, "I have responsibility but no power." The power belonged to Henry. More and more, after he gained total control of the company, it was the power to destroy.

The five millionth Ford car rolled off the assembly line on May 28, 1921. At that point fifty-six of every hundred cars sold in the United States were Model T's. But Henry's famous disdain for consumer sovereignty—"Any customer can have a car painted any color that he wants so long as it is black"—was beginning to take its toll. By 1925, Ford's share of the automobile market had fallen to 45 percent. The hot car was GM's Chevrolet, whose popularity had soared under the leadership of William S. Knudsen, an executive Henry had fired.

Inside the Ford Motor Company, two sides competed for power under Henry. Edsel and his brother-in-law, Ernest Kanzler, controlled operations at Highland Park. Charles Sorensen ruled with an iron fist at the Rouge. The key moment in the contest came on January 20, 1926, when Kanzler gave Henry a six-page typewritten memorandum pleading with him to recognize that the time had come to replace the Model T.

"I can write certain things that I find it difficult to say to you," Kanzler explained cautiously. "It is one of the handicaps of the power of your personality which you perhaps least of all realize, but most people when with you hesitate to say what they think."

Six months later, Kanzler was out of the company. Henry waited till Edsel and his family left on a trip to Europe. Then he said to an associate, "Well, by this time I think Edsel is several miles out to ocean, so I think tomorrow we can get rid of Kanzler." Edsel was informed by telegram. The message was clear: At the age of sixty-three, Henry still ruled.

Yet Kanzler's advice had been sound. On May 26, 1927, with Henry and Edsel aboard for photographers, the fifteen millionth Model T moved off the assembly line. The day before, the company had announced that it intended to replace the Model T with a new model. The changeover was traumatic. For four months, at a cost of $42 million a month in lost profits, the Ford Motor Company produced no new cars at all. In all, the estimated cost of the changeover was $250 million.

On December 1, 1927, Ford introduced its new car: the Model A. The car was a hit, but Henry's dream of reproducing the success of the Model T died early in the Depression: The days when a single model could dominate the market for two decades were gone. The last car with which Henry was deeply involved, the Ford V-8, went on display in May 1932. At that point few people could afford cars, and those few tended not to prefer Fords. By 1936 Ford's share of the U.S. automobile market had fallen to 22 percent, behind General Motors at 43 percent and Chrysler at 25 percent.

"It Was My Grandfather Who Killed My Father"

The story of the deterioration of management at Ford in these years is one of the most remarkable chapters in American industrial history. It is not merely the story of a father who destroyed his own son. It is also the story of a father who gave power to a thug rather than give it to his son.

Harry Bennett was twenty-four years old when he joined the Ford Motor Company in 1917. He was a wiry little man who had run away from home at sixteen to join the Navy and who, in the Navy, had been a champion boxer. He came to Henry's attention when he beat up a larger man in a fight on the factory floor. After a few more incidents of this kind, Henry made him head watchman at the Rouge, where he came to be known as Charles Sorensen's "puppy," although, as Peter Collier and David Horowitz have commented, "at times is seemed that 'mad dog' would have been more appropriate."

Henry was fascinated by Bennett's toughness. He liked the way Bennett talked out of the side of his mouth, like a gangster in a movie. He liked the fact that Bennett could tell him tales about the Detroit underworld. He did not mind when Bennett gave jobs to men such as Kid McCoy, a former prizefighter who had spent time in jail after murdering one of his ten wives, or when Bennett introduced him to men such as convicted murderer "Black Leo" Celuria, or when Bennett gave a food supply concession to Detroit mobster Chester "Chet" La Mare.

In 1927, Bennett became head of the Personnel Department at the Rouge—responsible not only for all hiring and firing but also for security. At about the same time, Henry's infatuation with Bennett reached the point where Henry often phoned him first thing in the morning or drove to work with him. Then, after the kidnapping of the Lindbergh baby in 1932, Henry put Bennett in charge of all security for the Ford family. Edsel's three sons found themselves trailed everywhere by men they sometimes called "Bennett's rats."

As director of personnel and security, William Greenleaf has written, Bennett "headed an organization that was in effect an intelligence apparatus; his Service Department was a force of plant police, labor spies, plug-uglies, and underworld figures." If the Ford Company in the 1930s sometimes resembled a totalitarian state, then Bennett's Service Department was its Gestapo.

Bennett was responsible for labor relations at Ford during one of the most tumultuous periods in American labor history. Henry Ford bitterly resisted the movement to organize a union of automobile workers at Ford in the 1930s. "Unions are organized by Jewish financiers, not labor," Henry charged. "A union is a neat thing for a Jew to have on hand when he comes around to get his clutches on industry."

In a confrontation with a Communist-organized "March on Hunger" in Dearborn in 1932, police fired on unarmed demonstrators after Bennett was hit on the head by a brick. Four demonstrators were killed and fifty wounded. Afterward, Henry gave Bennett all the money he wanted for his Service Department. Bennett built a private army that began to resemble the Praetorian Guard of ancient Rome. In 1937, *The New York Times* described it as "the largest private quasi-military organization in existence."

The year 1937 was an especially unhappy one. General Motors and Chrysler recognized the United Automobile Workers, but Henry refused, and he showed his intention of fighting on by naming Harry Bennett as the company's official negotiator. Then, on May 26, came one of the most famous confrontations in American labor history. Walter Reuther, Richard Frankenstein, and a few other union men and women had obtained permits to distribute leaflets outside the Rouge. Bennett's men surrounded and attacked them. The outnumbered unionists were brutally kicked and beaten. Photographers captured every kick, as well as unforgettable images of the dazed Reuther and Frankenstein, bleeding profusely, after the attack. "The Battle of the Overpass" became an immediate symbol of American industry at its most vicious.

Though the National Labor Relations Board condemned Ford's labor policies in December 1937, the company held out against the UAW until 1941. Intimidation and terror were Bennett's main weapons. On April 1, 1941, after Bennett had fired eight workers for union activities, the entire labor force at the Rouge—fifty thousand men—stopped working. At that point Henry agreed to allow an NLRB election. At the age of seventy-eight he had become so isolated that he seems actually to have been surprised when only 2.5 percent of his workers chose the "no union" option.

Henry was ready to shut down the company rather than accept the union, but his wife intervened. "Mrs. Ford was horrified," Henry told Sorensen. "She said she could not understand my doing anything like that. . . . She insisted that I sign what she called a peace agreement. If I did not, she was through. What could I do? . . . Don't ever discredit the power of a woman."

Even after the union arrived, Bennett's power grew. Henry had a minor stroke in 1938 and a more serious one in 1941. Bennett routinely claimed to act on the basis of private conversations with Henry—conversations that often did not take place. An electronic control board outside Bennett's office seemed the symbol of his influence. One executive recalled later:

You couldn't get a message to anybody without him seeing it. One could not hire, fire or transfer a man. I could not send a telegram if he did not wish me to do so. He had control of hiring and firing. He had control of transportation and communication. He had to approve all travel vouchers. . . . Regardless of where you were he knew about it. If you were in Europe he would know who you had dinner with on such and such an occasion. He had a spy system that was that thorough.

Edsel, ill with stomach problems that eventually turned into stomach cancer, could not overcome the combination of Bennett's scheming and Henry's distrust. "The hurtful thing," Edsel said to a friend, "is that Father takes Harry's word for everything and he won't believe me. Who is this guy, anyhow? Where did he come from?" Clara Ford echoed her son's bewilderment: "Who is this man Bennett who has so much control over my husband and is ruining my son's health?"

Edsel died at the age of forty-nine in May 1943. Like King Lear confronting the death of Cordelia, Henry was devastated. Something terribly unnatural had occurred. Everyone in the family understood what had happened, but neither Henry nor anyone else could understand *why* it had happened. One Ford executive recalled, "It was like watching a hog trying to eat its own farrow." Edsel's son Henry Ford II said much later, "It was my grandfather who killed my father. I know there was cancer. But it was also because of what my grandfather had put him through."

Endgame and Rebirth

The end of World War II, business historian Harold C. Livesay has written, found the Ford Motor Company "in the hands of a senile octogenarian and the vicious corporal of a goon-squad guard." Henry himself had become president again after Edsel's death, and Bennett's power kept growing. Edsel's chubby son Henry II, who turned twenty-eight in 1945, seemed no match for a street fighter who commanded his own army and who had been shrewd and tough enough to displace Charles Sorensen at Henry's right hand.

In this situation, the long-suffering women of the Ford family intervened decisively on behalf of Henry II. In 1941, Clara Ford had threatened to leave her husband of more than fifty years unless he recognized the UAW. Now, it seems, she made the same threat, only this time she insisted that he make Henry II president of the company. Her threat was backed by Edsel's widow, Eleanor, who said she would sell the stock she had inherited from Edsel—41.7 percent of the company—unless her son was put in charge immediately.

Henry II was named president of the Ford Motor Company on September 21, 1945. One of his first moves was to fire Harry Bennett. In the year that followed, he cleansed the company, firing more than a thousand of Bennett's men.

But much more needed to be done. In 1946 the Ford Motor Company was a case study in corporate rot. Decades of ruthless and capricious management had taken their toll. The company had not made a profit in fifteen years and was losing money at a rate of $1 million a day. Its share of the U.S. automobile market had dropped from 60 percent at the end of World War I to less than 20 percent at the start of World War II.

In *My Life and Work*, the ghostwritten autobiography he published in 1922, Henry had stated his philosophy of management: "No organization, no specific duties attaching to any position, no line of succession or authority, very few titles and conferences." He had meant what he said. Old-timers could recall the day when he had told his accountants that he saw no point in keeping ledgers: "Just put all the money we take in in a big barrel and when a shipment of material comes in reach into the barrel and take out enough money to pay for it."

Henry II hired a group of ten former Air Force officers led by Charles B. "Tex" Thornton, the youngest colonel in the history of the Army Air Force, to bring modern management techniques to Ford. As head of the Army Air Force's Office of Statistical Control under Assistant Secretary of War Robert A. Lovett, Thornton had been responsible for gigantic problems of scheduling and coordination.

At Ford, Thornton's group became known as the "Whiz Kids." It included future Ford presidents Arjay R. Miller and Robert S. Mc-Namara. After the group arrived on February 1, 1946, one of its first tasks was to assess the company's management systems. Thornton's team had known that the company had problems, but what they found astonished them. Millions of dollars were sitting in noninterest-bearing accounts in banks all over Michigan. Bookkeepers estimated accounts payable by using a yardstick to measure stacks of invoices. There was no system of cost accounting, no system of product development, no systematic scheduling of materials, no real market research, no real planning. One of the world's giant enterprises was being run like a mom-and-pop grocery

Henry Ford died at the age of almost eighty-four on April 7, 1947. Eleven years earlier, Henry and Edsel had established a small family foundation, the Ford Foundation, to avoid estate taxes and to ensure that the family would retain control of the company after their deaths. The foundation received most of the two estates in the form of Class A non-voting stock—an arrangement that made it the richest private foundation in the world, assured that the family's control of the company remained intact, and deprived the government of an estimated federal estate tax of $321 million.

In his life, Henry's attitude toward philanthropy had been well summarized in the title of one chapter in his autobiography: "Why Charity?" He had no patience, he wrote, "with professional charity or with any sort of commercialized humanitarianism. . . . Professional charity is not only cold but it hurts more than it helps. It degrades the recipient and drugs their self-respect." Many men failed because they lacked "gristle and bone." But charity would not help them. "Let every American become steeled against coddling. Americans ought to resent coddling. It is a drug. Stand up and stand out; let weaklings take charity."

Despite these misgivings, in his lifetime Henry gave almost $40 million to philanthropic causes, including about $10 million to build the Henry Ford Hospital in Detroit and close to $30 million to finance two projects that reflected his antiquarian interests: Greenfield Village, a miniature rural community; and the Henry Ford Museum.

Henry's real legacy, however, was the company he built and nearly destroyed. And even more than the company, his legacy was a lesson. Nowhere in the history of American business are the dangers of one-man rule more frighteningly demonstrated than in the decline of the Ford Motor Company in the last thirty years of Henry Ford's life.

CHAPTER 12

Alfred P. Sloan, Jr.: The Consummate Professional

The Organization Builders

In the period from 1924 to 1940, while Ford's share of the automobile market fell from 51 percent to 18 percent, General Motors' share rose from 18.8 percent to 47.5 percent. The blame for Ford's decline belongs largely to Henry Ford. The credit for GM's rise belongs largely to Alfred P. Sloan, Jr. In part the Ford Motor Company squandered the lead it had seized in the automobile industry, but the story of Ford's decline was not simply the story of the things Henry Ford did wrong. It also was the story of the things Sloan did right.

Business historian Alfred D. Chandler, Jr., has distinguished between "empire builders" and "organization builders" in American business. For the most part, Chandler argues, the empire builders of the late nineteenth and early twentieth centuries showed "little interest in fashioning a rational and systematic design for administering effectively the vast resources they had united under their control." To an empire builder like William Durant of GM, the details of administrative coordination seemed unimportant, whereas to an organization builder like Alfred Sloan, they seemed essential. After Durant led GM to the brink of collapse in 1920, it was Sloan who rescued the reeling company—rescued it not with charismatic leadership but with a precise, brilliant, comprehensive plan to restructure the organization, a plan that "transformed General Motors from an agglomeration of many business units . . . into a single, coordinated enterprise." In the history of American business, Sloan is the quintessential organization man, the consummate professional.

Alfred Pritchard Sloan, Jr., was born in New Haven, Connecticut, on May 23, 1875, the son of a well-to-do coffee and tea importer who moved the family to Brooklyn when Alfred was ten. After winning a reputation as a boy genius at Brooklyn Polytechnic Institute, Sloan graduated from the Massachusetts Institute of Technology with a B.S. in electrical engineering at the age of twenty, the youngest in his class.

After his graduation from M.I.T., Sloan tells us in *My Years with General Motors*, he took a job with the Hyatt Roller Bearing Company in New Jersey at a salary of $50 a month as "a kind of office boy, draftsman, salesman, and general assistant to the enterprise." He left to work with an early electric refrigerator firm, but returned in 1898 after his father and an associate bought control of Hyatt for $5,000, installed Alfred as general manager, and announced that they were giving him six months to make the company profitable.

Sloan met that challenge, and profits ceased to be much of a problem when manufacturers discovered that rear axles that turned on roller bearings worked wonderfully in automobiles. Ford became Hyatt's best customer; GM, its second best. By 1916 Sloan owned 75 percent of a company with an annual gross income of $10 million, yet he was worried. What if Ford, which represented half of Hyatt's sales, decided to make its own roller bearings? That same year, when William Durant called to ask whether he had ever thought of selling Hyatt, Sloan was ready to listen.

Durant had created General Motors as a holding company in 1908. Before long he controlled the Buick, Cadillac, Oldsmobile, and Oakland (later Pontiac) companies, along with nearly a dozen parts and accessories manufacturers. But the optimism that he never learned to restrain caused him to become overextended financially, and in 1910 he had been forced to turn over the management of the company to a banking syndicate headed by James J. Storrow of Boston.

With Louis Chevrolet, a Swiss-born mechanic and racing driver, Durant organized the Chevrolet Motor Company in 1911. Then, with profits from this venture and powerful new allies from Du Pont, he secretly bought stock in GM and regained the presidency in 1916. That same year Pierre Du Pont, one of the most highly respected men in American business, became GM's chairman.

With Du Pont's blessing, Durant ran the show. One of his first moves was to organize a new holding company, United Motors, as an umbrella for the parts and accessories companies he bought whenever he could. When GM purchased Hyatt for $13.5 million in 1916, Sloan became president of United Motors. The subsidiary firms included Dayton Engineering Laboratories Company, known as Delco. Charles F. Kettering of Delco, the engineering genius who had invented the self-starter in 1912, became one of Sloan's key associates. "Boss Ket" headed research and development at GM; invented the antiknock gasoline that makes possible high-compression engines; made numerous other contributions to the engineering of automobiles, locomotives, airplanes, and appliances; and, in 1945, joined Sloan in making the gift that established what is generally regarded as the nation's leading cancer research institute, the Sloan-Kettering Institute for Cancer Research in New York City.

At United Motors in 1916–19, Sloan fretted that, as he wrote later, Durant "was too casual in his ways for an administrator." In *Adventures of a White-Collar Man*, a memoir published in 1941, Sloan was candid about his reservations:

> From the time I became president of United Motors, I saw a great deal of Mr. Durant. I was constantly amazed by his daring way of making decisions. My business experience had convinced me facts are precious things, to be eagerly sought and treated with respect. But Mr. Durant would proceed on a course of action guided solely, as far as I could tell, by some intuitive flash of brilliance. He never felt obliged to make an engineering hunt for facts.

As a result, Sloan felt, GM made "many costly errors."

Despite his indifference to administration, Durant had built an empire. By 1919 GM was the fifth-largest industrial enterprise in the United States—a loosely knit confederation of dozens of automobile manufacturing and accessories companies. The looseness troubled Sloan: "I was particularly concerned that [Durant] had expanded General Motors between 1918 and 1920 without an explicit policy of management with which to control the various parts of the organization. . . . We did not have adequate knowledge or control of the individual operating divisions. It was management by crony, with the divisions operating on a horse-trading basis."

Durant was not troubled. He had built his automobile empire on the apparently sound assumption that the market for automobiles was unlimited. The only business problem that interested him was the problem of making enough automobiles to satisfy soaring demand. He had never worried much about the possibility that demand might fall. He had never worried much about the problems of coordinating his far-flung empire. "He was invariably optimistic," Sloan wrote later.

In 1920, Durant's optimism nearly destroyed GM. Failing to anticipate the postwar recession, GM's division managers continued to invest heavily in new plants and machinery to meet the next surge in demand. Instead, demand plunged. By November, sales had dropped to one-quarter of their level in early summer, and the company was having trouble finding cash to pay current invoices and to meet its payroll. To make matters worse, Durant tried to sustain GM's falling stock price by buying stock on credit—a maneuver that did not merely fail, but also left him owing $30 million to bankers and other creditors. On November 20, 1920, Durant resigned as president of GM. Ten days later, Pierre Du Pont, the chairman of the corporation and the representative of the largest shareholder (the Du Pont Company), was named to replace him.

As 1920 ended, GM's prospects looked bleak. As Sloan wrote in his autobiography, "The automobile market had nearly vanished and with it our income. . . . We were loaded with high-priced inventory and commitments at the old inflated price level. We were short of cash. We had a confused product line. There was a lack of control and of any means of control in operations and finance, and a lack of adequate information about anything."

Saving General Motors

What GM did have going for it was a comprehensive plan to correct its operating deficiencies. Sloan had drawn up the plan on his own initiative in late 1919 and early 1920, before the events that led to Durant's departure. When Pierre Du Pont took over as president of GM, one of his first acts was to review Sloan's proposal. Like Sloan, Du Pont was steady and conservative, a graduate of M.I.T. who favored an analytic, systematic approach to business. Sloan's organizational plan, the most famous in the history of American business, was approved by GM's Board of Directors on December 29, 1920, a month after Du Pont took command.

Sloan's recommendation for General Motors resembled in many ways the organization design that Pierre Du Pont had worked out as president of the Du Pont Company from 1902 to 1919. But, as Sloan observes in his autobiography, the two companies "proceeded from opposite poles." Du Pont had evolved from a too rigidly centralized type of organization, whereas GM was emerging from the chaos of almost total decentralization. Du Pont had needed to gain the advantages of decentralized operations without losing the advantages of centralized coordination. GM needed to gain the advantages of centralized coordination without losing the advantages of decentralization.

The great advantage of decentralization, in Sloan's view, was that it allowed each business unit to be run by the executives who knew it best. Thus it allowed key business decisions to be made by the executives who were best equipped to make them. Decentralization took advantage of the company's most important resource—its people. It encouraged individual initiative and judgment. It groomed executives. "A decentralized organization," Sloan wrote in a memo in 1921, "is the only one that will develop the talent necessary to meet the Corporation's big problems."

But Sloan did not advocate complete decentralization. What he wanted was decentralized operations with centrally coordinated control—"a happy medium in industrial organization between the extremes of pure centralization and pure decentralization." Coordination would be achieved through "interdivisional committees" (later called "policy groups") in areas such as engineering, purchasing, distribution, personnel, public relations, and research.

Sloan also assigned each operating division to one of four "groups"—Car, Accessory, Parts, and Miscellaneous—under the general supervision of a group vice president. But he carefully limited the role of the group executives: "I have never believed that a group as such could manage anything. A group can make policy, but only individuals can administer policy." Group executives were supposed to advise operating managers, but they were not supposed to make decisions for them. "The responsibility for the success or failure of each individual operation within the group lies entirely . . . with the General Manager of that particular operation who formulates all the detailed policies subject only to control in an advisory way by the General Manager of the group."

An Operations Committee was established to appraise the performance of the divisions. Here Sloan faced a final problem. In attempting to solve it, he addressed the paradox that lies at the heart of any scheme of decentralization with centrally coordinated control: "How could we exercise permanent control over the whole corporation in a way consistent with the decentralized scheme of organization?"

"It was on the financial side," Sloan writes in his autobiography, "that the last necessary key to decentralization with co-ordinated control was found." The key was the principle of return on investment, which furnished "the means to review and judge the effectiveness of operations." To Sloan, return on investment was not merely a measure of results. It also was "a strategic principle of business." But it was a principle that had to be understood in a sophisticated way: "The question is not simply one of maximizing the rate of return for a specific short period of time. . . . The fundamental consideration was an average return over a long period of time"—that is, "the highest return consistent with . . . a sound growth of the business."

Today, business historian Alfred D. Chandler, Jr., points out, the decentralized structure with centrally coordinated control has become "the accepted form of management for the most complex and diverse of American industrial enterprises." But in the days when Pierre Du Pont and Alfred Sloan struggled with the problems of structuring giant corporations, the decentralized, multidivisional design was a genuine innovation—something new in the history of economic organization. The kind of organization they created has grown familiar now, but it was not familiar when they created it. In their precise, rational, methodical ways, Du Pont and Sloan were innovators as bold as Picasso in painting or Stravinsky in music.

"A Car for Every Purse and Purpose"

On May 10, 1923, satisfied that the company had recovered from the crisis that nearly toppled it in 1920, Pierre Du Pont stepped down as president of GM. Sloan replaced him, serving as president until 1937 and then as chairman of the board from 1937 until his retirement at the age of eighty in 1956. With small modifications, the organizational design he put in place in the early 1920s remains intact to this day.

It was not only in the area of organizational structure that Sloan exercised a profound influence. In the area of product policy, too, he initiated a transformation from chaos to coherence.

Under Durant there had been "no established policy for the car lines as a whole," with the result that the different divisions competed with one another. The company had too many cars at some price levels and no cars at other levels. Sloan's sense of order found the system—or, rather, the lack of system—offensive. "It seemed to me that the intelligent approach would be to have a car at every price position, just the same as a general conducting a campaign wants to have an army at every point he is likely to be attacked."

Sloan felt that GM should make six standard models at six different price levels—"a car for every purse and purpose." But he was not satisfied merely to define a product line. He defined the line in a way that also defined a selling strategy. No passage in Sloan's autobiography shows better the clarity of his thinking than his explanation of this point: "Having thus separated out a set of related price classes, we set forth an intricate strategy which can be summarized as follows: We proposed in general that General Motors should place its cars at the top of each price range and make them of such a quality that they would attract sales from below that price, selling to those customers who might be willing to pay a little more for the additional quality, and attract sales from above that price, selling to those customers who would see the price advantage in a car of close to the quality of higher-priced competition. This amounted to quality competition against cars below a given price tag, and price competition against cars above that price tag."

This strategy, with its commitment to variety, was the strategy that routed Henry Ford in the 1920s. A critical factor in this period was the development of the closed-body automobile, which supplied the final blow to the Model T. With its light chassis, the Model T "was pre-eminently an open-car design." But an open-body automobile was not an all-weather automobile. GM's share of the automobile market rose from 18.8 percent in 1924 to 43.3 percent in 1927. In his autobiography, commenting on Ford's decline, Sloan pulls no punches: "The old master had failed to master change. Don't ask me why. There is a legend cultivated by sentimentalists that Mr. Ford left behind a great car expressive of the pure concept of cheap, basic transportation. The fact is that he left behind a car that no longer offered the best buy, even as raw, basic transportation."

Sloan on Sloan

A profound test of Sloan's skill as a chief executive came with the Depression of the 1930s. Having learned from Durant's failure in the slump of 1920, Sloan quickly slashed inventories when sales began to fall. At a time when many companies went out of business, GM made at least a small profit every year in the 1930s. It also paid dividends every year.

"No more than anyone else did we see the depression coming," Sloan observes in his autobiography. Yet, over the decade as a whole, the company paid shareholders $1.19 billion in dividends, compared with $797 million in the 1920s. At the same time, "net working capital rose from $248 million . . . to $434 million," while "capital employed rose slightly, from $954 million to $1,066 million." This record in a time of crisis was "perhaps the greatest payoff of our system of financial and operating controls."

The 1930s was also the period when GM officially embraced the policy of an annual change in car models. Procedures governing the production of new models were spelled out in a comprehensive manual first published in 1935. With its commitment to continuous, controlled change, GM's annual model change was the exact opposite of the design "freeze" that had killed the Model T in the long run.

Sloan was nearly ninety when he published his autobiography in 1963. At that point he took the opportunity to reflect on the growth of General Motors "as an institution in American economic life." In the forty-five years from 1918 through 1962, he noted, the number of GM employees had increased from twenty-five thousand to over six hundred thousand; the number of shareholders had increased from less than three thousand to more than one million; sales of cars and trucks produced in the United States and Canada had risen from 205,000 units to 4.491 million units; dollar sales had risen from $270 million to $14.6 billion; and total assets had grown from $134 million to $9.2 billion. In those forty-five years dividend payments had totaled nearly $10.8 billion, or 67 percent of total earnings.

These figures inspired Sloan to pay himself the most modest of tributes, disguised as a tribute to the organization he had built: "In an economy based on competition, we have operated as rational businessmen. . . . The result has been an efficient enterprise. . . . Our performance has been demonstrated day by day in our production and distribution of goods useful to the community. I shall be glad for General Motors to be judged by this performance."

The enterprise was efficient, Sloan added elsewhere, because it was "an objective organization," not "the type that gets lost in the subjectivity of personalities." In other words, the organization was efficient because Sloan had built it in his own image. The company that roared from behind to dominate the American automobile industry mirrored the personality of the man who fashioned it, no less than the Ford Motor Company mirrored the personality of Henry Ford. But there was a vital difference: After Sloan left, his successors did not have to smash the mirror.

CHAPTER 13

Madison Avenue

The Mass Market

Every economic system balances supply and demand. Mass production (the supply side of the equation) must be supported by mass consumption (the demand side). Together, mass production, mass distribution, and mass consumption meet in the modern mass market.

In straightforward histories of American business, the discussion of mass distribution usually precedes the discussion of mass production. The reason is obvious. In the business history of the United States, the infrastructure that supports mass distribution was completed before Henry Ford ever dreamed of mass-producing his Tin Lizzie.

The tough work was done in the nineteenth century. The development of a national transportation system (the railroads) and a national communications system (first the telegraph, later the telephone) made a mass market possible. The nation's economic development depended on these advances. Mass production would have been meaningless without a system of mass distribution.

Mass distribution in the United States began with agricultural products and standardized consumer goods. Until about 1850, old-fashioned mercantile firms still brought the nation's goods to market. In the 1850s and 1860s, these firms were challenged by commodity dealers in agricultural products and by full-line wholesalers in consumer goods. Then, in the 1870s and 1880s, mass retailers began to supplant the wholesalers.

The first of the modern mass retailers were the department stores, which started to emerge in the 1860s and 1870s. The critical factor was the growth of urban markets. In a few decades names such as Macy's and Gimbels in New York; John Wanamaker and Strawbridge & Clothier in Philadelphia; Filene's and Jordan Marsh in Boston; Marshall Field in Chicago; Hutzler's in Baltimore; Woodward and Lothrop in Washington, D.C.; Rich's in Atlanta; Neiman-Marcus in Dallas; and the Emporium and I. Magnin in San Francisco became household words and made fortunes for their founders.

Another type of mass retailer, the mail-order house, concentrated on rural America. Whereas urban consumers came to the department stores, the mail-order houses brought their wares to more isolated customers through catalogs. Montgomery Ward, founded in 1872 by Aaron Montgomery Ward and his brother-in-law George A. Thorne, was the first enterprise that marketed a wide variety of goods by mail. By 1887 it had a catalog of 540 pages with more than twenty-four thousand items listed.

Sears, Roebuck & Company, founded in 1887 to sell watches by mail, began to expand in the 1890s and passed Montgomery Ward as the top mail-order house in 1900. Under the leadership of Julius Rosenwald, who joined the firm as a partner in 1895, sales rose from $388,000 in 1893 to $11 million in 1900, $40 million in 1910, and $245 million in 1920. By the early years of the twentieth century, business historian Alfred D. Chandler, Jr., has pointed out, Sears was handling over one hundred thousand orders a day—"as many transactions as most traditional merchants in prerailroad days handled in a lifetime."

A third type of mass retailer, the chain stores, began to emerge after the Civil War, but their growth was not explosive until the twentieth century. In groceries, half a dozen chains had begun by 1900, including the Great Atlantic and Pacific Tea Company, the Grand Union Company, and the Great Western Tea Company. In low-priced variety stores, Woolworth's came first, followed by the chains begun by S. H. Kress in Memphis in 1896 and by S. S. Kresge in Detroit in 1899. Then, in the 1920s, as the rural market declined. Sears, Roebuck and Montgomery Ward organized enormous chains of retail stores. After World War II, the suburban shopping mall began to be a dominant feature of the American landscape.

Mass distribution in the twentieth century was not handled only by mass retailers. Many manufacturers built their own marketing and distribution networks. In these firms, Chandler observes, "the mass producer rather than the mass marketer took over the role of coordinating the flow of goods through the economy." In other words, mass production and mass distribution were united in giant organizations that internalized activities formerly carried out by separate enterprises. The big automobile companies with their global networks of suppliers and dealers are the best examples of these modern, vertically integrated enterprises.

The Adman Cometh

With the emergence of the modern mass market, marketing has become tremendously complex. In one textbook that is currently popular in American business schools, the chapter "Advertising Decisions" follows chapters titled "Price Decisions," "Channel Decisions," "Physical-distribution Decisions," and "Communications-promotion Decisions," not to mention such chapters as "Strategic Marketing," "Consumer Markets and Buyer Behavior," "Demand Measurement and Forecasting," "Market Segmentation and Targeting," "Product-mix and Brand Strategy," "New-Product Development Strategy," "Product Life-Cycle Strategy," and more.

Though advertising may all but disappear in a textbook, nothing is as visible, as audible, or as inescapable in our lives. For this reason, no aspect of marketing is more interesting than advertising. We hear advertisements before we understand what we are hearing; we remember advertisements years after we have forgotten when we first heard or saw them; we live out our lives among advertisements; we grow accustomed to advertisements as we grow accustomed to grass, air, and sunshine.

The first American advertising agency was founded by Volney B. Palmer in Philadelphia in 1841. Palmer charged newspapers a commission of 25 percent for selling advertising space to companies. In his *Reminiscences of the Advertising Business* an early agent, S. M. Pettingill, recalls Palmer as a consummate salesman: "He was . . . of good address, genial, and pleasant in manner. . . . He would generally enforce his words by some well-told stories, and get all parties into good humor and laughing heartily. He would end up by asking if he might be permitted to make out an estimate for the merchant's advertisement." Palmer eventually went mad—a sign, perhaps, that he paid a price for the charm that made him a good salesman.

One of the most important nineteenth-century advertising agents was

George P. Rowell, a farm boy from New Hampshire who founded his own agency in Boston in 1865. At the time, one major problem for advertisers was the difficulty of obtaining accurate estimates of circulation for various newspapers. In 1869 Rowell published the first edition of *Rowell's American Newspaper Directory*, with circulation estimates for over five thousand American and Canadian newspapers. Rowell's directory became a standard reference work, the forerunner of *N. W. Ayer & Son's Directory of Newspapers and Periodicals*. Later in his career Rowell founded *Printers' Ink*, which became a standard trade magazine for the emerging advertising industry.

Francis Wayland Ayer (the son in N. W. Ayer & Son) was responsible for another innovation that helped create the advertising business as we know it today. In 1875, Ayer introduced the "open contract," which established the agent's fee as a set commission—first 12.5 percent, later 15 percent—of the amount paid to the publisher. The "open" contract meant that the true rates charged by publishers were not kept secret from the advertisers who hired Ayer. This method of doing business eventually became the norm in the industry.

Ayer himself was a rather grim Baptist who irritated many of his colleagues. George Rowell complained that Ayer "thinks of work all the time, eats little, drinks nothing but water, [and] has no vices, small or large, unless overwork is a vice." All in all, Rowell felt, Ayer was "such a man as Oliver Cromwell would have been had Oliver been permitted to become an advertising agent."

Patent medicines were the first products to be widely advertised in the United States. According to Ralph Hower in his history of N. W. Ayer & Son, patent medicine advertising accounted for one quarter of the firm's revenues in the 1870s. Ayer handled advertising for such typical nineteenth-century products as Kennedy's Ivory Tooth Cement, which promised to make every man his own dentist; Compound Oxygen, which was said to cure every illness; and Rock and Rye, which offered a "Sure Cure for Lung Diseases" at $4.00 a gallon.

Probably the best known of the nineteenth-century patent medicines was Lydia Pinkham's Vegetable Compound, "The Positive Cure for All Female Complaints." Invented in 1875 by a Quaker housewife in Lynn, Massachusetts, the brew contained four kinds of roots, fenugreek seed, and a healthy dose of alcohol. It was said to cure every ill that troubled women, from menstrual cramps to difficult pregnancies. Even after Lydia Pinkham's death in 1883, advertisements urged women in need of help to write to her for answers to their problems.

The proliferation of low-priced, packaged consumer goods toward the end of the nineteenth century was probably the factor that contributed the most to the emergence of the advertising-saturated culture of the twentieth century. Branded goods that are sold nationwide require national advertising. Many companies that remain leading advertisers to this day first came on the scene in the last years of the nineteenth century, including Pillsbury, Quaker Oats, Eastman Kodak, Borden, H. J. Heinz, American Tobacco, Carnation, Campbell Soups, Procter & Gamble, and Colgate-Palmolive.

More than anything else, advertisers for the new national products sought a trademark or slogan that would make their product stand out from the crowd. Much that we still remember dates from this period. In 1877, for a cereal he called "Quaker Oats," Henry Parsons Crowell registered the trademark of a man in Quaker garb—the first registered trademark for a breakfast cereal. For Harley T. Procter's air-filled Ivory Soap, invented in 1882, advertisers came up with two of the most memorable phrases in advertising history: "It floats" and "99 and 44/100 percent pure." Also memorable was the slogan that helped to sell George Eastman's Kodak camera, invented in 1888: "You press the button; we do the rest" appealed to anyone who had ever struggled with a recalcitrant machine. For a prepackaged biscuit that the National Biscuit Company launched in 1898, N. W. Ayer & Son caught the public's fancy with "Lest you forget, we say it yet, Uneeda Biscuit." Consumers soon were offered Uwanta Beer, Itsagood Soup, and *Ureada Magazine*.

The enormous growth of consumer goods advertising late in the nineteenth century helped to create a new advertising medium, the mass-circulation magazine. In 1885 there were only four general magazines with a circulation of one hundred thousand or more. Two decades later there were twenty, with a combined circulation of 5.5 million. The leaders were two magazines published by Cyrus H. K. Curtis: *Ladies' Home Journal*, which reached nearly twice as many readers as any other adult magazine by the mid-1890s, and its counterpart for men, *The Saturday Evening Post*, whose circulation under editor George H. Lorimer rose from twenty-two hundred to two million in only fifteen years. By 1910, writes Stephen Fox in his history of American advertising, *The Mirror Makers*, "The magazine world had been transformed: a revolution prodded, celebrated, and paid for by advertising."

Curtis himself spent large sums advertising his magazines: "I want business men to advertise in the *Journal*," he explained, "and to show them that I believe in the principles which I advance, I advertise largely myself. . . . A man can never advertise too much." Finley Peter Dunne's curmudgeonly alter ego "Mr. Dooley" agreed, complaining that his favorite magazine had wasted a quarter of its pages on reading matter, with the result that its readers had suffered great inconvenience: "A man don't want to dodge around through almost inpenethrable pomes an' reform articles to find a pair iv suspinders or a shavin' soap." Being teased by Mr. Dooley was a kind of confirmation. The advertising age had arrived.

Hard Sell, Soft Sell

The advertising agencies of the 1870s were thinly staffed compared to their bustling successors. They had no full-time copywriters, no art directors, no market research experts, no account executives. They did not create ads but merely placed them.

The first "full service" advertising agency was founded by George Batten in New York in 1891. Batten offered his clients not merely assistance in placing ads but also in writing copy, preparing artwork, and supervising production. Batten's firm (Batten, Barton, Durstine & Osborne) became one of the advertising giants of twentieth century. In 1986 BBDO Worldwide was the fourth-largest agency in the world, with billings of $3.26 billion.

With the growth of full-service agencies came an increasing need for an individual who could mediate between clients and the creative staff of the agency. This need was met through the development of an executive whose role was to serve as an intermediary—the account executive. Invented by J. Walter Thompson, the position of account executive assumed crucial importance at the firm of one of the legendary figures of twentieth-century advertising, Albert D. Lasker.

Lasker's influence on advertising was so great that the first decades of the twentieth century have been called "The Age of Lasker." Born in Texas in 1880, the son of a German Jew whose ancestors had lived in the village of Lask in East Prussia, Lasker was made a partner in the Chicago firm of Lord & Thomas at the age of only twenty-four. His most notable gifts seem to have been his capacity for innovation and "his colossal assurance," as one of his associates commented, "that, given the same circumstances, nothing that he was doing could be done better."

In addition to his role in expanding the scope of the account executive, Lasker is credited with having made Lord & Thomas (later Foote, Cone & Belding) the prototype of the modern copy-oriented agency. "What goes into the space—that makes the difference," Lasker said in 1906. "Ninety percent of the thought, energy and cost of running our agency goes into copy. . . . Our copy staff costs us four times as much as that of any other agency."

Though he himself wrote no copy, Lasker hired not one but two of the most influential copywriters in advertising history. The first was John E. Kennedy, who was forty when, in 1904, the twenty-four-year-old Lasker hired him away from Dr. Shoop's Restorative at a salary of $16,000 a year. Kennedy preached an advertising gospel that focused squarely on sales. Good advertising, he argued, was "salesmanship-on-paper." It appealed to reason, offering the prospective customer a concrete "reason why" he or she should buy the advertised product. Its only aim was to sell. It did not care about "that Goldbrick of Advertising called 'General Publicity.' "

Through its commitment to "reason why" advertising, Lord & Thomas under Lasker became the largest advertising agency in the United States. "Mr. Kennedy is a one-idea man," the trade journal *Advertising & Selling* declared in 1909. "But his is a great idea. . . . His style is now the foundation stone of successful advertising." By that time Kennedy himself had left Lord & Thomas for a lucrative career as a free-lancer. But his replacement, Claude Hopkins, soon became the best-known copywriter of his time.

Hopkins built on the idea of advertising as salesmanship in print. "I consider advertising as dramatic salesmanship," he said. ". . . Advertising must be better than ordinary argument, just as a play must be stronger than ordinary life." To be effective, he added, an advertising campaign must focus on a single selling point: "You cannot chop a tree in two by hitting every time in a different place." Hitting a tree in the same place every time might be hard on the tree (a "hard sell"), but it got the job done.

Hopkins loved to work and claimed late in life that he had worked twice as hard as anyone else in the business. No one disputed him. Explaining his success, he said, "I steep myself in advertising. I read advertising, write advertising, think of advertising day and night." Thanks to Hopkins, the public learned that Quaker Puffed Wheat was "shot from guns" in the manufacturing process, that Pepsodent toothpaste attacked plaque, and that Schlitz beer came in bottles "washed with live steam" (so did other beers, but few people knew it). Hopkins's ads typically included a money-back guarantee, a premium, or a coupon for a free or cheap sample. So many coupons were distributed in ads written or influenced by Hopkins that "reason why" advertising is also known as "claim and coupon" advertising.

As the twentieth century proceeded, it became clear that fashion in advertising, like fashion in dress, did not progress in a line but moved in cycles. A period that favored the hard sell was sure to be followed by a period that favored the soft sell; a period that favored overstatement was sure to be followed by a period that favored understatement; a period that favored no-nonsense copy was sure to be followed by a period that favored fancy artwork; a period that favored logic and "reason why" was sure to be followed by a period that favored emotion, atmosphere, and image.

For instance, the Kennedy/Hopkins school was partly a reaction against a style of advertising popularized by Calkins & Holden, an agency founded by Ernest Elmo Calkins and Ralph Holden in 1901. Calkins & Holden specialized in campaigns that featured jingles and trade characters such as "The Arrow Collar Man" and Aunt Jemima, the black chef associated with pancakes. Their campaigns rarely offered the customer a reason to buy but were content simply to keep the product's name before the public, in ads that emphasized artwork rather than copy. The ads looked good and the jingles sounded good, but companies began to doubt how much they affected sales, and the Calkins & Holden style was supplanted by "reason why," with its insistence that "advertising should be judged *only* by the goods it is conclusively *known to sell*."

In time, however, the wheel of advertising fashion came full circle, and "reason why" began to seem stale. After all, critics charged, customers are not guided by reason alone. In the second decade of the twentieth century, Theodore F. MacManus championed a new style called "atmosphere" or "image" advertising and won a reputation as "the Claude Hopkins of soft sell."

MacManus's best-known work was done for General Motors, and his best-known ad—sometimes considered the greatest single ad ever written—appeared exactly once. In the fall of 1914, GM's top car, the Cadillac, was being challenged in an advertising campaign that focused on problems Cadillac was having with its new V-8 engine. MacManus responded with an ad that contained no illustration but consisted entirely of copy under the headline "The Penalty of Leadership." The copy did not mention Cadillac, nor did it mention automobiles. Instead, it used language to create an aura:

> In every field of human endeavor, he that is first must perpetually live in the white light of publicity. Whether the leadership be vested in a man or in a manufactured product, emulation and envy are ever at work. . . . The leader is assailed because he is a leader, and the effort to equal him is merely added proof of that leadership. Failing to equal or to excel, the follower seeks to deprecate and to destroy. . . . There is nothing new in

this. It is as old as the world and as old as the human passions. . . . And
it all avails nothing. If the leader truly leads, he remains—the leader. Mas-
ter-poet, master-painter, master-workman, each in his turn is assailed, and
each holds his laurels through the ages. That which is good or great makes
itself known, no matter how loud the clamor of denial. That which deserves to live—lives.

"The Penalty of Leadership" sought to persuade not through arguments but through atmosphere. Instead of offering reasons to buy, it
sought to create for Cadillac a mystique that transcended reason. Unlike
Claude Hopkins, who insisted that in advertising "Style is a handicap,"
MacManus assaulted the reader with "poetical" flourishes that would have
appalled any real poet. Though the ad ran only once (in *The Saturday
Evening Post* of January 2, 1915), it had an immediate effect on sales, and
for years GM was flooded with requests for reprints. When *Printers' Ink*
asked its readers to name the greatest ad of all time in 1945, "The Penalty of Leadership" won by a landslide.

Though a tension exists, the conflict between "reason why" advertising and "image" advertising is not as severe as it may seem at first glance.
Savvy advertisers eventually realized that each style had its place. As
Stephen Fox observes, "The Hopkins style worked best for small, frequently purchased items like cigarettes, toothpaste, and soap that could
be cheaply offered as samples and sent through the mail. . . . The
MacManus style was best applied to large, expensive, durable items with
prestige associations, bought infrequently and seldom on impulse. Surrounded by what MacManus called 'an invisible cloud of friendly, favor-
able impressions,' the product would all but sell itself at the proper time."

An advertising style that combined the "reason why" and "atmosphere" approaches was developed by Stanley and Helen Resor at the
J. Walter Thompson agency after J. Walter Thompson himself retired
in 1916. With Stanley Resor as president of the agency and his wife as
the star copywriter, JWT soared into first place in total billings in the
1920s—a position it held for half a century.

Products that the Resors helped to make famous include Crisco vegetable shortening, Lux soap flakes, Yuban coffee, Cutex nail polish, and
Fleishmann's Yeast. For Pond's cold cream, Helen developed a famous
series of ads with testimonials from some of the best-known women in
the world. The series began when the eccentric *grande dame* of New York
society, Mrs. Oliver H. P. Belmont, consented to appear in exchange
for a contribution to one of her favorite charities. An ad featuring the
Queen of Romania brought 9,435 replies; an ad featuring Mrs. Reginald
Vanderbilt topped the queen by drawing 10,325 replies; and an ad fea-

turing the Duchess de Richelieu topped everyone by drawing 19,126 replies.

Helen Resor's best-known ad was for Woodbury's Facial Soap. The atmosphere in the ad was provided by a painting of an attractive high-society couple in evening dress. Beneath the alluring image, under the headline "A skin you love to touch," came seven paragraphs of "reason why" copy, plus the kind of offer Claude Hopkins loved: for ten cents, a week's supply of soap and an eight-color reproduction of the painting. The campaign was a sensation. "The phrase sings itself into your memory," one writer gushed in the *Atlantic Monthly*. "The pictures of this famous series have probably been seen by more people at one time than any others ever painted." Years later, Albert Lasker said that the three most important events in advertising history were Ayer's development of the open contract, his own promotion of "reason why" advertising, and the use of sex appeal in Helen Resor's Woodbury's campaign. The public gave its own testimonial: Sales of the soap increased by 1,000 percent in eight years.

Reeves, Rubicam, Burnett, and Ogilvy

A comprehensive history of advertising in the twentieth century might show in detail, as Stephen Fox has shown in *The Mirror Makers*, how cycles of hard sell and soft sell have succeeded one another through the years. The cycles occur, Fox argues, not because one style is intrinsically better than the other but because the public craves novelty. After one style has dominated for a while, people grow bored and stop responding to it, at which point the style that has been out of favor is suddenly experienced as new and fresh.

Probably the best-known disciple of Claude Hopkins in recent years was copywriter Rosser Reeves, who led the Ted Bates agency through a period of tremendous growth in the 1950s. Reeves was noted for his dedication to the Unique Selling Proposition, as in his campaigns for M&M candies ("melt in your mouth, not in your hands") and for Colgate toothpaste ("cleans your breath while it cleans your teeth"). He also was known for his devotion to the hard sell, as in the widely admired ads for Anacin aspirin that showed a crashing hammer, a tightly coiling spring, and a bolt of blazing electricity in the skull of a headache victim. "Salesmanship in print," Reeves said, is "still the best definition of advertising. If a copywriter isn't a salesman, then he is a bad copywriter."

The "image" style of advertising associated with Theodore MacManus also has had influential followers, including Raymond Rubicam, who masterminded the growth of Young & Rubicam in the 1930s, and Leo Burnett, the leader of the "Chicago school" that emerged as a major force in the 1950s. Under Rubicam, Y&R invented Elsie the Cow as a motherly symbol for the Borden Company, lured George Gallup from Northwestern University to conduct market research surveys, and came up with "The Instrument of the Immortals" as a suitably classy slogan for Steinway pianos. By 1940, only J. Walter Thompson exceeded Y&R in annual billings.

Like Rubicam, Leo Burnett spurned "reason why" advertising in favor of soft-sell appeals that relied on trade characters such as the Pillsbury Doughboy, Tony the Tiger, and the Jolly Green Giant. Burnett's most famous character was a cowboy, the Marlboro Man, who was introduced in 1955 to persuade consumers that filter cigarettes were not for sissies. Burnett took pride in his agency's capacity to invent characters that appealed to ordinary people, and he made a point of contrasting the work that came out of Chicago with the work produced by the sophisticates on Madison Avenue: "Our sod-busting delivery, our loose-limbed stand and our wide-eyed perspective make it easier for us to create ads that talk turkey to the majority of Americans," he said. "I like to think that we Chicago ad-makers are all working stiffs. I like to imagine that Chicago copywriters spit on their hands before picking up the big, black pencils."

As Helen Resor had combined the "reason why" and "atmosphere" approaches at J. Walter Thompson in the 1920s, so the most celebrated advertising man of the past fifty years, David Ogilvy, sought to develop a synthesis that would take the best from both approaches. Born near London in 1911, the son of a mother whom he described as a "beautiful and eccentric Irishwoman" and a father whom he described as "a Gaelic-speaking highlander, a classical scholar, and a bigoted agnostic," Ogilvy lived as a child in Lewis Carroll's house in Guildford, England, but the family was not rich. Ogilvy's early work experience included a position as an apprentice chef at $7.00 a week in Paris and a stint as a door-to-door salesman of cooking stoves in Scotland.

The job as a stove salesman inspired Ogilvy to write a pamphlet, *The Theory and Practice of Selling the Aga Cooker*, that won him a position with the London advertising agency Mather & Crowther, where his older brother Francis already worked as an account executive. In 1928 David persuaded the agency to send him to the United States to study American advertising. Ogilvy, Stephen Fox writes, "arrived as an exponent of the British image school of whimsy and soft sell," but he soon fell under the spell of Rosser Reeves, who lent him a copy of Claude Hopkins's *Scientific Advertising* and preached the "reason why" gospel to him. "My admiration for these two opposite schools tore me apart," Ogilvy recalled decades later. "It took me a long time to reconcile what I learned from both of them."

Reeves's influence reached beyond work. The tweedy, pipe-smoking Englishman liked Reeves's wife, asked to meet her sister, and wound up becoming Reeves's brother-in-law. What had been intended as a one-year visit in America became a stay that lasted some forty years.

As associate director of George Gallup's Audience Research Institute at Princeton, Ogilvy conducted over four hundred national opinion surveys in three years—an experience that, he writes in *Confessions of an Advertising Man*, "gave me more insight into the habits and mentality of the American consumer than most native copywriters can bring to bear." What especially impressed him was Gallup's research on "the factors which make people *remember* what they read." In later years he was irritated when he found himself "type-cast as a good copywriter, but an ignoramus in every other department." He felt that his strength "was not copy at all, but research."

After serving in British Security during the Second World War, Ogilvy spent several happy years as a farmer in the Amish country near Lancaster, Pennsylvania. When it became apparent that he could not earn a living from the land, however, he decided to start his own agency. Hewitt, Ogilvy, Benson & Mather opened for business in September 1948 with a few small British accounts.

Though Ogilvy considered himself a convert to the "reason why" tradition, his agency won its first great success with a fabulously successful "image" campaign. A small clothing firm in Maine approached the agency to develop advertising for its shirt. Ogilvy produced an ad that showed the shirt on a middle-aged, moustached gentleman with a black patch over one eye. The eye patch, he explained to the client, made the model look "like a very real and interesting person, instead of a conventional dummy. . . . It is a small matter, but it may make a big difference." The first ad in the series appeared in *The New Yorker* on September 22, 1951. Soon the Hathaway factory in Maine was swamped with orders for its shirts.

For four years, Ogilvy's ads featuring the man in the Hathaway shirt appeared only in *The New Yorker*. "As the campaign developed," Ogilvy recalled in *Confessions of an Advertising Man*, "I showed the model in a series of situations in which I would have liked to find myself: conducting the New York Philharmonic at Carnegie Hall, playing the oboe, copying a Goya at the Metropolitan Museum, driving a tractor, fencing, sailing, buying a Renoir, and so forth." The first ad contained five paragraphs of reason-why copy, but by 1956 the ad ran without a word. "Customers," Stephen Fox comments, "were buying an image, not a sales pitch."

An image, too, was what Ogilvy sold in a second series of famous advertisements, this one for Schweppes quinine water. The bushy-bearded "man from Schweppes" in the ads was Schweppes's own advertising manager, Commander Edward Whitehead. Whitehead's beard, like the model's eye patch in the Hathaway ads, was a small matter that made a big difference. Sales soared, and with them Ogilvy's reputation. But the success of his "image" advertisements was not an unmixed pleasure for Ogilvy. "I have become the symbol," he complained in 1956, "for a school of advertising which I deplore."

Ogilvy joined the "image" and "claim" approaches in a celebrated ad for Rolls-Royce that appeared in 1958. The image was the car itself, without "baronial halls or footmen"—the Rolls portrayed, Ogilvy explained to Rolls's executives, as "an acceptable symbol of *American* life." The headline—"At 60 miles an hour the loudest noise in this new Rolls-Royce comes from the electric clock"—emphasized the quality of Rolls's engineering. Below, in tiny print, came nineteen items of "reason why" copy—nineteen items whose aim was "to give the reader *facts*—more facts than the Detroit manufacturers put into their advertisements." Through facts "set down austerely, without adjectives," Ogilvy told Rolls's executives, the company would assert its position of "supreme leadership." His strategy worked. The year the ad appeared, sales rose by 50 percent.

Ogilvy's *Confessions of an Advertising Man*, a brisk, witty, anecdote-crammed memoir and primer published in 1963, sold over four hundred thousand copies in its first five years in print and over a million copies in twenty, thus becoming the best-selling advertising book of all time. In one of the most interesting passages in the book, Ogilvy renounced "image" advertising: "I have never admired the *belles lettres* school of advertising which reached its pompous peak in Theodore F. MacManus' famous advertisement for Cadillac, 'The Penalty of Leadership,' and Ned Jordan's classic, 'Somewhere West of Laramie.' Forty years ago the business community seems to have been impressed by these pieces of purple prose, but I have always thought them absurd; they did not give the reader a single *fact*."

Though he poked fun at Raymond Rubicam's famous slogan for Squibb ("The priceless ingredient of every product is the honor and integrity of its maker"), Ogilvy pronounced Rubicam "probably the best agency head in history" and ranked him as second only to Claude Hopkins among copywriters. Rubicam returned the compliment: "You are Claude Hopkins," he wrote to Ogilvy after he received the book, "enriched with an intellect and an Oxford education."

In 1964 Ogilvy's agency merged with Mather & Crowther of London to form Ogilvy & Mather, with Ogilvy as chairman. By this time, however, Ogilvy's years as a supersalesman were taking their toll. To a friend he wrote, "I have developed an almost uncontrollable distaste for my job: the paper, the unappreciative clients, the perpetual fire-fighting, the humbug." More and more, he spent his time at the French château he had purchased in 1967. He was a legend, but not a complacent one. When he looked back on his life in 1976, his tone was a mixture of modesty and resignation, with perhaps a touch of sadness: "I didn't have the brains to be a historian," he told an interviewer. "Of all the things that were open to me, advertising was the best. It's the only thing in my whole life I've been any good at."

The Consumption Ethic

The growth of the advertising industry in the second half of the twentieth century has been phenomenal. Total advertising expenditures in the United States rose from $5.7 billion in 1950 to nearly $12.0 billion in 1960, $19.5 billion in 1970, $53.5 billion in 1980, and $102.1 billion in 1986. That $102.1 billion represented 56.7 percent of total worldwide advertising expenditures. For every man, woman, and child in the United States in 1986, a total of $424.07 was spent on advertising. That figure compared with $242.43 per capita in Finland, $150.81 per capita in Japan, $81.02 per capita in France, $53.73 per capita in Italy, and $13.67 per capita in Brazil.

Large companies spent the bulk of the money. The top ten advertisers spent $8.6 billion in 1986. Procter & Gamble led with total advertising expenditures of $1.435 billion, followed by Philip Morris with $1.364 billion, Sears, Roebuck with $1.005 billion, RJR Nabisco with $935 million, General Motors with $839 million, Ford with $648 million, Anheuser-Busch with $644 million, McDonald's with $592 million, K Mart with $590 million, and PepsiCo with $581 million. The nation's thirty-third–largest advertiser was the federal government, which spent $300 million to promote everything from the Postal Service to the Statue of Liberty coin campaign.

Contrary to popular belief, the leader among advertising media was not television but newspapers. A total of $27 billion was spent on newspaper advertising in 1986, compared to $22.6 billion on television advertising, $17.1 billion on direct mail advertising, $6.9 billion on radio advertising, and nearly $5.5 billion on magazine advertising.

Also contrary to popular belief, Madison Avenue on the East Side of Manhattan was no longer the center of the advertising world. In 1989, the Ogilvy Group and N. W. Ayer announced that they were moving to lower-rent facilities on unfashionable Eighth Avenue in New York City. With their departure, only two of the nation's sixteen largest agencies remained on Madison Avenue.

Those large agencies were very large, indeed. In 1945, only two agencies, J. Walter Thompson and Young & Rubicam, billed over $50 million. In 1986, each of the top ten agencies billed over $2.0 billion, led by Young & Rubicam with total worldwide billings of $4.19 billion. Total billings of U.S. advertising agencies rose from $23.0 billion in 1980 to $48.3 billion in 1987.

To look only at U.S. agencies is to miss the larger story, however. The big shift in the advertising world in recent years has not been the move of American agencies away from Madison Avenue, but the purchase of American agencies by foreign giants. A British firm, the WPP Group, bought J. Walter Thompson for $566 million in 1987 and the Ogilvy Group for $864 million in 1989, while its chief rival, the British firm Saatchi & Saatchi, acquired such notable American agencies as Dancer Fitzgerald Sample, Backer & Spielvogel, and Ted Bates Worldwide. These acquisitions, *The Sunday Times* of London commented in an editorial, had "exposed the full nakedness of the greatest names on Madison Avenue." In advertising, as in automobiles and electronics, the United States had seemed "invulnerable and majestic," but in reality it was "shabby, inefficient and self-satisfied, an emperor with no clothes."

An extraordinary aspect of the massive expenditure on advertising in modern times is that no one knows for sure what effect it has. Critics of advertising frequently charge that it has an enormous impact. For instance, in *The New Industrial State* John Kenneth Galbraith asserts that "The industrial system is profoundly dependent on commercial television and could not exist in its present form without it." Why? Because producers depend upon "a relentless propaganda on behalf of goods in general." No citizen escapes the assault: "From early morning until late at night, people are informed of the services rendered by goods—of their profound indispensability. . . . Even minor qualities of unimportant commodities are enlarged upon with a solemnity which would not be unbecoming in an announcement of the combined return of Christ and all the apostles. More important services, such as the advantages of whiter laundry, are treated with proportionately greater gravity."

In the absence of this "massive and artful persuasion," Galbraith argues, "increasing abundance might well have reduced the interest of people in acquiring more goods. . . . No one would have pressed upon them the advantages of new packages, new forms of processed foods, newly devised dentifrices, new pain-killers, or other new variants on older products. Being not pressed by the need for these things, they would have spent less reliably of their income and worked less reliably to get more. The consequence—a lower and less reliable propensity to consume—would have been awkward for the industrial system."

Advertisers reply that the critics overestimate the power of advertising. They point out that market research shows that only a tiny fraction of viewers can name the brand they saw advertised on television three minutes ago. They note, too, that while there is plenty of evidence to suggest that advertising can get people to try a bad product once, there is no evidence to suggest that it can get them to try it a second time. With regard to the power of advertising to influence product choices, defenders of advertising point out, the critics consistently claim more than the advertisers themselves. The critics imagine that advertisers can influence product choices, whereas the advertisers themselves seek nothing more than to influence *brand* choices.

One point that seems incontestable is that advertising fills our minds in a unique way. In recent years we have heard much discussion about deficiencies in the education of America's young people. According to one much-publicized study, two thirds of our seventeen-year-olds do not know when the Civil War occurred. Half cannot identify either Stalin or Churchill. One third do not know that Columbus sailed for the New World before 1750. Three fourths cannot identify Walt Whitman or Henry David Thoreau. And so on.

These studies tell us what we do not know, but not what we know. The answer, it seems clear, is that we know advertising. The same college students who identify Socrates as a Native American chief and the Great Gatsby as a magician would have little difficulty, one suspects, recognizing the celebrities who appear on the popular Miller Lite ads or humming GM's anthem of the 1980s, "The Heartbeat of America."

The pervasiveness of advertising, combined with pitiless repetition, gives some of it remarkable staying power. "Lucky Strike Means Fine Tobacco" . . . "I'd Walk a Mile for a Camel" . . . "I Dreamed I was WANTED in my Maidenform Bra" . . . "Put a Tiger in your Tank"

. . . "Don't Leave Home Without It"—if we emptied the head of the average American in the second half of the twentieth century, surely this is the stuff that would spill out. These odds and ends, these scraps, shreds, tidbits, jingles, slogans—these are the common coin of the American consciousness, the shared language that ties us together no matter what else divides us.

A second point that seems incontestable is that advertising encourages what might be called a consumption ethic. No matter what else it might tell us, all advertising tells us that it is good to consume. This is a point that elicits a measure of agreement even among writers who generally view the world through quite different ideological spectacles.

In *The Culture of Narcissism*, for instance, liberal commentator Christopher Lasch writes that advertising

> manufactures a product of its own: the consumer, perpetually unsatisfied, restless, anxious and bored. [Advertising] serves not so much to advertise products as to promote consumption as a way of life. . . . It upholds consumption as the answer to the age-old discontents of loneliness, sickness, weariness, lack of sexual satisfaction; at the same time, it creates new forms of discontent peculiar to the modern age. . . . Is your job boring and meaningless? Does it leave you with feelings of futility and fatigue? Is your life empty? Consumption promises to fill the aching void.

By comparison, conservative commentator Irving Kristol, in *Two Cheers for Capitalism*, laments what the modern world has done to the kind of person he calls "the bourgeois citizen." This admirable individual, Kristol writes, "used to exist in large numbers, but now is on the verge of becoming an extinct species. He has been killed off by bourgeois prosperity, which has corrupted his character from that of a *citizen* to that of a *consumer*." Modern capitalism "incites ever more unreasonable expectations, in comparison with which the actuality of the real world appears ever more drab and disconcerting." More and more, it is as "a consumer's utopia that our bourgeois society presents itself to its people."

Advertising was not the only factor that promoted the rise of the consumption ethic. There was a time, economist Shlomo Maital has pointed out, when America was full of old-fashioned cash registers with bells that rang when their doors opened and little signs that said, "In God We Trust, All Others Pay Cash." With the coming of modern, mass-produced durable goods such as automobiles and refrigerators came an explosion of sales on the installment plan. "Buy now, pay later" became one of the most famous phrases in American life. Credit sales were assisted by the mass marketing of plastic money in the form of credit cards: Diner's Club, VISA, American Express, Carte Blanche, MasterCard, and so on. An ad for the American Express card that appeared in 1948 caught the reader's eye with a big black headline: "NO CASH." Below, in smaller type, came the sales pitch: "Now you can drive any brand new car of your choice *without putting a penny down.*"

More than any other factor, perhaps, easy buying on the installment plan has undermined traditional attitudes toward debt. Not that we admit it. Opinion surveys show that many Americans feel uncomfortable about buying on credit. We simply ignore our discomfort when it comes time to buy. The prevailing attitude was captured perfectly long before it prevailed, by humorist Artemus Ward: "By happy and live within your means, even if you have to borrow to do it."

Mass production is the engine that throbs at the heart of modern American society. Mass consumption, promoted by advertising and made possible—indeed, made easy—through the mass availability of credit, is the fuel that drives the engine. When consumer demand fails, as it did during the Depression, the system breaks down. But even when the economy runs smoothly, the pressure to consume tears at our souls, since we cannot escape the fact that we are, culturally, the descendants of Puritans. As sociologist Daniel Bell has observed, "Saving . . . is the heart of the Protestant ethic." Under the guidance of that ethic, "Being moral meant being industrious and thrifty. If one wanted to buy something, one should save for it."

By the 1950s, the consumption ethic had triumphed: "The culture was no longer concerned with how to work and achieve, but with how to spend and enjoy." In an odd way, high consumption is the price we must pay for our high-powered economy, even if it divides our souls. It is the price we must pay because, as Bell notes, "the one thing that would utterly destroy the new capitalism is the serious practice of deferred gratification."

A revival of deferred gratification does not seem much of a risk, however. For more than a century, advertisers have labored mightily to make sure that thrift is the last thing on any American's mind. By the end of the 1980s it was clear to anyone who was paying attention that Americans had forgotten how to save. Against all odds, the United States had become the world's largest debtor nation. Advertising is not entirely to blame, but it has done its share to lull us into contented indebtedness. Living beyond our means has become a national habit.

CHAPTER 14

The Literature of Success in the Twentieth Century

Old Wine in New Bottles

The United States that was emerging in 1900 differed greatly from Benjamin Franklin's America. It was not a world of shopkeepers and farmers, but a world of giant enterprises. Rockefeller had built Standard Oil; J. P. Morgan and Andrew Carnegie were about to collaborate in the birth of U.S. Steel; and Henry Ford was working on a machine that would use up oil and steel in unprecedented quantities. Men with special skills were needed to manage the organizations that would dominate the industrial world of the twentieth century. The future, we can see in retrospect, belonged not to graduates of the school of hard knocks but to young men like Alfred P. Sloan, Jr., with degrees from places like M.I.T.

We might imagine that the advice of get-ahead writers would change to reflect changing conditions. For a long while, however, it did not change. Ambitious youths in 1900 received much the same advice they had received a century before. Three works of enormous popularity— Russell H. Conwell's *Acres of Diamonds*, Elbert Hubbard's *A Message to Garcia,* and George Horace Lorimer's *Letters from a Self-Made Merchant to*

His Son—show how the influence of Benjamin Franklin persisted in a world he never imagined.

Russell Conwell was only eighteen years old when, in 1861, he delivered his sermon-lecture *Acres of Diamonds* for the first time. By the time he died in 1925, he had given the speech more than six thousand times and earned more than $8 million in royalties and lecture fees from it. In the days before radio and television, Conwell reached an audience of millions and became a national celebrity.

Like most good sermons, *Acres of Diamonds* makes its point dramatically, through a parable. It tells the story of a farmer named Al Hafed, who lived in ancient Persia. One day an old priest informs the farmer that a diamond no larger than his thumb could purchase a dozen farms. Immediately Al Hafed becomes a poor man—"poor because he was discontented, and . . . discontented because he thought he was poor." He sells his farm and embarks on a search for diamonds.

The search is a disaster. Al Hafed "began," Conwell tells us, "very properly, with the Mountains of the Moon, and came down through Egypt and Palestine. Years passed. He came over through Europe, and, at last, in rags and hunger, he stood a pauper on the shores of the great Bay of Barcelona; and when that great tidal wave came rolling in through the Pillars of Hercules, he threw himself into the incoming tide and sank beneath its foaming crest, never again to rise in this life."

But the death of the wanderer is not the end of the story. One day the man who purchased Al Hafed's farm leads his camel to drink from the stream in the garden. As the camel buries its nose in the water, the man sees a flash of light in the sand: "Thus were discovered the wonderful mines of Golconda. . . . Had Al Hafed remained at home and dug in his own cellar or garden, or under his own wheat fields, he would have found acres of diamonds."

Having made his basic point that "The acres of diamonds of which I propose to speak today are to be found in your homes, or near to them, and not in some distant land," Conwell proceeded to cite other examples—as many as he needed to fill his talk. In this part of the lecture, logic mattered little. The fact that John Jacob Astor had made his fortune after wandering from Germany to the United States did not stop Conwell from holding him up as a model. Conwell's grip on his audience depended on emotion, not consistency. When the time came to bring the talk to a close, his biggest problem was to remember where he was speaking: "Now then," he would boom, "I say again that the opportunity to get rich, to attain unto great wealth, is here in ——— now, within the reach of almost every man and woman who hears me speak tonight. . . . There never was a place on earth more adapted than the city of ———— today, and never in the history of the world did a poor man without capital have such an opportunity to get rich quickly and honestly as he has now in ————."

Though today he is most likely to be remembered as the founder and first president of Temple University in Philadelphia, in his own time Conwell was best known, as historian Richard M. Huber has commented, as "America's greatest salesman of opportunity." *Acres of Diamonds* was one of the most popular speeches ever given in the United States. The reason for its popularity is not hard to see. The message that Conwell shared with his eager audiences was a message of reassurance. America had not changed since Franklin strolled the streets of Philadelphia. Any man could succeed, if only he tilled his own garden.

An incident in the Spanish-American War inspired Elbert Hubbard's *A Message to Garcia*, which may have reached an audience even larger than the one reached by *Acres of Diamonds*. "Next to Benjamin Franklin's *Way to Wealth*," Huber writes, "*A Message to Garcia* was the most effective and widely distributed tract in the history of success literature."

Hubbard was born in a tiny farming community near Bloomington, Illinois, in 1856. After early success as the sales manager for a soap company, he developed literary ambitions and, at the age of thirty-six, sold his share in the soap business. Soon he was editing his own magazine, *The Philistine*. Under the influence of English aesthete William Morris, he also founded the Roycroft Shops in East Aurora, New York. The shops were dedicated to the idea that a revival of medieval craftsmanship might soften the evils of the Industrial Revolution. Hubbard became known as "the sage of East Aurora."

His son convinced Hubbard that the unsung hero of the Spanish-American War was Lieutenant Andrew Rowan, who had fought his way across Cuba to take a vital message from President McKinley to General Calixto García Íñiguez, the leader of the Cuban insurgents against Spain. Rowan's deed inspired Hubbard to dash off a sermonette of some fifteen hundred words, which he published in the March 1899 issue of *The Philistine*.

What especially impressed Hubbard, he explains in *A Message to Garcia*, was the attitude Rowan had brought to his assignment. Though he knew only that Garcia was "somewhere in the mountain fastnesses of Cuba," the lieutenant did not waste time asking questions. He simply "took the letter, sealed it up in an oilskin pouch, strapped it over his heart, in four days landed by night off the coast of Cuba from an open boat, disappeared into the jungle, and in three weeks came out on the other side of the island, having traversed a hostile country on foot and delivered his letter to Garcia."

As in war, so in business. Character, Hubbard says, is what young men need to succeed—"a stiffening of the vertebrae which will cause them to be loyal to a trust, to act promptly, concentrate their energies, do the thing—'Carry a message to Garcia!' "

But character is a rare commodity. Here Hubbard cites his own experience as an employer: "No man who has endeavoured to carry out an enterprise . . . but has been well-nigh appalled at times by the imbecility of the average man—the inability or unwillingness to concentrate on a thing and do it." For every man who is capable of getting a job done without fuss, a dozen provide nothing but "slipshod assistance, foolish inattention, dowdy indifference, and half-hearted work."

Genius may fail, A *Message to Garcia* suggests, but any man with a proper attitude can succeed. "It is not book learning young men need, nor instruction about this and that." Determination conquers all obstacles. "My heart goes out," Hubbard concludes, "to the man who does his work when the 'boss' is away as well as when he is home. And the man who, when given a letter for Garcia, quietly takes the missive, without asking any idiotic questions, and with no lurking intention of chucking it into the nearest sewer, or of doing aught else but deliver it. . . . Civilization is one long, anxious search for just such individuals."

A *Message to Garcia* struck a note that the public—especially employers—seemed eager to hear. The issue of *The Philistine* that carried it sold out in only three days. A month later, Theodore Roosevelt struck the same note in a speech in Chicago: "I wish to preach, not the doctrine of ignoble ease but the doctrine of the strenuous life." America, Hubbard and Roosevelt suggested, had not outgrown the work ethic. Character still mattered. Initiative, self-reliance, and drive would still prevail.

Most magazine articles disappear, but A *Message to Garcia* lived on. More than a million copies were distributed by the New York Central Railroad, in a special reprint that also carried railroad advertising. Many employers gave copies to their employees. In the Russo-Japanese War in 1904, Japanese soldiers found copies in the knapsacks of slain Russians. Hubbard died in the sinking of the *Lusitania* on May 7, 1915, but the message he jotted down in an hour in 1899 has not died. Altogether it is estimated that forty million copies have been printed, in forty or fifty different languages.

Whereas *Acres of Diamonds* and *A Message to Garcia* were only a few pages long, George H. Lorimer needed a whole book to preach his version of the get-ahead gospel. *Letters from a Self-Made Merchant to His Son*, first published as a series of articles in *The Saturday Evening Post* in 1901, made Lorimer one of the most popular business-advice writers in American history.

Born in Louisville, Kentucky, in 1868, Lorimer was editor in chief of *The Saturday Evening Post* from 1899 until his death in 1936. Under his direction, *The Post* both mirrored and helped to shape the culture of the swiftly growing middle class. "Lorimer is *The Post* and *The Post* is Lorimer," said its publisher, Cyrus H. K. Curtis, who hired Lorimer shortly after he bought *The Post* for $1,000 in 1898, with the hope that Lorimer could create a men's magazine that would match the success of Curtis's *Ladies' Home Journal*.

At the time *The Post* was, in the words of Lorimer's biographer John Tebbel, "more of a memory than a magazine." Lorimer's strategy for revitalizing the ailing monthly included a new emphasis on business fiction. Business, he felt, dominated the lives of most Americans, yet the nation's novelists rarely dealt with it. Most writers preferred romance, whereas Lorimer felt that in fiction "the struggle for existence is the loaf, love or sex is the frosting on the cake."

When he had trouble finding writers who could supply the kind of fiction he wanted, Lorimer decided to supply it himself. The result was *Letters from a Self-Made Merchant to His Son*, which ran serially in 1901 and 1902; was published in book form in 1902; became a best seller in the United States, England, and Germany; and eventually, says Tebbel, "was translated into more languages and was more generally circulated in all parts of the world than any book of American authorship since *Uncle Tom's Cabin*."

Lorimer's book consists of letters written by a street-smart merchant, John Graham, "familiarly known . . . as 'Old Gorgon Graham,' " to his spoiled son Pierrepont, "facetiously known to his intimates as 'Piggy.' " Graham is a pork baron modeled on Philip D. Armour, for whom Lorimer had worked before he became a journalist. The book can still be read with pleasure, largely because Lorimer made Graham so appealing. Gruff and sensible, the Gorgon is an American original, a kind of business version of Harry Truman. Much of his advice is delivered in a plain style that still pleases. "Remember . . . that it's easier to look wise than to talk wisdom. Say less than the other fellow and listen more than you talk." "Money talks—but not unless its owner has a loose tongue. . . . Poverty talks, too, but nobody wants to hear what it has to say." "Jack was one of these charlotte-russe boys, all whipped cream and sponge cake and high-priced flavoring extract, without any filling qualities." "Education will broaden a narrow mind, but there's no known cure for a big head. The best you can hope is that it will swell up and bust."

With the plain style goes a plain message. Hard work pays; laziness does not. Whether something "pays" is, of course, the only measure of its worth. A passage about college shows Old Gorgon applying this principle: "Does a College education pay? Does it pay to feed in pork trimmings at five cents a pound at the hopper and draw out nice, cunning, little 'country' sausages at twenty cents a pound at the other end? . . . You bet it pays. Anything that trains a boy to think and think quick pays. Anything that teaches a boy to get the answer before the other fellow gets through biting the pencil, pays."

Though it can make a difference in life, college is not foolproof. "College doesn't make fools; it develops them. It doesn't make bright men; it develops them. A fool will turn out a fool, whether he goes to college or not. . . . And a good, strong boy will turn out a bright, strong man."

To keep his son from turning into a full-fledged fool, Old Gorgon comes down hard when Pierrepont shows signs of extravagance: "The cashier has just handed me your expense account for the month, and it fairly makes a fellow hump-shouldered to look it over. When I told you that I wished you to get a liberal education, I didn't mean that I wanted to buy Cambridge. Of course the bills won't break me, but they will break you unless you are very, very careful."

Work, Lorimer suggests, is the proper antidote to the perils of higher education. "I have no fears for you," Old Gorgon writes to Pierrepont, "after you've been at work for a few years, and have struck an average between the packinghouse and Harvard." But the old man wants the best for his son, and the best means starting at the bottom: "The only sure way that a man can get rich quick is to have it given to him or to inherit it. You are not going to get rich that way—at least, not until after you have proved your ability to hold a pretty important position with the firm; and, of course, there is just one place from which a man can start for that position with Graham & Co. . . . That place is the bottom."

Pierrepont dutifully begins at the bottom, but it takes him a while to acquire a taste for labor. Echoing Franklin, Old Gorgon warns the boy, "Your time is money—my money—and when you take half an hour of it for your own purposes, that is just a petty form of petty larceny." Golf may be a pleasant diversion, but "a young fellow who wants to be a boss butcher hasn't much daylight to waste on any kind of links except sausage links." Hardworking ancestors matter only if they serve as models: "A man's as good as he makes himself, but no man's any good because his grandfather was."

Halfhearted effort inspires contempt. "I would feel a good deal happier over your showing," Old Gorgon fumes, "if you would make a downright failure or a clean-cut success once in a while, instead of always just skimming through this way. It looks to me as if you were only trying half as hard as you could and in trying it's the second half that brings results. . . . Of course, you are bright enough to be a half-way man, and to hold a half-way place at a half-way salary by doing half the work you are capable of, but you've got to add dynamite and ginger and jounce to your equipment if you want to get the other half that's coming to you. . . . You've got to get up every morning with determination if you're going to get to bed with satisfaction. You've got to eat hog, think hog, dream hog—in short, go the whole hog if you're going to win out in the pork-packing business."

In the end Pierrepont settles down, begins to do well on the job, and meets a girl he wants to marry. Old Gorgon is delighted. Like college, marriage pays: "A married man is worth more salary than a single one, because his wife makes him worth more. He's apt to go to bed a little sooner and to get up a little earlier; to go a little steadier and to work a little harder than the fellow who's got to amuse a different girl every night, and can't stay at home to do it."

Lorimer's book inspired a host of imitations and parodies, with titles such as *Letters from a Son to His Self-Made Father; Letters from a Self-Made Chorus Girl to Her Hand-Made Mother; Letters from a Tailor-Made Daughter to a Home-Made Mother; Letters from a Custom-Made Son to His Ready-Made Father;* and, much later, Will Rogers's *Letters of a Self-Made Diplomat to His President.* The imitations were a kind of tribute, but the fact that Lorimer was so easy to imitate may have a deeper significance. By the first decade of the twentieth century, the imitations suggest, the self-made man was beginning to seem a ready-made cliché. New times demanded new wine. The market soon supplied it.

"TO THINK SUCCESS BRINGS SUCCESS"

In his fine study *The American Idea of Success*, Richard M. Huber distinguishes the "character ethic" with its emphasis on thrift, prudence, and hard work from two quite different types of success thinking that emerged as powerful influences in the twentieth century. He calls these other approaches the "mind power ethic" and the "personality ethic."

In the United States, the mind power ethic is familiar to many people through such twentieth-century titles as Napoleon Hill's *Think and Grow Rich* and Norman Vincent Peale's *The Power of Positive Thinking*. But the American interest in the power of mind goes back to much earlier times.

Phineas Parkhurst Quimby, born in Lebanon, New Hampshire, in 1802, was the best-known early proponent of mental healing in the United States. Quimby maintained that all illness results from mistaken beliefs and can be cured through right thinking. Mental healing, Quimby taught, is the only healing that rests on a solid foundation. Jesus' cures were mind cures.

After Quimby's death in 1866, the mind-cure movement developed along two lines. One line, Christian Science, was a religion founded, organized, and strictly controlled by a former patient and disciple of Quimby, Mary Baker Eddy. The second line, generally called New Thought, was a loose coalition of groups that believed in some form of mental healing but did not accept Mrs. Eddy's *Church Manual* as divinely inspired.

Once New Thought had affirmed that sickness was a mental phenomenon that could be cured by mental means, it did not take much of a leap to conclude that other woes might have the same origin and might be cured in the same way. The leap was made by a writer named Prentice Mulford in a series of pamphlets written in the late 1880s and eventually published under the title *Your Forces and How to Use Them*. Mulford became the first of the mind-power writers who focused on success in business.

"Your thought," Mulford tells his readers, "is an invisible substance, as real as air, water, or metal. . . . As you learn how this power really acts; as you learn how to hold, use and control it,—you will do more profitable business, and accomplish more in an hour than now you may do in a week." Idleness is not necessarily wicked: "To think persistent resolve, to think persistent push in your one aim and purpose,—to simply think it, and do nothing else,—will create for you a power as certain to move and effect results as the jackscrews placed under the heaviest building will move it upward." In short, Mulford suggests, the way to wealth is mental: "TO THINK SUCCESS BRINGS SUCCESS."

In the early years of the twentieth century, mind power was emphasized in many books by one of the most prolific success writers of all time, Orison Swett Marden. Between 1894 and his death in 1924, Marden published over forty-five books on the subject of getting ahead, with titles such as *Every Man a King, He Can Who Thinks He Can, Be Good to Yourself, Everybody Ahead, Success Fundamentals, The Miracle of Right Thought, The Victorious Attitude,* and *How to Get What You Want.*

Marden was born in New Hampshire in 1850, lost both of his parents before he was seven, and endured a wretched childhood as a "hired boy" in a series of unsympathetic families. Hope came when he discovered, at fourteen, the British self-improvement writer Samuel Smiles. Smiles's *Self-Help,* Marden recalled later, "was a perpetual delight to me, and I treasured it as if it were worth its weight in diamonds, reading and rereading the precious pages until I had almost committed them to memory. . . . The stories of poor boys climbing to the top so thrilled and inspired me that I then and there resolved to get out of the woods—to get an education at any cost—and to make something of myself!"

Education became a passion. Always holding down one or two jobs outside of school, Marden earned a Bachelor of Arts degree from Boston University in 1877, a Bachelor of Oratory and a Master's degree from Boston University in 1879, an M.D. from Harvard in 1881, and an LL.B. from Boston University Law School in 1882.

Having thus equipped himself for a career in medicine or law, Marden went into the hotel business, and by 1892 he was running four hotels in three states. Then disaster struck. One hotel burned down; five cases of smallpox caused another to be quarantined. In 1893, having fallen deeply in debt, Marden decided to restore his fortunes by writing a book about success.

The result was *Pushing to the Front: Or, Success Under Difficulties,* published by Houghton Mifflin in 1894. The book is an old-fashioned affirmation of the character ethic. "A great check-book can never make a great man," Marden tells his readers; ". . . *character is success, and there is no other.*" The most popular of Marden's books, *Pushing to the Front,* went through twelve printings in its first year and later was translated into twenty-five languages. It did especially well in Japan, where, one American was told, "Among ourselves we often call it the Japanese Bible."

In 1897 Marden founded a magazine, *Success*, to provide an outlet for the ideas that spilled from him at a rate of three thousand to four thousand words a day. Circulation rose to some three hundred thousand, but the magazine was forced out of business in 1911 as a result of muckraking articles that offended important creditors. A second magazine, *New Success*, was founded in 1918, stayed away from muckraking, and survived until a few years after Marden's death.

Like many other success writers, Marden affirmed mind power on vaguely religious grounds, as in this passage in *Prosperity: How to Attract It* (1922): "Everything in man's life, everything in God's universe . . . follows a divine law, and the law of prosperity and abundance is just as definite as the law of gravitation, just as unerring as the principles of mathematics. It is a mental law. Only by thinking abundance can you realize the abundant, prosperous life that is your birthright."

Success is our birthright because God wants us to succeed: "Success is every human being's normal condition; he was made for success; he is a success machine, and to be a failure is to pervert the intention of his Creator." Anyone can tap the power that produces success. It is only necessary to "keep your supply pipes wide open by the consciousness of your oneness with the One, your connection with the All Supply."

Marden even goes so far as to propose a biological theory of mind power. In *Training for Efficiency* (1913) he asserts that "Innumerable experiments have established the fact that all healthful, hopeful, joyous, encouraging, uplifting, optimistic, cheerful thoughts improve the cell life of the entire body. . . . The brain cells are constantly bathed in the blood, from which they draw their nourishment, and when the blood is loaded with the poison of fear, worry, anger, hatred, or jealousy, the protoplasm of those delicate cells becomes hard and is thus materially injured."

Fortunately, people can counter the poison of negative thinking through self-treatment. In *How to Get What You Want* (1917), Marden explains exactly how to administer the antidote: "When giving a self-treatment, always get by yourself and talk to yourself in a firm, decided tone of voice, just as if you were speaking earnestly to some one else whom you wished to impress with the great importance of what you were saying. Addressing yourself by name, say: 'You are a child of God, and the being He made was never intended for the sort of weak, negative life you are leading. God made you for success, not failure. . . . Don't disgrace your Maker by violating His image, by being everything but the magnificent success He intended you to be.' "

It is difficult to overestimate the appeal exerted by messages of this kind. In an article about Marden published in 1926, H. L. Mencken estimates that Marden's writings in book form "must have reached a total sale of twenty million copies," including three million in twenty-five languages other than English. Noting that he has encountered translations of Marden's books "on the news-stands of remote towns in Spain, Poland, and Czecho-Slovakia," Mencken cannot resist exclaiming, "How many false hopes he must have raised in his day!"

Success writers who emphasize mind power do not always depend on a pipeline to some supernatural source of power supply. A secular version promoted by Frenchman Émile Coué enjoyed a remarkable vogue in France, England, and the United States in 1922–23. Coué, a chemist blessed with what one journalist described as "the face of a dehydrated fox . . . wizened and solid and twinkling and inscrutable and shrewd and winning," presented his ideas in a popular book titled *Self-Mastery Through Conscious Autosuggestion.*

Autosuggestion, Coué says, is a method of self-improvement based on the proposition that "Man is what he thinks." The technique is simple: "*As long as you live*, every morning before getting up, and every evening as soon as you are in bed, you must shut your eyes, so as to concentrate your attention, and repeat twenty times . . . *Every day, in every respect, I am getting better and better.*" In a slightly different form ("Day by day, in every way, I am getting better and better") Coué's slogan spread so rapidly that it became, one magazine reported, "the stock phrase of the country almost overnight."

Freudian and pseudo-Freudian ideas have taken some odd twists when American promoters got hold of them. For instance, in the 1920s an outfit called the Psycho-Phone Company offered ambitious Americans an opportunity to "GET THE THINGS YOU WANT—WHILE YOU SLEEP." A 1929 advertisement cited by Richard Huber asks, "Are you only half alive, sickly in body, doing unpleasant work, beset with marriage problems, with never quite enough money to do what you want?" No matter. For $190 you can purchase the Psycho-Phone, "an automatic suggestion machine which reaches your unconscious mind while you are asleep. . . . Through liberating your unconscious powers you can make yourself over according *to your own specifications*. You can develop your power to get *money*, and the *things and conditions necessary to your highest development.*"

The Psycho-Phone Company was not an isolated phenomenon. In the

1950s essentially the same appeal was made in promotional materials that advertised recordings sold by a company in Los Angeles. No matter "what you have been striving for," the Cambridge Institute declared, "whether it be better health, financial success, vibrant personality improvement . . . YOU WILL BEGIN TO ACHIEVE IT. . . . From now on, your every hope, your every wish, your every prayer, will be accomplished and fulfilled thru the tremendous powers of your very own sub-conscious mind." Best of all, the company said, this fulfillment would come through a "completely *new method*" that requires "NO EFFORT ON YOUR PART!" Everything would be done by listening to records, "WHILE YOU RELAX!"

To win without working, to grow rich "WHILE YOU RELAX!"— this was a promise that was not often heard in the United States before 1900. After 1900 it was heard more and more frequently.

Though the mind-power philosophy does not require a religious base, the best-known formulation of the philosophy in the twentieth century has come from a minister.

Norman Vincent Peale was born in 1898 in Bowersville, Ohio. After graduating from Ohio Wesleyan University in 1920 and from the Boston University Divinity School, Peale was ordained as a minister in the Methodist Church and, in 1924, was assigned to a tiny church in Brooklyn. In three years Peale increased church membership from forty to almost nine hundred, raised $100,000 to build a new church, and made his Sunday school the largest in the borough. In 1932, after an equally successful stint as head of the University Methodist Church in Syracuse, he took over as minister of one of the oldest evangelical churches in the country, the Marble Collegiate Church at Fifth Avenue and Twenty-ninth Street in Manhattan.

At Marble Collegiate, Peale soon was drawing sixteen hundred worshipers to hear his Sunday sermons. Yearning for a larger audience, he published two books in the 1930s, but it was not until *A Guide to Confident Living*, published in 1948, that he began to hit his stride as an author. He followed with a book that was not merely a success but also a phenomenon. *The Power of Positive Thinking* ranked fifth among nonfiction best sellers in 1952, first in 1953, first in 1954, and second in 1955. By 1956 it had passed every book except the Bible as the all-time nonfiction best seller.

Peale's message is the basic message of mind power. "You can think your way to failure and unhappiness," he tells his readers, "but you can also think your way to success and happiness. The world in which you live is not primarily determined by outward conditions and circumstances but by thoughts that habitually occupy your mind. . . . If you think in negative terms you will get negative results. That is the simple fact which is at the basis of an astonishing law of prosperity and success. In three words: Believe and succeed."

Earlier success writers often focused on young people. Peale does not write for the young as much as he writes for people facing middle age. He understands fatigue: "The blows of life, the accumulation of difficulties, the multiplication of problems tend to sap energy and leave you spent and discouraged." He also understands fear: "Lack of self-confidence apparently is one of the great problems besetting people today. . . . Everywhere you encounter people who are inwardly afraid, who shrink from life, who suffer from a deep sense of inadequacy and insecurity, who doubt their own powers. Deep within themselves they mistrust their ability to meet responsibilities or to grasp opportunities. . . . Thousands upon thousands go crawling through life on their hands and knees, defeated and afraid."

To the defeated and afraid, Peale offers hope. "In most cases," he affirms, "such frustration of power is unnecessary. . . . you are less defeated than you think you are." Indeed, Peale assures his readers, his book "is written to suggest techniques and to give examples which demonstrate that you do not need to be defeated by anything, that you can have peace of mind, improved health, and a never-ceasing flow of energy. . . . These assertions, which may appear extravagant, are based on bona-fide demonstrations in actual human experience."

Some critics charged that "Pealism" was a profound distortion of Christianity. In a special preface written after his book had sold several million copies, Peale protested that he advocated positive thinking "not as a means to fame, riches or power, but as the practical application of faith to overcome defeat and accomplish worthwhile creative values in life." In the book itself, however, the reader is rarely allowed to forget the link between positive thinking and a positive payoff. A woman who sells vacuum cleaners from door to door becomes a supersaleswoman, Peale reports, by saying before every call, "If God be for me, then I know that with God's help I can sell vacuum cleaners." Who can dispute it? Peale asks.

Like Lorimer's *Letters from a Self-Made Merchant to His Son, The Power of Positive Thinking* inspired its share of parody. The jeering reached its peak in 1955 with the publication of Anna Russell's *The Power of Being a*

Positive Stinker and Bernard W. Shir-Cliff's *The Power of Negative Thinking*, which recommended the Negative Thinker's Basic Credo: "I don't wanna. Therefore I ain't gonna!"

But the satires did not have nearly as large an audience as the straight message. In the 1950s, according to one poll, nineteen out of twenty Americans said they believed in God. Almost as many, it seems, believed in Norman Vincent Peale. At one point, when Peale asked a saleswoman how his book was doing compared to the Kinsey report, she gave him glad tidings: "You know, success is much more popular than sex this year." It was as if God sold books even more effectively than He sold vacuum cleaners.

The Power of Personality

Mind power is not the only success philosophy that has produced best sellers in the twentieth century. At the same time that the number of books emphasizing character has declined, the number emphasizing personality has soared. Sometimes, too, there have been odd combinations. In *Masterful Personality* (1921), for instance, Orison Swett Marden recommends using mind power to develop a personality that will pay off in business: "YOU CAN COMPEL PEOPLE TO LIKE YOU!" he affirms. ". . . It's the smile that boosts you up the ladder."

Similarly, Norman Vincent Peale, citing the case of an executive who says that he goes to church to "get his batteries charged," explains that faith animates every dynamic personality. "When in spiritual contact with God through our thought processes, the Divine energy flows through the personality, renewing the original creative act. When contact with the Divine energy is broken, the personality gradually becomes depleted." A man plugged into the Divine is like "an electric clock connected with an outlet." His energy never fails.

One of the most remarkable works in the history of American success literature was published by advertising executive Bruce Barton in 1925 and reached the top of the nonfiction best-seller list in 1926. It is *The Man Nobody Knows*—a portrait of Jesus as a winning personality.

A minister's son, Barton was born in 1886 in rural Tennessee and was educated at Amherst, where his classmates voted him "most likely to succeed." He spent a hectic decade as an editor and journalist. Then, in the fall of 1918, he met a couple of advertising men, Alex Osborn and Roy Durstine, in a fund-raising drive to benefit the United War Work

Campaign. Early in 1919 a new advertising agency, Barton, Durstine & Osborn, opened on Madison Avenue. BDO quickly became one of the most successful agencies in the country, with clients such as General Electric, General Motors, and Lever Brothers. (A merger with the George Batten company in 1928 added the second B in BBDO.)

In an introductory note, Barton explains the impulse that led him to write *The Man Nobody Knows*. As a boy, he says, he had objected to the image of a "sissified" Jesus presented to him in Sunday school. Years later, after he had become a businessman, he decided to "read what the men who knew Jesus personally said about him . . . read about him as though he were a new historical character, about whom I had never heard anything at all." The result was a revelation—"A Discovery of the Real Jesus."

Far from being an ineffective "lamb of God," Barton's Jesus is, first of all, an outstanding executive. The key to his success is the "blazing conviction" that always is the essence of leadership. The man at the top must inspire his followers, and Jesus "had the voice and manner of the leader—the personal magnetism which begets loyalty and commands respect."

Part of Jesus' appeal as a leader came from his physical strength, Barton says. Those who portray Jesus as a lamb "never feel the rich contagion of his laughter, nor remember how heartily he enjoyed good food, nor think of what his years of hard toil must have done to his arms and back and legs." Barton's Jesus is an "outdoor man." When he throws the money-changers out of the temple, he shows strength that is more than moral: "As his right arm rose and fell, striking its blows with that little whip, the sleeve dropped back to reveal muscles as hard as iron. No one who watched him in action had any doubt that he was fully capable of taking care of himself."

Another remarkable aspect of Barton's Jesus is his gregariousness. "Theology has reared a graven image," Barton complains, "and robbed the world of the joy and laughter of a great companion." Jesus "loved to be in the crowd." Some Sunday school teachers may promote a killjoy Jesus, but in fact "He was the most popular dinner guest in Jerusalem!"

Along with his skill as an organizer, his physicality, and his sociability, Barton emphasizes Jesus' ability as an advertiser. The parables are "the most powerful advertisements of all time"—condensed, simple, sincere, dramatic. "Take any one of the parables, no matter which—you will find that it exemplifies all the principles on which advertising text books are written. . . . Always a picture in the very first sentence; crisp, graphic language and a message so clear that even the dullest cannot escape it. . . . Every advertising man ought to study the parables of Jesus . . . schooling himself in their language." The best among them is the parable of the Good Samaritan—"the greatest advertisement of all time."

Finally, according to Barton, Jesus is "the founder of modern business." At the age of twelve, Barton notes, when Mary and Joseph found Jesus disputing with old men in the temple, he answered their scolding with, "Wist ye not that I must be about my Father's *business?*" Barton asks, "What did he mean by business?" And he answers that to Jesus, business was service—the same discovery "proclaimed in every sales convention as something distinctly modern and up to date." As the first proponent of the service concept of business, Barton declares, Jesus set the stage for such luminaries as George Perkins of New York Life Insurance Company, Henry Ford, and Theodore Vail of AT&T.

It is easy to make fun of Bruce Barton, but his book does what he says it will do—provides a fresh look at one of the world's most familiar faces. It is true that, as Richard Huber says, *The Man Nobody Knows* "soaked the idea of success in the sanctity of the New Testament." But it is not true that the book is silly or stupid, or that it affirms shallow values. Summarizing Jesus' message, Barton writes, "If he says that there are things more vital than merely making money, let no one question his authority. He was handed the wealth of a nation and handed it back again. . . . 'There is a success which is greater than wealth or titles,' he says. 'It comes through making your work an instrument of greater service, and larger living to your fellow men and women. *This* is my Father's business and he needs your help.' "

Barton adds a judgment that clearly reflects his own experience: "You know men whose health is gone; men whose taste for reading and music and art is gone. Men who have literally no interests in life beyond the office which has become a mere treadmill whereon their days are ground away. . . . In the process of being successful they have sacrificed success. Never once forgetting themselves they have forgotten everything else. This is not Jesus' idea of what a life should be."

In the years after the publication of *The Man Nobody Knows*, Barton's aspirations led him to be less and less active in business and more and more active in politics. From 1937 to 1941 he served as a Republican congressman from Manhattan, but his isolationist views won him the enmity of Franklin Roosevelt, who skewered Barton and two colleagues—"Martin, Barton, and Fish"—with a speech that made as large

an impression as any of Barton's advertisements. Today Barton is remembered chiefly as the author of a book that is both one of the oddest
ever written about Christianity and one of the oddest ever written about
business—a book that, it seems safe to say, could have been written only
by an American, and perhaps only by a minister's son who was also an
advertising man.

"If You Want to Gather Honey"

Barton insists that Jesus was "a great Companion," a super guy who
would have been welcome company on any fishing trip. If being popular
meant so much, what could ordinary people do to achieve it? Barton did
not tackle that question, but Dale Carnegie did.

Carnegie was born in 1888 on a farm in Maryville, Missouri, picked
strawberries for five cents an hour as a boy, and earned a reputation as
a debater at the State Teachers' College in Warrensburg, Missouri. After
several false starts in business (most notably a job selling bacon, soap,
and lard for Armour & Company in the Badlands of South Dakota), he
moved East to study oratory and, he hoped, to become a Chatauqua
lecturer.

In 1912 Carnegie persuaded the director of the Young Men's Christian
Association at 125th Street in Manhattan to allow him to teach a night
course in public speaking. The course did not merely succeed, it also
grew into probably the most successful venture in the history of American adult education. As of 1985—thirty years after Carnegie's death—
three million people around the world had graduated from courses
offered by the Dale Carnegie Institutes, and approximately two thousand new students enrolled weekly. The graduates included Lee Iacocca,
the loquacious chairman of Chrysler, who declared in his autobiography
that he had been a "shrinking violet" until he took the Carnegie course
in public speaking as a young manager at Ford.

As he taught public speaking, Carnegie realized that he was teaching
more. "I beg of you not to think of this as a public speaking course," he
would tell his students. "Think of it as a course in destroying fear and
building self-confidence. Think of it as a course in human relations. Think
of it as a new way of life." The businessmen who came to his courses to
learn how to speak in public, Carnegie saw, often suffered from feelings
of insecurity and inferiority. They were afraid. The winners in business
and in life, they felt, were the people with winning personalities, the

people who could walk into a room full of strangers, light it with a smile, and leave with a room full of friends.

Carnegie developed a lecture, "How to Win Friends and Influence People," that addressed the fear he saw in his students. Out of the lecture came a book, published in 1936. The book became an immediate hit, selling more than a third of a million copies in the first six months of the Depression year of 1937. What was more remarkable, the book kept selling. For two years it sold at a rate of five thousand copies per day. For ten years it appeared on the best-seller list of *The New York Times*. The paperback edition, published by Pocket Books in 1940, became the first paperback in history to sell more than a million copies. In all, more than seventeen million copies had sold worldwide by 1989. The book has been translated into more than thirty languages and dialects, including Afrikaans, Gujarati, Punjabi, and Burmese. Dale Carnegie is the Babe Ruth of success literature.

How to Win Friends and Influence People focuses on a theme that can be stated in three words: success through personality. "Dealing with people," Carnegie explains in his introduction, "is probably the biggest problem you face, especially if you are a businessman." He has written his book, he declares, to provide "training in the fine art of getting along with people in everyday business and social contacts."

What is most striking about *How to Win Friends and Influence People* is what it does not include. Carnegie says little about hard work or any of the other old-fashioned virtues, except to insist that competence alone will not take anyone far: "One can . . . hire mere technical ability in engineering, accountancy, architecture or any other profession at fifty to seventy-five dollars a week. The market is always glutted with it. But the man who has technical knowledge *plus* the ability to express his ideas, to assume leadership, and to arouse enthusiasm among men—that man is headed for higher earning power."

What is the way to arouse enthusiasm? Carnegie first answers in the negative. The way *not* to arouse enthusiasm is to criticize. This is the whole point of Carnegie's opening chapter, memorably titled "If You Want to Gather Honey, Don't Kick Over the Beehive." In human relations, Carnegie tells his readers, criticism is the equivalent of kicking over the beehive. "Criticism is futile because it puts a man on the defensive, and usually makes him strive to justify himself. Criticism . . . wounds a man's precious pride, hurts his sense of importance, and arouses his resentment." "When dealing with people, let us remember we are not dealing with creatures of logic. We are dealing with creatures of emotion, creatures bristling with prejudices and motivated by pride and vanity." "If you and I want to stir up a resentment tomorrow that may rankle across the decades and endure until death, just let us indulge in a little stinging criticism—no matter how certain we are that it is justified."

What, then, is "the big secret of dealing with people"? The secret is praise. "Of course," Carnegie writes, "you are interested in what you want. You are eternally interested in it. But no one else is. The rest of us are just like you: We are interested in what we want." And what we want more than anything is to feel good about ourselves. "People would think they had committed a crime if they let their families or employees go for six days without food; but they will let them go for six days, and six weeks, and sometimes sixty years without giving them the hearty appreciation that they crave almost as much as they crave food . . . the kind words of appreciation that would sing in their memories for years like the music of the morning stars."

Carnegie cites the example of the blue ribbons that his father won for his hogs and pedigreed cattle: "The hogs didn't care about the ribbons they had won. But Father did. These prizes gave him a feeling of importance." He also cites the example of one of the few men then alive who were paid a salary of $1 million a year, Andrew Carnegie's lieutenant Charles Schwab. When he was asked how he aroused enthusiasm among his employees, Schwab replied, "There is nothing else that so kills the ambitions of a man as criticisms from his superiors. I never criticize anyone. I believe in giving a man incentive to work. So I am anxious to praise but loath to find fault. If I like anything, I am hearty in my approbation and lavish in my praise."

A smile, Dale Carnegie suggests, is an executive's most potent weapon. The whole heart of his success philosophy is captured in an anecdote about an employer who took one of Carnegie's courses. "For years," Carnegie says of this man, "he had driven and criticized and condemned his employees without stint or discretion. Kindness, words of appreciation and encouragement were alien to his lips. After studying the principles discussed in this book, this employer sharply altered his philosophy of life. His organization is now inspired with a new loyalty, a new enthusiasm, a new spirit of team work. Three hundred and fourteen enemies have been turned into 314 friends."

Carnegie's other books—*How to Stop Worrying and Start Living, How to Develop Self-Confidence and Influence People by Public Speaking*, and so on— repeat the same basic message. Appreciating other people is the best way of making them feel good about themselves, which is the best way of making them feel good about management, which is probably the best way of making sure that management won't kick over the beehive. The wheel of good feeling can revolve forever, and with it the wheel of fortune. Personality is the engine that keeps the wheel in motion. Praise is the oil that makes the engine purr. Everyone can be a winner as long as everyone smiles.

"Personality Always Wins the Day"

Arthur Miller's play *Death of a Salesman* offers an unusual glimpse of the shift that has been traced in this chapter—the shift from the character ethic to the personality ethic.

Miller's protagonist, Willy Loman, is a traveling salesman who has come to the end of the road. Miller shows his audience what Willy is— a foolish, suffering, self-deluded man—but he leaves the audience to imagine how he became what he is. He shows the death of a salesman, but he leaves the audience to imagine the forces that shaped the salesman's life. The success literature that a man like Willy might have read in his youth helps to fill that background.

Willy dies in his early sixties, so he would have been born in the middle 1880s—1885, let's say—the year when the Dictaphone and the speedometer were invented and when William Dean Howells published *The Rise of Silas Lapham*—a portrait of a harassed businessman that is not likely to have come to Willy's attention.

What would have come to Willy's attention? It is easy to imagine him being excited by the success literature that flourished in his youth. Stories like William B. Woodbridge's "That Something" might have thrilled any young man. "What is it that keeps the underdog down?" Woodbridge asks. "What is it that the upper ten possesses that the under ten thousand does not possess?" And he answers: "Faith, Confidence, Power, Ambition, and more." Above all, a young man needs "*that something*"— the will to win, the will to success, the will to say, "I WILL." This is "the talisman of success," which every ambitious youth should "write upon your memory in letters of fire."

Willy would have been about seventeen when George Lorimer published his *Letters from a Self-Made Merchant to His Son.* It is easy to imagine Willy reading the letters in a copy of *The Saturday Evening Post* that his father had brought home. When Willy lashes out at his disappointing son Biff, he sounds much like Old Gorgon Graham complaining that his son Pierrepont seems satisfied to be a half-way man, holding a half-way place at a half-way salary. When Pierrepont works in sales, Old Gorgon gives him advice that foreshadows the advice Willy later gives Biff: "It isn't enough to be all right in this world; you've got to look all right as well, because two-thirds of success is making people think you are all right."

Willy would have been forty, in his prime, when Bruce Barton hit the best-seller list with *The Man Nobody Knows*—a book that thousands of salesmen must have read in snatches on the road. The portrait of Jesus as a supreme salesman was meant for men like Willy: "Every one of His conversations, every contact between His mind and others, is worthy of the attentive study of any sales manager." No doubt Willy would have noticed that, above all, Barton's Jesus is well liked—"the most popular dinner guest in Jerusalem."

In Willy's view, to be not merely liked but "well liked" is the deepest secret of success in business. Popularity excuses all deficiencies. Summing up his qualms about someone he knows well, Willy says, "Charley is not—liked. He's liked, but he's not—well liked."

If Willy read only one book in 1937, it might have been Dale Carnegie's *How to Win Friends and Influence People*—a book that summarized everything Willy believed and confirmed everything he was trying to teach his children. "Six Ways to Make People Like You," "Twelve Ways to Win People to Your Way of Thinking," "Nine Ways to Change People Without Giving Offense or Arousing Resentment": Willy did not need to read Carnegie's best seller; he could have written it.

In one of the rare nights when he was not on the road, it is easy to imagine Willy reading Dale Carnegie out loud to his boys at the dinner table. "Actions speak louder than words," Carnegie declares, "and a smile says, 'I like you. You make me happy. I am glad to see you.' . . . An insincere grin? No. That doesn't fool anybody. . . . I am talking about a real smile, a heart-warming smile, a smile that comes from within, the kind of a smile that will bring a good price in the market place." And so on—for eight pages! Once you have read Dale Carnegie on the subject of smiling, you may find yourself listening as if for the first time to the famous speech a friend makes at Willy's funeral: "Willy was a salesman. And for a salesman, there is no rock bottom to the life. He don't put a bolt to a nut, he don't tell you the law or give you medicine. He's a man way out there in the blue, riding on a smile and a shoeshine. And when they start not smiling back—that's an earthquake."

* * *

Of all the success literature Willy might have heard or read, the most tantalizing to consider is Russell Conwell's *Acres of Diamonds*. The fascination lies in its possible relation of Conwell's sermon to the story of Willy Loman's rich brother Ben.

Ben's story is extremely strange. When Willy was about four, we learn, his father, a flute peddler, abandoned the family. Ben set out to find the father in Alaska, but, being blessed with "a very faulty view of geography," he traveled South, so, he explains, "instead of Alaska, I ended up in Africa." No matter. "When I was seventeen I walked into the jungle, and when I was twenty-one I walked out. And by God, I was rich."

Ben is presented as a fabulous character, and his story has all the qualities of fable—a fable of pure dumb luck. But, of course, Willy doesn't see it that way. To Willy, Ben is "a genius . . . success incarnate!" The dizzy kid who didn't know North from South is converted, by the alchemy of money, into a man of masterful purpose: "There was a man started with the clothes on his back and ended up with diamond mines."

Diamond mines! Ben's story, some people in Arthur Miller's early audiences might have realized, turns Russell Conwell's *Acres of Diamonds* upside down. Willy Loman has dug in his own cellar, tilled his own garden, put in thirty-four years with one firm—and for what? For nothing. By contrast, Willy's brother Ben ventured boldly into the world like Conwell's Al Hafed, but instead of plunging to his death, he stumbled upon diamond mines. There may be a message here, but it is not a reassuring one. The message seems to be that in addition to being blind, Fortune enjoys a good joke, especially a joke that gnaws the heart.

To anyone who looks at *Death of a Salesman* with the history of American success literature in mind, what is most striking about Willy is that the success tradition that is based on character means nothing to him. He puts his faith not in character but in personality. Biff cannot fail, Willy thinks, because "He's got spirit, personality . . . personal attractiveness." "Personality always wins the day." "The man who makes an appearance in the business world, the man who creates personal interest, is the man who gets ahead." "Be liked and you will never want." "It's not what you say, it's how to say it." "It's not what you do. It's who you know and the smile on the face." And so on, till the day he dies. From Willy we do not hear one word about character, nor do we hear one word in praise of honesty, even as a matter of policy. Indeed, when young Biff "borrows" a football from the high-school locker room, Willy sanctions the theft with a characteristic explanation of the coach's failure to punish the young star: "That's because he likes you. If somebody else took the ball there'd be an uproar."

To Willy, being popular is not merely the best policy; it's the only policy. The need to be well liked is the nearest thing to a religion in Willy's life. At the emotional heart of the play, when Biff falls sobbing at Willy's feet after a confrontation that leaves the audience as shaken as it leaves the father and son, a stunned Willy exclaims with astonishment, "Biff—he likes me!" only to be corrected by his wife: "He loves you, Willy."

In the United States in the twentieth century, a man like Willy Loman might have read Russell Conwell, Elbert Hubbard, George H. Lorimer, Bruce Barton, Dale Carnegie, and dozens or hundreds of others, but none of them could tell him what to do when he was old and his smile had failed him. Faith might have helped, but Willy has no faith, and personality is not much of a rock on which to build a life.

Some literary critics have dismissed Arthur Miller as a purveyor of middle-brow melodrama, but the audiences who keep his work alive may see something the critics have missed. When Dustin Hoffman starred in a revival of *Death of a Salesman* in New York City in 1984, I asked an executive in his early fifties whether he intended to go. His face turned ashen. "No," he whispered. "I can't bear to. It reminds me of my father."

In the success literature of the twentieth century, Americans heard less and less about thrift, discipline, and hard work. They heard more and more about success through mind power or through the power of a winning personality. No doubt positive thinking helped many people, and no doubt a smile helped many others. Yet, like drugs that do little harm in the short run but wreak havoc if taken for extended periods, these success philosophies may have had unintended side effects. The title of a long-running musical in the 1960s, *How to Succeed in Business Without Really Trying*, neatly suggests what was happening to the work ethic in the United States as the nation grew more affluent. To succeed without trying: The title may have been a joke, but to many Americans in the second half of the twentieth century—which is to say, to many of Willy Loman's children and grandchildren—it was also a secret hope. The success literature that fed that hope was not wine. It was soda pop.

CHAPTER 15

Dissenting Voices: 1920–1945

Sinclair Lewis

In the twentieth century, as in the nineteenth, the voices that celebrated business values were countered by voices of doubt and dissent. No one denied that business had shaped American life in vital ways. The questions that interested the critics were questions of value. How did the United States measure up as a civilization? What kind of people was it producing? What kind of lives did they live? Had business exercised not merely a shaping but also a warping influence?

These questions were addressed with special fervor in the work of a tall, skinny redhead who became, in 1930, the first American to win the Nobel Prize for Literature. Sinclair Lewis was born in Sauk Centre, Minnesota, in 1885, the son of a country doctor. In the twelve years after he graduated from Yale in 1907, Lewis traveled restlessly around the United States; worked briefly in a number of editorial positions; and published four novels, none of them now remembered. Then, in 1920, he published *Main Street*. "It was," says Lewis's biographer Mark Schorer, "the most sensational event in twentieth-century American publishing history."

Main Street is a portrait of Gopher Prairie, Minnesota—a town of a few thousand that, Lewis emphasizes, might have been any of "ten thousand towns from Albany to San Diego." From the start, Lewis makes it clear that his portrait of Gopher Prairie also is a portrait of a civilization. And from the start he makes it clear that he will draw the portrait with his tongue set firmly in his cheek. "Main Street," he writes in an introductory note, "is the climax of civilization. That this Ford car might stand in front of the Bon Ton Store, Hannibal invaded Rome and Erasmus wrote in Oxford cloisters."

Lewis's heroine, Carol Milford, is an orphan who moves to Gopher Prairie after marrying the town physician, Dr. Will Kennicott. She soon discovers that she is "a woman with a working brain and no work," and she discovers that Gopher Prairie is a town where people live in "serene ignorance," worshiping "the Tribal God mediocrity." In the middle of the novel, Lewis sums up the vision of "tragic futility" that, he says, Carol felt but could not quite formulate:

> Doubtless all small towns, in all countries, have a tendency to be not only dull but mean, bitter, infested with curiosity. . . . But a village in a country which is taking pains to become altogether standardized and pure, which aspires to succeed Victorian England as the chief mediocrity of the world, is no longer merely provincial. . . . It is a force seeking to dominate the earth. . . . Sure of itself, it bullies other civilizations, as a traveling salesman in a brown derby conquers the wisdom of China and tacks advertisements of cigarettes over arches for centuries dedicated to the sayings of Confucius.
>
> Such a society functions admirably in the large production of cheap automobiles, dollar watches, and safety razors. But it is not satisfied until the entire world also admits that the end and joyous purpose of living is to ride in flivvers, to make advertising-pictures of dollar watches, and in the twilight to sit talking not of love and courage but of the convenience of safety razors.

The uniformity of style and thought that troubled Emerson in Concord in 1850 has become, in Lewis's view, a national disease. "The universal similarity," he suggests:

> . . . is the physical expression of the philosophy of dull safety. Nine-tenths of the American towns are so alike that it is the completest boredom to wander from one to another. Always west of Pittsburgh, and often, east of it, there is same lumber yard, the same railroad station, the same Ford garage, the same creamery, the same box-like houses and two-story shops.

Carol finds the uniformity unbearably oppressive. On an outing, while the men converse "with the sedate pomposity of the commercialist," she reflects that "In details the men were unlike, yet they said the same things in the same hearty monotonous voices. You had to look at them to see which was speaking." When Will decides that he wants a new house, it turns out that "what he wanted was a house exactly like Sam Clark's, which was exactly like every third new house in every town in the country: . . . a house resembling the mind of a merchant who votes the party ticket straight and goes to church once a month and owns a good car."

What has made Main Street so dull? The narrowness of opinion, Lewis suggests, as well as "the demand for standardized behavior coming in waves from all the citizens," is rooted in the forces that have shaped the American character. The Midwest is "double-Puritan—prairie Puritan on top of New England Puritan." But the Puritanism of 1912, when the action of the novel begins, is a shell: "In Gopher Prairie it was not good form to be holy except at a church, between ten-thirty and twelve on Sunday." What Main Street really worships, as the town atheist points out to Carol, is money. "The dollar-sign has chased the crucifix clean off the map."

In *Babbitt*, published in 1922, Lewis continues the satiric assault on business values that he had begun in *Main Street*. This time the setting is not a small town but a great midwestern city, Zenith, a thriving metropolis whose "towers . . . were neither citadels nor churches, but frankly and beautifully office buildings."

Lewis's central character, George F. Babbitt, is one of the most meticulously described characters in American literature. Lewis lingers over the details of Babbitt's life with an attentiveness that can only spring from perfect love or perfect spite. We do not merely learn, for instance, that Babbitt's alarm clock awakens him. We learn that "It was the best of nationally advertised and quantitatively produced alarm-clocks, with all modern attachments, including cathedral chime, intermittent alarm, and a phosphorescent dial." We learn, too, that "Babbitt was proud of being awakened by such a rich device. Socially it was almost as creditable as buying expensive cord tires."

Similarly, when Babbitt puts on his suit, we learn that it is "well cut, well made, and completely undistinguished." When Babbitt puts on his shoes, we learn that they are "black laced boots, good boots, honest boots, standard boots, extraordinarily uninteresting boots." When Babbitt puts on his spectacles, we learn that they have "huge, circular, frameless lenses of the very best glass," that the earpieces are "thin bars of gold," and that in his spectacles Babbitt radiates the authority of "the modern business man; one who gave orders to clerks and drove a car and played occasional golf and was scholarly in regard to Salesmanship."

In his bathroom—"an altogether royal bathroom of porcelain and glazed tile and metal sleek as silver"—Babbitt is revealed as a man "whose god was Modern Appliances." Material goods are more than conveniences to him. "Just as he was an Elk, a Booster, and a member of the Chamber of Commerce, just as the priests of the Presbyterian Church determined his every religious belief and the senators who controlled the Republican Party decided . . . what he should think . . . so did the large national advertisers fix the surface of his life, fix what he believed to be his individuality. These standard advertised wares—toothpastes, socks, tires, cameras, instantaneous hot-water heaters—were his symbols and proofs of excellence; at first the signs, then the substitutes, for joy and passion and wisdom."

Zenith, a city consecrated to business, is full of men whose lives are devoted "to the economic purpose of Selling—not of selling anything in particular . . . but pure Selling." Babbitt himself, Lewis tells the reader in a famous sentence, "made nothing in particular, neither butter nor shoes nor poetry, but he was nimble in the calling of selling houses for more than people could afford to pay."

Babbitt's ethics are the ethics of his tribe. He is honest, but "not too unreasonably honest." He understands the value of flexibility: "He advocated, though he did not practise, the prohibition of alcohol; he praised, though he did not obey, the laws against motor-speeding; he paid his debts; he contributed to the church, the Red Cross, and the Y.M.C.A.; he followed the custom of his clan and cheated only as it was sanctified by precedent; and he never descended to trickery—though, as he explained . . . 'Course I don't mean to say that every ad I write is literally true or that I always believe everything I say when I give some buyer a good strong selling-spiel.' "

Babbitt's ethical standards are "practical." They do not require that he "refuse to take twice the value of a house if a buyer was such an idiot" that he failed to bargain. Nor do they require that he decline to take part in "the secret buying of real-estate options for certain . . . street-traction officials." After his candidate triumphs in a local election, Babbitt does turn down opportunity to fill several minor positions in the city government, but only because he prefers "advance information about the extension of paved highways."

The uniformity that vexed Carol Kennicott in Gopher Prairie is no less oppressive in Zenith. Babbitt's bedroom, for instance, is "a masterpiece among bedrooms, right out of Cheerful Modern Houses for Medium Incomes. Only it had nothing to do with the Babbitts, nor with any one else. . . . It had the air of being a very good room in a very good hotel."

This uniformity in the realm of material goods is matched by a uniformity of thought and tone in the realm of ideas. In the smoking compartment of a Pullman railway car, Babbitt converses with a group of traveling businessmen—the sort of men he classifies as "the Best Fellows You'll Ever Meet—Real Good Mixers." The men, Lewis notes, "all had the same ideas and expressed them always with the same ponderous and brassy assurance." In the same way, at a cocktail party in Zenith, the men proclaim their views "with the booming profundity of a prosperous male repeating a thoroughly hackneyed statement about a matter of which he knows nothing."

These hackneyed views are brought together brilliantly, in the middle of the novel, in a speech that Babbitt makes at the annual "Get-Together Fest of the Zenith Real Estate Board." In a memoir written years later, literary critic Alfred Kazin commented on Lewis's "understanding of the great American spiel" as well as his "uncanny and bizarre powers" of mimicry: "When he sprang up to do one of his imitations," Kazin recalls, "the amount of personal electricity he poured into the . . . apartment was astonishing. There was a snap, a clatter, a shock—above all, an eruption. . . . Nothing I had enjoyed in vaudeville, amusement parks, or among the silver-voiced snake-oil salesmen who in my youth peddled patent medicines had prepared me for the angry energy of Lewis's delivery. It was merciless. It left you stunned."

No monologue in Lewis's novels is more merciless than Babbitt's speech to the Real Estate Board. Here the gift of satiric mimicry is applied to Babbitt's Chamber of Commerce mentality with a zest that clearly is meant to kill:

> Every intelligent person [Babbitt says] knows that Zenith manufactures more condensed milk and evaporated cream, more paper boxes, and more lighting-fixtures than any other city in the United States. . . . But it is not so universally known that we also stand second in the manufacture of package-butter, sixth in the giant realm of motors and automobiles, and somewhere about third in cheese, leather findings, tar roofing, breakfast food, and overalls! . . . When I add that we have an unparalleled number of miles of paved streets, bathrooms, vacuum cleaners, and all the other signs of civilization; that our library and art museum are well supported

and housed in convenient and roomy buildings; that our park-system is more than up to par . . . then I give but a hint of the all-round unlimited greatness of Zenith! . . .

But the way of the righteous is not all roses. . . . The worst menace to sound government is not the avowed socialists but a lot of cowards who work under cover—the long-haired gentry who call themselves "liberals" and "radicals" and "non-partisan" and "intelligentsia" and God only knows how many other trick names! . . . The American business man is generous to a fault, but one thing he does demand of all teachers and lecturers and journalists: if we're going to pay them our good money, they've got to help us by selling efficiency and whooping it up for rational prosperity! And when it comes to these blab-mouth, fault-finding, pessimistic, cynical University teachers, let me tell you that during this golden coming year it's just as much our duty to bring influence to have these cusses fired as it is to sell all the real estate and gather in all the good shekels we can.

Not till that is done will our sons and daughters see that the ideal of American manhood and culture isn't a lot of cranks sitting around chewing the rag about their Rights and their Wrongs, but a God-fearing, hustling, successful, two-fisted Regular Guy, who belongs to some church with pep and piety to it, who belongs to the Boosters or the Rotarians or the Kiwanis, to the Elks or Moose or Red Men or Knights of Columbus or any one of a score of organizations of good, jolly, kidding, laughing, sweating, upstanding, lend-a-handing Royal Good Fellows, who plays hard and works hard, and whose answer to his critics is a square-toed boot that'll teach the grouches and smart alecks to respect the He-man and get out and root for Uncle Samuel, U.S.A.!

Lewis also shows his powers of imitation in a model sales letter written by Babbitt ("SAY, OLD MAN! I just want to know can I do you a whaluva favor?"); a hilarious series of advertisements for mail-order courses ("Mr. P. R., formerly making only eighteen a week in a barber shop, . . . is now pulling down $5,000 as an Osteo-vitalic Physician"); a perfect, two-page spoof of a Dale Carnegie ad ("$ $ $ $ $ $ $ $ . . . POWER AND PROSPERITY IN PUBLIC SPEAKING"); and a "highbrow" ad written for an automobile called the Zeeco by Zenith's renowned poet and advertising agent, T. Cholmondeley Frink ("Speed—glorious Speed. . . . Listen, brother! You'll never know what the high art of hiking is till you TRY LIFE'S ZIPPINGEST ZEST—THE ZEECO!").

Advertising jargon permeates Babbitt's world. An economist for the Zenith Street Traction Company is proud to be known as "the guy that put the con in economics." T. Cholmondeley Frink is proud to be known as the creator of "Ads that Add." A good slogan, Babbitt assumes, can sell anything. Zenith is not merely Zenith. It's "Zenith the Zip City—

Zeal, Zest, and Zowie." Even religion must be marketed. The pastor at Babbitt's church tells his congregation that "the real cheap skate is the man who won't lend to the Lord!" and publishes a newspaper editorial titled "The Dollars and Sense Value of Christianity." When Babbitt is appointed to a committee whose function is to boost church member-ship—or, as Babbitt puts it, "getting out and drumming up custom-ers"—he shows his business acumen by recommending that the Sunday school hire "a real paid press-agent" to preach "the value of the Prayer-life in attaining financial success."

Beneath the pep and optimism of Zenith's businessmen, Lewis sug-gests, beneath the incessant boosting and selling, some men feel an uneasiness. "You know," says Babbitt's best friend, a roofing salesman named Paul Riesling, "my business isn't distributing roofing—it's prin-cipally keeping my competitors from distributing roofing. Same with you. All we do is cut each other's throats and make the public pay for it!"

But it's not merely business that makes Paul uneasy; it's also the timidity and dullness of the lives dominated by business. "Take all these fellows we know," Paul says to Babbitt one day at the Zenith Athletic Club, "the kind right here in the club now, that seem perfectly content with their home-life and their businesses, and that boost Zenith and the Chamber of Commerce. . . . I bet if you could cut into their heads you'd find that one-third of 'em are sure-enough satisfied with their wives and kids and friends and their offices; and one-third feel kind of restless but won't admit it; and one-third are miserable and know it. They hate the whole peppy, boosting, go-ahead game, and they're bored by their wives and think their families are fools—at least when they come to forty or forty-five they're bored—and they hate business. . . ."

The crushing dullness of the typical businessman's life exists, Lewis suggests, despite virtually nonstop activity—or, to be more precise, the appearance of nonstop activity. It is hard to say when the phrase "rat race" came into common use, but it is clear that the concept, if not the phrase, was one that Lewis would have embraced:

> As [Babbitt] approached the office he walked faster and faster, mutter-ing, "Guess better hustle." All about him the city was hustling, for hus-tling's sake. Men in motors were hustling to pass one another in the hustling traffic. Men were hustling to catch trolleys, with another trolley a minute behind, and to leap from the trolleys, to gallop across the sidewalk, to hurl themselves into buildings, into hustling express elevators. Men in dairy lunches were hustling to gulp down the food which cooks had hustled to fry. Men in barber shops were snapping, "Jus' shave me once over. Gotta

hustle." . . . Men who had made five thousand, year before last, and ten
thousand last year, were urging on nerve-yelping bodies and parched brains
so that they might make twenty thousand this year; and the men who had
broken down immediately after making their twenty thousand dollars were
hustling to catch trains, to hustle through the vacations which the hustling
doctors had ordered.

Among them Babbitt hustled back to his office, to sit down with nothing much to do except see that the staff looked as though they were
hustling.

In the last third of the novel, Babbitt is shaken by the tumultuous
doubt and distress that later generations would come to call a "midlife
crisis." After eating a rotten clam, he is forced to lie still for two days,
and lying still turns out to be dangerous: "He beheld, and half admitted
he beheld, his way of life as incredibly mechanical. Mechanical business—a brisk selling of badly built houses. Mechanical religion—a dry,
hard church, shut off from the real life of the streets, inhumanly respectable as a top-hat. Mechanical golf and dinner-parties and bridge and conversation. . . . mechanical friendship—back-slapping and jocular, never
daring to essay the test of quietness."

All his working life, Babbitt has understood that time is money. Now
he realizes that time is also time, and that for him time is running out.
" 'I'll be fifty in three years,' " he reflects with a mixture of gloom and
resolution. " 'Sixty in thirteen years. I'm going to have some fun before
it's too late. I don't care! I will!' "

Babbitt revolts as vigorously as a middle-aged businessman can. He
has an affair with a woman exotically named Tanis Judique, falls in with
Tanis's bohemian crowd, repents his old "life of barren heartiness," leaves
his office in midafternoon "with a vicious determination to do what he
pleased," and, when a strike hits, even goes so far as to suggest that far
from being "a lot of bomb-throwing socialists and thugs," the striking
workers seem to be normal fellows with normal aspirations.

In the end his revolt fizzles. The good businessmen of Zenith organize
a Good Citizens' League "to put the kibosh on cranks"—which is to say,
to put the strikers back in their proper places. Babbitt hesitates to join,
and he soon discovers that he cannot march to a different drummer without paying a price. He loses business, loses employees, loses friends, is
not invited to an important poker party, is not invited to speak at the
Chamber of Commerce dinner.

"The independence," Lewis writes, "seeped out of him." At last, with
profound relief, Babbitt joins the League, and "Within two weeks no

one . . . was more violent regarding . . . the crimes of labor unions, the perils of immigration, and the delights of golf, morality, and bank-accounts than George F. Babbitt." But he understands—understands with a terrible clarity—that his spirit has been broken: " 'They've licked me; licked me to a finish!' " he whimpers. His defeat is complete: "He felt that he had been trapped into the very net from which he had with such fury escaped and, supremest jest of all, been made to rejoice in the trapping."

In his Nobel Prize acceptance speech in 1930, Lewis commented on the supreme jest that, he felt, often faces the American satirist in a culture saturated and dominated by business. The American artist, he said, "is oppressed ever by something worse than poverty—by the feeling that what he creates does not matter, that he is expected by his readers to be only a decorator or a clown, or that he is good-naturedly accepted as a scoffer whose bark probably is worse than his bite and who probably is a good fellow at heart." In any case, the artist knows that his work "certainly does not count in a land that produces eighty-story buildings, motors by the million, and wheat by the billions of bushels."

It was a prophetic speech. To be accepted as a scoffer whose bark was worse than his bite was, in fact, Lewis's fate in the years that followed. In his later books, Alfred Kazin complained in *On Native Grounds* in 1942, Lewis's iconoclasm became "tedious and safe. . . . He had lampooned Babbittry easily enough; but when the Babbitts themselves were threatened, he rushed forward to defend them." Mark Schorer came to the same conclusion in the mammoth biography of Lewis that he published in 1961: "How often, . . . in his own sentimentality and Philistinism, he settled for the very stolidity in American life that he castigated! . . . He loved what he deplored."

There is some truth to these comments. For all his jeering, Lewis was not a mean-spirited writer. His satire is both biting and benevolent. He wanted Carol Kennicott to be happy. He wanted George Babbitt to live a fuller life. To say that he loved what he deplored goes too far. But it does not go too far to say, as Lewis himself said in 1950, that he loved America but did not like it.

It certainly seems absurd to state, as Alfred Kazin does in *On Native Grounds*, that Lewis's work is the work of a novelist "fundamentally uncritical of American life." A more balanced view might judge Lewis as Carol Kennicott judges herself at the end of *Main Street:* " 'This Community Day makes me see how thoroughly I'm beaten. . . . But I have won in this: I've never excused my failures by sneering at my aspirations. . . . I do not admit that Main Street is as beautiful as it should be! I do not admit that Gopher Prairie is greater or more generous than Europe! I do not admit that dish-washing is enough to satisfy all women! I may not have fought the good fight, but I have kept the faith.' " Lewis may have faltered in his later novels, but in his best fiction he not only fought the good fight and kept the faith as he saw it; he also created a body of work that endures.

The Agrarians

Sinclair Lewis's revolt against business was a revolt in support of liberal ideas and in opposition to suffocating conventions. At the same time that Lewis pressed his attack against everything "genteel and traditional and dull" in American life, another revolt was brewing. But this revolt was inspired by impulses that differed sharply from Lewis's. It assailed business in support of traditions that Lewis disdained and in opposition to ideas that Lewis cherished.

This revolt was led by a group of southern writers who came to be called "the Agrarians" and who poured out their contempt for the modern world in a collection of essays published in 1930 under the title *I'll Take My Stand*. Considering what a tiny band it was, the Agrarians included an extraordinary number of gifted writers, included John Crowe Ransom, Allen Tate, Andrew Lytle, Stark Young, Donald Davidson, and Robert Penn Warren. In addition to the essays on various aspects of southern life that make up the body of the book, *I'll Take My Stand* contained a passionate introductory manifesto, on which the twelve contributors collaborated. In this introduction the group stated the principles that explained their opposition to the "American industrial ideal" and their support of the southern or agrarian way of life.

What distinguished the Agrarians' vision was its scope and its severity. In the modern age, the Agrarians argued, neither men nor women stand in a "right relation" to history, to nature, to one another, or to God. Industrialism is an "evil dispensation" that piles up material goods yet does not provide a good life. As the elder statesman of the group, John Crowe Ransom, writes in his contribution to *I'll Take My Stand*, "Industrialism is a program under which men, using the latest scientific paraphernalia, sacrifice comfort, leisure, and the enjoyment of life to win Pyrrhic victories from nature at points of no strategic importance. . . . Industrialism is an insidious spirit, full of false promises. . . . Only a community of tough conservative habit can master it."

What especially disturbed the Agrarians was the quality of life in modern industrial society. In the introduction in which they summarized their common convictions, they examined the quality of work in America, the quality of leisure in America, and the quality of consumption in America, and they found little that they liked. They found little because they examined these aspects of American life from the perspective of the highest standard they could apply. As Stark Young wrote in his essay, "It all comes down to the most practical of all points—what is the end of living? . . . It may be that the end of man's living is not mere raw Publicity, Success, Competition, Speed and Speedways, Progress, Donations, and Hot Water, all seen with a capital letter. There are also more fleeting and eternal things to be thought of; more grace, sweetness and time; more security in our instincts, and chance to follow our inmost nature. . . ."

From this perspective, the world looked very different than it looked from the perspective of, say, Henry Ford. Take the example of work. Industrialism, the Agrarians point out in their introduction, "is generally quite sure that the saving of labor is a pure gain"—a conclusion that assumes that "labor is an evil" and thus abandons the possibility that labor might be "one of the happy functions of human life." But what happens when a labor-saving device or machine is introduced into an industrial process? We might expect that labor would become more leisurely. "But the modern laborer has not exactly received this benefit under the industrial regime. His labor is hard, its tempo is fierce, and his employment is insecure." Industrialism seeks ever-expanding production, but there its vision ends: "Labor is one of the largest items in the human career; it is a modest demand to ask that it may partake of happiness." Industrialism never thinks to make this demand.

Consider, next, the quality of modern leisure. "It is common knowledge," Donald Davidson writes in his essay, "that . . . the kind of leisure provided by industrialism is a dubious benefit. It helps nobody but merchants and manufacturers, who have taught us to use it in industriously consuming the products they make in great excess over the demand. Moreover, it is spoiled, as leisure, by the kind of work that industrialism compels. The furious pace of our working hours is carried over into our leisure hours, which are feverish and energetic. We live by the clock. Our days are a muddle of 'activities,' strenuously pursued. We do not have the free mind and easy temper that should characterize true leisure."

Finally, consider not merely the quality of modern leisure but also the quality of the consumption that increasingly fills that leisure—the consumption that the apologists of industrialism offer as "the grand end which justifies the evil of modern labor." True, the Agrarians concede in their introduction, "We have more time in which to consume, and many more products to be consumed." But in the same way that our labor is not leisurely, so our consumption is not leisurely: "The tempo of our labors communicates itself to our satisfactions, and these also become brutal and hurried." What we lose in our hustle-bustle society, John Crowe Ransom grieves, is "that leisure which conditions the life of intelligence and the arts."

The positive value that the Agrarians proposed in opposition to industrialism was the life of the independent farmer—not merely an agrarian life, but an agrarian life that is not hurried and not mechanized, or at least not insanely mechanized. Agrarianism is seen as "the best and most sensitive of vocations" because it places those who practice it in a natural relation—a "right relation"—to nature.

In proposing to wean men from their attachment to the soil, Ransom writes, "industrialism sets itself against the most ancient and the most humane of all the modes of human livelihood." The farmer "identifies himself with a spot of ground," whereas the urban industrial worker is rootless. Both for the individual and for society, the difference between a rooted and a rootless life is the difference between an ordered and a disordered life. "A man can contemplate and explore, respect and love, an object as substantial as a farm or a native province. But he cannot contemplate nor explore, respect nor love, a mere turnover, . . . a pile of money, a volume of produce, a market, or a credit system. It is into precisely these intangibles that industrialism would translate the farmer's farm. It means the dehumanization of his life."

What about the dehumanization of the slave system? Slavery, Ransom writes, "was a feature monstrous enough in theory, but, more often than not, humane in practice"—an assertion he does not bother to document. In any case, Ransom sees slavery as a horror that has passed, whereas industrialization is a horror that is rushing to ruin the land he loves. In one eloquent passage, Ransom sums up the whole quarrel between the Agrarians and the defenders of industrialism. The issue, he makes clear, is an issue of definition—the definition of what constitutes a civilized life: "There are a good many faults to be found with the old South, but hardly the fault of being intemperately addicted to work and to gross material prosperity. The South never conceded that the whole duty of man was to increase material production, or that the index to the degree of his culture was the volume of his material production. His business seemed to be rather to envelop both his work and his play with a leisure which permitted the activity of intelligence."

The Agrarians were sensible men who did not expect to restore the past, any more than Henry Adams had expected to halt the Dynamo. "The South must be industrialized," Ransom conceded, but he hoped that it might be industrialized "to a certain extent only, in moderation." As befitted a man steeped in the classics, Ransom believed in a middle way, as the Greeks had believed in it. Stark Young took the same moderate stance, but he expressed himself less moderately: "We can accept the machine, but create our own attitude toward it," he wrote. "There is no reason why Southern people, however industrialized, should bolt the whole mess as it stands."

To bolt the whole mess was easier, however, than pursuing a middle way. "The South has thrown its lot squarely with the machines and factories," literary critic and historian Louis D. Rubin, Jr., wrote in his introduction to a new edition of *I'll Take My Stand* published in 1962. ". . . Today the suburbs of Nashville, Richmond, Charleston, and Mobile are scarcely distinguishable from those of Buffalo, Trenton, Indianapolis, and Hartford."

Statistics tell the story. As a percentage of total population, the farm population in the United States fell from 41.9 percent in 1900 to 2.2 percent in 1986. In the South, the total farm population rose from 14.2 million in 1900 to nearly 17.2 million in 1935, but by 1980 the number had fallen below 1.8 million. As a percentage of total population, the farm population of the South fell from 58.0 percent in 1900 to less than 2.4 percent in 1980.

Moreover, the farms that remained, in the South and elsewhere, tended increasingly to be large and heavily industrialized—"essentially a factory in the field," as the *Encyclopaedia Britannica* puts it. In *I'll Take My Stand*, John Crowe Ransom foresaw this development with uncanny accuracy: "After the war," he noted, "the Southern plantations were often broken up into small farms. These have yielded less and less of a living, and it is said that they will never yield a good living until once more they are integrated into large units. But these units will be industrial units . . . worked with machinery, and manned not by farmers living at home, but by 'labor.' " In the slow seasons, Ransom added with rueful irony, "the laborers will have to work in factories, which henceforth are to be counted on as among the charming features of Southern landscape."

And so it has come to pass. Manufacturing and mechanized agriculture flourish in the New South. Tennessee itself, where so many of the Agrarians forged their anti-industrial philosophy at Vanderbilt University, has embraced industrialism with special fervor. Eleven years after Ransom's death in 1974, Tennessee governor Lamar Alexander announced proudly that General Motors had chosen Spring Hill, Tennessee, over one thousand other towns in thirty-seven other states as the site of a new $5 billion automobile plant for its much-heralded car of the future called Saturn. "Dozens of other governors had been bidding for the Saturn facility against Mr. Alexander," *The New York Times* reported. *The Times* noted, too, that only a few years earlier the Japanese auto company Nissan had chosen Smyrna, Tennessee, as the site of its largest American manufacturing plant.

In 1930, Ransom had described industrialism as "a foreign invasion of Southern soil, which is capable of doing more devastation than was wrought when Sherman marched to the sea." In 1985 Governor Alexander greeted the news that GM had picked Tennessee for its giant plant with the words. "We welcome you, we're proud of you, we're flattered that you chose Tennessee. We want Saturn people to feel like they're Tennesseans from the day they arrive." In the land of lost causes, the Agrarian movement to stem the industrial tide had been, in the end, just another lost cause.

The Modern Corporation and Private Property

One of the wonders of American intellectual history is the number of different angles from which business has been attacked. In the nineteenth century, Thoreau attacked it from the perspective of a radical individualism, whereas the participants in such cooperative experiments as Brook Farm, Fruitlands, and the Oneida Community attacked it from the perspective of a communal ideal. In the twentieth century, the muckrakers criticized the robber barons and the giant trusts, whereas Sinclair Lewis offered a critique of small-town business and the small-town business mentality. Lewis was a liberal who loved "progressive" ideas. The Agrarians were conservatives who condemned industrialism from the perspective of pastoral values and who believed that, in the words of John Crowe Ransom. "The American progressive principle . . . was a principle of boundless aggression against nature."

Only two years after the Agrarians stated their case against industrialism, an economist and a law professor examined the American economic scene from a completely different perspective and, without ever questioning either the value of industrialism or the role of industrialism in American life, reached conclusions that troubled them as much as industrialism itself troubled the Agrarians.

These conclusions are summarized in one of the most influential books ever written about American business. *The Modern Corporation and Private Property*, by Adolf A. Berle, Jr., and Gardiner C. Means, was published in 1932, one of the bleakest years in American economic history. But the book was conceived in the boom year 1927, when the thirty-two-year-old Berle received a grant from the Laura Spelman Rockefeller Foundation to collaborate with an economist on a study of the role of corporations in American life. When they began work on their book, Berle and Means could not have imagined the circumstances that would exist when it appeared. Nor could they have imagined that those circumstances would help make Berle, in the words of his biographer Jordan Schwarz, "the Marx of the 'New Deal Revolution.' "

Berle (pronounced "burly") was clearly the senior partner in the collaboration. Born in 1895, the son of one of New England's leading theologians, he was a child prodigy who entered Harvard College at the age of fourteen and who was the youngest graduate in the history of the Harvard Law School when he received his degree in 1916 at the age of twenty-one. At twenty-three he was an adviser on Russian affairs at the Paris peace talks, where his colleagues included such young luminaries as Walter Lippmann, Allen and John Foster Dulles, and Samuel Eliot Morison.

In the 1920s Berle published a series of articles on corporate law and finance that quickly earned him a reputation as one of the nation's most brilliant legal scholars. This work led to the proposal that won the 1927 grant from the Laura Spelman Rockefeller Foundation. As his collaborator, Berle chose Gardiner Means, a friend who had just completed a master's degree in economics at Columbia University and who would go on to have a distinguished career of his own as an academic economist.

For more than two hundred years, the fundamental argument in favor of free enterprise has been that elucidated in Adam Smith's *The Wealth of Nations* and famously summarized in the metaphor of the "invisible hand." Every individual "who employs his capital in the support of domestic industry," Smith writes in Book IV, Chapter II of his opus, "necessarily endeavours so to direct that industry, that its produce may be of the greatest possible value." But the wants and needs of other individuals, as revealed by the prices they are willing to pay, define what the community truly values. Thus the pursuit of self-interest, disciplined by competition and directed by shifting conditions of supply and demand, leads to the best possible economic result for society as a whole. The individual "neither intends to promote the public interest, nor knows how much he is promoting it. . . . [H]e intends only his own gain, and he is in this, as in many other cases, led by an invisible hand to promote an end which was no part of his intention." Indeed, by pursuing his own interest the individual "frequently promotes that of society more effectually than when he really intends to promote it."

Berle and Means do not challenge this argument in its application to the world of Adam Smith. But they do challenge it in its application to the world of the modern corporation. That challenge, backed not by the furious rhetoric of the muckrakers but by a quiet marshaling of facts, is what made *The Modern Corporation and Private Property* an explosive book.

In part, the challenge to Adam Smith in *The Modern Corporation* is based on Adam Smith himself. "When Adam Smith talked of 'enterprise,' " Berle and Means point out, "he had in mind as the typical unit the small individual business in which the owner, perhaps with the aid of a few apprentices or workers," did the work. In the case of the joint-stock corporation with dispersed ownership, Smith felt, the invisible hand was likely to fail. "The directors of such companies . . . ," he wrote, "being the managers rather of other people's money than of their own, it cannot well be expected that they should watch over it with the same anxious vigilance with which the partners in a private copartnery . . . watch over their own. . . . Negligence and profusion, therefore, must always prevail, more or less, in the management . . . of such a company."

This issue—which Berle and Means describe as "the divorce of ownership from control"—was not one that Smith needed to address in detail at a time when England was essentially a nation of shopkeepers. But conditions had changed dramatically since *The Wealth of Nations* was published in 1776. In the United States in 1800, Berle and Means point out, "Manufacturing industry lay almost wholly outside the corporate field, being represented by only six corporations." By 1900, two thirds of all manufactured products in the United States were made by corporations, and by 1932, Berle and Means estimate, the figure had risen to nearly 95 percent.

The quasi-public corporation—"a corporation in which a large measure of separation of ownership and control has taken place through the multiplication of owners"—is the dominant economic institution of the modern world. As giant corporations grow ever more giant, economic power tends "more and more to concentrate in the hands of a few corporate managements," while "ownership continually becomes more dispersed." Moreover, the separation of ownership from control "produces a condition where the interests of owner and of . . . manager may, and often do, diverge, and where many of the checks which formerly operated to limit the use of power disappear."

In other words, what we see in the modern world is "the dissolution of the old atom of ownership into its component parts." The assumption that the invisible hand of self-interest guarantees economic efficiency no longer holds, because "it is no longer the individual himself who uses his wealth," but salaried managers with interests and motives of their own. "The explosion of the atom of property destroys the basis of the old assumption that the quest for profits will spur the owner of industrial property to its effective use. It . . . challenges the fundamental economic principle of individual initiative in industrial enterprise."

With the separation of ownership from control, the invisible hand divides into two hands, engaged, perhaps, in a tug-of-war. On the one side we have "a large body of security holders . . . who exercise virtually no control over the wealth which they or their predecessors . . . have contributed to the enterprise." On the other side we have the professional managers who actually run the enterprise and who "may hold the power to divert profits into their own pockets," with the result that "There is no longer any certainty that a corporation will in fact be run primarily in the interests of the stockholders."

The divorce of ownership and control in the modern corporation, Berle and Means assert, "may fairly be said to work a revolution." That revolution has destroyed the unity of property and raised doubts about the theory of the invisible hand. What is even more important, the world of Adam Smith has given way to the world of the giant corporation. "When we speak of business enterprise today, we must have in mind primarily these very units which seemed to Adam Smith not to fit into the principles which he was laying down for the conduct of economic activity. How then can we apply the concepts of Adam Smith in discussing our modern economy?"

The separation of ownership from control in large corporations would not have alarmed Berle and Means if, as in Adam Smith's day, those

POOR RICHARD'S LEGACY

corporations had played only a minor role in the economy. But it had been obvious for at least half a century that large corporations played a major role. Indeed, it had been so obvious that few people had tried to define what "major" meant in terms of assets and dollars. Berle and Means looked closely at the numbers and made their readers look.

What was a "large" corporation in the modern world? In terms of assets, Berle and Means point out, "the American Telephone and Telegraph Company would be equivalent [in 1927] to over 8,000 average sized corporations, and both the United States Steel Corporation and the Pennsylvania Railroad Company to over 4,000. . . . Clearly such great organisms are not to be thought of in the same terms as the average company. Already the Telephone Company controls more wealth than is contained within the borders of twenty-one of the states in the country."

To evaluate the role of these giant enterprises in the modern economy, Berle and Means present a list of the two hundred largest non-banking corporations in the United States. Using gross assets controlled by a corporation as the measure of its wealth, they find that as of January 1, 1930, the two hundred largest nonbanking corporations controlled roughly 49.2 percent of total *corporate* wealth in the United States; that they controlled roughly 38.0 percent of total *business* wealth in the United States; and that they controlled roughly 22.0 percent of the total *national* wealth.

These figures put the issue of the concentration of economic power in stark perspective: "There were over 300,000 nonfinancial corporations in the country in 1929. Yet 200 of these, or less than seven hundredths of one percent, control nearly half the corporate wealth."

This concentration of economic power "is made even more significant," Berle and Means assert, "when it is recalled that as a result of it, approximately 2,000 individuals out of a population of one hundred and twenty-five million are in a position to control and direct half of industry." Within the corporate system "there exists a centripetal attraction which draws wealth together into aggregations of constantly increasing size, at the same time throwing control into the hands of fewer and fewer men."

What is implied by this description of economic concentration is, again, a challenge to the validity of Adam Smith's arguments if they are applied to circumstances he never imagined. "When Adam Smith championed competition as the great regulator of industry, he had in mind units so small . . . that no single unit held an important position in the market."

But the development of the modern industrial economy has made it "necessary to think, to a very important extent, in terms of . . . huge units" rather than in terms of a multitude of small units. Traditional economic theory has become inadequate. Fundamental changes in the structure of the economy demand fundamental changes in the way we think about economic life.

Much of the argument to this point has been descriptive. But Berle and Means were not content merely to describe. The emergence of giant corporations in the modern world, they observe at the start of their final chapter, "involves a concentration of power in the economic field comparable to the concentration of religious power in the mediaeval church or of political power in the national state." And thus the emergence of giant corporations poses a giant problem—the problem of "power and its regulation." Throughout human history, "a constant warfare has existed between the individuals wielding power, in whatever form, and the subjects of that power. Just as there is a continuous desire for power, so also there is a continuous desire to make that power the servant of the bulk of the individuals it affects. . . . How will this demand be made effective?"

To answer this question, Berle and Means write, "would be to foresee the history of the next century." They cannot describe what has not yet occurred. But on the subject of "power and its regulation" they are prepared to offer a prescription.

What they prescribe is a middle way between socialism and capitalism—a middle way that is often described with the phrases "state capitalism" or "corporate liberalism." The conditions they have outlined, Berle and Means assert, have "cleared the way for the claims of a group far wider than either the owners or the control. They have placed the community in a position to demand that the modern corporation serve not alone the owners or the control but all society."

This middle way "offers a wholly new concept of corporate activity." Neither the claims of ownership nor those of management should prevail against the interests of the community. In order to ensure that the economic power of the giant corporations shall be "the servant of the bulk of the individuals it affects," the state is justified in insisting that "the 'control' of the great corporations should develop into a purely neutral technocracy, balancing a variety of claims by various groups in the community and assigning to each a portion of the income stream on the basis of public policy rather than private cupidity." As Berle put the matter in *The New York Times* on March 4, 1934, "Our problem is to maintain individualism by balancing economic concentration—specifically, big banks, big corporations, big industrial units—with enough State police power to make them our servants instead of our masters."

It is important to note that Berle's attitude toward big business differed sharply from the attitude of another ardent critic of large corporations, Louis Brandeis. Whereas Brandeis considered bigness a curse, Berle considered it an irreversible fact. Whereas Brandeis wanted to use the power of government to break up large economic units, Berle wanted to use the power of government to regulate and discipline them. It is no accident that one of the bitterest rivalries within the Roosevelt administration was the rivalry between Berle and Brandeis's disciple Felix Frankfurter.

Even before *The Modern Corporation and Private Property* appeared, Berle had been asked to join Columbia professors Raymond Moley and Rexford Guy Tugwell in the famous "brain trust" advising New York Governor Franklin Delano Roosevelt during the presidential campaign of 1932. It was Berle who drafted the speech that has been described as "the manifesto of the New Deal" and "the most momentous of the campaign"—the address calling for "an economic declaration of rights" that Roosevelt made at the Commonwealth Club of San Francisco on September 23, 1932.

Published by Macmillan in November 1932, *The Modern Corporation* was greeted with overwhelming enthusiasm. The review in *The Nation* called the book "epoch-making," and noted lawyer Jerome Frank declared that the work of Berle and Means would "perhaps rank with Adam Smith's *Wealth of Nations* as the first detailed description in admirably clear terms of the existence of a new economic epoch." On the front page of the *New York Herald Tribune* book review, historian Charles A. Beard proclaimed that the book was a "masterly achievement of research and contemplation" that might be "the most important work bearing on American statecraft between the publication of the immortal *Federalist* . . . and the opening of the year 1933." By the spring of 1933, *Time* was calling *The Modern Corporation* "the economic Bible of the Roosevelt Administration."

Guided by these comments, it would be easy to overstate the impact of *The Modern Corporation*. The New Deal would have occurred even if Berle and Means had not supplied an economic Bible for it. The force behind the New Deal was Roosevelt—not a book, not Berle, not the brain trust. It is true that, as Jordan Schwarz says in his biography of Berle, *The Modern Corporation* "laid the ideological foundations for much of the New Deal's industrial, banking, and finance legislation." But it is also true that Roosevelt would have acted with or without ideological foundations.

Nevertheless, an accident of timing made *The Modern Corporation* one of the most famous books of its time. More important, *The Modern Corporation* became a cultural phenomenon—a work that shaped the opinions of opinionmakers, was absorbed by the general culture, and influenced the ideas of millions of people who never read or even heard of it. Anyone who has read John Kenneth Galbraith has received a heavy dose of Berle and Means. Anyone who opens the best work ever written on the subject of American business history, Alfred D. Chandler, Jr.'s, *The Visible Hand,* meets an immediate reminder of the challenge to Adam Smith in "the pioneering work" of Berle and Means. In the world of the university, every academic study of the distribution of corporate wealth in the United States begins where Berle and Means left off. In the general culture, the various lists of America's five hundred largest corporations that appear annually in *Fortune* and *Forbes* descend directly from Berle and Means's study of America's two hundred largest corporations.

Perhaps the most impressive testimony to the persistent influence of *The Modern Corporation* was a conference sponsored by the Hoover Institution in 1982, on the fiftieth anniversary of the book's publication. Midway through the triumphant first term of the most conservative president since the 1920s, some of the nation's most brilliant conservative economists took the time to assail both the work of Berle and Means and the "astonishingly uncritical" reception of that work in the 1930s. The conference was remarkable not merely for the vigor of the attacks by the book's critics but also for the vigor of the counterattack by Gardiner C. Means, his lust for intellectual combat undiminished at the age of eighty-six.

Adolf A. Berle, Jr., died in 1971, after a long and varied career in government and as an author. It would be a pity to discuss his work without saying a few words about his unusual personality. The prodigy who had entered Harvard at the age of fourteen grew up to strike many who encountered him as testy, arrogant, and obnoxious. He was also daring—a man who got away with sending letters to FDR that began with the salutation "Dear Caesar." Berle's father had been a bright light in what has been described as "the golden age of Massachusetts aristocratic liberalism." As we near the end of the twentieth century, it is difficult to remember or imagine what "aristocratic liberalism" might mean, but an incident that occurred in the 1960s gives a hint. A magazine named *Avant-Garde* invited Berle and other celebrities to contribute to a feature, "The Most Hated Man." Berle's reply was, indeed, testy, arrogant, and obnoxious. It was also aristocratic and liberal. He wrote, "I have the same emotion for Hatred that I have for leprosy, syphillis, gangrene and other degenerative diseases. So I nominate *Avant-Garde* and its editor who propose to sell Hatred for profit." None of the other contributors said anything that anyone remembers.

John L. Lewis

The concentration of economic power that troubled Berle and Means was not balanced, in 1932, by any increase in the power of organized labor. Indeed, the fat years of the 1920s had been lean years for labor, with total union membership declining from 5.0 million in 1920 to 3.6 million in 1930, and membership in the American Federation of Labor declining from a 4.1 million to slightly less than 3.0 million.

It is difficult to overstate the extent of the business collapse between 1929 and 1933. In that period the number of manufacturing enterprises in the United States declined from 133,000 to 72,300; industrial income declined from $29 billion to $2.9 billion; and production itself declined nearly 48 percent. Roughly one third of the nation's wage earners were unemployed at the end of 1932. In the big cities of the North, unemployment approached 50 percent. Bread lines and soup lines stretched for blocks; grim-faced men searched hopelessly for work or sold apples from pushcarts; and thousands of homeless workers and their families lived on city dumps in shacks made of scrap metal and egg crates— "Hoovervilles."

Federal legislation to provide a "new deal" for labor began to be passed even before the inauguration of Franklin Delano Roosevelt as president in March 1933. Ending a struggle that had raged for four decades, the Norris-La Guardia Act of 1932 limited the use of injunctions in labor disputes except in cases that threatened the national security. At the same time, the act made "yellow dog" contracts (contracts that required the worker to agree not to join a union) unenforceable in federal courts.

Then, on June 16, 1933, on the last day in that period of frenzied legislative activity that became known as Roosevelt's "Hundred Days," Congress passed the National Industrial Recovery Act (NIRA), which established the Public Works Administration and the National Recovery Administration and guaranteed the right of workers "to organize and bargain collectively through representatives of their own choosing." Labor historian Irving Bernstein has called the NIRA "the spark that rekindled unionism within American labor." With government committed to the basic principle of collective bargaining in labor relations, the stage was set for a period of tremendous change.

In this time of ferment, the most important labor leader in the United States was John L. Lewis, the head of the United Mine Workers (UMW). A burly, barrel-chested man with a booming voice and a bushy-browed face set in a permanent frown, it was Lewis, more than any other man, who completed the unfinished business of the American labor movement—the organization of the nation's industrial workers.

The son of Welsh immigrants, Lewis was born in 1880 in the coal-mining hamlet of Cleveland, Iowa, completed all but the last year of high school, and went to work in the mines at the age of seventeen. After becoming active in the affairs of the UMW in 1908, Lewis rose rapidly through a series of appointed offices in the union hierarchy. In 1920, at forty, he was elected president of the UMW, the largest union in the nation and the largest, at the time, in the American Federation of Labor. He remained the head of the UMW, inside the AFL and later outside, for forty tumultuous years.

In the 1920s Lewis behaved curiously for a man who would soon be reviled as one of the nation's most dangerous radicals. He supported the Republican administrations of Warren Harding and Calvin Coolidge and endorsed the candidacy of Herbert Hoover in 1928. Far from being a visionary or a deep thinker, he gave every indication of being a man who was content to take advantage of any opportunities that happened to come his way. Autocratic by temperament, he expelled his enemies from the UMW and ended the decade with his command unchallenged. He also ended the decade with a reputation, as historian David Brody later wrote, of being "merely a labor boss of the most conventional kind, and a largely discredited one at that."

The 1930s were different. The miseries that the Depression inflicted on American workers also opened enormous new opportunities. Lewis did not become any more visionary or any less autocratic in the 1930s, but he saw the opportunities and seized them.

Unlike most AFL affiliates, the UMW was not a craft union but an industrial union—an organization that embraced all workers at the job site, whether they were skilled or unskilled. Lewis saw that the unrest stirred by the Depression, along with the friendly attitude of the Roosevelt Administration and the legislative support provided by the National Industrial Recovery Act of 1933 and the National Labor Relations Act of 1935, created a unique opportunity to organize the nation's vast corps of unskilled industrial workers.

To Lewis's consternation, however, the AFL seemed willing to let the opportunity slip away. Under the cautious leadership of William Green, the AFL continued to be less interested in organizing unskilled workers than in protecting the claims of the established craft unions. At the AFL convention in San Francisco in 1934, union leaders promised to launch vigorous organizing drives in the mass-production industries, but by the time the AFL met again in Atlantic City in October 1935, Lewis was convinced that the promise had been a lie. The AFL's leaders, Lewis charged in a sensational address to the convention on October 16, had been guilty of "a breach of faith and a travesty of good conscience." Industrial unions were "dying like the grass withering before the autumn sun." The AFL policy of always favoring the craft unions was bankrupt. For twenty-five years the AFL had followed this policy, and for twenty-five years every effort to organize America's industrial workers had broken upon this "rock of utter futility." In its relations with the unskilled workers in the mass-production industries, the AFL had compiled "a record of constant, unbroken failure."

With the old-fashioned oratorical flair that could mesmerize even his adversaries, Lewis asked his audience to remember the promises made the year before at the convention in San Francisco: "At San Francisco they seduced me with fair words. Now, of course, having learned that I was seduced, I . . . am ready to rend my seducers limb from limb." The delegates were about to vote on a minority report that recommended organizing workers in mass-production industries upon industrial and plant lines rather than craft lines. "Heed this cry," Lewis urged, ". . . that comes from the hearts of men." If the minority report was rejected, "despair will prevail where hope now exists. . . . High wassail will prevail at the banquet tables of the mighty."

As Lewis had anticipated, the convention rejected his plea. Three weeks later, on November 9, Lewis announced the creation of a Committee for Industrial Organization (CIO) to encourage the formation of industrial unions within the AFL. Lewis's effort was an act of open defiance, and the unions affiliated with the CIO were suspended at the AFL convention in October 1936. But it was not until November 1938 that the CIO (with the initials now standing for Congress of Industrial Organizations) officially became a separate entity.

Although other labor leaders were involved in the creation of the CIO, Lewis was clearly the dominant figure. In the fifteen crucial months from June 1936 to September 1937, the CIO spent $1.4 million more than it took in. In the same period, labor historians Melvyn Dubofsky and Warren Van Tine point out, the UMW alone gave $1.24 million to support CIO operations. "There can be no doubt that Lewis created the CIO," they conclude. "Without Lewis's generosity . . . there would have been no CIO."

Lewis's efforts paid off in a series of dramatic breakthroughs in the winter of 1936–37. A six-week sit-down strike at the huge GM plant in Flint, Michigan, produced a major victory when GM signed a contract with the United Automobile Workers on February 11, 1937. Just nineteen days later, on March 2, secret negotiations produced a pathbreaking contract with the U.S. Steel Company. On April 6 Chrysler yielded to the UAW after a brief series of sit-down strikes.

By the end of 1937, the CIO was larger than the AFL, with over 2.5 million workers in its affiliated unions, including 500,000 steelworkers, 400,000 textile workers, 375,000 autoworkers, 250,000 members of the ladies' garment workers union, and 200,000 members of the Amalgamated Clothing Workers. The total number of American workers who belonged to unions rose from 4,164,000 at the end of 1936 to 7,218,000 by the end of 1937, an increase of 73.3 percent. Thanks largely to John L. Lewis, the percentage of the total nonagricultural work force that belonged to unions more than doubled from 1936 through 1939.

In the late 1930s John L. Lewis was a central figure in American life—a man whose deep bass voice on the radio was almost as familiar as the voice of the president. Lewis was a man of action, capable of ruthlessness and even of physical brutality. He also was a man of powerful ego who, one journalist said, had come to believe that his own birthday should be celebrated instead of Christmas. "To ask Lewis to exercise magnanimity," writer John Chamberlain commented, "to ask him to be humble, is just about as futile as trying to get gold from pyrites or blood from a turnip."

Lewis's career after the triumphs of 1937 was as erratic as the man himself. The only stable element in the story is Lewis's volatile personality. In 1940, unhappy with the Roosevelt Administration's preparations for war and with its apparent indifference to the unfinished business of the New Deal, Lewis not only endorsed the presidential candidacy of Wendell Willkie, he also declared that Roosevelt's reelection would be "a national evil of the first magnitude" and announced that he would resign as president of the CIO if America's industrial workers repudiated his leadership by voting for FDR. After Roosevelt was reelected, Lewis not only carried out his threat but also, early in 1942, pulled the UMW out of the CIO. Then, in 1943, responding to the grievances of miners over policies that, Lewis said, fattened industry and starved labor, Lewis defied the government by leading nearly half a million soft-coal miners in a series of strikes that appeared to threaten the war effort. According to some historians, Lewis actually exercised a moderating influence in this episode, but his role was not appreciated. Once a hero to the vast majority of working Americans, he became one of the most hated men in the nation. "Speaking for the American soldier," the Army newspaper *Stars and Stripes* declared in an editorial, "John Lewis, damn your coal-black soul!"

In 1946–50 Lewis led a series of strikes that focused on the establishment of health, welfare, and retirement programs for the union's miners. Twice, in 1946 and 1948, the courts imposed large fines on the union and ordered striking workers to return to the mines. Twice Lewis was convicted of contempt for ignoring a court injunction. Then, in the 1950s, confrontation was replaced by accommodation. Coal faced vigorous competition from other sources of energy. As demand declined, the union's bargaining power diminished. Lewis's appetite for conflict seemed to diminish, too. Now in his seventies, Lewis became a labor statesman who advocated "cooperative capitalism," won praise from Herbert Hoover for his enlightened leadership, and turned the UMW, according to his biographer Melvyn Dubofsky, "into a friendly collaborator of the mine owners."

One of Lewis's most obvious failures was his failure to prepare the UMW to carry on without him. After his retirement as president of the union early in 1960, he was succeeded by the union's seventy-three-year-old vice president, Thomas Kennedy. Kennedy was followed, in 1964, by W. A. "Tony" Boyle, who, as Lewis's "administrative assistant" after 1948, had won a reputation as being little more than a loyal thug. On December 30, 1969, some six months after Lewis's death at eighty-nine, Boyle's chief adversary in the union, Joseph A. "Jock" Yablonski, was shot to death, along with his wife and daughter, at their home in Clarkesville, Pennsylvania. Four years later Boyle was convicted of conspiracy to murder Yablonski. By that time, despite reports that Lewis had considered Boyle "the worst mistake I ever made," it seemed clear that, as Melvyn Dubofsky and Warren Van Tine write in their biography of Lewis, "despotism . . . and a contempt for the law ranked high among the legacies the ancient leader passed on to his successors."

John L. Lewis was always a towering and often a baffling figure—a formidable foe who was also, at times, his own worst enemy. The most serious students of his career seem to have found him more rather than less perplexing as they learned more about him. A good case can be made for the proposition that no simple explanation accounts for him. A good case also can be made for any of half a dozen simple explanations. The simplest of all—that he did the best he could for the miners who trusted him to represent them—might not be far from the truth. "Think of me as a coal miner," he said once, "and you won't make any mistakes."

But a good case also can be made for the proposition that Lewis's service to the miners was like the service of a Tammany Hall politician to his constituents. In the end, Lewis may have been an enigma even to himself. "I value this portrait," he said when he was given an oil painting of himself in 1963. Then, looking at the image, he added, "I am going to have a hard time reading all the facets of his character."

In a broader perspective, the arc of Lewis's career mirrors the arc of the labor movement as a whole in the twentieth century. In the same way that the challenge of competing energy sources led to a decline in the strength of the UMW in the 1950s, so, in the 1970s and 1980s, the challenge of changing economic circumstances has led to a decline in the importance of labor unions. In 1960 nearly one third of American workers belonged to unions. By 1987 that figure had dropped to 17.0 percent. More than sixteen million workers belonged to AFL-CIO unions when the great federations finally merged under George Meany and Walter Reuther in 1955. By 1987 that figure had fallen by 3.3 million, to slightly under 12.7 million. What's more, the trend is expected to continue. Blue-collar employment in the manufacturing sector is steadily declining, while the fastest growth in the labor force is occurring among service workers, who historically have been difficult to organize. Some forecasters predict than only 13 percent of the nonagricultural labor force will belong to unions in the year 2000—the lowest percentage since 1930.

These circumstances suggest that John L. Lewis is not likely to be challenged, much less supplanted, as the most important labor leader of the twentieth century in the United States. He may have been labor's last lion. In 1940, Lewis's Labor Day speech on radio drew an audience of twenty-five million Americans. Today, in a nation whose population has nearly doubled, it is difficult to imagine that any labor leader could draw an audience half that size.

Horatio Alger with a Switchblade

The literature of the 1930s was largely a literature of social protest. Not much of this literature can be read with pleasure today. With their eyes focused, as Edmund Wilson has remarked, on a society that "seemed actually to be going to pieces," most writers of fiction in this period lost the capacity to create vivid characters. But in 1941 a twenty-seven-year-old Dartmouth graduate named Budd Schulberg published a novel that featured a character as memorable as Sinclair Lewis's Babbitt. Sammy Glick is a rat, but *What Makes Sammy Run?* is not merely a portrait of a rat. It is also, as Schulberg wrote in the famous last sentence of the novel, "a blueprint of a way of life that was paying dividends in America in the first half of the twentieth century."

Schulberg came from a family of immigrants whose experience in the United States followed the classic rags-to-riches pattern. His grandfather on his father's side, Schulberg reports in *Moving Pictures: Memories of a Hollywood Prince*, was, by the testimony of Schulberg's father, "a bum" who would "pick up a dollar a day as a sandwich man—a fellow who walks the street with a sandwich-board slung around his neck." His mother's family came to America "on the run from the Cossacks who terrorized their native Dvinsk, the lowly village-sister of Minsk and Pinsk that was in Poland or Sweden or Germany or Russia as the tides of history changed the flags but not the bottom-dog status of the Jews in the ghetto near the river Dvina."

Schulberg's father, Ben (later known as B.P.), was one of those "second-generation ghetto children" with a special fire burning in his belly. Always the smartest student in his class, he won a prize for the best short story by a schoolboy in New York City and, after lack of money forced him to drop out of City College, got a job as a copyboy for Franklin Pierce Adams, whose column "The Conning Tower" was one of the most widely read of its time.

One of B.P.'s jobs, "the lowest on the paper," was to review the one-reel movies that were starting to be shown in the nickelodens of the Lower East Side. By the age of twenty-two, B.P. had written hundreds

of screenplays, and when Budd was born in 1914, his father was working for one of the first film tycoons, Adolph Zukor, for "the lordly salary
of fifty dollars a week." Before long B.P. himself was a tycoon—the head
of production at Paramount. It was B. P. Schulberg who coined the
phrase "America's Sweetheart" to describe Mary Pickford, who discovered Cary Grant, and who brought to Hollywood the man who later
wrote the screenplay for *Citizen Kane*, Herman Mankiewicz. It was B.P.'s
wife, Adeline, who built the first beach house at Malibu.

Growing up, Budd Schulberg wrote later, "I . . . believed that Western Civilization had its center at the corner of Vine Street and Hollywood Boulevard." Hollywood was his playground. When he went to
Dartmouth, he recalls in his autobiography, "My mind was about as
empty a vessel as ever needed to be filled. I had yet to read Veblen's
Theory of the Leisure Class. Hell, I *was* the leisure class." But he also knew
Hollywood from the inside, which means that he knew about the dingi-
ness, vulgarity, ambition, and greed that lay behind the glamor. When
he sat down to write a novel about success in America, it was natural
for him to set most of the action in the town he knew best, and when
the book was done, it was natural for him to be pleased by the response
of Dorothy Parker: "I never thought anyone could put Hollywood—the
true shittiness of it—between covers."

Sammy Glick is introduced to the reader at the age of sixteen—"a
little ferret of a kid, sharp and quick," who works as a copy runner at
the newspaper in New York where the novel's narrator, Al Manheim,
writes a theater column. Watching Sammy run, Manheim quickly
realizes that the hyperactive teenager sees the world as a race, and
before long he asks the question that haunts that novel: "What makes
Sammy run?"

Sammy is more than a hard worker. He is a schemer and a back-
stabber, driven by "some angry, volcanic force erupting and overflowing
deep within him." In his rise to the top, every step is accompanied by
some lie, trick, or betrayal. He gets his own column in the newspaper
by making Manheim look bad, and he gets his invitation to Hollywood
by stealing a story idea from a bumbling young writer who doesn't even
realize that Sammy is using him.

Manheim tries to convince Sammy that "We can't live in this world
like a lot of cannibals trying to swallow each other," but Sammy laughs
him off. Even before he has gotten out of his teens, Sammy's face gives
"an impression of arrogance and a fierce aggressiveness." It is "a face that

reminded you of an army, full of force, strategy, single will and the kind of courage that boasts of never taking a backward step." Soon it begins to settle into "a permanent sneer"—a sneer that betrays "an incredible contempt for other human beings, not only for . . . his everyday acquaintances, but for strangers too, the back of a taxi driver's neck at which he yelled instructions, people he pushed out of the way in a crowd. . . ."

In Hollywood Sammy displays a gift for self-promotion that might have made P. T. Barnum jealous. At the restaurant where he takes Manheim for lunch after Manheim gets a job writing for one of the studios, Sammy reveals himself as a champion networker, "on speaking terms with everybody, the parking attendant, the hat-check girl who could have been a stand-in for Jean Harlow, the headwaiter. . . ." He stops to chat with gossip columnist Louella Parsons, then explains to Manheim, "The first thing I did when I got to town was call her up and give her an item for her column. That's a good habit to get into because every couple of times you can slip her a story about yourself too." After lunch Sammy makes "one of those bumble-bee exits, buzzing from table to table on his way out."

Sammy continues to rise—"a swift little rodent" whose chief weapons are "a fabulous gall," "a mouth energetic and loud," "a violent passion for his own future," and a monumental indifference to conventional moral scruples. "Going through a life with a conscience," he tells Manheim, "is like driving your car with the brakes on." Sammy himself goes through life with his cigar "stuck out in front of him like a cannon leveled at the world." Manheim watches him with a mixture of horror and fascination, wondering, in the words of one of Sammy's discarded girlfriends, "what would happen if Sammy used all that energy and imagination to create something—not just to devise ways of reaching the top without creating anything."

Getting to the top is all that interests "Kid Get-Ahead." In a world that "is run with all the rules and restrictions of a rough-and-ready free-for-all," scruples do not pay. When Manheim is ordered to work on a screenplay with an overweight writer named George Pancake, Sammy gives him a glimpse of the way a real operator works:

> If you turn in one treatment with both your names on it and that fat swish lets the producer know he did all the writing, you're dead. If you want to play it cozy, write a treatment of your own without letting Pancake know and then get to your producer alone and tell him you thought

Pancake was so far off the line it seemed faster to straighten it out yourself. That way you've got a chance of scaring him into bouncing Pancake off the picture and grabbing yourself a solo screen credit.

Much of Sammy's energy is devoted to getting credit for work other people do. If he advanced merely through street-smart strategems that left no one wounded, he would be nothing more than an amusing scoundrel. But he leaves a trail of victims behind him. In addition to being clever, he is callous, vulgar, and ruthless, and he does not care how many lives he wrecks in his "undeclared war against the world," his "blitzkrieg against his fellow men."

Though he knows how hard Sammy runs, Manheim does not know what makes him run until he takes a trip into Sammy's past. After losing his job because he has tried to organize a Screenwriters' Guild, Manheim returns to his newspaper in New York. There he makes an excursion to the Lower East Side, searching for an answer to the question of what has turned Samuel Glickstein into Sammy Glick.

Manheim finds Sammy's mother and his older brother Israel on Rivington Street "in a tenement laced with corroded fire-escapes and sagging washlines." After learning that Sammy sends them a check every month but never writes, Manheim finds others who allow him to piece together the story of Sammy's childhood. But it is not the story of a childhood. It is the story of a child who was never young, like the boys Manheim sees fighting in a schoolyard: "The little boys did not fight like children. . . . They fought grimly, weaving, jabbing, dancing away. . . . These were not children but seasoned battlers, battle-scarred veterans of seven or eight, for the East Side is like one gigantic prize-ring through the ropes of which everyone has to climb at birth."

In the end Manheim feels not only that he has learned something about Sammy but also that he has "learned something about the machinery that turns out Sammy Glicks." In Hollywood he had thought about "the horror of a foetus called Sammy Glick sprinting out of his mother's womb, turning life into a race in which the only rules are fight for the rail and elbow on the turns and the only finish line is death." Now he decides that the real horror is the world that spawned Sammy:

I thought of Sammy Glick rocking in his cradle of hate, malnutrition, prejudice, suspicions, amorality, the anarchy of the poor; I thought of him as a mangy little puppy in a dog-eat-dog world. I was modulating my hate for Sammy Glick from the personal to the societal. I no longer even hated

Rivington Street but the idea of Rivington Street, all Rivington Streets of all nationalities allowed to pile up in cities like gigantic dung heaps smelling up the world, ambitions growing out of filth and crawling away like worms. I saw Sammy Glick on a battlefield where every soldier was his own cause, his own army and his own flag, and I realized that I had singled him out not because he had been born into the world any more selfish, ruthless and cruel than anybody else . . . but because in the midst of a war that was selfish, ruthless and cruel Sammy was proving himself the fittest, the fiercest and the fastest.

Manheim winds up with a double view of Sammy. On the one hand he sees him as a "frantic marathoner" who cannot stop running—a missile hurtling through life with no more control over his flight than a cannonball shot out of a cannon. On the other hand, he sees him as a man responsible for the destruction he dishes out and for the loneliness that engulfs him in the end. Thinking of the message that he wishes he could have gotten across to Sammy as he rushed by, "hitting-and-running his way to the top," Manheim thinks about the dark side of individualism: "I thought of all the things I might of told him. . . . It had to be all you, all the way. You had to make individualism the most frightening ism of all. You act as if the world is just a blindfold free-for-all. Only the first time you get it in the belly you holler brotherhood. But you can't have your brothers and eat them too. You're alone, pal, all alone. That's the way you wanted it, that's the way you learned it. . . . All alone in sickness and in health, for better or for worse . . . till death parts you from your only friend, your worst enemy, yourself."

Schulberg tried to make *What Makes Sammy Run?* a book not merely about an individual but also about a type, not merely about Sammy Glick but also about "all the Sammy Glicks" who lived by the creed "Do it to them before they do it to me." After the book came out, Schulberg wrote in the Afterword to a new edition published in 1978, he was delighted to see how well he had succeeded. "As the mail began to pour in, I began to realize that Sammy Glick was not a Hollywood phenomenon. From advertising agencies in New York, insurance companies in Hartford, mail-order houses in the Middle West, people were writing to express their conviction that I could not have written *Sammy* without personal knowledge of their own mail-room boy who had run over their backs to become office manager."

As the years passed, Schulberg reports, something odd happened. To his astonishment, he discovered that being called a Sammy Glick was no longer necessarily an insult. "Now self-confident young men come up to shake my hand because 'I learned so much from your book; it helped me get ahead.' "

Sammy Glick, Schulberg concludes,

has become a candidate for the Junior Chamber of Commerce—Horatio Alger with a martini in one hand and a switchblade in the other. . . . In a culture that has replaced right or wrong with winning or losing, Sammy is no longer an anti-hero. . . . No longer the immigrant outsider, now the quintessential American, Sammy runs on into the twenty-first century. And the book I thought I had written as a warning against antisocial behavior is in danger of becoming a business manual, a fictionalized how-to version of a current best seller, *Looking Out for Number One*.

Many readers may wonder whether, in the real world of American business, amoral go-getters do as well as Schulberg suggests in *What Makes Sammy Run?* There is reason to doubt that they do. But there can be no doubt that Schulberg succeeded in creating a character that readers recognize and never forget. Every rat race must have a rat. Sammy Glick's way of life may not have been the only way that was "paying dividends in America in the first half of the twentieth century," but it seems to have been one way. At one point Manheim says of Sammy, "He rankled. He was like a splinter festering under my skin." Nearly half a century later, the splinter still festers. When he created Sammy Glick, Budd Schulberg touched a nerve. To think that business inspired, in a single generation, protests as diverse as the protests of Sinclair Lewis, the Agrarians, Adolf A. Berle, Jr., and Gardiner C. Means, John L. Lewis, and Budd Schulberg is to realize what deep anxieties and suspicions seethed in American minds and hearts in the first half of the twentieth century, directly alongside the buoyant optimism and bouncy affirmations that animated the literature of success.

CHAPTER 16

The Triumph of IBM

The Consummate Corporation

In the American company that has towered above all others in the twentieth century, Sammy Glick would not have lasted one day. If Budd Schulberg had grown up in Armonk rather than in Hollywood, and if his father had been the head of sales at IBM rather than the head of production at Paramount, it seems certain that the young writer would have reached sharply different conclusions about the kind of man who succeeds and the kind of behavior that pays off in the modern world.

The Industrial Revolution, many historians have noted, took place in two stages. The first stage used machines to ease the burden of manual drudgery. The cotton gin, power loom, and sewing machine that revolutionized textile manufacture; the reaping and threshing machines that revolutionized agriculture; the steam engines, electrical engines, and internal-combustion engines that revolutionized transportation; the telegraph and telephone that revolutionized communications; the washing and drying machines, refrigerators, dishwashers, and garbage-disposal machines that revolutionized household labor; the machine tools that revolutionized the very process of making machines—all of these belong to the first stage.

The second stage of the industrial revolution—sometimes called the second industrial revolution or the postindustrial revolution—used machines to reduce the burden of intellectual drudgery. Machines that have revolutionized clerical and managerial work; machines that have revolutionized the way we tabulate, count, compute, analyze, record, retrieve, and transmit data; machines that can convert data to information and information to knowledge; machines that can act upon the data they have analyzed, or tell human beings to act upon it, or tell other machines to act upon it—all of these belong to the second stage.

The first stage of the industrial revolution transformed our relations with matter. The second stage transformed our relations with data. To a remarkable extent, a single corporation has dominated this second stage. From its start as an unlikely conglomeration of companies that made meat slicers, butcher scales, coffee grinders, time clocks, and primitive tabulating machines, the International Business Machines Corporation has become in less than eighty years the world's most profitable industrial enterprise. Operating in more than one hundred countries, IBM collects 40 percent of the revenue and 70 percent of the profit from the world's information-processing industry. But IBM is more than a giant. It is a legend—the most widely admired corporation of the twentieth century.

The corporation we now know as IBM was formed in 1911 as the Computing-Tabulating-Recording Company (CTR), a holding company that controlled three business-machine manufacturers: the Computing Scale Company, a firm that produced grocery scales, meat slicers, and cheese slicers; the Tabulating Machine Company, a firm that produced electromechanical tabulating machines; and the International Time Recording Company, a firm that produced time clocks.

Of the three, the most important was the Tabulating Machine Company. It was founded in 1896 by Dr. Herman Hollerith, an engineer who had worked briefly in the U.S. Census Office and who later had taught at M.I.T. For the 1890 census, Hollerith devised a system of recording and storing information through holes punched in columns on cards. He also devised a series of electromechanical machines to punch, tabulate, and sort cards at high speed. Thanks to Hollerith's tabulating machines, tasks that previously had taken armies of clerical workers months to complete could be done in weeks by a small group of machine operators.

From one perspective, the story of IBM is a story of spectacular technological innovation. The story moves from Hollerith's punched-card machines to the vacuum-tube calculators of the 1940s to the mighty electronic computers of the 1980s with speeds measured in billionths of a second. The story moves from the wires, wheels, and levers of Hollerith's machines to the transistors that replaced vacuum tubes in the 1950s to the "solid logic technology" of the 1960s, the "integrated circuit technology" of the 1970s, and the "high density technology" of the 1980s. Today, research scientists at IBM talk not only about circuits and chips but also about "fractal geometry," "ballistic electron-transfer techniques," "Superconducting Quantum Interference Devices," "Scanning Tunneling Microscopy," and the "11 Gigaflops machine . . . designed to operate at a peak speed of 11 billion floating point operations per second."

As dazzling as the technological story is, however, it does not take us to the heart of IBM's success. IBM has not always made better machines than other companies, and it has not always led the way in developing new technologies. But it has led the way in marketing new technologies and in satisfying the people who lease or buy its systems. Other companies have excelled at creating machines. IBM has excelled at creating customers.

"Sell and Serve"

In 1962, Thomas Watson, Jr., who by then had succeeded his father as chairman and chief executive officer of IBM, gave a fascinating series of lectures at the Columbia University Graduate School of Business. The lectures, later published under the title A Business and Its Beliefs, advanced the thesis that "the most important single factor in corporate success" is not technology, not strategy, not structure, but the corporation's commitment to "a sound set of beliefs."

"Beliefs," Watson said, "must always come before policies, practices, and goals. The latter must always be altered if they are seen to violate fundamental beliefs. The only sacred cow in an organization should be its basic philosophy of doing business." This is the "final and most important lesson" to be learned from the history of IBM.

IBM's basic philosophy, Watson added, "is largely contained in three simple beliefs." First is "respect for the individual . . . the simple belief that if we respected our people and helped them to respect themselves the company would make the most profit." Second is a belief in "major attention to service. . . . *We want to give the best customer service of any company in the world.*" Third is a belief in the continuous "drive for superiority." This is "the force that makes the other two effective. *We believe that an organization should pursue all tasks with the idea that they can be accomplished in a superior fashion.*"

The business philosophy that shaped IBM was defined by a man who began his career as a bookkeeper for a butcher shop; who then worked (at eighteen) as a traveling salesman of pianos, organs, and sewing machines; who rose swiftly through a series of sales positions at the National Cash Register Company; and who, at forty, found his life in ruins after he himself was convicted of conspiracy in restraint of trade, sentenced to a year in jail, and dismissed from his position as head of sales at NCR. This same man recovered to become, in the words of Peter Drucker, "the seer and, very largely, the maker of what we now call postindustrial society and one of the great social innovators in American history."

Thomas J. Watson, Sr., was born in 1874 in a rural community near Corning, New York. His father, a lumber dealer, wanted him to become a lawyer, but Watson was drawn to business. At the National Cash Register Company, he learned from a master, John H. Patterson. A flamboyant autocrat with a genius for salesmanship, Patterson has been described as "an amalgam of St. Paul, Poor Richard, and Adolf Hitler." Under Patterson's leadership, NCR established itself as the dominant business-machine company of its time.

The only problem, for Patterson himself, Watson, and about thirty other NCR executives, was that the company's success was achieved in part through violations of the nation's antitrust laws. After his conviction in 1913, Watson might well have gone to jail if nature had not intervened. While the verdict was being appealed, Dayton, Ohio, was hit by one of the most devastating floods in American history. Patterson led a brilliant relief effort. A short while later, after the U.S. Court of Appeals reversed the decision of the lower court, the government dropped the case against NCR rather than prosecute again the sixty-five-year-old business czar who had fed and housed thousands of homeless Daytonians and who, according to one report, had stood waist-deep in swirling waters to fight the flood.

Even before the conviction was reversed, Patterson had fired Watson. The reasons scarcely matter. In the early 1900s, to be fired by John Patterson was almost a badge of honor. In addition to firing the man who built IBM, Patterson fired Hugh Chalmers and Edward Jordan, who went on to found automobile companies; Ivan Macauley, who went on to head the Packard Motor Car Company; and Charles Kettering, who went on to become an engineering legend at General Motors. To the extent that he is remembered today, John Patterson is most often remembered as a man who trained and then dismissed some of the ablest executives of the twentieth-century.

Hired in 1914 as general manager of the recently organized Computing-Tabulating-Recording Company, Watson was named president in 1915 after the Court of Appeals overturned his conviction. He promptly set to work building an organization that would mirror in many ways the organization Patterson had built at NCR. There was one difference, however. At the first big sales convention after he joined his new company, Watson addressed the subject of ethics. "You must not do anything that's in restraint of trade," he told his sales force, nor anything that could be "construed by anybody as unfair competition. . . . No man ever won except in the one honest, fair, and square way in which you men are working."

There is always a temptation to dismiss executive rhetoric, but the history of IBM under Watson and his successors suggests that he meant exactly what he said. This does not mean, of course, that every employee believed him or that every employee has acted as he recommended. But the company itself has taken a clear stand. In IBM's "Business Conduct Guidelines," a booklet now given to everyone who joins the company, the message is plain: "Business today is being called upon as never before to explain its actions, provide reasons for its decisions and speak out clearly on where it stands on ethical behavior. . . . If there is a single, overriding message in these guidelines, it is that IBM expects every employee to act, in every instance, according to the highest standards of business conduct."

Is this merely corporate hot air, too abstract to offer useful guidance? IBM may fear that it sounds that way. In a memo recently distributed to 400,000 employees, the company tried to make the same point in a more personal way: "You are responsible for your actions, and this responsibility will not always be an easy one. The next time you have an ethical dilemma, you might try this test. Ask yourself: If the full glare of examination by associates, friends, even family, were to focus on your decision, would you remain comfortable with it? If you think you would, it probably is the right decision."

A salesman himself, Watson concentrated on making CTR a sales-oriented, customer-oriented, market-oriented enterprise. At CTR, the salesman was king, which meant that the customer was king. Every employee quickly learned that the company depended on sales and that sales depended on service. One of Watson's favorite slogans, "Sell and Serve," put the company's whole philosophy in a nutshell.

In 1924, CTR's name was changed to the International Business Machines Corporation—good evidence that Watson developed a global perspective long before it became fashionable. But Watson's most dramatic gift was for inspiring his sales force. "Father used showmanship," Thomas Junior recalled later. ". . . He staged band concerts and picnics and made scores of speeches. Almost every kind of fanfare was tried to create enthusiasm."

Slogans played a large role in Watson's strategy for selling his business philosophy to a vital group of customers—his own employees. The slogans were standard fare, but they set the tone for the company. "Aim High." "Make Things Happen." "Never Feel Satisfied." "We Sell and Deliver Service." "We Forgive Thoughtful Mistakes." "A team that won't be beat, can't be beat." "A company is known by the men it keeps." "You have to put your heart in the business and the business in your heart." "Time lost is time gone forever." "Pack your todays with effort—extra effort. Your tomorrows will take care of themselves."

Most famous of all was the simple slogan "THINK." According to biographical material supplied by IBM, Watson introduced the slogan at NCR when, after hearing the words "I didn't think" one time too often, he told a meeting of salesmen, " 'I didn't think' has cost the world millions of dollars." At IBM, "THINK" signs appeared everywhere—on every desk, on walls and bulletin boards, on company publications, carved in stone on company buildings.

In addition to the company slogans, there were company songs, which were published in company songbooks and sung, often, at company songfests. Banquets and sales conventions often concluded with the company anthem, "Ever Onward!"

> EVER ONWARD—EVER ONWARD!
> That's the spirit that has brought us fame!
> We're big, but bigger we will be,
> We can't fail for all can see
> That to serve humanity has been our aim!
> Our products now are known in every zone,
> Our reputation sparkles like a gem!
> We've fought our way through—and new
> Fields we're sure to conquer too
> For the EVER ONWARD IBM.

To show that the company appreciated its employees, Watson established One Hundred Percent Clubs for salesmen who had met their quotas and Quarter Century Clubs for employees who had demonstrated the absolute loyalty that Watson prized. Memberships in IBM country clubs were available to employees for one dollar a year. But there was more to Watson's philosophy of management than songs, slogans, sales contests, and clubs. The hoopla and fanfare were related, in Watson's view, to the core belief in respect for the individual. Watson's methods may seem corny today, but he was a man who would have understood perfectly Dale Carnegie's comment on the prizes that his father won for his hogs: "The hogs didn't care about the ribbons they had won. But Father did. These prizes gave him a feeling of importance."

Paradoxically, it was Watson's concept for respect that led him to adopt policies that made IBM seem to many observers the most regimented of all American companies. Watson wanted his employees both to respect themselves and to be respected by others, and in pursuit of these goals he insisted upon standards of dress and grooming—white shirts, dark suits, neat hair, shined shoes—that soon gave IBM the appearance of being a company of clones. What seemed most bizarre to Watson's contemporaries was his demand that both his sales workers and his service workers should meet these standards. Watson himself never understood the criticism that came his way on this subject. "Clothes don't make the man," he would say, "but they go a long way toward making a businessman." He was moved, however, by a concern that transcended business and that probably was rooted in his own experiences as a salesman: "I want my IBM salesmen to be people to whom their wives and their children can look up," he explained in an interview in 1939. "I don't want their mothers to feel that they have to apologize for them or have to dissimulate when they are being asked what their son is doing."

An observer who looked beyond the white shirts and dark suits might have seen at IBM in the 1930s some practices that were both more startling and more significant. There was, for instance, an emphasis on continuous employee training that was most unusual for the time. Even more remarkable, at the heart of the Great Depression IBM refused to lay off workers, showing a commitment to its employees that most Americans now associate with the policy of "lifetime employment" that is commonly practiced by sophisticated Japanese companies.

No one who has studied the career of Thomas Watson, Sr., can doubt that he was paternalistic, but at least it was the paternalism of a father who cares deeply about his children. In a brilliant portrait published in *Esquire* in 1983, Peter Drucker put Watson's career in perspective, comparing him both with his most distinguished contemporary and with his most formidable successors:

> Watson was actually one year older than Alfred Sloan. But whereas Sloan in the Twenties created modern management by building General Motors, and with it the modern "big corporation," Watson ten years later and quite independently created the "plant community" that we know to be the successor to Sloan's "big business enterprise" of the Twenties. He created in the Thirties the social organization and the work community of the postindustrial society.
>
> The first ones to see this . . . were the Japanese. Again and again I have been laughed at in Japan when I talk about Japan's management embodying Japanese values. "Don't you realize," my Japanese friends say, "that we are simply adapting what IBM has done all along?" And when I ask how come, they always say, "When we started to rebuild Japan in the Fifties, we looked around for the most successful company we could find— it's IBM, isn't it?"

Monopoly?

Two weeks after Franklin Delano Roosevelt took office as president in 1933, the U.S. Justice Department filed suit against two giants of the business-machines industry, IBM and Remington-Rand, under the antitrust provisions of the Sherman Act and the Clayton Act. The heart of the case was the charge that IBM and Remington-Rand had "combined to restrain commerce" by requiring firms that leased their machines also to purchase punch cards from them, and by agreeing not to compete against one another in certain markets.

Remington-Rand agreed to accept any judgment entered against IBM, but IBM fought the charges. Over the next three years, as the case dragged on, some interesting facts emerged. IBM leased 85.7 percent of all tabulating machines, 86.1 percent of all sorting machines, and 81.6 percent of all punch-card machines in use in the United States. These machines gobbled up cards at an incredible rate, so that by the mid-1930s, IBM was selling more than four billion cards a year, at a price of $1.05 per thousand.

IBM argued that the "tying clauses" that required firms that leased its machines also to purchase its cards were a "reasonable control of the commerce in cards," because defective cards supplied by other vendors might make it difficult to operate or maintain IBM's machines. The court ruled against IBM, in a decision sustained by the U.S. Supreme Court on April 27, 1936. Despite this ruling, IBM continued to make large profits from the sale of cards, in part because it cut its prices to scare away potential competitors.

At the same time that the government was fighting IBM in court, it was considering IBM's bid to undertake what Thomas Watson, Jr., later described as "one of the greatest bookkeeping operations of all times." The Social Security Act of 1935 required that the government keep tabs on wages earned by every American worker, and keeping tabs meant using tabulating machines. IBM won the contract, which meant that IBM linked itself to the only true growth industry of the 1930s—the government. FDR's New Deal spawned dozens of new agencies to administer hundreds of new programs. By the time the government filed its next suit against IBM, late in 1952, 95 percent of the government's punch-card machines were leased from the company it was suing.

Again the Justice Department charged IBM with monopolizing the market for tabulating machines and punch cards, and again it demanded an end to IBM's policy of only leasing its machines. The suit infuriated Thomas Watson, Sr., but Thomas Junior, now the company's president, took a different view. Tabulating machines and punch cards, Thomas Junior felt, were the products of the past. IBM might benefit if it negotiated an agreement that freed the company to concentrate on developing products that would matter in the future—the new electronic computers.

Under a consent decree signed in 1956, IBM did not admit that it had violated any law, but it agreed to change certain business practices. In the future it would sell its machines as well as lease them; it would license patents to competitors who were willing to pay for them; and it would reduce significantly its share in the punch-card market.

As Thomas Watson, Jr., had foreseen, these concessions hurt little. By 1965, IBM had captured 65.3 percent of the market in the computer industry, whereas the combined market share of its seven largest competitors, sometimes called the "Seven Dwarfs," was 34.0 percent. The Seven Dwarfs included firms as formidable as Sperry Rand, Control Data, Honeywell, Burroughs, General Electric, RCA, and NCR. To make matters even more embarrassing for these challengers, IBM's profits and its profit margins were as impressive as its market share. Among America's blue-chip companies, "Big Blue," as it often was called, was the bluest.

Given the degree of IBM's market dominance, it was inevitable, perhaps, that the government would sue again. The suit was filed by the U.S. Justice Department on January 17, 1969, and was resolved nearly thirteen years later, on January 8, 1982, when the assistant attorney general in charge of the Antitrust Division announced that his staff had reviewed the evidence and concluded that "the case is without merit and should be dismissed."

Most analysts agree that the government was right to withdraw the suit. In the words of economist Carl Kaysen, "The government's argument was based on erroneous conceptions of competition and a grossly inadequate understanding of the facts." By charging that IBM had erected insurmountable barriers to entry into the computer industry, and by offering as evidence depositions from a large number of companies that had not existed when the original suit was filed, the government killed its own case.

A number of private companies also filed antitrust cases against IBM in this period. In many instances, business historian Robert Sobel has pointed out, "the complaining parties asked for damages that exceeded their net corporate worths," so that "the firm's major asset wasn't its patent, product, or anything else that appeared on the balance sheet," but rather its lawsuit against IBM. What was involved, in other words, was a corporate version of ambulance chasing. Thirteen of the fourteen judges who ruled in these cases decided in favor of IBM. The decision of the fourteenth was reversed on appeal.

"Ever Onward!"

IBM's worldwide gross revenues passed $1 billion for the first time in 1957. In 1985 the figure reached $50.7 billion—more, according to *The Wall Street Journal*, than the gross domestic product of Greece, Iceland, Ireland, New Zealand, Portugal, or Turkey. At the same time IBM's stock-market capitalization stood at $95.7 billion—more than the total capitalization of the stock markets in Switzerland ($90.3 billion), France ($78.5 billion), or Italy ($64.7 billion). IBM was more than merely a big multinational corporation. It was a colossus—a multinational corporation that dwarfed many nations.

What was most striking about this giant, perhaps, was not how much it had changed in the scale and scope of its operations but how little it had changed in its basic philosophy. Thomas Watson, Jr., emphasized this point in 1962 when he focused on "the ideas that helped build IBM" in his lectures at Columbia Business School. "The starched collar is gone," he said, "along with our company songs. . . . But in its attitude, its outlook, its spirit, its drive, IBM is still very much the same company it has always been and that we intend it shall always be. For while everything else has altered, our beliefs remain unchanged."

The continuous effort to live up to its beliefs, Watson added, had given IBM a reputation as the supreme example of a service-oriented, customer-oriented company. "Years ago we ran an ad that said simply and in bold type: IBM Means Service. I have often thought it our very best ad. It stated clearly just exactly what we stand for. . . . The main aim of our business is service, to help the customer solve his problems no matter how many problems this may create for us."

The IBM Way, a book published in 1986 by F. G. "Buck" Rodgers, a retired vice-president formerly responsible for IBM's worldwide marketing activities, reinforces the sense that the company remains firmly committed to a set of beliefs defined by Thomas Watson, Sr., in the days when it sold time clocks and meat slicers. One chapter is titled "Service, Service, Service . . . and More Service." In a chapter titled "Creating a Totally Sales-Oriented Environment," Rodgers writes, "At IBM, *everybody sells!* . . . Every employee has been trained to think that the customer comes first—everybody from the CEO, to the people in finance, to the receptionists, to those who work in manufacturing. . . . Any IBM employee you might meet . . . should treat you as if his or her job depended on your satisfaction."

Whatever other changes may have occurred, Rodgers emphasizes that IBM has not forgotten the importance of showing that it appreciates employees who excel and that it has not grown too sophisticated for old-fashioned methods of recognition: "At a company affair, a suitcase or a small wheelbarrow filled with a large number of dollar bills may be dumped on a table as the emcee invites the recipient to 'Please come here and pick up your money!' Then the emcee explains what outstanding support to the marketing function occasioned this award."

Even in the matter of dress, IBM has changed less than might be expected of a company that prides itself on its leadership in a field where new technologies are developed with dazzling speed. One of the first questions outsiders ask him, Rodgers writes, "is not about IBM's size or its products or its history, but rather: 'Is it true that IBM requires you to wear a dark conservative suit, winter or summer, a white shirt and a quiet tie?' " IBM has no written policy that tells a person how to dress, Rodgers says, "But to be completely truthful, there is an unwritten dress code that's as effective as if it were engraved in steel—or as if it had a loaded gun behind it."

The testimony of Thomas Watson, Jr., in 1962 and of Buck Rodgers in 1986 may tell us how IBM looks to insiders or it may merely tell us how insiders want us to think it looks—that is, it may merely tell us the company line. It is important, therefore, also to consider the testimony of outsiders.

Some testimony of this kind appears in one of the best-selling business books of the 1980s, *In Search of Excellence*, an examination of well-run companies written by a pair of management consultants, Tom Peters and Robert H. Waterman, Jr. In a chapter that emphasizes the importance of being "close to the customer," Peters and Waterman pay special attention to IBM and to the "swarm effort" that sometimes results from IBM's commitment to service. They quote a data-processing executive at a firm in Atlanta that uses IBM equipment: " 'I remember the last time we had trouble. In hours the horde descended, from everywhere. . . . At least four were from Europe, one came from Canada, one from Latin America. That's just where they happened to be.' " Customer after customer testifies that Buck Rodgers is serious when he says that he wants every proposal to be "overwhelmingly cost-justifiable from the customer's standpoint."

In a chapter titled "Productivity Through People," Peters and Waterman examine the philosophy of "respect for the individual" that Thomas Watson, Jr., described as "the most important" of the company's three basic beliefs. "IBM's total history," they conclude, "is one of intense people orientation." Comparing the IBM of the 1920s with the IBM of the 1980s, they write, "There is not much to add to the early Watson stories, except for the remarkable fact that IBM has stayed about the same. The open door policies, the clubs, the simplicity, the homilies, the hoopla, and the training are as intense in relation to the styles of today as they were fifty or sixty years ago."

The history of IBM is not simply a history of triumph. Now and then the company has stumbled, but it never has lost stride for long. It may or may not have competed unfairly, but it certainly has competed fiercely. In a sense, its basic strategy has been to be tough on competitors by being even tougher on itself. In the future, Buck Rodgers says, IBM's goal is to be "*the* most efficient and effective in everything it does—*the* low-cost producer, *the* low-cost seller, *the* low-cost servicer and *the* low-cost administrator."

Anyone who wants to compete is welcome to try, but no one should expect IBM to yield without a fight. Rodgers writes, "When I'm asked, 'What products does IBM sell?' I answer, 'IBM doesn't sell products. It sells solutions.' . . . Everything IBM does is influenced by its effort to excel in value-added service. If a customer is lost, you can bet it's not because of IBM's apathy or smugness. And you can also bet that IBM takes its competition seriously. If they intend to take away a customer, they'll have to care about that customer as much as IBM does."

The heart of IBM's success is its dedication to sustaining a particular kind of corporate culture—a culture that coddles the customer. Reading about IBM, even a doubting Thomas may begin to feel a sneaking fondness for it. How much it does right at a time when so many American companies seem to do nothing right! An uneasiness persists only because everyone associated with IBM seems to say the same wonderful things and to have the same wonderful attitudes. On trips to IBM sales conventions abroad, business historian William Rodgers reports, Thomas Watson, Sr., often would declare exultantly, "This might just as well be one of the conventions back home." Returning to New York, Watson would say: "Our people over there looked just the same to me. They said the same things, they had just the same qualities." Fifty years later IBM's people still say the same things, and even if they no longer sing the old songs, "Ever Onward!" still seems to be the music to which they march.

CHAPTER 17

Dissenting Voices: 1945–1990

The Organization Man in an Age of Plenty

In the eyes of skeptical observers, the very success of an enterprise like IBM raises troubling questions. While Budd Schulberg was worrying about the ferocious individualism of "all the Sammy Glicks," other writers, looking at American life, saw not rampant individualism but a new kind of conformity. Books such as David Riesman's *The Lonely Crowd* (1950), C. Wright Mills's *White Collar* (1951), Sloan Wilson's *The Man in the Gray Flannel Suit* (1955), William H. Whyte, Jr.'s, *The Organization Man* (1956), and Alan Harrington's *Life in the Crystal Palace* (1959) explored this subject.

All of these writers were responding, in one way or another, to the increasing dominance of large organizations in the lives of Americans. This subject commanded keener and keener scrutiny as the age of the robber barons receded. As has been noted in an earlier chapter, business historian Alfred D. Chandler, Jr., has commented on the importance of distinguishing between "empire builders" and "organization builders" in the history of American business. At IBM, both Watsons played a role in both tasks, but that situation was unique. The pattern of development at General Motors was more typical. William Durant built the empire, but he could not run it. Alfred P. Sloan, Jr., saved the enterprise by creating the organization that kept the empire from collapsing.

The organization men who attracted attention in the 1950s were the inheritors of structures that men like Sloan had designed. Their task was not to build an empire, nor even to build an organization, but to occupy an office. In the giant enterprises of the twentieth century, Chandler observes in *The Visible Hand*, administrative structures were developed that "had a permanence beyond that of any individual or group of individuals who worked in them. Men came and went. The institution and its offices remained."

What kind of men (for they were still mostly men in the 1950s) sat in these offices? One point on which everyone agrees is that they were not risk-takers. As early as 1944, Donald K. David, dean of Harvard Business School, sounded a warning that has been heard again and again in the 1980s. "I am afraid," he said, "that over a period of years the Harvard Business School has turned out far too many men who have sought the shelter and security of positions in large corporations. . . . The environment at our school has, I am afraid, discouraged rather than encouraged a venturesome spirit and a willingness to take risks."

Talking to managerial trainees in the middle 1950s, William H. Whyte, Jr., was struck by the same lack of adventurousness. "Frequently," he notes in *The Organization Man*, "they talk of finding a sort of plateau—a position well enough up to be interesting but not so far up as to have one's neck outstretched for others to chop at." Something of the same attitude is apparent in the scene in which Tom Rath, the hero of *The Man in the Gray Flannel Suit*, explains to his boss why he has second thoughts about a promotion to a more demanding job: "I don't think I'm the kind of guy who should try to be a big executive," Rath says. ". . . I don't want to give up the time. I'm trying to be honest about this. I want the money. Nobody likes money better than I do. But I'm just not the kind of guy who can work evenings and weekends and all the rest of it forever. . . . I'm not the kind of person who can get all wrapped up in a job—I can't get myself convinced that my work is the most important thing in the world."

To be sure, it is not risk that Rath objects to, but the price that must be paid to succeed in what was increasingly regarded as the corporate rat race. Nevertheless, the effect is the same. Rather than run the race, Rath is willing to accept, even embrace, a comfortable position in the grandstand. In a limited way, Rath's renunciation is the twentieth-century equivalent of Bartleby's "I would prefer not to."

An aversion to risk was not the only charge leveled against the organization men of the 1950s. In addition, it was commonly said, the men in the gray flannel suits were dull. They looked alike, lived alike, and thought alike.

Sociologist David Riesman thought that dullness flourished because Americans grew up in a society that was becoming increasingly "other-directed"—that is, a society that developed in its typical members a "tendency to be sensitized to the expectations and preferences of others." In a memorable stroke, Riesman made this concept come alive by citing, as an example of other-direction, Tolstoy's character Stepan Arkadyevitch Oblonsky in *Anna Karenina:*

> Stepan Arkadyevitch [Tolstoy writes] took in and read a liberal newspaper, not an extreme one, but one advocating the views held by the majority. And in spite of the fact that science, art, and politics had no special interest for him, he firmly held those views on all subjects which were held by the majority and by his paper, and he only changed them when the majority changed them—or, more strictly speaking, he did not change them, but they imperceptively changed of themselves within him.
>
> Stepan Arkadyevitch had not chosen his political opinions or his views; these political opinions and views had come to him of themselves, just as he did not choose the shapes of his hats or coats, but simply took those that were being worn. And for him . . . to have views was just as indispensable as to have a hat.

In the United States in the twentieth century, Riesman argues, other-direction is the typical orientation of the new middle class—"the bureaucrat, the salaried employee in business, etc." In contrast, inner-direction was the typical orientation of the old middle class—"the banker, the tradesman, the small entrepreneur." In business, inner-directed men were the empire-builders of the nineteenth century—"ambitious, energetic, self-reliant men engaged in transforming physical nature, instituting large-scale formal organization, and revolutionizing technology." But inner-directed people, in Riesman's view, are becoming rarer and rarer. Other-direction is the orientation that is needed to function effectively in groups, to be a team player, to thrive in large organizations.

Riesman elaborates the distinction between inner-directed and other-directed types through two vivid metaphors. The inner-directed person, he says, "has early incorporated a psychic gyroscope which is set going by his parents and can receive signals later on from other authorities who resemble his parents. He goes through life . . . obeying this internal piloting." The other-directed person, on the other hand, "learns to respond to signals from a far wider circle than is constituted by his parents. The family is no longer a closely knit unit to which he belongs but merely part of a wider social environment to which he early becomes attentive. . . . This control equipment, instead of being like a gyroscope, is like a radar."

The attention that is paid to signals coming from other people, Riesman makes clear, leads to a conformity that is rooted in "an exceptional sensitivity to the actions and wishes of others." More than anything else, the other-directed individual "seeks adjustment. That is, he seeks to have the character he is supposed to have, and the inner experiences as well as outer appurtenances that are supposed to go with it." In his relations with others, he "seeks not fame . . . but the respect and, more important than the respect, the affection" of his peers. He is terrified of standing out: "To outdistance [his colleagues], to shine alone, seems hopeless, and also dangerous." It is better to fit in, to melt into the crowd. Far from seeing the United States as a nation of Sammy Glicks, Riesman sees it as a nation of chameleons.

By the time William Whyte published *The Organization Man* in 1956, complaints about conformity had become so common that Whyte takes pains to distance himself from them. "This book is not a plea for nonconformity," he declares in his introduction. "Such pleas have an occasional therapeutic value, but as an abstraction, nonconformity is an empty goal. . . . There will be no strictures in this book against 'Mass Man'— a person the author has never met—nor will there be any strictures against ranch wagons, or television sets, or gray flannel suits. They are irrelevant to the main problem, and, furthermore, there's no harm in them."

The main problem, Whyte says, is not the "surface uniformities" and "outward forms" that have been so widely condemned. The main problem is to find ways to foster a genuine individualism in our world of giant enterprises—an "individualism *within* organization life." We need "to know how to co-operate with The Organization but, more than ever, so do we need to know how to resist it. . . . We need not worry that a counteremphasis will stimulate people to an excess of individualism."

Part of the difficulty, Whyte argues, is that modern organizations hold people who work in them not in an iron but a velvet grip. The organization man is not presented with "a case of whether he should fight against black tyranny or blaze a new trail against patent stupidity. . . .

The real issue is far more subtle. For it is not the evils of organization life that puzzle him, *but its very beneficence*" (Whyte's italics).

What Whyte means by "beneficence" is made clear in Alan Harrington's *Life in the Crystal Palace*, probably the most memorable "inside" portrait of modern corporate life ever written. "I went into my job at the corporation with a poor spirit," Harrington tells his readers. "I was suspicious of large companies, and swore that nobody was going to turn me into a robot. . . . When I arrived, everyone turned and smiled, and they all came over to say how glad they were that I was with them. The boss took my arm and had me in for a long talk. 'We want you to be happy here,' he said earnestly. 'Is there anything we can do? Please let us know.' "

On top of the decency of his colleagues, Harrington discovers that the corporation itself is decent:

> We have a fine pension fund, a fantastically inexpensive medical program . . . , and a low-premium life-insurance policy for double your salary. The company will invest five per cent of your pay in blue-chip stocks and contribute on your behalf another three per cent. The company picks up half of your luncheon check. . . . It is practically impossible to be fired. . . . We are taken care of from our children's cradles to our own graves. We move with carefully graduated rank, station, and salary through the decades.

No one need ever take a risk that is not shared: "In our daily work most of us have not made an important decision in years, except in consultation with others."

A price is paid, of course, for this comfortable existence. Harrington lists some symptoms of contentment: "You find that you are planning your life defensively, in terms of savings plans and pensions. . . . You become much less impatient over inefficiency, shrug your shoulders and accept it as the way things are. . . . Your critical faculties become dull; . . . it seems unsporting to complain." In addition, Harrington finds himself becoming "easygoing and promiscuously nice," with "a harmless word for everyone."

This amiability—"our talent for being extremely friendly without saying anything to each other"—is one of the hallmarks of life in Harrington's company. No Sammy Glicks run loose: "We are serene. . . . Cutting out the other fellow and using tricks to make him look bad is hardly ever done." It is agreeable to be cushioned from competition, but, again, a price is paid. "As the years go by, the temptation to strike out on your own or take another job becomes less and less. . . . If you have been in easy circumstances for a number of years, you feel that you are out of shape. Even in younger men the hard muscle of ambition tends to go slack, and you hesitate to take a chance in the jungle again."

In short, Harrington's company is a womb. Harrington understands that working in a womb is not necessarily good for people. He also understands that people who have worked in a womb for a long while are not necessarily good for the organization. In a chapter about the corporation's willingness, in the name of humanity, to carry a certain amount of deadwood, Harrington asks, "Has there ever been a society that has perished from too much mercy? I think the Crystal Palace is running that risk." Life can be too easy, too comfortable. "No matter how generous their pension plans may be, employees of a thick-headed, fat-bottomed corporation are living in a fool's paradise."

This comment suggests why, in 1990, the literature of the 1950s seems both familiar and quaint. All of it was written in the happy days after World War II when America's business muscle went unchallenged, and most of it assumed that this situation would last forever. In the 1950s and early 1960s, American writers worried about anomie and alienation, they worried about conformity, and they worried about the problems associated with "permanent" prosperity, but no one worried about our ability to compete in world markets or about the future of the automobile industry. Titles like *The Affluent Society* (John Kenneth Galbraith, 1958) and *Abundance for What?* (David Riesman, 1964) appeared on the best-seller lists. By 1990, the cushion of blubber that once separated American managers from the realities of economic competition had all but melted away. It was difficult to sustain an interest in addressing the problems that afflict an "age of plenty" (Riesman, 1958) in a period like the 1980s, when General Motors announced that it would cut its white-collar work force by 25 percent, General Electric decided it could not compete in consumer electronics, and companies such as CBS Records, Columbia Pictures, and Firestone Tire and Rubber were sold to Japanese investors.

John Kenneth Galbraith

In the decades since World War II, the economic thinker who has done the most to bring a dissenting perspective to the attention of the American public has been John Kenneth Galbraith. With his wry style, his contempt for conventional views, and his taste for skewering his opponents, Galbraith has been the Veblen of his time.

Galbraith was born in 1908 in a Scotch farming community in Ontario, Canada. In an introduction to a new edition of Veblen's *The Theory of the Leisure Class* published in 1973, Galbraith comments on the psychological similarities between the Scotch farmers he had known in his youth and the Scandinavian farmers in the midwestern community that produced Veblen. Both the Scotch and the Scandinavian farm children, Galbraith recalls, "were taught to think that claims to social prestige based on . . . vacuous criteria were silly. We regarded the people of the towns not with envy but amiable contempt. On the whole we enjoyed letting them know."

Amiable contempt, and the enjoyment of letting others know about it, became hallmarks of Galbraith's career. After receiving a bachelor's degree in agricultural economics from Ontario Agricultural College in 1931 and a Ph.D. in economics from the University of California at Berkeley in 1934, Galbraith taught at Harvard and Princeton and spent a year as a social science research fellow at Cambridge University in England. His height—six feet, eight inches—disqualified him for serving in the armed forces during World War II, but he spent two years administering wartime price controls as an official at the Office of Price Administration in Washington. After serving in other government agencies and working for *Fortune* magazine on and off from 1943 through 1947, he resumed teaching at Harvard in 1948. There he remained for most of the rest of his career, except for a stint as ambassador to India under President Kennedy.

Galbraith's career as a writer took a decisive turn in 1952. In that year he published two books. One of them, *American Capitalism: The Concept of Countervailing Power*, was published by Houghton Mifflin for a general audience. The other, *A Theory of Price Control*, was published by Harvard University Press for an academic audience. In an interview with David Halberstam in 1967, Galbraith recalled the lesson he learned from the experience. *A Theory of Price Control* was, he says, "the best book I ever wrote in many ways. It was a tough technical essay and maybe fifty people read it and it had absolutely zero influence. I made up my mind then that I was not going to invest any more of my time that way. From now on I would put in an extra year on the writing to engage a larger audience, and because of that the other economists would have to react to me. My work would not be ignored."

More than twenty books followed over the next thirty-five years, along with a steady stream of op-ed pieces and magazine articles. Galbraith irritated many academic economists, including quite a few who sympathized with much that he said. But he got the larger audience he had wanted.

The heart of Galbraith's thought is contained in *The Affluent Society*, published in 1958; *The New Industrial State*, published in 1967; and *Economics and the Public Purpose*, published in 1973. Though there is some repetition, each book builds on what has come before.

The Affluent Society is the first book in which Galbraith flourishes the style that made him famous. It is a style much like Veblen's—witty, derisive, aggressive. Much of the wit is directed against the commonplaces of classical and neoclassical economic thought—what Galbraith calls "the conventional wisdom."

Economic thinking, Galbraith tells his readers, suffers not from "original error but uncorrected obsolescence. . . . Familiarity may breed contempt in some areas of human behavior, but in the field of social ideas it is the touchstone of acceptability."

In classical economics, Galbraith observes, nothing is more crucial than the theory of competition. This theory, familiar to every student of elementary economics, describes the blessings that follow from free competition in a market where prices are determined by the interaction of supply and demand. This model applied fairly well to the economy of England in the time of Adam Smith. But it does not apply, Galbraith says, echoing Berle and Means, to the modern world of giant corporations. Whereas the theory of competition calls for many firms in a market, in real life often there are few firms. Whereas the model "called for a price that no firm controlled, in real life some firms, at least, seemed to have quite considerable discretionary power over price. And unions were not without power of their own."

In addition, Galbraith argues, the ideas of the great classical economists were developed in an age of comparative scarcity. These ideas "began to take their modern form in the late eighteenth and nearly nineteenth centuries," against a background of "centuries-old stagnation relieved . . . by increasing wealth, but wealth not of the many but the few." The economists who built on the work of Adam Smith did not foresee an age of widespread affluence. In the hands of Thomas Malthus and David Ricardo, the tradition of classical economics was also a "tradition of despair," as is clearly seen in Ricardo's famous "iron law" of wages—the theory that rising population will inevitably drive wages down to the subsistence level. In the modern world, with its high level of manufacturing productivity, life has been much better than Malthus or Ricardo imagined it ever could be. Yet proponents of the conventional wisdom continue to assert "the myth that production . . . is the central problem of our lives."

In Galbraith's view, then, the conventional wisdom fails on two major counts: first, because it blindly applies the theory of perfect competition to an economy dominated by a small number of enterprises; and second, because it blindly affirms the paramount importance of production at a time when goods are abundant, when "more die in the United States of too much food than of too little," and when "no one can seriously suggest that the steel which comprises the extra four or five feet of purely decorative distance on our automobiles is of prime urgency."

Beyond these deficiencies, the conventional wisdom fails because it affirms a theory of consumer demand that is "illogical and meretricious and in degree even dangerous." According to classical economics, the consumer is king. The consumer's preferences determine which products will succeed and which will fail in the free market. In fact, Galbraith argues, modern advertising and salesmanship aim "to bring into being wants that previously did not exist." Indeed, "outlays for the manufacturing of a product are not more important in the strategy of modern business enterprise than outlays for the manufacturing of demand for the product." Through advertising and related activities, business "creates the wants it seeks to satisfy." But, Galbraith says, the vast expenditure that is devoted to the manufacture of desires undercuts the theory of consumer sovereignty. "If the individual's wants are to be urgent they must be original with himself. . . . One cannot defend production as satisfying wants if that production creates the wants."

In addition to undermining the theory of consumer sovereignty, the manufacture of wants through mass marketing undermines the old-fashioned economic virtues of thrift, prudence, and deferred gratification. "The immediate danger in the way wants are . . . created," Galbraith writes in a chapter that now seems prophetic, "lies in the related process of debt creation. . . . It would be surprising indeed if a society that is prepared to spend thousands of millions to persuade people of their wants were to fail to take the further step of financing these wants, and were it not then to go on to persuade people of the ease and desirability of incurring debt to make these wants effective. This has happened." As a result, Galbraith predicts, "Our march to higher living standards will be paced, as a matter of necessity, by an ever deeper plunge into debt."

Having completed his attack on classical economic theory, Galbraith is prepared to reach conclusions and to make recommendations. His main conclusion is that a thoughtless reliance on the conventional wisdom is cheating us. We live by illusions, and "Illusion is a comprehensive ill. . . . The affluent country which conducts its affairs in accordance with rules of another and poorer age . . . forgoes opportunities."

The heart of the problem, in Galbraith's view, is the distrust of public expenditure that goes along with the sanctification of private enterprise in the gospel of the conventional economic thought. As a consequence of this distrust, our lives are not as agreeable as they might be. We suffer from a systematic overproduction of trivial goods and underinvestment in public goods. In a famous passage, Galbraith describes the result:

> The family which takes its mauve and cerise, air-conditioned, power-steered, and power-braked automobile out for a tour passes through cities that are badly paved, made hideous by litter, blighted buildings, billboards, and posts for wires that should long since have been put underground. They pass on into a countryside that has been rendered invisible by commercial art. . . . They picnic on exquisitely packaged food from a portable icebox by a polluted stream and go on to spend the night at a park which is a menace to public health and morals. . . . Is this, indeed, the American genius?

In essence, Galbraith's aim in *The Affluent Society* is to make the case for redressing this imbalance. "To furnish a barren room is one thing," he concludes. "To continue to crowd in furniture until the foundation buckles is quite another." In the conventional view, vacuum cleaners are essential, whereas sanitation workers to clean our streets are "an unfortunate expense." The result is that "our houses are generally clean and our streets generally filthy." The situation confounds common sense. To care about production without caring about what is produced is to condemn ourselves to picnic forever by polluted streams.

As he completed work on *The Affluent Society*, Galbraith tells his readers in the Foreword to *The New Industrial State*, "another and larger world began obtruding itself on my thoughts." This was the world of giant corporations, a world in which "far from being the controlling power in the economy, markets were more and more accommodated to the needs and convenience of business organizations." *The New Industrial State* focuses on this world. In relation to *The Affluent Society*, Galbraith says, it stands "as a house to a window. This is the structure; the earlier book allowed the first glimpse inside."

As its title indicates, *The New Industrial State* pays special attention to the relationship between large corporations and the state. Here, Galbraith is particularly concerned with corporations whose chief customer is the government. He argues that "The line that now divides public from so-called private organization in military procurement, space exploration and atomic energy is so indistinct as to be nearly imperceptible." A symbiosis has developed. The industrial system is not something that can be properly understood as standing apart from the state, nor can the state be properly understood as standing apart from the industrial system. Each must be understood as "part of a much larger complex." President Eisenhower rightly underscored the dangers posed by this situation when he warned, in his farewell address, against "the acquisition of unwarranted influence, whether sought or unsought, by the military-industrial complex."

In conclusion, Galbraith combines a warning with an exhortation. "If we continue to believe that the goals of the industrial system . . . are coordinate with life," he writes, "then all of our lives will be in the service of these goals. . . . Our wants will be managed in accordance with the needs of the industrial system; the policies of the state will be subject to similar influence; education will be adapted to industrial need. . . . All other goals will be made to seem . . . unimportant or asocial."

But we have a choice. If other goals are strongly asserted, then "the industrial system itself will be subordinated to the claims of these dimensions of life. . . . Men will not be entrapped by the belief that apart from the goals of the industrial system . . . there is nothing important in life. . . . The industrial system will fall into its place as a detached and autonomous arm of the state, but responsive to the larger purposes of the society." This, of course, is the road that Galbraith recommends.

In *Economics and the Public Purpose*, Galbraith offers the fullest and most clearly organized explication of his views. What is new in *Economics and the Public Purpose* is Galbraith's open embrace of what he calls sometimes "a new socialism," sometimes "the new socialism," and sometimes even "The New Socialism." This socialism, he asserts, is "urgent and even indispensable" in some sectors of the economy. "The new socialism allows of no acceptable alternatives; it cannot be escaped except at the price of grave discomfort, considerable social disorder, and, on occasion, lethal damage to health and well-being."

In particular, Galbraith advocates socialism for activities "which do not lend themselves to organization by the planning system and which are not rendered competently by the market system"—for instance, housing, public transportation, and health services. "The only solution for these industries is full organization under public ownership"—a solution that, Galbraith hastens to add, is already being adopted in piece-meal and haphazard fashion.

In addition, Galbraith advocates socialism in areas where the line between the state and the industrial system blurs. For instance, he recommends public ownership of large weapons firms. "The change is one of form rather than substance," he writes. Firms such as General Dynamics and Lockheed "do virtually all of their business with the government." The government absorbs their losses, and the government comes to their rescue if they falter. "The large weapons firms are already socialized except in name; what is here proposed only affirms the reality." As a rule of thumb, Galbraith suggests, any corporation "doing more than half of its business with the government should be converted into a full public corporation."

It might seem that Galbraith is merely arguing, as he did in *The Affluent Society*, for an expansion of the public sector. In fact, his position has grown substantially more complex. The state itself, he now believes, "is a major part of the problem." The new socialism will work only if the state is "broken free from the control of the planning system." The problem is that the planning system encompasses both a number of giant firms and the "symbiotic bureaucracies" in government. The solution is "the emancipation of the state from the control of the planning system."

Here Galbraith runs into trouble. The emancipation of the state, he says, is crucial—"a massive but central assumption." "Given the . . . emancipation of the state, [various] lines of public action become possible." But how can Galbraith's readers accept so massive an assumption as "given"? Galbraith does not tackle that question. At exactly the point of greatest practical difficulty, he turns his attention to other affairs.

Much can be said, and much has been said, in opposition to Galbraith's views. In *Galbraith and Market Capitalism*, English economist David Reisman (not to be confused with American sociologist David Riesman) provides a fair-minded summary of the most important objections. "Galbraith is best understood," Reisman concludes, "when regarded neither as a serious economist nor as what Paul Samuelson has called 'noneconomist's economist,' but rather as an economic sociologist and a social philosopher." What is crucial is that readers recognize the danger of being carried away by the force of Galbraith's rhetoric rather than the force of his arguments: "Galbraith's attack on textbook economics must be recognized for what it is—an important plank in a normative, pro-Statist political platform. . . . It is not in essence the attack of an economist seeking to purify his subject but that of a social critic seeking to transform his society."

Another common complaint has been that Galbraith is much less original than he wants his readers to think. Galbraith's debts to Veblen, to Berle and Means, and to English writer R. H. Tawney are obvious, and frequently acknowledged by Galbraith. Still, it is true that Galbraith delights in attacking sacred cows, even if the cows already have taken quite a beating. As British economist G. C. Allen comments, "He puts forth as if they were novel and heretical various propositions about industrial society which have been accepted as commonplaces by many economists for several decades."

Finally, many academic economists have attacked Galbraith for being insufficiently rigorous—for being so enamored of the big picture that he loses the command of detail that is needed to ensure that the picture is accurate. Economics, Robert Solow of M.I.T. wrote in a celebrated critique of *The New Industrial State*, makes progress through the work of determined "little-thinkers." The big thinkers tend to be wrong in a thousand little ways. Galbraith, Solow said in an interview years later, "will be remembered as an historian and a philosopher, but I don't think he will be primarily remembered as an economist. Economics is becoming more and more a technical subject like dentistry. Ken is not going to strike the future as a great dentist."

This dart is on target, but it misses the heart of Galbraith's work. Galbraith is at his best when he is attacking hypocrisy, as in his comment, in an article in *Harper's* in 1964, on the search for a "superior moral justification for selfishness" that always seems to accompany the renunciation of government action on behalf of "special" interests:

> It is an exercise which always involves a certain number of internal contradictions and even a few absurdities. The conspicuously wealthy turn up urging the character-building value of privation for the poor. The man who has struck it rich in minerals, oil, or other bounties of nature is found explaining the debilitating effect of unearned income from the State. The corporation executive who is a superlative success as an organization man weighs in on the evils of bureaucracy. . . . Socialized medicine is condemned by men emerging from Walter Reed Hospital. Social Security is viewed with alarm by those who have the comfortable cushion of inherited income.

In the long run, Galbraith's survival, like the survival of Thorstein Veblen and Henry George, will depend on the energy of his indignation and on his sting as a polemicist. It is as an enemy of cant, rather than as an economic thinker or as a proponent of specific remedies for specific ills, that Galbraith is likely to influence future generations.

Citizen Nader

Writing in the early 1930s, Adolf A. Berle, Jr., and Gardiner C. Means looked to government to counter the dangers of concentrated corporate power. A generation later, John Kenneth Galbraith also looked to government, but less optimistically. "The problem is organization itself, whether public or private," he wrote in *Economics and the Public Purpose*. Galbraith hoped vaguely that an enlightened citizenry might retrieve the state for public purposes. Citizens would do this by challenging "the symbiotic goals of the planning system and the public bureaucracy."

In the modern world of giant organizations described by Berle, Means, and Galbraith, it was difficult to imagine that any one man or woman could make much difference. But, starting in the early 1960s, one man did make a difference. One measure of Ralph Nader's impact is that book-length biographies of him began to appear when he was still in his thirties. The title of an early biography, *Citizen Nader*, says much about the role Nader played—or, as his critics have often said, the role to which he appointed himself.

Nader was born in Winsted, Connecticut, in 1934, the youngest of four children of Lebanese immigrants. His parents ran a restaurant and bakery and taught their children to be passionate about politics. "When I went past the Statue of Liberty," Nathra Nader explained years later, after his son had become famous, "I took it seriously."

A childhood friend, author David Halberstam, gives us a glimpse of Nader in grammar school: "Ralph was . . . argumentative," Halberstam recalls. "You can't talk about a pedantic nine-year-old kid, but that was the quality he had. He would make you define your terms outside the windows of the fourth grade." When most boys his age were reading sports magazines, Nader was reading the *Congressional Record*. "I read all the muckraker books before I was fourteen," he says.

At Princeton in the early 1950s, Nader majored in Far Eastern Studies; paid $35 a month for the cheapest room on campus; and once, legend has it, registered his protest against the dress code by attending class in a bathrobe. In his junior year he wrote a letter to the *Daily Princetonian* about the sparrows that were being killed when trees on campus were sprayed with DDT. The editors did not publish the letter because, they explained to him, they could not see any reason to get upset about a few dead birds. "If that's what it does to the birds," the budding activist replied, "what do you think it's doing to *us*?"

After Princeton, Nader attended Harvard Law School. Many of his classmates were preparing for careers as corporate lawyers. Harvard Law, Nader commented later, "never raised the question of sacrifice. Nothing! . . . The icons were Holmes and Cardozo and Learned Hand . . . the staid, the dry, those who were respected by the power structure. Who the hell says a lawyer has to be like that?"

Harvard was followed by six months in the Army as a cook at Fort Dix, New Jersey. Before he returned to civilian life, Nader went to the PX and purchased twelve pairs of low-cut black Army dress shoes for $6.00 a pair and four dozen pairs of calf-length black socks. Decades later, no article about Nader seemed complete unless it mentioned that he had not bought new shoes or socks since he left Fort Dix.

Nader opened a law office in Hartford, Connecticut, in 1959, but the conventional practice of law seems never to have interested him. From 1961 to 1964, working as a free-lance journalist, he traveled in Europe, the Soviet Union, Africa, and Latin America. Then, in 1964, he accepted an invitation from Daniel Patrick Moynihan, the assistant secretary of labor for policy planning, to join Moynihan's staff as a consultant on highway safety, a subject that had interested Nader since law school.

While working for Moynihan, Nader signed a contract to write a book about automobile safety. *Unsafe at Any Speed*, published in 1965, became the most influential work of journalism in the muckraking tradition since the days of Ida Tarbell and Upton Sinclair. Much that Nader wrote was anticipated in an article that Moynihan himself had published in the *Reporter* magazine in 1959. Indeed, a number of books on automobile safety were published at about the same time as Nader's, but, as Charles McCarry notes in *Citizen Nader*, "Only Nader's was struck by lightning." The bolt was not hurled by the gods. It was hurled by General Motors.

Nader had struck the first blow. In the first chapter of his book, he focused on a hair-raising series of accidents involving a popular GM sportscar, the Corvair. The Corvair, Nader charged, was an extremely dangerous vehicle, and GM knew it. It might have been fair to say that the Corvair's engineers "designed a vehicle but forgot about the driver," except that "They did not forget the driver; they ignored him." The Corvair was an elegant death trap. "It took General Motors four years . . . and 1,124,076 Corvairs before they decided to do something for all unsuspecting Corvair buyers by installing standard equipment to help control the car's handling hazards." When lawsuits started to be filed, "General Motors denied the charges, and instead blamed the accidents involved on driver negligence." The whole affair, Nader wrote, added up to "one of the greatest acts of industrial irresponsibility in the present century."

Moreover, in Nader's view, the problem went far beyond a single model. Disdain for the safety of consumers was standard in the automobile industry. The free market could not be relied on to correct the problem because "the free market has been seriously compromised by a concentrated industry capable of substantially defining the standards of the marketplace." In essence, the public did not demand better cars because the public did not know what awful cars it was getting. "The public has never been supplied the information nor offered the quality of competition to enable it to make effective demands through the marketplace and through government for a safe, non-polluting and efficient automobile that can be produced economically."

The solution, Nader said, was government action to force safety standards upon an industry that, left to its own devices, had demonstrated an appalling contempt for the lives of its customers. "Only the federal government can undertake the critical task of stimulating and guiding public and private initiatives for safety. . . . The public which bears the impact of the auto industry's safety policy must have a direct role in deciding that policy."

Even before *Unsafe at Any Speed* was published, General Motors had decided that Ralph Nader was a man it might someday want to discredit. Therefore, GM had taken the action that, apparently, it considered natural in the face of a challenge. It had hired a detective to look into Nader's personal life.

Nader's personal life, as it happened, was quite unusual. He was a bachelor who lived in a low-rent rooming house, owned no television set, owned no automobile, never read novels or went to the movies, and often forgot to eat. He cared about nothing, it seemed, except his work. His last car had been a 1949 Studebaker that he owned at Harvard Law School. GM's investigators did their best, but the worst that could be said about Nader's personal life was that he did not have one.

On February 11, 1966, GM's private eyes made the mistake of following a man who looked like Nader into the New Senate Office Building, where they were challenged by Senate security officers. A month later, with the story about to break, GM issued a press release acknowledging that its general counsel had "authorized a routine investigation . . . to determine if Ralph Nader was acting on behalf of litigants or attorneys in Corvair design cases pending against General Motors."

Senator Abraham Ribicoff of Connecticut, the chairman of a Senate subcommittee that was working on automobile safety, promptly called James M. Roche, the president of General Motors, to testify about the investigation under oath at a meeting of the subcommittee. At the hearing, Ribicoff and Senator Robert Kennedy of New York expressed the opinion that GM's press release had been an effort to mislead the American people. The investigation had not been a "routine" attempt to find out whether Nader was acting on behalf of litigants in Corvair design cases. During the testimony of the chief investigator, Vincent Gillen, Ribicoff exploded: "Your entire investigation, Mr. Gillen, had to do with trying to smear a man, the question of his sex life, whether he belonged to any left-wing organization, whether he was anti-Semitic, whether he was an oddball, whether he liked boys instead of girls. The whole investigation was to smear an individual, and I can't find anything of any substance in your entire investigation that had anything to do . . . with Corvair cars."

James Roche publicly apologized to Nader, but the investigation was a spectacular blunder. GM's attempt to discredit Nader did not merely make him famous; it also established his reputation as a lone crusader, pure and incorruptible. In the eyes of James Roche, Nader was "one of the bitter gypsies of dissent who plague America." But in the eyes of the American public, Nader was a David who had taken on the corporate Goliath and brought it to its knees. GM's snooping created a climate that led directly to the National Traffic and Motor Vehicle Safety Act of 1966. But that was not all. With the fame and credibility that GM had furnished, Ralph Nader was put in a position to make a career of citizenship.

The subject of *Unsafe at Any Speed* was automobile safety, but the larger theme was corporate accountability. From the start, Nader was especially concerned with the kind of market failure that is likely to arise when a commodity is subject to what economists call "external effects" or "externalities." As defined in one widely used textbook (Robert A. Samuelson and William D. Nordhaus, *Economics*, 12th edition), "An externality or spillover effect occurs when production or consumption inflicts incidental costs or benefits on others; that is, costs or benefits are imposed on others yet are not paid for by those who impose them."

Examples include air and water pollution, drunk drivers, and risks from unsafe factories or nuclear power plants.

Unlike many economists, Nader has a gift for talking and writing about externalities in language that ordinary people can understand. On the first page of *Unsafe at Any Speed*, for instance, he talks about externalities in the automobile industry: "Highway accidents were estimated to have cost this country in 1964, $8.3 billion in property damage, medical expenses, lost wages, and insurance overhead expenses. . . . But these are not the kind of costs which fall on the builders of motor vehicles . . . and thus [they] do not pinch the proper foot. Instead, the costs fall to users of vehicles, who are in no position to dictate safer automobile design."

Nader is not merely capable of talking about externalities in a concrete way; he also is capable of making the concept of corporate responsibility—corporate citizenship—concrete. "What if you owned a boarding house employing two or three people?" he would ask audiences in the early 1970s. "If you insisted on being treated the way big industrialists are, you could dump your garbage into the streets. Then if the authorities say stop, you can say no—that would decrease your profits, force you to lay off your employees. If they persist, you can threaten to set up your business in another neighborhood, giving its economy a boost and leaving the present neighborhood depressed. That's precisely what Union Carbide does. Why should it be impossible to toilet-train Union Carbide?" (This speech was made a decade before the release of forty tons of poison gas from a Union Carbide plant in Bhopal, India, that killed more than three thousand people and injured an estimated two hundred thousand, in the world's worst industrial accident to that time.)

Despite his reputation as a lone crusader, Nader's influence probably would have waned quickly if he had not demonstrated, in the years after GM made him a national figure, extraordinary skills as an organization-builder. Starting in 1969, he created a remarkable network of activist organizations, with names such as Public Citizen, the Corporate Accountability Research Group, the Public Interest Research Group, the Health Research Group, the Litigation Group, Congress Watch, and the Center for Study of Responsive Law. These organizations were staffed by bright, hardworking, underpaid young men and women whom the press soon dubbed "Nader's raiders."

A former raider, Jonathan Rowe, later recalled the outpouring of mail and support that Nader received from ordinary Americans who had come to look upon Nader as the one man they could trust in Washington. To help with one study, Rowe reports, "a group of truck drivers drove seven hours from upstate New York to show us firsthand evidence of the safety violations in which their companies were engaged. 'Look here, Ralph, look at these logs. They're makin' us run twelve, thirteen hours—can't make those runs in the time they say. Guys are takin' pills to stay up, then it's booze to go to sleep. Look at these equipment reports, Ralph. I've been reporting this brake problem for months now and look at this. Nothin'. People are gonna get killed, Ralph. We gotta do something.' "

In the early 1970s, reports by teams of Nader's raiders, and by Nader himself with various collaborators and associates, streamed out in a seemingly endless series. A few titles suggest how far the movement ranged: *The Nader Report on the Federal Trade Commission; The Chemical Feast: Report on the Food and Drug Administration; Vanishing Air: The Report on Air Pollution; Water Wasteland: The Report on Water Pollution; The Closed Enterprise System: The Report on Antitrust Enforcement; Bitter Wages: The Report on Disease and Injury on the Job; The Company State: The Report on Du Pont in Delaware; Damming the West: Report on the Bureau of Reclamation; The Last Stand: Nader Study Group Report on the National Forests; Who Runs Congress?; Corporate Power in America; The Consumer and Corporate Accountability; Taming the Giant Corporation.*

These were not academic studies that no one read. Within a year after the publication of *The Chemical Feast*, the three top officials at the Food and Drug Administration resigned, the federal government banned cyclamates from soft drinks, and manufacturers stopped putting MSG in baby food. Between 1966 and 1973 Congress passed more than two dozen pieces of consumer, environmental, and regulatory legislation that were influenced by Nader and his raiders, including the Wholesome Meat Act, the Natural Gas Pipeline Safety Act, the Federal Coal Mine Health and Safety Act, the Wholesome Poultry Safety Act, the Occupational Safety and Health Act, the Safe Water Drinking Act, the Consumer Product Safety Act, and the Freedom of Information Act.

Along with the legislative legacy, there is a permanent organizational legacy. "By design," Jonathan Rowe wrote in 1985, "the Nader network has become an institution; Exxon doesn't go home and the consumer advocates can't either." Nader's watchdogs did not merely watch the giant business firms; they also watched Congress; they watched the executive branch of government; they watched the courts; and they watched the government's regulatory commissions. The theme of corporate accountability stretched to become the theme of institutional accountability.

* * *

Naturally, Nader has made plenty of enemies over the years. "No thoughtful person can question that the American economic system is under broad attack," U.S. Supreme Court justice Lewis Powell wrote a few years before his appointment to the Court. Nader, Powell added, is "perhaps the single most effective antagonist of American business." In the view of conservative commentator Irving Kristol, "Nader takes no responsibility. He only attitudinizes." Nader and his disciples are "constantly scaring people by exaggerating the dimensions of real problems. You end up with overregulation."

Even sympathizers concede that Nader's approach can lead to too much regulation. Nader, former raider Michael Kinsley wrote in *The New Republic* in 1985, has developed "the classic zealot's worldview, paranoid and humorless, and his vision of the ideal society—regulations for all contingencies of life, warning labels on every french fry . . . —is not one many others would care to share with him." Yet, Kinsley adds, "No living American is responsible for more concrete improvements in the society we actually do inhabit than Ralph Nader." Nader's achievements are "as immutable as FDR's. President Reagan may inveigh against burdensome government regulation, just as he inveighs against government spending. . . . But he would no more get the government out of the business of protecting consumers, workers, and the environment than he would dismantle Social Security."

Nader himself, in the late 1980s, continued to work with the dogged intensity of the man who had decided, decades earlier, that the causes he cared about required "total commitment." Always the activist, he tries to win recruits wherever he goes. In speeches to adult audiences, he emphasizes the power that consumers can wield if they act together. "To get in the mood," he urges, "the next time you go to Sears and they give you a form to fill out, cross out everything you don't like and put in things you do like, such as doubling the warranty. Or go to the supermarket resolved not to buy anything but just walk up and down the aisles taking notes. When the manager approaches you, inform him that you represent a group of several hundred households and that if his store passes, your group will call to set up an appointment to negotiate on such things as the nutritional value of the food he carries."

In speeches to student audiences, Nader often begins with, "How many of you are hungry to become fighters for justice in America?" To students he also says, "Almost every significant breakthrough has come from the spark, the drive, the initiative of one person. You must believe this." Consumer issues often seem narrow, but not when Nader talks about them. In his formulation they blend into larger issues of citizenship, power, and accountability. He once defined his goal as "nothing less than the qualitative reform of the industrial revolution." Asked what he does for pleasure, he replies, "Trying to make a democracy work better—what could be more pleasurable?" Asked what makes him so singleminded, he replies, "Is it so implausible, so distasteful, that a man would believe deeply enough in his work to dedicate his life to it?" To the critics who condemned or dismissed him as a "self-appointed consumer advocate," he rightly might have asked, as Jonathan Rowe has pointed out, whether he should "have gotten an official appointment before presuming to act like a citizen."

Sinclair Lewis, the Agrarians, Adolf A. Berle, Jr., Gardiner C. Means, John L. Lewis, Budd Schulberg, David Riesman, William A. Whyte, Jr., Sloan Wilson, Alan Harrington, John Kenneth Galbraith, Ralph Nader—merely to list these names is to suggest the range of criticism that American writers and activists have directed against business in the twentieth century. No one factor links the critics except, perhaps, an unspoken assumption that when they attack business, they are attacking a target of towering and indomitable strength. The notion that American business might be in any way weak or shaky, a tottering giant, is not a notion that was ever entertained by any of these dissenters. Nor, indeed, was there ever much reason to entertain it, until the giant began to sway.

CHAPTER 18

Poor Richard Revisited

Whatever Happened to Yankee Know-how?

In 1985, twenty million people visited Tsukuba Science City in Tsukuba, north of Tokyo, to view an $840 million celebration of recent scientific and technological progress. According to *The Wall Street Journal*, the fair was a tribute to the "awesome gains in technology" that have made Japan one of the world's leading economic powers. "The U.S. was there, too," *The Journal* reported, "but its exhibits were overshadowed by those of the Japanese. By this time, the U.S. also was losing to Japanese rivals in semiconductor memory chips, piling up huge trade deficits with Japan, and was on the verge of becoming a debtor nation."

The United States has not always fared so poorly at international trade expositions. Indeed, America's industrial and technological proficiency dominated the New York World's Fair of 1964–65, the New York World's Fair of 1939–40, and the Chicago World's Columbian Exposition of 1893. And it was at the world's first big industrial fair, the Great Exhibition staged at London's Crystal Palace in 1851, that European observers caught their first glimpse of America's coming of age as a manufacturing power.

To be sure, the United States did not dominate the Crystal Palace Great Exhibition. As historian Nathan Rosenberg has noted, "In spite of continued obeisance to the idea of Yankee ingenuity, it cannot be overstressed that America in the first half of the nineteenth century was still primarily a borrower of European technology." At the Crystal Palace, beneath a cardboard eagle that invited ridicule, the American entry in the midcentury "tournament of industry" included much that was not industrial at all: Indian corn, preserved peaches, maple sugar, and so on.

But the display did not end with peaches and sugar. Revolvers made by Samuel Colt, locks made by Alfred Hobbs, and reapers made by Cyrus McCormick deeply impressed British manufacturers. "It is beyond all denial," *The Times* of London conceded after the exhibition had run for several months, "that every practical success of the season belongs to the Americans. Their consignments showed poorly at first, but came out well upon trial. Their reaping machine has carried conviction to the heart of the British agriculturist."

What especially struck foreign observers was the proficiency of American manufacturers in the use of machine tools. "If these cunning American devisements are a portent of that nation's future capabilities," John Stuart Mill wrote in a letter to a London scientific journal late in 1851, "we in this country have good cause to be concerned for the well-being of our industrial treasure. Every sign points to the prospect of these Americans creating a colossus of industry the size of which is beyond the ability of current imagination to grasp."

A similar conclusion was reached by a committee of British experts who toured a variety of American manufacturing establishments in 1855. American factories, the committee reported, were distinguished by the "adaptation of special tools to minute purposes," "the ample provision of workshop room," "systematic arrangement in the manufacture," "the progress of material through the manufactory," and the "discipline and sobriety of the employed." Americans, the committee predicted, would be formidable competitors in the years to come. The "contriving and making of machinery has become so common in [the United States] . . . that unless the example is followed at home . . . it is to be feared that American manufacturers will before long become exporters . . . to England."

No doubt Benjamin Franklin would have found much to gratify his Yankee heart if he could have heard these prophesies or wandered the aisles of the Crystal Palace Great Exhibition. After all, he was an inventor himself, whose proposal for the establishment of the Pennsylvania Academy included the recommendation that all students should study not only "The History of *Commerce*" but also "*Mechanicks* . . . to be in-form'd of the Principles of that Art by which weak Men perform such Wonders, Labour is sav'd, Manufactures expedited, &c."

Franklin would have been less pleased, one imagines, if he had sur-veyed the scene in the 1980s. Yankee know-how seemed to have meta-morphosed into Yankee don't-know-how. The story was told in dozens of magazine and newspaper articles, crammed with statistics that soon became depressingly familiar to any American who was paying attention.

The seriousness of the American decline was suggested by a Labor Department study of average yearly productivity gains among eight in-dustrial nations from 1973 to 1984. The United States ranked dead last, with an average annual gain of 2.1 percent. Ahead came France at 6.4 percent, Belgium at 6.2 percent, Japan at 5.9 percent, the Netherlands at 4.6 percent, Italy at 3.8 percent, West Germany at 3.4 percent, and Great Britain at 2.3 percent.

In head-to-head competition with its strongest rival, Japan, the United States also fared badly. Between 1960 and 1973, U.S. productivity in the manufacturing sector grew at an average annual rate of 3.2 percent, whereas Japanese productivity rose an astonishing 10.3 percent a year. Both countries slipped somewhat between 1973 and 1985, but Japan con-tinued to improve its productivity at a far faster rate than the United States. The United States managed average annual increases of 2.2 per-cent, compared with 5.6 percent for Japan.

Starting in the middle 1980s, there were signs that American manu-facturers were doing better. But by that time the nation had saddled itself with such a load of debt that increased productivity merely made it easier to pay the interest we owed to foreign lenders, who could use their gains to invest in new plant and equipment or to buy big chunks of American real estate. America, many observers felt, had put itself up for sale, and at bargain prices.

To make matters worse, in many industries the American decline in manufacturing productivity has been translated into a tremendous de-cline in market share. For instance, between 1970 and 1989 American manufacturers saw their share in the consumer electronics market plunge from 100 percent to less than 5 percent. American consumers bought phonographs, color TV's, and VCR's in great quantities, but they rarely bought them from American manufacturers. Americans had invented the transistor, but Japan dominated the world market in miniaturized elec-tronics. Americans had done pioneering work in semiconductor technology, but Japan dominated the world market in semiconductors. More often than not, American-made goods were not even made by American machine tools anymore. The American share of the U.S. market in machine tools dropped from 100 percent in 1970 to 35 percent in 1987.

The poor performance of America's manufacturers had other implications. In the long run a nation's standard of living depends on its rate of productivity growth. In the United States, the per capita GNP grew at an average annual rate of 2.4 percent between 1948 and 1968, whereas the average rate of increase declined to only 1.4 percent over the next twenty years. So the nation was richer in 1988 than it had been in 1968, but it was not nearly as rich as it would have been if it had sustained a higher rate of productivity growth.

What this meant, in concrete terms, was that the nation did not have as large a pie as it might have had to divide among the purposes that competed for its attention—to feed its hungry, house its homeless, care for its sick, provide for its elderly, invest in its young, preserve its environment, defend its borders, support its friends, oppose its foes, incarcerate its criminals, or even simply squander in the pursuit of happiness.

Lagging productivity meant more than lost opportunities, however. It also meant pain. Between January 1981 and January 1986, 10.8 million Americans lost their jobs because of plant shutdowns and employment cutbacks. True, more Americans than ever before were working in the 1980s. But more American families than ever before felt that they needed a double income to make ends meet.

The decline of America's manufacturing prowess has implications, too, for the kind of work Americans will be doing in the future. By the year 2000, according to Labor Department forecasters, only 15.2 percent of all nonagricultural jobs will be in manufacturing, down from 26.1 percent in 1972. Nearly four jobs of five will be in the relatively low-paying service sector, up from 67.8 percent in 1972. The American economy still produces jobs, but to an alarming extent the jobs it produces, as Chrysler chairman Lee Iacocca has pointed out, are jobs sweeping up around Japanese computers.

The causes of America's manufacturing problems are easy to identify and hard to remedy. Part of the blame must be assigned to labor, which has pressed for higher wages without showing much concern for quality or productivity. Between 1960 and 1985, labor costs per unit of output increased by 2.4 times in both the United States and Japan. In the same period, output by Japanese workers increased over nine times while output by American workers increased only 2.3 times. In a period when Asian workers won a reputation for producing high-quality goods that sold at low prices, American workers won a reputation for producing so-so goods that sold at high prices.

Labor is not the only problem, however. Management has played its part in the disaster. Though the United States has improved in recent years, through most of the 1970s Japan and West Germany spent far more on research and development as a percentage of GNP. American managers have been slower to adopt new technologies than their major foreign competitors, and they have been less aggressive in investing in new plant and equipment. In recent years the average age of American factories actually has risen, from 13.8 years in 1980 to 15 years in 1988.

The American failure to invest more heavily in research and development has had a predictable effect on American patents and other evidences of technological leadership. Of the twenty-four most significant new drugs introduced in the United States in the 1970s, according to The Wall Street Journal, only thirteen were developed in American laboratories. Foreign inventors have captured nearly half of U.S. patents in recent years, up from 35 percent in 1975. In 1982 more U.S. patents were granted to General Electric than to any other company. By 1987, General Electric ranked fourth, behind three Japanese companies: Canon, Hitachi, and Toshiba.

Complacent labor, complacement management, a low rate of investment in research and development and in state-of-the-art plant and equipment—altogether, it has not been a winning strategy for the United States. The nation exported more than it imported every year from 1946 to 1970. Since then the pendulum has swung the other way, and violently. The U.S. balance on merchandise trade plunged from a surplus of $2.6 billion in 1970 to a deficit of $144.3 billion in 1986. In the latter year the United States ran a trade deficit with almost every one of its major trading partners, though it did manage a surplus of $45 million in trade with the basket-case economies of Eastern Europe.

America's difficulties in meeting the challenge of foreign competition do not merely reflect the relatively poor performance of American labor and management. They also are a consequence of the high cost of capital in the United States. In 1984, for instance, the real cost of capital in the United States was 7.5 percent, three times the cost of capital in Japan. This factor, many economists argue, is the final link in the chain that is dragging down America's productivity.

Why has the cost of capital been so high? The answer lies not in economics but in culture—in deeply rooted patterns of American behavior. To be more precise, the answer lies in recent patterns of spending and saving. Of everything that might have astonished Benjamin Franklin if he had visited the United States in the 1980s, it seems safe to say that nothing would have astonished him more than the nation's love affair with debt.

Whatever Happened to Thrift?

"Remember," Franklin advised his countrymen, "that Money is of a prolific generating Nature. Money can beget Money, and its Offspring can beget more. . . . He that kills a breeding Sow, destroys all her Offspring to the thousandth Generation. He that murders a Crown, destroys all that it might have produc'd, even Scores of Pounds."

On this point the American people have never ceased to agree with Franklin, at least in theory. American attitudes were measured in an interesting series of polls conducted by the Gallup Organization in the late 1970s. Asked about the propriety of buying on credit, six of ten respondents answered that it was "not OK or never OK." Asked whether "credit is a valuable asset which should be used to let [people] live the kind of life they want to live" or whether "credit is something that is best to use as little as possible," seven of ten answered that "Credit should be used as little as possible."

These attitudes, as economist Shlomo Maital has pointed out, seem to have virtually no impact on behavior. Installment debt, for instance, has risen from about 8 percent of disposable personal income in the 1950s to 17 percent in recent years. Total consumer credit rose from $5.6 billion at the end of World War II to $139.4 billion in 1970, before soaring to $723.6 billion in 1986. For most Americans, using credit "as little as possible" has involved almost nothing in the way of self-discipline or self-denial.

The other side of this energetic borrowing is a low rate of personal savings. In 1987, personal savings as a percentage of disposable income were 3.9 percent in the United States. That figure compared with 5.6 percent for the United Kingdom, 12.2 percent for West Germany, 13.0 percent for France, and 16.5 percent for Japan. Thrift may still be a virtue that Americans honor, but it is not one they practice.

Personal debt is only one part of the problem. Corporate debt also has risen sharply in recent years. Corporate liquid assets (cash and cash equivalents) have fallen from about 15 percent of GNP in the 1950s to 7.5 percent today. This corporate borrowing, like individual borrowing, is not necessarily bad. If it is used for research and development, new plant and equipment, or other productivity-enhancing investments, debt should pay off in the long run. But if it is not used wisely, debt can sink a company. The 1980s saw an unprecedented boom in the use of corporate "junk bonds": high-risk, high-yield bonds that the major bond-rating services considered highly speculative. By 1987 a total of $145 billion of the $550 billion in corporate bonds outstanding were classified as "junk."

These bonds were favorite instruments in a business (high-debt or "leveraged" buyouts) that was dominated by a new breed of wheeler-dealer, the most celebrated of whom was Michael Milken of the Wall Street firm Drexel Burnham Lambert. As the 1980s ended, Milken's legal difficulties diverted attention from the fact that after several years of furious activity, no one could say for sure whether leveraged buyouts strengthened or weakened either the firms involved or the nation as a whole. While economists, legislators, and Wall Street professionals debated that point, nonprofessionals watched the game with their fingers crossed, hoping that "junk bonds" would not live up to their name when the economy faltered. A recession intensified by a wave of junk-bond defaults was not a prospect that anyone relished.

Anxiety deepened in the fall of 1989, when the prices of junk bonds plunged as junk-bond defaults for the year soared past the $3 billion mark. In a front-page article on September 18, 1989, under the headline "The Party's Over: Mounting Losses Are Watershed Event for Era of Junk Bonds," *The Wall Street Journal* reported that "The heyday of the junk bond . . . seems to be coming to an end. . . . More and more acquisitions and buy-outs from the last decade appear to be highly unsound, and are running into what appear to be insurmountable debt problems." Junk-bond investors, said corporate raider Carl Icahn, "are going to have to pay the piper." For a while, *The Journal* concluded, "the junk-bond market seemed to be a liquid public market. Now, it is being exposed for what it really is: A place where highly risky loans to lower quality companies are traded."

Along with high levels of individual and corporate debt, the 1980s witnessed an extraordinary surge in government debt. Though he advocated a constitutional amendment that would require the federal government to balance its budget, President Reagan himself never came close to submitting a budget that was balanced, and, indeed, during the Reagan era the federal government consistently ran up deficits of well over $100 billion a year. The total federal debt rose from $1.0 trillion in 1981 to $2.58 trillion in 1988—$11,565 for every man, woman, and child in the United States. As a percentage of GNP, the total federal debt had fallen from 122.5 percent in 1945 to 33.6 percent in 1981. By 1988 it was back up to 54.9 percent.

By that time, too, American taxpayers paid well over $100 billion a year merely to meet the interest on the federal debt. That was as much as the federal government spent on Medicare, health, and international affairs combined, and almost half as much as it spent on Defense. Nearly one dollar out of five spent by the federal government was spent on interest payments.

A thousand years from now an historian in a nation that does not yet exist, seeking to understand the failed civilizations of the distant past, may study the last years of the twentieth century in the United States as avidly as Gibbon studied Rome under Nero or Caracalla. What will be most striking, perhaps, will be the degree to which ideology supplanted thought in the discussion of vital issues, including the discussion of the nation's finances. After years of advocating fiscal restraint, people who called themselves conservatives suddenly decided that deficits did not matter. After years of not caring about deficits, people who called themselves liberals suddenly decided that deficits mattered a great deal. Having exchanged wardrobes, participants in the debate hastened to charge that their opponents were dressed in rags. In the rare moments when the discussion focused on issues, each side made a habit of asserting that the flimsiest guesses, hopes, and prejudices were proven and eternal truths.

The deficit, it seems safe to say, is a bomb that might or might not explode. In another time or place, our future Gibbon might conclude, a nonpartisan consensus might have prevailed: that the most prudent response to a bomb that might or might not go off is to treat it as if it will. This dull argument—call it "better safe than sorry"—has fallen on deaf ears in the 1980s.

The nation, it seems, only musters the will to act in the face of a pressing crisis. This has worked well enough in the past, but the debt may be a bomb that goes off not with a bang but with a long, slow whimper. The scenario that haunts many American economists is this: Our low level of savings leads to a low level of investment; the low level of investment leads to a low level of productivity growth; the low level of productivity growth makes it more difficult to pay off the debt; the difficulty of paying the debt lowers the amount available for savings; and so on, through the cycle again. Instead of a day of reckoning, we may have a century of reckoning.

Economic scenarios are subject to many uncertainties. What seems indisputable is that Americans have grown accustomed to living beyond their means. By saving much less than we might, in effect we are borrowing from our children to throw a party for ourselves. The insidious ailment that is sapping our nation's strength was memorably described by Richard Darman, George Bush's budget director, when he said that we suffer from "now-nowism," a "shorthand label for our collective shortsightedness, our obsession with the here and now, our reluctance to address the future." Darman was not the only naysayer. The message we are sending to future generations, *The New York Times* declared in an editorial on February 5, 1989, is smug, self-satisfied, and self-serving: *"Dear Grandchildren: We leave you an America that's poorer and shabbier than it could have been if we had paid our own way. But what the hell, it's good enough."*

Looking Out for Number One

The way to wealth, Franklin had told his countrymen, "depends chiefly on two words: INDUSTRY and FRUGALITY." By the end of the 1980s, it was clear that the nation's main competitors worked harder and saved more than Americans did. One reason, perhaps, was the kind of advice that Americans were reading in the books that told them how to succeed.

Many of these books were shamelessly cynical. The distance that separates Robert J. Ringer's *Looking Out For #1*, a best seller of the late 1970s, from the self-help writings of Benjamin Franklin, Dale Carnegie, or Norman Vincent Peale—to take a diverse lot—is quite extraordinary.

"Clear your mind," Ringer advises his readers as they begin his book. ". . . Forget foundationless traditions, forget the 'moral' standards others may have tried to cram down your throat, forget the beliefs people may have tried to intimidate you into accepting as 'right.' Allow your intellect to take control as you read, and, most important, think of yourself—Number One—as a unique individual. . . . You and you alone will be responsible for your success or failure."

The heart of Ringer's book is a "philosophy" that might have come straight from the mouth of Sammy Glick. The message is served to the reader in little bundles that Ringer calls "theories." These include, for

instance, the "Screwor-Screwee" theory ("The screwor is always the other
guy; the screwee is always you"); the "Zip-the-Lip" theory ("If you've
got something good going, *shut up!*"); and the "Tend-To" theory ("Most
people have a tendency to believe their own bullshit: when you start
believing yours, you're in a state of mind that is dangerous to your well-
being"). There is much more, but these are the highlights in a book of
342 pages.

Michael Korda is more sophisticated and entertaining than Ringer,
but no less cynical. "All life is a game of power," Korda announces in
the opening pages of *Power! How to Get It, How to Use It* (1975). "The
object of the game is simple enough: to know what you want and get it.
The moves of the game, by contrast, are infinite and complex, although
they usually involve the manipulation of people and situations to your
advantage." The truth that no reader can ever afford to forget, Korda
adds, is that "your gain is inevitably someone else's loss, your failure
someone else's victory."

Having informed his readers that they live in a world in which "the
Puritan work-ethic seems irrelevant," Korda focuses his attention on status and power symbols, in chapters with titles like "The Power Dynamics of Office Parties," "Phone Me in the Limo," and "A Gold-Plated
Thermos Is a Man's Best Friend." Whereas Ringer specializes in street
smarts for minor-league hustlers, Korda addresses a corporate audience:
"It is useful to learn to sit still while others are fidgeting—many a businessman has benefited from his rocklike immobility in times of crisis."
Korda has little to say about managing people or managing a business,
but a subject like "Foot Power" brings out the best in him: "Powerful
people generally wear simple shoes—Peal & Co., Ltd., five-eyelet shoes
from Brooks Brothers, for example, and always put the laces in straight,
not crisscrossed."

Like Ringer and Korda, Betty Lehan Harragan presents herself as a
teacher of harsh truths in *Games Mother Never Taught You: Corporate
Gamesmanship for Women*, a widely read book published in 1977. " 'Working' is a game women never learned to play," Harragan declares, and her
book purports to offer a map of "no-woman's land"—the world of American business—to women who have stumbled or plunged into that world
"as if . . . into a foreign territory."

Harragan's basic argument is that, not knowing the rules of the game,
many women have been saps in the business world. Like Ringer and
Korda, she is an advocate of "me first" thinking. For instance, after noting what she describes as an "excessive devotion to duty" among women

in the work force, Harragan needs only three sentences to demolish the illusion that "pitching in" is a virtue in business: "Redoing someone else's work is not your job. Assuming responsibility outside the parameters of your function is not your job. . . . Someone else's failure to perform is not your problem."

Harragan offers her readers no-nonsense advice about subjects that range from the proper response when an interviewer asks about current salary ("lie") to the proper attitude toward salary negotiations ("substantial raises have little to do with ability or achievement and nothing to do with personal self-worth"). As usual in the success literature of recent years, the whole emphasis is on being savvy—which is to say, the whole emphasis is on symbols and "gamesmanship."

Of course, it is difficult to say how much books influence behavior. Perhaps the most that can be said is that books help to create a climate of opinion, and at the same time they reflect a climate that is shaped by other factors. In the eighteenth and nineteenth centuries, for instance, the climate was shaped by the Puritan ethic that not only sanctioned success but also sanctioned the qualities of character that were presumed to lead to success—industry, frugality, sobriety, honesty, perseverance, punctuality, reliability, and so on.

Later, as affluence weakened the influence of Puritanism, the emphasis shifted away from character. Success, Americans were told, would come through a winning personality (Dale Carnegie) or through a winning attitude (Norman Vincent Peale). Then, in the 1970s, there was another shift. The literature of success got nasty. After the Vietnam War, a flurry of assassinations, and the wreck of the Nixon presidency, it was easy to be cynical, and cynicism dominated the success literature of the 1970s. Forget about character, forget about personality, forget about positive thinking. What mattered was to be savvy, and being savvy meant looking out for number one.

In the 1980s, the me-first ethic was put on vivid display as the largest insider-trading scandal in the history of American business slowly unraveled. The story began to break in 1986, when several young investment bankers were permanently barred from working in the securities industry on charges that they had illegally traded stocks on the basis of "inside" knowledge. Next came the fall of Ivan Boesky, one of the leading wheeler-dealers of the 1980s. Boesky agreed to pay a fine of $50 million and to return $50 million in illegal profits, was barred from the securities industry for life, and was sentenced to three years in jail amid speculation that the government had let him off easy.

Boesky was a big fish, but by 1989 it was clear that federal prosecutors might yet land a bigger one. In a deal announced just before Christmas 1988, Drexel Burnham Lambert, the fifth-largest securities firm in the United States, agreed to plead guilty to six counts of mail, wire, and securities fraud, to pay a record fine of $650 million, and to cooperate with the government in its investigation of the head of Drexel's lucrative junk-bond department, Wharton graduate Michael Milken. In March 1989 the government filed a ninety-eight-count felony indictment against Milken on charges of racketeering, conspiracy, mail fraud, and other illegal activities. Milken, who had received $550 million in salary and other compensation from Drexel Burnham Lambert for the year 1987 alone, continued to deny he had done anything wrong. It was difficult to forget, however, that Drexel had denied that it had done anything wrong almost up to the moment it announced it was pleading guilty.

The insider-trading scandal of the 1980s was not the first that ever hit Wall Street, but the extent of the scandal shocked even seasoned observers. John Shad, the chairman of the Securities and Exchange Commission, was so disturbed by "the large number of graduates of leading business schools who have become convicted felons" that in 1987 he made a gift of $20 million to Harvard Business School to establish a program in ethics. In *The New York Times* on July 27, 1987, Shad explained the point that, in his view, business schools were failing to teach: "In sum, ethics pays: It's smart to be ethical." Cynics may wonder why this straightforward utilitarianism needs to be backed by $20 million, but Harvard was happy to accept the gift.

The Bottom Line

More than a decade has passed since I emerged from Michael Milken's alma mater with the thought that I wanted to study business in a more fundamental way than business school had ever permitted. At first I imagined that my explorations might resolve the tension within me—a tension I experienced sometimes as a clash of dissenting and affirming voices, sometimes as a dream in which Huck Finn and Ben Franklin struggled for my soul. Later I decided that the conflict was permanent. I could not resolve the tension, any more than America itself can resolve it.

I think that the clashing voices will always be with us, and, though the battle may exhaust us, I think it also may make us stronger. In any case, I'm glad to have the perspective that comes from having listened to the ardent ghosts of the American past. When I read Robert Ringer or Michael Korda, I'm glad I can imagine what Benjamin Franklin would have thought of them. When I read the latest article about the decline of America's manufacturing competitiveness, followed by the latest article about the "merger mania" of the 1980s under the influence of various corporate raiders, I'm glad I can recall the comment of Thorstein Veblen, "The typical American businessman watches the industrial process from ambush, with a view to the seizure of any item of value that may be left at loose ends. Business strategy is a strategy of 'watchful waiting,' at the centre of a web; very alert and adroit, but remarkably incompetent in the way of anything that can properly be called 'industrial enterprise.' "

Similarly, when I see people living on the streets of New York City in the 1980s, and when I read about Malcolm Forbes transporting six hundred of his closest friends to Morocco for a $2 million bash in honor of his own birthday, or when I hear that Donald Trump is considering the purchase of a blimp to go along with the jet, the yacht, and the helicopter that are on call to speed him from his 50-room, $20 million triplex penthouse in Manhattan to his 45-room Georgian manor in Greenwich, Connecticut, or to his 130-room hideaway in West Palm Beach, Florida, I can't help recalling how Henry George, visiting New York in the winter of 1868–69, "saw and recognised for the first time the shocking contrast between monstrous wealth and debasing want." And I can't help remembering the alarm George sounded: "So long as all the increased wealth which modern progress brings goes but to build up great fortunes, to increase luxury, and make sharper the contrast between the House of Have and the House of Want, progress is not real and cannot be permanent." It is not merely the misery on the streets that worries me. It is the misery in the souls of the people who walk by.

On the other hand, when I hear simpleminded attacks on the greed of the 1980s, I'm glad that we have a conservative like Michael Novak to remind us that affluence is not inherently immoral. Novak quotes Max Weber's answer, in *The Protestant Ethic and the Spirit of Capitalism*, to the notion that greed is the soul of capitalism: "It should be taught in the kindergarten of cultural history that this naive idea of capitalism must be given up once and for all. Unlimited greed for gain is not in the least identical with capitalism, and is still less its spirit."

What is the bottom line? as people in business like to ask. Sometimes I imagine that all Americans, heading toward the twenty-first century, are guests at a party even more spectacular than the one Malcolm Forbes threw for himself in Morocco. Benjamin Franklin is there, along with John Jacob Astor, Cornelius Vanderbilt, John D. Rockefeller, Andrew Carnegie, Jay Gould, J. P. Morgan, Henry Adams, Henry James, Thorstein Veblen, Sinclair Lewis, and many, many more. The din is terrific. Donald Trump is making a deal with John Jacob Astor; Lee Iacocca has buttonholed Henry Ford; Thorstein Veblen is reading *What Makes Sammy Run?*; Calvin Coolidge announces that the business of America is business; William James denounces the bitch-goddess Success; Dale Carnegie explains how to win friends and influence people; and Melville's Bartleby declares that he, for one, would prefer not to.

It's a grand party, full of fascinating people. The only problem is that we're borrowing extravagantly to pay for it. "Fools make Feasts," Benjamin Franklin warned, "and wise Men eat them." As our party roars on, it's a warning that few people seem able to hear. Perhaps we have lost not merely the capacity to work and to save but also the capacity to listen, not merely the discipline to deny ourselves for the future but also the discipline to learn from the past. If we continue to squander our inheritance, our most precious bequest to our grandchildren may well be a copy of *Poor Richard's Almanack*, to show them where we went wrong.

Sources

GENERAL BACKGROUND

For a broad view of the history of American business, the best source is Alfred D. Chandler, Jr., *The Visible Hand* (Cambridge, Mass.: Harvard University Press, 1977). In depth and scope, Chandler's work is unrivaled.

The Coming of Managerial Capitalism: A Casebook on the History of American Economic Institutions (Homewood, Ill.: Richard D. Irwin, 1985), edited by Chandler and Richard S. Tedlow, provides a compilation of materials used in teaching the core course on American business history to students in the M.B.A. program at Harvard Business School. Not many people will want to read this book from cover to cover, but I have found it invaluable.

Another invaluable book that is not likely to be read from cover to cover is *The American Heritage History of American Business and Industry* (New York: American Heritage, 1972), edited by Alex B. Groner and the editors of *American Heritage* and *Business Week*. Lavishly and lovingly illustrated, ably written, and beautifully designed, this is the best book I know for the general reader who wants to see the story of American enterprise unfold, in vivid detail, from the farms and plantations of Colonial days to the conglomerates of the late 1960s.

Many journalists and nonacademic historians have written engagingly, though not always reliably, about the tycoons of the nineteenth century. For the perspective of a leading muckraker, see Gustavus Myers's three-volume *History of the Great American Fortunes* (Chicago: Charles H. Kerr & Company, 1910). Matthew Josephson's *The Robber Barons* (New York: Harcourt Brace Jovanovich, 1934) was strongly influenced by Myers. It is worth reading, but it must be read skeptically. Stewart H. Holbrook's *The Age of the Moguls* (Garden City, N.Y.: Doubleday, 1953) is vigorous and unpretentious—a good book. For the period from 1890 to 1935, see Frederick Lewis Allen's *The Lords of Creation* (New York: Harper & Brothers, 1935).

Sigmund Diamond's *The Reputation of the American Businessman* (Cambridge, Mass.: Harvard University Press, 1955) examines in detail the public comment that followed the deaths of Stephen Girard, John Jacob Astor, Cornelius Vanderbilt, J. P. Morgan, John D. Rockefeller, and Henry Ford. The general reader may not relish this book, but no one who writes about these titans should miss it.

INTRODUCTION

Richard Darman's speech was given at the National Press Club in July 1989 and can be obtained from the Office of Management and Budget in Washington, D.C. For commentary, see Alan Murray, "The Outlook," *The Wall Street Journal*

(July 31, 1989), sec. 1, p. 1, and Bernard Weintraub, "White House," *The New York Times* (August 25, 1989), sec. A, p. 11.

CHAPTER 1: BENJAMIN FRANKLIN: "THE WAY TO WEALTH"

A handsome paperback edition of Franklin's autobiography has been published by Yale University Press (New Haven, Conn., 1976). It includes a fine introduction and notes by Leonard W. Labaree, et al., the editors of the definitive edition of Franklin's papers published by Yale University Press.

In a Signet Classic paperback edited by L. Jesse Lemisch (New York: New American Library, 1961), readers will find the full text of the autobiography and a wonderful selection of Franklin's other writings, including the full texts of "Advice to a Young Tradesman," "The Way to Wealth," and the "Standing Queries for the Junto." This little book is a bargain that Franklin would have appreciated. Also a bargain, though a more expensive one, is the 1,600-page volume of Franklin's writings published by the Library of America (New York: 1987).

The best biography of Franklin, and one of the best biographies ever written by or about any American, is Carl Van Doren's *Benjamin Franklin* (New York: The Viking Press, 1938). Other biographers have written good books about Franklin. This is a great book.

Most of the best essays about Franklin are collected in *Benjamin Franklin: A Profile*, edited by Esmond Wright (New York: Hill and Wang, 1970). See also *Benjamin Franklin and the American Character*, edited by Charles L. Sanford (Boston: D. C. Heath, 1955).

A note for literary archaeologists: Max Weber (as translated by Talcott Parsons) quotes the version of "Advice to a Young Tradesman" that appears in the Sparks edition of Franklin's works published in 1840. I have reprinted the paragraphs that Weber quotes exactly as they appear in the Parsons translation. Weber also quotes several short paragraphs from Franklin's "Necessary Hints to Those That Would be Rich." I have omitted these, but I have added the final paragraph of "Advice to a Young Tradesman" as it appears in the Yale University Press edition.

CHAPTER 2: JOHN JACOB ASTOR: "A SELF-INVENTED MONEY-MAKING MACHINE"

For the life of John Jacob Astor, I have relied upon Arthur D. Howden Smith, *John Jacob Astor: Landlord of New York* (Philadelphia and London: J. B. Lippincott, 1929); Virginia Cowles, *The Astors* (London: Weidenfeld and Nicolson, 1979); and John D. Gates, *The Astor Family* (Garden City, N.Y.: Doubleday, 1981).

For Astor's business activities, the best source is the two-volume biography by Kenneth Wiggins Porter, *John Jacob Astor, Business Man* (Cambridge, Mass.: Harvard University Press, 1931). Readers who want a sophisticated business perspective but less detail should see the chapter on Astor in Chandler and Tedlow, *The Coming of Managerial Capitalism*.

CHAPTER 3: CORNELIUS VANDERBILT: "I NEVER CARED FOR MONEY"

For the life of Cornelius Vanderbilt, I have relied heavily on Wheaton J. Lane's superb biography, *Commodore Vanderbilt: An Epic of the Steam Age* (New York: Alfred A. Knopf, 1942). I have also consulted Wayne Andrews, *The Vanderbilt Legend* (New York: Harcourt, Brace, 1941); Matthew Josephson, *The Robber Barons;* Stewart H. Holbrook, *The Age of the Moguls;* Maury Klein, *The Life and Legend of Jay Gould* (Baltimore: Johns Hopkins University Press, 1986); Sigmund Diamond, *The Reputation of the American Businessman;* Henry Adams and Charles Francis Adams, Jr., *Chapters of Erie and Other Essays* (Boston: James R. Osgood, 1871); the biography of Vanderbilt in the *Dictionary of American Biography;* and *The American Heritage History of American Business and Industry.* For a complete account of the storm precipitated by Vanderbilt's will, see Frank Clark, "The Commodore Left Two Sons," *American Heritage,* April 1966.

CHAPTER 4: THE LITERATURE OF SUCCESS IN THE NINETEENTH CENTURY

For the discussion in this chapter, I owe a large debt to Irwin G. Wyllie's *The Self-Made Man in America* (New York: The Free Press, 1954). This is a wonderful book. I also recommend John G. Cawelti's *Apostles of the Self-Made Man* (Chicago and London: University of Chicago Press, 1965) and Richard M. Huber's *The American Idea of Success* (New York: McGraw-Hill, 1971). For Horatio Alger, see Gary Scharnhorst, *Horatio Alger, Jr.* (Boston: Twayne, 1980) and Gary Scharnhorst and Jack Bates, *The Lost Life of Horatio Alger, Jr.* (Bloomington: Indiana University Press, 1985).

CHAPTER 5: DISSENTING VOICES: 1850

The Modern Library has published a fine selection of Thoreau's most important work: *Walden and Other Writings,* edited by Brooks Atkinson (1937; reprinted New York: Random House, 1950). Ralph Waldo Emerson's "Thoreau," reprinted in *The Portable Emerson,* edited by Mark Van Doren (New York: Viking, 1946), is a fascinating reminiscence. For readers with a special interest in Thoreau's economic thought, see the chapters on that subject in Vernon L. Parrington's *Main Currents in American Thought,* Vol. II: *The Romantic Revolution in America, 1800–1860* (New York: Harcourt, Brace, 1927) and Leo Stoller's *After Walden: Thoreau's Changing Views on Economic Man* (Stanford, Calif.: Stanford University Press, 1957).

For the history of Brook Farm, I have relied on V. F. Calverton, *Where Angels Fear to Tread* (Indianapolis, Ind.: Bobbs-Merrill, 1941), 197–224; Ralph Waldo Emerson, "Historic Notes of Life and Letters in New England" in *The Portable Emerson,* 536–43; Vernon L. Parrington, *Main Currents in American Thought,* Vol. II, 346–50; Van Wyck Brooks, *The Flowering of New England* (New York: Random House, 1936), 242–51; and Edith Roelker Curtis, "A Season in Utopia," *American Heritage* (April 1959). For the constitution of the Brook Farm Association, see *The Annals of America,* Vol. 7 (Chicago: Encyclopaedia Britannica, 1976). Hawthorne on manure is quoted in Vernon L. Parrington, Jr., *American Dreams*

(Providence, R.I.: Brown University Press, 1947). See also the entries "Brook Farm" and "George Ripley" in the *Encyclopaedia Britannica* and in *The Oxford Companion to American Literature*, edited by James D. Hart, 4th ed. (New York: Oxford University Press, 1965).

For the publication history of "Bartleby" and a good discussion of the story, see "Resources for Discussing Herman Melville's Tale, 'Bartleby, the Scrivener,' " prepared by Merton M. Sealts, Jr. (Madison: The Wisconsin Humanities Committee, 1982). For "Bartleby" itself, see *Selected Writings of Herman Melville* (New York: Random House, 1950).

The Confidence Man: His Masquerade, edited by H. Bruce Franklin (Indianapolis, Ind.: Bobbs-Merrill, 1967) is an excellent edition with very helpful notes.

CHAPTER 6: JOHN D. ROCKEFELLER: "BOUND TO BE RICH!"

Allan Nevins's two-volume *John D. Rockefeller: The Heroic Age of American Enterprise* (New York: Charles Scribner's Sons, 1940) is the definitive biography. Nevins has gathered more material than any other biographer, but he gives Rockefeller the benefit of almost every doubt. For a less flattering perspective and for a taste of two fiery muckrakers, see Henry Demarest Lloyd's *Wealth Against Commonwealth* (New York: Harper & Brothers, 1894) and Ida M. Tarbell's *History of the Standard Oil Company* (New York: Harper & Brothers, 1904). Tarbell is more reliable than Lloyd.

Robert L. Heilbroner's "The Grand Acquisitor," *American Heritage* (December 1964), is a brilliant short biography of John D. Rockefeller, Sr. For the story of the Rockefeller family through three generations and partway through the fourth, see Peter Collier and David Horowitz, *The Rockefellers: An American Dynasty* (New York: Holt, Rinehart, and Winston, 1976).

Rockefeller's *Random Reminiscences of Men and Events* is now available in a handsome edition published jointly by the Rockefeller Archive Center and the Sleepy Hollow Press (Tarrytown, N.Y., 1984). These reminiscences first appeared as a series of articles that ran monthly, from October 1908 through April 1909, in *The World's Work*, a magazine published by Doubleday, Page & Company. A special attraction of the Sleepy Hollow edition is that it reproduces the rare and fascinating photographs that appeared in the magazine. For an inside account of the genesis of Rockefeller's autobiography, see Frank Nelson Doubleday, *The Memoirs of a Publisher* (Garden City, N.Y.: Doubleday & Company, 1972).

The reader with a special interest in the development of American industry should see the chapter on Standard Oil in Chandler and Tedlow, *The Coming of Managerial Capitalism*. For background on Frederick T. Gates and an excerpt from his autobiography, see Allan Nevins, "The Man Who Gave Away Rockefeller's Millions," *American Heritage* (April 1955).

CHAPTER 7: ANDREW CARNEGIE: "I COULD HAVE SLAIN KING, DUKE, OR LORD . . ."

Harold Livesay's *Andrew Carnegie and the Rise of Big Business* (Boston: Little, Brown, 1975) is the best biography. For a muckraker's perspective, see James H. Bridge, *The Inside History of the Carnegie Steel Company* (New York: 1903). Robert

Heilbroner's "Epitaph for the Steel Master" (*American Heritage*, August 1960) is an excellent short biography.

First published in 1920, Carnegie's autobiography was recently made available in paperback (Boston: Northeastern University Press, 1986). Of Carnegie's other writings, the most interesting are *Triumphant Democracy* (New York: Charles Scribner's Sons, 1886), *The Gospel of Wealth and Other Timely Essays* (New York: Century Company, 1900), and *The Empire of Business* (Garden City, N.Y.: Doubleday, Page & Company, 1902).

CHAPTER 8: J. PIERPONT MORGAN: "AND TO THINK HE WAS NOT A RICH MAN!"

The best biography of Morgan is Frederick Lewis Allen's *The Great Pierpont Morgan* (1949; reprinted New York: Harper & Row, 1965). Also entertaining though not as elegant in style are Andrew Sinclair's *Corsair* (Boston: Little, Brown, 1981) and Stanley Jackson's *J. P. Morgan* (Briarcliff Manor, N.Y.: Stein and Day, 1983). Max Lerner's "Jupiter in Wall Street" (*American Mercury*, July 1930) offers a fine portrait in few words.

For the reader with a special interest in financial affairs, Vincent P. Carosso's *The Morgans* (Cambridge, Mass.: Harvard University Press, 1987) is indispensable. See also the chapter on Morgan in Chandler and Tedlow, *The Coming of Managerial Capitalism.*

For Morgan as a collector, see Aline B. Saarinen, *The Proud Possessors* (1958; reprinted New York: Vintage, 1968); Francis Henry Taylor, *Pierpont Morgan as Collector and Patron, 1837–1913* (New York: The Pierpont Morgan Library, 1957); and Frederick B. Adams, Jr., *An Introduction to the Pierpont Morgan Library* (New York: 1964).

Herbert L. Satterlee's *J. Pierpont Morgan: An Intimate Portrait* (New York: The Macmillan Company, 1939) lives up to its title, though the reader in search of perfect truth must remember that Satterlee was the husband of Morgan's daughter Louisa.

CHAPTER 9: OPULENCE

For the mansions of the Gilded Age, see Wayne Andrews, *Architecture, Ambition and Americans* (New York: Harper & Brothers, 1955) and Edward L. Kirkland's essay "The Big House" in *Dream and Thought in the Business Community, 1860–1900* (Ithaca, N.Y.: Cornell University Press, 1956).

For the mansions of Fifth Avenue, see Grace M. Mayer, *Once upon a Mile* (New York: Macmillan, 1958); Fred W. McDarrah, *Museums in New York* (New York: E. P. Dutton, 1967); and the essays by S. C. Burchell and Henry Hope Reed in *New York, N.Y.* (New York: American Heritage, 1968).

The best way to understand Newport is to go there. If you also want to read, see Cleveland Amory, *The Last Resorts* (New York: Harper & Brothers, 1952); Richard O'Connor, *The Golden Summer* (New York: G. P. Putnam's Sons, 1974); Nancy Sirkis, *Newport: Pleasures and Palaces* (New York: The Viking Press, 1963); Bertram Lippincott, *Indians, Privateers, and High Society* (Philadelphia and New York: J. B. Lippincott, 1961); and Antoinette F. Downing and Vincent J. Scully,

Jr., *The Architectural Heritage of Newport, Rhode Island, 1640–1915* (Cambridge, Mass.: Harvard University Press, 1952). Lovers of urbane prose will not want to miss the chapters on Newport in Henry James, *The American Scene* (1907; reprinted New York: Harper & Brothers, 1946).

Entertaining minibiographies of Ward McAllister appear in O'Connor, *The Golden Summer*, pp. 37–48; Amory, *The Last Resorts*, pp. 185–90; and Amory, *Who Killed Society?* (New York: Harper & Brothers, 1960), pp. 114–19. See also McAllister's pompous autobiography, *Society As I Have Found It* (1890; reprinted New York: Arno Press, 1975).

For tales of high living in the Gilded Age and afterward, see Amory, *Who Killed Society?;* Holbrook, *The Age of the Moguls;* Lucius Beebe, *The Big Spenders* (Garden City, N.Y.: Doubleday, 1966); Albert Stevens Crockett, *Peacocks on Parade* (New York: Sears Publishing Company, 1931); and Joseph J. Thorndike, Jr., *The Very Rich* (New York: American Heritage, 1976).

CHAPTER 10: DISSENTING VOICES: 1865–1915

The Theory of the Leisure Class is easily available, but it is hard to get hold of Veblen's other books. Viking would perform a service if it reprinted *The Portable Veblen* (New York: 1948), a fine anthology with an excellent introduction by Max Lerner. The best biography of Veblen is Joseph Dorfman, *Thorstein Veblen and His America* (New York: The Viking Press, 1934). For a consideration of Veblen in the context of other social theorists see John P. Diggins, *The Bard of Savagery: Thorstein Veblen and Modern Social Theory* (New York: Seabury Press, 1978).

See also the minibiography of Veblen by Max Lerner in the *Dictionary of American Biography;* the section on Veblen in Alfred Kazin's *On Native Grounds* (1942; reprinted Garden City, N.Y.: Doubleday, 1956); the chapter on Veblen in Robert Heilbroner's *The Worldly Philosophers* (1953; reprinted New York: Simon & Schuster, 1972); C. Wright Mills's introduction to the Mentor edition of *The Theory of the Leisure Class* (New York, 1953); Robert Lekachman's introduction to the Viking Compass edition of *The Theory of the Leisure Class* (New York, 1967); John Kenneth Galbraith's introduction to the Houghton Mifflin edition of *The Theory of the Leisure Class* (Boston, 1973); and John P. Diggins's chapter on Veblen in *American Writers*, Supplement I, Part II (New York: Charles Scribner's Sons, 1979).

Any study of Henry George must begin with *Progress and Poverty* (1879; New York: Robert Schalkenbach Foundation, 1966). The best biography is Charles Albro Barker's *Henry George* (New York: Oxford University Press, 1955). See also two biographies by George's children: Henry George, Jr., *The Life of Henry George* (Garden City, N.Y.: Doubleday & McClure, 1900); and Anna George de Mille, *Henry George: Citizen of the World* (Chapel Hill: University of North Carolina Press, 1950).

The reader who is not a specialist may enjoy the discussion of George in Robert Heilbroner's *The Worldly Philosophers;* David Hapgood's "The Tax to End All Taxes," *American Heritage* (April 1978); and my own "The Man Who Raised Hell," *American Heritage* (October–November 1986).

Steven B. Cord's *Henry George: Dreamer or Realist?* (Philadelphia: University of Pennsylvania Press, 1965) is an invaluable study of the response to George's ideas by economists and other social scientists from 1880 to 1965. See also Richard W. Lindhold and Arthur D. Lynn, Jr., eds., *Land Use Taxation: The Progress and Poverty Centenary* (Madison: University of Wisconsin Press, 1982); Robert V. Andelson, ed., *Critics of Henry George: A Centenary Appraisal of Their Strictures on Progress and Poverty* (London: Associated University Presses, 1979); and C. Lowell Harriss, "Lessons of Enduring Value: Henry George a Century Later," *American Journal of Economics and Sociology*, Vol. 44, No. 4 (October 1985).

For the life of Henry Adams, see *The Education of Henry Adams* (1918; reprinted Boston: Houghton Mifflin, 1961) and Ernest Samuels, *Henry Adams* (3 vols.; Cambridge, Mass.: Harvard University Press, 1948–64). For the life of Charles Francis Adams, Jr., see *An Autobiography, with a Memorial Address Delivered November 17, 1915, by Henry Cabot Lodge* (Boston: Houghton Mifflin, 1916) and Edward Chase Kirkland, *Charles Francis Adams, Jr.: The Patrician at Bay* (Cambridge, Mass.: Harvard University Press, 1965).

Anyone with an interest in American business history and a taste for brilliant prose will want to sample the essays in Henry Adams and Charles Francis Adams, Jr., *A Chapter of Erie and Other Essays* (Boston: James R. Osgood, 1871). For a superb account of Charles's career as a regulator, see Thomas McCraw, *Prophets of Regulation* (Cambridge, Mass.: Harvard University Press, 1984).

For the career of William James of Albany as well as the attitudes toward business of Henry James, Sr., and William James, I have relied on Howard M. Feinstein, *Becoming William James* (Ithaca, N.Y.: Cornell University Press, 1984). This is an unusually interesting example of a psychologically oriented biography, written by a psychiatrist who is an adjunct professor of psychology at Cornell University.

One could spend a lifetime studying the role of money in Henry James's novels and stories. For one scholar's perspective, see Donald L. Mull, *Henry James's "Sublime Economy": Money as Symbolic Center in the Fiction* (Middletown, Conn.: Wesleyan University Press, 1973). John Berryman's comment about *The American* appears in his Afterword to Theodore Dreiser's *The Titan* (1914; New York: New American Library, 1965).

Foster Rhea Dulles, *Labor in America* (New York: Thomas Y. Crowell, 1949) is an excellent history of labor in the United States through the Second World War. For a Marxist perspective see Anthony Bimba, *The History of the American Working Class* (1927; reprinted New York: Greenwood Press, 1968). For a brief history, see Chandler and Tedlow, *The Coming of Managerial Capitalism*, Chaps. 19–20.

For the Wobblies, see Paul F. Brissenden, *The I.W.W.* (1919; reprinted New York: Russell & Russell, 1957) and Patrick Renshaw, *The Wobblies* (Garden City, N.Y.: Doubleday, 1967).

Many of the most important articles by the muckrakers are reprinted in Arthur and Lila Weinberg, eds., *The Muckrakers* (New York: Simon & Schuster, 1961). This volume contains a very useful bibliography. For additional background and commentary see Richard Hofstadter, *The Age of Reform* (New York: Vintage, 1955), 186–214; C. C. Regier, *The Era of the Muckrakers* (Chapel Hill: University of North Carolina Press, 1932); Louis Filler, *Crusaders for American Liberalism* (New York: Harcourt, Brace, 1939); and David M. Chalmers, *The So-*

cial and Political Ideas of the Muckrakers (New York: Citadel Press, 1964). Also see the autobiographies of Ray Stannard Baker, S. S. McClure, Lincoln Steffens, Mark Sullivan, and Ida Tarbell.

John D. Rockefeller was the most muckraked man who ever lived. For judicious assessments of the attacks by Lloyd, Tarbell, and Lawson, see Allan Nevins, *John D. Rockefeller: The Heroic Age of American Enterprise,* Vol. II, 52–59, 331–42, and 520–29.

CHAPTER 11: HENRY FORD: THE CONSUMMATE CRANK

The best biography of Henry Ford is a three-volume study by Allan Nevins and Frank Ernest Hill: *Ford: The Times, the Man, the Company* (New York: Charles Scribner's Sons, 1954); *Ford: Expansion and Challenge, 1915–1933* (New York: Charles Scribner's Sons, 1957); and *Ford: Decline and Rebirth, 1933–1962* (New York: Charles Scribner's Sons, 1963).

Despite significant inaccuracies and omissions, there is fascinating material in the three volumes that Ford wrote in collaboration with ghostwriter Samuel Crowther: *My Life and Work* (Garden City, N.Y.: Doubleday, Page, 1922); *Today and Tomorrow* (Garden City, N.Y.: Doubleday, Page, 1926); and *Moving Forward* (Garden City, N.Y.: Doubleday, Doran, 1930).

Two of Ford's tough lieutenants wrote autobiographies that must be approached with caution: Harry Bennett as told to Paul Marcus, *We Never Called Him Henry* (New York: Fawcett, 1951) and Charles Sorensen, *My Forty Years with Ford* (1956; reprinted New York: Crowell-Collier, 1962).

William Greenleaf, a professor of history who worked as a research associate for the Nevins-Hill biography, has written a superb short biography of Ford for the *Dictionary of American Biography*. Allan Nevins's "Henry Ford—A Complex Man" (*American Heritage*, December 1954) and Harold Livesay's chapter "The Insolent Charioteer" in *American Made* (Boston: Little, Brown, 1979) are fine short portraits of Ford that ought not to be read until the reader already knows the basic facts about him. Readers with a taste for psychohistory should consult Anne Jardim, *The First Henry Ford: A Study in Personality and Business Leadership* (Cambridge, Mass.: The M.I.T. Press, 1970).

The 1980s have witnessed the publication of several big books that cover more than one generation of the Ford family. See Peter Collier and David Horowitz, *The Fords: An American Epic* (New York: Summit Books, 1987); Robert Lacey, *Ford, the Men and the Machine* (Boston: Little, Brown, 1986); and David Halberstam, *The Reckoning* (New York: William Morrow, 1986).

Most discussions of manufacturing technology at Ford are rudimentary. For an analysis that goes much deeper, see David A. Hounshell, *From the American System to Mass Production, 1800–1932: The Development of Manufacturing Technology in the United States* (Baltimore: Johns Hopkins University Press, 1984). This is a fascinating book with wonderful photographs and an especially suggestive chapter titled "The Limits of Fordism."

CHAPTER 12: ALFRED P. SLOAN, JR.: THE CONSUMMATE PROFESSIONAL

Sloan published two autobiographies: *Adventures of a White-Collar Man*, in collaboration with Boyden Sparkes (Garden City, N.Y.: Doubleday, Doran, 1941);

and *My Years with General Motors*, edited by John McDonald and Catharine Stevens (Garden City, N.Y.: Doubleday, 1963). The second is much the better of the two, perhaps in part because Alfred D. Chandler, Jr., early in the career that saw him become America's leading business historian, served as consulting historian and research associate.

The story of the transformation of General Motors under Sloan in the 1920s is told in fascinating detail in Chandler's *Strategy and Structure: Chapters in the History of the American Industrial Enterprise* (Cambridge, Mass.: The M.I.T. Press, 1962). This book is essential reading for anyone interested in organizational design or in the evolution of giant enterprise in the United States. I also highly recommend Peter F. Drucker's pioneering study of GM, *Concept of the Corporation* (1946; reprinted New York: Mentor, 1972). For good short biographies of Pierre du Pont and Alfred Sloan, see Harold C. Livesay, *American Made*.

CHAPTER 13: MADISON AVENUE

For the history of advertising in the United States I have relied heavily on Stephen Fox's excellent book *The Mirror Makers* (New York: William Morrow, 1984). To a lesser extent I have drawn upon Martin Mayer, *Madison Avenue, U.S.A.* (New York: Harper & Brothers, 1958); James Playsted Wood, *The Story of Advertising* (New York: Ronald Press, 1958); and Michael Schudson, *Advertising: The Uneasy Persuasion* (New York: Basic Books, 1984). A good account of the recent acquisition of American agencies by British firms appears in Randell Rothenberg, "Brits Buy Up the Ad Business," *The New York Times Magazine* (July 2, 1989).

For the rise of mass distribution in the United States see Alfred D. Chandler, Jr., *The Visible Hand*, 207–39. For statistics on total advertising expenditures, the largest agencies, and the companies that spend the most on advertising, see *Louis Rukeyser's Business Almanac* (New York: Simon & Schuster, 1988), 355–63. For the advertisements themselves see Julian Lewis Watkins, *The 100 Greatest Advertisements* (1949; reprinted New York: Dover, 1959). For Ogilvy on Ogilvy see *Confessions of an Advertising Man* (1963; reprinted New York: Atheneum, 1983).

For a maverick economist's perspective on advertising and larger issues related to it, see Chapter 18, "The Management of Specific Demand," and Chapter 20, "The Regulation of Aggregate Demand," in John Kenneth Galbraith, *The New Industrial State* (1967; 2nd ed., rev., New York: Mentor, 1972). Christopher Lasch discusses advertising in *The Culture of Narcissism* (New York: W. W. Norton, 1979), 135–40. Irving Kristol's comments are from "Utopianism, Ancient and Modern" in *Two Cheers for Capitalism* (1978; reprinted New York: Mentor, 1979), 143–59.

Michael Schudson says much of interest about the role of advertising as an institution in *Advertising: The Uneasy Persuasion*. I recommend especially Chapter 4, "An Anthropology of Goods," and Chapter 5, "Historical Roots of Consumer Culture." For a stimulating discussion of consumer psychology and behavior see Shlomo Maital, *Minds, Markets, & Money* (New York: Basic Books, 1982). For a brilliant discussion of the consumption ethic see Daniel Bell, *The Cultural Contradictions of Capitalism* (New York: Basic Books, 1976), 54–84.

CHAPTER 14: THE LITERATURE OF SUCCESS IN THE
TWENTIETH CENTURY

For my discussion of the literature of success in the twentieth century I have relied heavily on Richard M. Huber's *The American Idea of Success* (New York: McGraw-Hill, 1971). Huber's comparison of the character ethic, the mind power ethic, and the personality ethic seems to me brilliant and illuminating.

Russell H. Conwell's *Acres of Diamonds* and Elbert Hubbard's *A Message to Garcia* can be found in Volumes 11 and 12 of *The Annals of America* (Chicago: Encyclopaedia Britannica, 1976). George H. Lorimer's *Letters from a Self-Made Merchant to His Son* (Boston: Small, Maynard, 1902) and Bruce Barton's *The Man Nobody Knows* (Indianapolis, Ind.: Bobbs-Merrill, 1925) are still available in many libraries. Norman Vincent Peale's *The Power of Positive Thinking* (New York: Prentice-Hall, 1952) and Dale Carnegie's *How to Win Friends and Influence People* (New York: Simon & Schuster, 1936) are available in paperback in most bookstores, as is Arthur Miller's *Death of a Salesman*.

For background about George H. Lorimer, see John Tebbell, *George Horace Lorimer and The Saturday Evening Post* (Garden City, N.Y.: Doubleday, 1948). For background about Bruce Barton, see Huber, *The American Idea of Success*, 196–209, and Stephen Fox, *The Mirror Makers*, 101–12. My discussion of Willy Loman appeared in a slightly different form in "If Willy Loman Read Books, He'd Have Read These," *The New York Times*, Arts & Leisure Section (May 13, 1984), p. 8.

CHAPTER 15: DISSENTING VOICES: 1920–1945

The best biography of Sinclair Lewis is Mark Schorer's *Sinclair Lewis: An American Life* (New York: McGraw-Hill, 1961). Schorer also has written afterwords to the Signet Classic editions of both *Main Street* and *Babbitt*, and he has edited a useful collection of critical essays about Lewis for the *Twentieth-Century Views* series (Englewood Cliffs, N.J.: Prentice-Hall, 1962).

Lewis's Nobel Prize acceptance speech can be found in Volume 15 of *The Annals of America* (Chicago: Encyclopaedia Britannica, 1976), pp. 62–70.

For Alfred Kazin's early critical views on Lewis see *On Native Grounds* (1942; reprinted Garden City, N.Y.: Doubleday, 1956), 173–80. For Kazin's personal recollections of Lewis and for his later critical views see "Sinclair Lewis Got It Exactly Right," *American Heritage* (October–November 1985).

Notable critiques of Lewis include Vernon L. Parrington, "Sinclair Lewis: Our Own Diogenes," in *Main Currents in American Thought*, Vol. 3 (New York: Harcourt, Brace, 1930), 360–69; and Walter Lippman, "Sinclair Lewis," in *Men of Destiny* (New York: Macmillan, 1927), 71–92.

For background about the Fugitives and the Agrarians I have relied on my own undergraduate thesis, "Robert Penn Warren's Development as a Philosophical Novelist," written at Harvard in 1971–72. See also Donald Davidson, "The Thankless Muse and Her Fugitive Poets," in *Southern Writing in the Modern World* (Athens: University of Georgia Press, 1958); Allen Tate, "*The Fugitive* 1922–25: A Personal Recollection Twenty Years After," *Princeton University Library Chron-*

icle 3 (April 1942); and John L. Stewart, *The Burden of Time: the Fugitives and the Agrarians* (Princeton, N.J.: Princeton University Press, 1965).

My primary source is *I'll Take My Stand: The South and the Agrarian Tradition* by Twelve Southerners (1930; reprinted Gloucester, Mass.: Peter Smith, 1976). This edition reprints Louis D. Rubin, Jr.'s, excellent introduction to the Torchbook edition (New York: Harper & Row, 1962).

Statistics relating to the economic development of the South in the twentieth century come from *Statistical Abstract of the United States 1988*, Tables 1052–58; *Historical Statistics of the United States, Colonial Times to 1970*, Part I, Series A, 195–209, Series K, 1–16, and Series K, 17–81; and the *State and Metropolitan Area Data Book 1986*, Table C.

For background on the Saturn factory see William E. Schmidt, "Tennessee's Governor Winning Political Friends, and Industry," *The New York Times* (August 4, 1985), Section 1, Part 1, p. 20, col. 1; and Leanne Waxman, "Saturn Takes 'Tentative' Out of Saturn Project," Associated Press (November 20, 1985).

Adolf A. Berle, Jr., and Gardiner C. Means, *The Modern Corporation and Private Property* (New York: Macmillan, 1932), ought to be read by anyone interested in the history of economic thought in the twentieth century. The spirited attacks on *The Modern Corporation* delivered at the conference sponsored by the Hoover Institution in 1982, as well as Means's spirited counterattack, are reprinted in the *Journal of Law and Economics*, Vol. XXVI, No. 2 (June 1983).

For the life of Berle see Jordan Schwarz, *Liberal: Adolf A. Berle and the Vision of an American Era* (New York: The Free Press, 1987). In addition to a great deal of serious analysis, this book contains one piece of delightful gossip. In 1960 Berle's son Peter married Lila Field Wilde, a great-great granddaughter of Cornelius Vanderbilt. "It should not be held against her," the father of the groom declared.

The standard biography of John L. Lewis is Melvyn Dubofsky and Warren Van Tine, *John L. Lewis: A Biography* (New York: Quadrangle, 1977). The best short biography is Robert H. Zieger, *John L. Lewis: Labor Leader* (Boston: Twayne, 1988). For the perspective of a well-known populist organizer see Saul Alinsky, *John L. Lewis: An Unauthorized Biography* (New York: G. P. Putnam's Sons, 1949).

For background see Foster Rhea Dulles, *Labor in America* (New York: Thomas Y. Crowell, 1949); Joseph G. Rayback, *A History of American Labor*, expanded and updated (1959; reprinted New York: Macmillan, 1968); Irving Bernstein, *The Lean Years: A History of the American Worker, 1921–33* (Boston: Houghton Mifflin, 1960); Irving Bernstein, *The Turbulent Years: A History of the American Worker, 1933–41* (Boston: Houghton Mifflin, 1970); and Chandler and Tedlow, *The Coming of Managerial Capitalism*, Chap. 20.

For statistics on union membership and related matters see *Historical Abstract of the United States*, Part I, Series D, 927–51; *Statistical Abstract of the United States 1989*, Tables 682 and 684; and *Louis Rukeyser's Business Almanac* (New York: Simon & Schuster, 1988), 60–75.

For the full story of Budd Schulberg's Hollywood childhood as well as a fascinating look at the early days of the movie business see Budd Schulberg, *Moving Pictures: Memories of a Hollywood Prince* (Briarcliff Manor, N.Y.: Stein and Day, 1981). For Schulberg's later thoughts about *What Makes Sammy Run?* see

SOURCES   353

the Modern Library edition published in 1952 and the Penguin edition published
in 1978. For a brief biography of Schulberg see Josephine Zadofsky Knopp,
"Budd Schulberg," *Dictionary of Literary Biography*, Vol. 28: *Twentieth-Century
American-Jewish Fiction Writers*, edited by Daniel Walden (Detroit: Gale Research
Company, 1984), 280–84.

CHAPTER 16: THE TRIUMPH OF IBM

For the history of IBM see William Rodgers, *Think: A Biography of the Watsons
and IBM* (London: Weidenfeld & Nicolson Limited, 1969), and Robert Sobel,
IBM: Colossus in Transition (New York: Times Books, 1981). See also "Behind the
Monolith: A Look at IBM," *The Wall Street Journal*, Section 2 (April 7, 1986).
For a fine short portrait of Thomas Watson, Sr., see Peter F. Drucker, "Thomas
Watson's Principles of Modern Management," *Esquire*, December 1983, pp.
194–202.

IBM itself has produced some excellent background material, especially for
readers with an interest in technology. See "IBM . . . Yesterday and Today"
(1984), "IBM Innovation" (1987), "Innovation in IBM Computer Technology"
(1987), and "How One Company's Zest for Technological Innovation Helped
Build the Computer Industry" (1984). See also "International Business Machines
Corporation," a lengthy article prepared by IBM itself, in *Encyclopedia of Computer
Science and Technology*, Volume 15 Supplement, edited by Jack Belzer, Albert G.
Holzman, and Allen Kent (New York and Basel: Marcel Dekker, Inc., 1979).

For IBM's business philosophy see Thomas J. Watson, Jr., *A Business and Its
Beliefs* (New York: McGraw-Hill, 1963) and F. G. "Buck" Rodgers with Robert
L. Shook, *The IBM Way* (New York: Harper & Row, 1986). See also the com-
ments about IBM in Thomas J. Peters and Robert H. Waterman, Jr., *In Search
of Excellence: Lessons from America's Best-Run Companies* (New York: Harper &
Row, 1982).

A comprehensive study of the government's 1969–82 antitrust case against
IBM is presented in Franklin M. Fisher, John J. McGowan, and Joen E. Greenwood, *Folded, Spindled, and Mutilated* (Cambridge, Mass.: The MIT Press, 1983).
This is a book for sophisticated readers with a special interest in the complex
economic issues posed by the case.

CHAPTER 17: DISSENTING VOICES: 1945–1990

For the organization man see David Riesman with Nathan Glazer and Reuel
Denney, *The Lonely Crowd* (New Haven, Conn.: Yale University Press, 1950);
C. Wright Mills, *White Collar* (New York: Oxford University Press, 1951); Sloan
Wilson, *The Man in the Gray Flannel Suit* (New York: Simon & Schuster, 1955);
William H. Whyte, Jr., *The Organization Man* (New York: Simon & Schuster,
1956); and Alan Harrington, *Life in the Crystal Palace* (New York: Alfred A.
Knopf, 1959).

For the facts of John Kenneth Galbraith's life and some sense of the shape of
his career see Robert Sobel, *The Worldly Economists* (New York: The Free Press,
1980). For critical perspectives on Galbraith's work see Robert M. Solow, "The
New Industrial State or Son of Affluence," *The Public Interest*, No. 9 (Fall 1967);

Charles H. Hession, *John Kenneth Galbraith and His Critics* (New York: New American Library, 1972); Milton Friedman, *From Galbraith to Economic Freedom* (London: Institute of Economic Affairs, 1977); and David Reisman, *Galbraith and Market Capitalism* (New York and London: New York University Press, 1980).

For positive views of Ralph Nader see Charles McCarry, *Citizen Nader* (New York: Saturday Review Press, 1972) and Hays Gorey, *Nader and the Power of Everyman* (New York: Grosset & Dunlap, 1975). For a strongly negative view see Ralph de Toledano, *Hit & Run* (New Rochelle, N.Y.: Arlington House, 1975). Short articles about Nader that are especially worth reading include Ken Auletta, "Ralph Nader, Public Eye," *Esquire* (December 1983); Jonathan Rowe, "Ralph Nader Reconsidered," *Washington Monthly* (March 1985); Michael Kinsley, "Saint Ralph," *The New Republic* (December 9, 1985); and Robert J. Samuelson, "The Aging of Ralph Nader," *Newsweek* (December 16, 1985). See also the section about Nader in David Halberstam, *The Reckoning* (New York: William Morrow, 1986), 497–505.

Chapter 18: Poor Richard Revisited

For a brief report on Tsukuba Science City see *The Wall Street Journal*, Special Section on Technology (November 14, 1988), p. 26. For the Crystal Palace Exhibition see *The American Heritage History of American Business and Industry*, 133–34, and David A. Hounshell, *From the American System to Mass Production, 1800–1932* (Baltimore: Johns Hopkins University Press, 1984), 16, 24. For the report of British experts in 1855 see Hounshell, 61–65.

On the general subject of American industrial development in the nineteenth century see Otto Mayr and Robert C. Post, eds., *Yankee Enterprise* (Washington, D.C.: Smithsonian Institution Press, 1981). Nathan Rosenberg's comment on "Yankee ingenuity" comes from his essay in this volume. John Stuart Mill is quoted in Thomas Kiernan, *The Road to Colossus* (New York: William Morrow, 1985), 119.

In my discussion of America's productivity in recent years, as well as my discussion of corporate and government debt, most of the statistics come from *Louis Rukeyser's Business Almanac*. See also C. Jackson Grayson, Jr., and Carla O'Dell, *American Business: A Two-Minute Warning* (New York: The Free Press, 1988) and Carl G. Thor, *Perspectives 89* (Houston: American Productivity & Quality Center, 1989).

For a worried analysis of foreign investment in the United States see Martin and Susan Tolchin, *Buying into America: How Foreign Money Is Changing the Face of Our Nation* (New York: Times Books, 1988). See also Robert B. Reich, "Corporation and Nation," *The Atlantic* (May 1988), 76–81.

Statistics on market share, patents, and drug approvals come from *The Wall Street Journal*, Special Section on Technology (November 14, 1988), 23. The figures on per capita GNP come from *Fortune* (February 2, 1987), 24.

For the balance of merchandise trade see *Statistical Abstract of the United States 1988*, Table 1328. For total consumer credit, see *Historical Abstract of the United States*, Vol. II, Series X, 551–60, and *Statistical Abstract of the United States 1988*, same series.

For a fine discussion of American attitudes toward debt see Shlomo Maital, *Minds, Markets, and Money* (New York: Basic Books, 1982), 138–43. For the personal savings rates of different nations see Karen Elliott House, "Though Rich, Japan Is Poor in Many Elements of Global Leadership," *The Wall Street Journal* (January 30, 1989), 1.

For an examination of the "merger mania" of the 1980s, covering subjects such as junk bonds, leveraged buyouts, risk arbitrage, and insider trading, see John Brooks, *The Takeover Game* (New York: Twentieth-Century Fund/E. P. Dutton, 1987). For the career of Michael Milken see Connie Bruck, *The Predators' Ball: The Junk Bond Raiders and the Man Who Staked Them* (New York: American Lawyer/Simon & Schuster, 1988).

For a full-length explication of the view that is presented in the "Dear Grandchildren" editorial see Benjamin M. Friedman, *Day of Reckoning* (New York: Random House, 1988). For a clearly written but less comprehensive discussion, written from a perspective much influenced by Friedman, see Jonathan Rauch, "Is the Deficit Really So Bad?" *The Atlantic* (February 1989), 36–42. For a conservative affirmation that deficits do not matter see Norman Podhoretz, "The Deficit: A Phony Issue," New York *Post* (January 31, 1989), 21.

For the literature of success in recent years see Robert J. Ringer, *Looking Out For #1* (New York: Fawcett World Library, 1977); Michael Korda, *Power!* (1975; reprinted New York: Ballantine Books, 1976); Michael Korda, *Success!* (1977; reprinted New York: Ballantine Books, 1978); and Betty Lehan Harragan, *Games Mother Never Taught You* (1977; reprinted New York: Warner Books, 1978).

For the insider trading scandals of the 1980s I have relied on easily located articles in *Time, Newsweek, The New York Times, The Wall Street Journal, Business Week, Fortune,* and *Forbes.*

The comment by Michael Novak comes from "Greed Does Not Explain It," *Forbes* (April 3, 1989), 56. Novak quotes Max Weber, *The Protestant Ethic and the Spirit of Capitalism,* translated by Talcott Parsons (1958; reprinted New York: Charles Scribner's Sons, 1976), 17.

Index